DEMOCRATIC POLITICAL THEORY

DEMOCRATIC POLITICAL THEORY

J. Roland Pennock

PRINCETON UNIVERSITY PRESS
PRINCETON, NEW JERSEY

Published by Princeton University Press, Princeton, New Jersey
In the United Kingdom: Princeton University Press, Guildford, Surrey

Library of Congress Cataloging in Publication Data will be .
found on the last printed page of this book
This book has been composed in Linotype Baskerville
Clothbound editions of Princeton University Press books
are printed on acid-free paper, and binding materials are
chosen for strength and durability
Printed in the United States of America by Princeton
University Press, Princeton, New Jersey

*To my Swarthmore College Students
of Political Theory*

Contents

viii

CHARTS

FIGURE

Preface

It is my primary aim in this book to get things straight about democratic theory, with all the help I can muster from theorists, past and present. I also try to show how theorists of various periods and of widely varying metaphysical and other assumptions fit into the picture, often arriving at the same or similar conclusions as far as concerns the justification or operation of democratic institutions of government. But the study is primarily analytic rather than genetic. Democratic theorists are not dealt with as wholes (whereby something is lost), but as they contribute something to an understanding of democratic theory considered as a body of theoretical propositions about democratic institutions (whereby, I believe, something is gained).

No claim is made that any single body of coherent theory is *the* theory of democracy. No such claim could be sustained. Essentially the fact of the variety of more or less systematic theories of democracy is dealt with in two ways. One way, while considering the body of democratic thought as a family of theories, is to analyze certain tensions within that body of thought. There are, for instance, tensions not only between liberty and equality but also within each of these concepts. The other way makes use of two typologies of democratic theory: one based on how political power is distributed and controlled, the other relating to the primary values that each theory presumes ought to control, or in fact do control, political behavior. This method is applied to a series of generic problems encountered in the operation of democratic institutions. In each case, I examine the fit between each of the theories and the lessons derivable from a study of the problem in question. In conclusion, I draw some of these findings together, along with others, in the effort to sustain a coherent theory of democracy. The various theories referred to are "pure types" and it is perhaps not surprising that a viable theory of democracy, in my opinion at least, turns out to be one that, especially in the case of the "motivational" theories, borrows from more than one of the types.

This book represents a long-term investment and my intellectual debts to many people have been mounting, with interest compounded daily. No matter how the reader may evaluate it, I shudder to think what it would have been like without their assistance. Since, in most cases, each of the persons I shall gratefully name has read only one or two chapters, even without the customary acceptance on my part of full responsibility for what appears here it would be impossible to locate the blame elsewhere for any of my errors of omission or commission. The following political scientists and philosophers have been generous with their time and of great assistance with their criticisms· Charles R. Beitz, John R. Champlin, John W. Chapman, Monique W. Clague, Richard E. Flathman, Charles E. Gilbert, Raymond F. Hopkins, Nannerl O. Keohane, James R. Kurth, John D. Lewis, Robert F. Lyke, Maurice Mandelbaum, Hans F. Oberdiek, and David G. Smith. William E. Connolly and Dennis F. Thompson each read the whole manuscript, courtesy of Princeton University Press, and gave me the invaluable benefit of their detailed criticisms and suggestions. To all of these scholars and to Sanford G. Thatcher, philosophy and social science editor of the Press, I owe a deep debt of gratitude. For great assistance in overcoming my stylistic inadequacies, I am likewise deeply indebted to Robert E. Brown of the Press. I should also record that except for the generous leave policy of Swarthmore College the gestation period for this book would have been even longer than it was. To the College I also owe thanks for financial assistance for typing and clerical chores.

Three chapters borrow heavily from material I have previously published. I am grateful to the editors and publishers of *The Monist* (parts of Chapter Five), to Lieber-Atherton (much of Chapter Eight), and to Washington University (a substantial portion of Chapter Twelve), for permission to use those materials here.

It is perhaps worthy of note here that the major section of the book draws heavily upon empirical materials and that I strongly believe it is important for a theoretical work —certainly for the kind of theoretical endeavor undertaken here—to do so. Melanson and King put it well when they remarked that theory which is "directly and self-consciously related to reality is to a greater extent its own master and is less likely to be the handmaiden of intuition, ideology, or utopian aspirations."[1]

Swarthmore College   J.R.P.

[1] Philip H. Melanson and Lauriston R. King, "Theory in Comparative Politics: A Critical Appraisal," *Polit. Studies*, 4 (1971), 205-231, 226.

Introduction

THIS book aims to clarify, to classify, to evaluate democratic theory, and, as far as is possible, to distinguish empirical propositions from evaluative ones, not to keep them permanently separated, but to show how they interrelate and to bring each to bear upon the other. Too often democratic theory has seemed obscure because of fuzzy language, tacit assumptions, and unnecessary entanglement with metaphysical propositions. Too often also, the world of theory and the world of practice have been permitted to travel in different orbits. It is hoped that the present attempt to correct these deficiencies will contribute both to the clarity and to the rigor of theory in this field and also to its realism.

Of equal importance and closely related to the objectives just mentioned is the attempt to relate major types of democratic theory to certain general operational problems confronting all democratic governments. In some cases a consideration of the problem areas will be relevant to an evaluation of the theories; in other cases the theories help in understanding the problems; either way, I believe, the confrontation of general democratic theory and the analysis of such specific problems as "responsiveness," "representation," or "leadership" is enlightening.

What is "democratic theory"? The phrase is often used as though it stood for a clearly demarcated and agreed upon body of doctrine; but that is far from the case. Even the question of what topics it should include, almost as much as what is to be said about any given topic, is the subject of wide disagreement. It has been quite properly called "a loosely knit family of ideas."[1]

Democratic theory is a part of the general corpus of political theory (itself a rather indeterminate body of material). It is, of course, the part that deals, in one way or another, with democracy, a term defined in the following chapter. It does not include the broadest concerns of political theory. No attention will be given to questions of methodology, per se; nor will the influence of theory on behavior or of behavior on theory receive more than passing notice. Likewise, what might be called the sociology of democratic theory, the theory of the conditions under which it develops and of what determines its various forms, will not be considered here. The subject of ideology, so popular today, and of democratic ideology in particular will also be largely ignored.

After three chapters devoted to the definition of democracy and to the basic tensions within that concept (liberty and equality; individualism and collectivism), the rest of the volume will be devoted to two kinds of democratic theory—"justificatory" and "operational"—the bulk of it concerning the latter. For the purposes of this book at least, this classification is superior to the more familiar "normative"/"empirical" dichotomy. "Normative" is ambiguous; or at the very least it is too broad a category for present purposes. Since laws as well as moral principles are "norms," it includes legal as well as ethical analysis. A study of the nature and location of democratic sovereignty would come under the "normative" head, as would the analysis of the role of law in a democracy. Although no systematic consideration will be given to legal norms in this book, another kind of nonethical norm will receive some attention: hypothetical-deductive reasoning, reasoning based upon a model, or set of simplified assumptions, generally having to

[1] Douglas W. Rae and Michael Taylor, *The Analysis of Political Cleavages* (New Haven: Yale University Press, 1970), p. 5.

xviii

do with the nature of man.[2] This type of reasoning is normative in the sense that it yields propositions of the following type: if the nature of man is so-and-so, and if the desired objective is such-and-such, then the following rules (norms), which might take the form of a constitution, ought to be observed.

While I have referred to the last-mentioned type of reasoning as normative but nonethical, and thus falling outside of the "justificatory" category, it is or may be a mixture. It utilizes two kinds of assumptions, one of which (about the nature of man) is empirical and the other of which (about the "desired objective") may also be interpreted as empirical (as long as it is simply a matter of fact about what is desired), but which is easily transposed into an ethical norm (when it is argued or assumed that a particular objective or set of objectives is desirable, meaning "worthy of being desired" or "ought to be desired").

"Empirical theory" also seems to be an undesirable concatenation of words. Physicists, for example, are commonly classified as either "theorists" or "empiricists." In the first case they are concerned with the formulation and elaboration of theory. "Empiricists," on the other hand, make observations and conduct experiments both for the purpose of providing materials for further analysis and for the purpose of testing propositions derived from theory. (Of course in physics, as in politics, the same scholar may engage in both kinds of activity.) In the case of physics, I would suppose, all theorists are "empirical" theorists in the sense that they are developing theory from, or for application to, data derived from the senses. Political theorists do the

2 As I am using the term, a "model" may, but need not be, cast in mathematical form. Thomas Hobbes derived his propositions from a model of natural man, as did Rousseau; though neither of them attempted to reduce them to mathematical form. Herbert Simon, in his *Models of Man* (New York: Wiley, 1957) finds resort to mathematical formulations useful if not essential, as do many other theorists today.

same, but this kind of activity may not be their exclusive concern; they may also be seeking to *justify* certain political institutions. To this end they may be seeking to demonstrate or persuade their audience that certain experiences or certain states of being are more valuable than others and that certain political institutions are essential for realizing these objectives, or perhaps are of ultimate value in themselves. Also they may or may not make use of empirical data.

Probably the bulk of theoretical work being done by American political scientists today falls in the class of nonjustificatory theory. I refer to this kind of theory—insofar as it is democratic theory—as "operational" political theory. It seeks to explain, ideally to predict, the operation of political institutions. It may rely upon insight or "understanding," making use of the whole body of political experience rather than attempting to analyze and measure it, for this purpose. This method, often referred to as "humanistic" (as contrasted with "scientific") is especially attractive to those who believe that any attempt, however provisional, to separate "facts" from "values" goes contrary to the nature of reality and is bound to lead to false or misleading results. More commonly today, theories of political (and democratic) operations tend to be "scientific" in their approach. Rather than trying to derive insight by sensing political experience as a whole, they break it up, measure it as best they can, and then, by finding generalizations, by making assumptions and developing theories from which can be derived testable propositions, construct a body of explanatory and, where possible, predictive theory. Equally, however, they may derive their testable propositions from model building, as defined above, without recourse to empirical data.

Finally, one other reason for preferring the term "operational" to "empirical" to designate nonjustificatory theory is the fact that some nonjustificatory theory other than model building contains very little empirical content. So it is with the kind of theory developed by the followers of Talcott Parsons. The work of David Easton proceeds at a high level of abstraction, yet it does relate to the operation of the political system.[3]

Operational democratic theory may be developed at any level of generalization, from the most "narrow-gauge" and fact-related to the most general and abstract. Easton's theory is an example of the latter. Examples of the former are so numerous and various that to select one as typical would be highly arbitrary, but one might mention the theory, propounded by Wilson and Banfield, that the higher his income group the more likely is a voter to support the public interest even when it conflicts with his own private interest.[4]

Democratic theories may be classified in many other ways. At a later point, a chapter is devoted to that subject. The plan of this book, however, will be to deal in turn, in the "operational" chapters, with a series of major topics or problems with which an operating democracy must contend, generally testing each theory by reference to how well it fits an analysis of the problem in question, and, in one case, using the theories to throw light on the best solution of the problem. Decisions once made must be executed, administered, and, frequently, adjudicated. However, since these stages of the governmental process take us far beyond what is distinctively democratic, they will not be discussed here.

Certain recurring themes will crop up from time to time and it may be helpful to call attention to them now. First, it will be found that a wide variety of ethical and meta-ethical theories all lend support to the democratic ideal. Second, while democratic theory contains within it sig-

[3] See, especially, David Easton, *A Systems Analysis of Political Life* (New York: Wiley, 1965).

[4] James Q. Wilson and Edward G. Banfield, "Public-Regardingness as a Value Premise in Voting Behavior," *Amer. Polit. Sci. Rev.*, 58 (1964), 876-887.

nificant tensions—they might be called "contradictions" in Marxist language—it is my contention that they are *only* tensions, often matters of emphasis, not antinomies. Finally, the types of democratic theory, as elaborated below, have varying applicability to various circumstances and aspects of democracy. Each contains important elements of truth; the differences can largely be reduced to matters of emphasis.

DEMOCRATIC POLITICAL THEORY

CHAPTER I

What Is Democracy?

BOTH etymology and history suggest that the primary meaning of democracy—certainly at least its original meaning—relates to a form of government. According to the classical tradition it is government by the many, as contrasted with government by one or a few.[1] Other meanings, as implied for instance by Plato's description of the democratic man, were derived either by extensions of the original meaning to other applications than the political or by applying the term to attributes of existing democracies and their citizens. Herodotus defined it as the "rule of the many" (sometimes translated as "the multitude's rule") and also as a society in which "equality before the law" prevails and where the holder of political office "is answerable for what he does."[2] The *OED* defines it as "government by the people; that form of government in which the sovereign power resides in the people as a whole, and is exercised either directly by them . . . or by officers elected by them. In modern use often more vaguely denoting a social state in which all have equal rights, without hereditary or arbitrary differences of rank or privilege."[3]

One of the earliest formulations of the principle behind the more modern usage to which the *OED* refers was given a famous formulation by Colonel Rainborough in the

[1] The classic Greeks distinguished between the good and perverted forms of government, and, later, Polybius coined a separate term, *ochlocracy*, for democracy's perversion, the arbitrary rule of the many.

[2] Herodotus, *History of the Persian Wars*, trans. Rawlinson, Modern Library edition (New York: Random House, 1942), Bk. III, chap. 80, p. 252.

[3] (Oxford: Clarendon Press, 1933, 1961).

Putney Debates, when he declared that "the poorest he . . . hath a life to live, as the greatest he."[4] Rainborough went on to say that "every man that is to live under a government ought first by his own consent to put himself under that government."[5] Spelled out in modern idiom, the ideals to which this leading Leveller was giving expression in mid-seventeenth-century England were those of the supreme value of the individual and of individual autonomy. These values were attributed to all individuals, without distinction; each must count equally. Moreover, the value, or the "dignity," as it is often called, of the individual demands that, in some sense, he shall be master of his own fate. What is ultimately best for him is for him to decide. Thus the twin democratic ideals of liberty and equality are both derived from the notions of human dignity and autonomy (which, in turn, they imply); and democracy is, in this sense at least, a profoundly individualistic doctrine.[6]

Yet democracy's individualism merges easily with that third element of the democratic triumvirate of values, fraternity. Respect for the worth of each individual, the basic humanism of democracy, means that violence, and indeed

[4] A.S.P. Woodhouse, ed., *Puritanism and Liberty* (Chicago: University of Chicago Press, 1951), p. 53.

[5] Ibid.

[6] From the great philosophical tradition, the name of Immanuel Kant should be mentioned in this connection. Although he is (rightly) not thought of as a democratic political theorist, his basic ethical doctrines are in almost perfect accord with Rainborough's and thus are fundamental to democratic theory. I refer to the second formulation of the Categorical Imperative, that no man should be treated only as a means to another man's ends, and to his doctrine of autonomy. For the former, see Immanuel Kant, *The Metaphysics of Ethics*, trans. Semple (Edinburgh: Clark, 1886), p. 40. And for the latter, note his admiring reference to "a constitution allowing *the greatest possible human freedom* in accordance with laws by which *the freedom of each is made to be consistent with that of all others. . . .*" *Critique of Pure Reason*, trans., Kemp Smith (London: Macmillan, 1953), p. 312, (B373). (Italics in original.)

4

all coercion, is considered evil, even when necessary.[7] Decisions affecting the whole group should preferably be made by consensus. Authority should not operate in such a way as to put any member of the society at a political disadvantage because of his economic or social status. Communication should be full and free, regardless of rank and power.[8]

The emphasis on communication is important and calls for some elaboration. Discussion has been said by some to be the essence of democracy. Thus A. D. Lindsay declares that "when men who are serving a common purpose meet to pool their experience, to air their difficulties and even their discontents, there comes about a real process of collective thinking." Again, he remarks, "Observe further that the moment we take discussion seriously, we are committed to the view that we are concerned not primarily to obtain or register consent, but to find something out."[9]

Finally, we must add the element of human development. This idea, frequently articulated by John Dewey, is encapsulated in C. B. Macpherson's statement that the aim of democracy is "to provide the conditions for the free development of human capacities, and to do this equally for all members of the society."[10] As the quotation implies, de-

[7] Some modern democrats, as will appear later, would hold that coercion may be good for the individual coerced, as well as for others, even when practiced by the state. But even they would be valuing coercion for its consequences, not for itself. The individualist, on the other hand, holds that liberty is good in itself as well as for its consequences.

[8] These aspects of the democratic ideal, in addition to certain others not mentioned here, such as an atmosphere of freedom that permits and even encourages emotional expression, are well put in Warren G. Bennis and Philip E. Slater, *The Temporary Society* (New York: Harper & Row, 1968), p. 4.

[9] Lindsay, *The Essentials of Democracy* (Philadelphia: University of Pennsylvania Press, 1929), pp. 36, 37.

[10] Macpherson, *The Real World of Democracy* (Oxford: Clarendon Press, 1966), p. 58.

velopment may be thought of as so closely connected with liberty as not to require separate enumeration.

This democratic ideal of liberty-cum-equality-and-fraternity (including free and full discussion of common problems and interests), with roots deep in the Judeo-Christian tradition, is, in the popular sense of the term, idealistic; and it shares the vagueness that commonly attaches to ideals.[11] As with ideals generally, it may be approximated in practice in varying degrees. Also it is applicable to all kinds of social relations outside of the realm of politics. At the same time, it has become more basic than the more precise and probably prior meaning of "government by the people." As applied to the polity, then, the definition of democracy as an ideal may be phrased as "government by the people, where liberty, equality, and fraternity are secured to the greatest possible degree and in which human capacities are developed to the utmost, by means including free and full discussion of common problems and interests."

The procedural definition, likewise beginning with "government by the people," renders this phrase more precise by relating it to a set of procedures rather than to certain values. An extreme version of this type of definition is found in the work of Y. Murakami. He defines democracy as "a social decision function *consisting of and only of voting procedures.*" More precisely, he declares, "a social decision function $F(D_1, D_2, \ldots, D_n)$ is called a *democracy,* if the function can be expressed only by voting operators—without any resort to negations and constants—and the

11 Without explicitly mentioning liberty and equality, Lucius Garvin expresses most of what I have been trying to say in the following sentence: "Democracy exists in full stature . . . when a people, using the techniques of full and informed discussion, seek to achieve the best common life and do so in a spirit which attests that the very process of seeking has already brought substantial fulfillment." *A Modern Introduction to Ethics* (Boston: Houghton Mifflin, 1953), p. 528.

function is nondictatorial, where nondictatorship is defined as follows: . . . 'A social decision function $F(D_1, D_2, \ldots, D_n)$ is called *nondictatorial*, if there is no individual whose preference is always adopted by the society.' "[12]

A less technical but still fairly precise procedural (or operational) definition of democracy will be adopted here. It runs along the following lines. A democracy is rule by the people where "the people" includes all adult citizens[13] not excluded by some generally agreed upon and reasonable disqualifying factor, such as confinement to prison or to an asylum for the mentally ill, or some procedural requirement, such as residency within a particular electoral district for a reasonable length of time before the election in question. "Rule" means that public policies are determined either directly by vote of the electorate or indirectly by officials freely elected at reasonably frequent intervals and by a process in which each voter who chooses to vote counts equally ("one person, one vote") and in which a plurality is determinative.

It will be noted that this definition includes majority rule in the sense of nonminority rule, which is to say that no specified minority can rule. It does not, however, include the requirement of rule by a bare majority (nor does it select from among various possible definitions of majority rule).[14] In other words, it does not rule out a requirement that decisions can be made only by an extraordinary or "qualified" majority (nor does it rule out decisions by pluralities less than a majority). Some students of democratic theory would insist on bare-majority rule as part of

[12] Murakami, *Logic and Social Choice* (New York: Dover Publications, 1968), pp. 28-29.

[13] Citizenship must be open to all residents of the country, subject to reasonable requirements.

[14] See below, pp. 370-374 and, for a more technical treatment, the articles by Gerald H. Kramer and Arthur Kuflik in J. Roland Pennock and John W. Chapman, eds., *Due Process*, NOMOS XVIII (New York: New York University Press, 1977), Chaps. 10 and 11.

the definition, insisting that it is implied by the equality or "one person, one vote" rule.[15] This question will be treated more fully at a later point (Chapters Nine and Ten). Even at this stage, however, it is important to sketch the reasoning in support of the definition as stated. A Quaker business meeting is normally conducted on the basis of reaching decisions by what is called "the sense of the Meeting." Although this term includes a slight area of vagueness, it approximates a unanimity requirement. Everyone is entitled to have his say; and, if he feels strongly enough about the matter, he can generally exert a veto. Obviously the system works only where either substantive or procedural consensus is high. That is to say, either differences of opinion must not be very great or dissenters must place a high enough value upon the communal spirit that they will stand aside and not exercise their veto once it becomes clear they are destined to remain a hopeless minority. The point to be noted here is that this procedure is generally thought of not as undemocratic but as *especially* democratic. Nor is it confined to the business transactions of these "peculiar people," as the Quakers sometimes call themselves. On the contrary, families, committees, and other small groups with strong internal ties not infrequently accept similar procedures and consider that in showing this high regard for the opinion of each individual they are behaving very democratically.

Just as the requirement of a qualified majority (even unanimity, at the extreme) may not be looked upon as undemocratic, so also bare-majority rule under certain circumstances may seem undemocratic. Suppose, for instance, a bare majority comprises a fixed coalition. No group or individual not included in this coalition is ever on the winning side, in spite of the fact, let us assume, that their interests and preferences are sharply at odds with those of the winning coalition. "One person, one vote," under these cir-

15 See for instance Willmoore Kendall, *John Locke and the Doctrine of Majority-Rule* (Urbana: University of Illinois Press, 1941).

cumstances, makes a travesty of the equality principle. From the point of view of the minority, at least, dictatorship is none the less so for being that of a majority. One must look beyond the forms, the procedures, to actual operation, at least in such an extreme situation. Similarly the unanimity rule might be considered undemocratic if a single individual or the same small group were able to exercise their veto power in such a way as to block all or most of the desires of the great majority.

The point of the last two paragraphs is not simply to defend the contention that it runs counter to general usage to stipulate a definition of democracy that entails the right of a bare majority to rule. The point is also, and even more significantly, that when a particular procedural definition runs afoul of some more general and substantive aspect of the democratic ideal, it is the former that tends to give way. Whatever may historically have come first, if we search our usages and our feelings, we shall find that it is to the democratic ideals of individual worth, autonomy, and equality that we appeal in case of doubt as to whether or not a particular practice is democratic. For certain purposes where precision is required, as in modeling, stipulative definitions, which must be procedural if they are to be precise, are valuable, indeed indispensable. But when the "democraticness" of a particular institution or practice is called into question, an appeal beyond procedures and stipulations to ultimate ideals is always in order and tends to be overriding. This is so because a stipulative definition is arbitrary; it is always open to the question Why? The search for an answer to that question leads inevitably to purposes, to ideals.

Similarly, the egalitarian and libertarian ideals of democracy may be used to justify more complicated definitions of democracy (especially of "liberal democracy") than that advanced here. Most of the contents of the American Bill of Rights, including especially the freedoms of expression and association, plus such other provisions of the

Constitution as the Equal Protection clause and the limitation on suspending the writ of *habeas corpus*, are so closely related to the preservation of equality and liberty that a case can be made for including them in the definition of democracy itself. Some would go even further and incorporate in the definition the idea of competitive political parties as an institutional insurance that the right of association will be utilized to make certain that issues will be formulated and debated during the process of decision making, thus making effective the concept of "rule" by the majority. However, I here follow the simpler practice of excluding these corollaries of liberal democratic ideals from the formal or procedural definition of democracy, while reserving the right to override this definition by appeal to the substantive (ideal) concept whenever a democracy as here defined fails so substantially to approach its ideals that to call it "democratic" seems farcical. Certainly people's views as to what seems "farcical" will differ, being affected especially by their views of the possible. The proposed definition does qualify the word *elected* by the term *freely*, although it might be argued that this usage is redundant. In fact, it points to further problems. In what sense must citizens be "free" to vote if they choose? Legally free, to be sure. But suppose the government closes its eyes to physical coercion by groups of private citizens? Suppose the coercion is economic? Or suppose, instead, that large numbers of citizens are so apathetic that they do not exercise their franchise, whether from ignorance, conviction that their cause is hopeless, or sheer laziness? Or again, suppose they have not used their freedom of association to organize themselves effectively into competing political parties? These are hazy areas. If we say that "freely" in our definition means "legally free," then the uncertainty relates to the point at which we would say that the procedurally democratic polity was so far removed from the democratic ideal as to cease to deserve the name "democracy."

Problems also arise in connection with the requirement

10

that votes should count equally. Suppose my vote and yours are each counted as one vote, but that my vote is one millionth of the number required to elect a representative in my district and that yours, in your district, is one hundred thousandth of enough to achieve the same objective. Are our votes equal? Are they made so by the fact that I may (can?) move to your district if I like? The United States Supreme Court has said no to these questions, but of course absolute equality in this sense can never be achieved. And suppose your vote is more influential because you are better educated, better endowed with brains, or with the qualities that produce political effectiveness? Suppose that inequalities of wealth enable certain groups to command highly disproportionate use of the means of communication and persuasion? And does it matter whether those inequalities of wealth were produced by inheritance, luck, superior ability, hard work, or greater thrift? Generally these questions indicate the existence of points (highly indeterminate) beyond which one would be inclined to appeal from a technical definition, whatever its terms, to the democratic ideal.

The practice of having both an ideal and a practical or technical definition, the first of which tends to be substantive and the second formal or procedural, is by no means uncommon. For instance, we might say of a university properly incorporated and authorized to grant degrees by the appropriate authority (in the United States, a state or the federal legislature), that even though it is *technically* a university, it is not *"really"* a university, because it has no graduate schools, or those it has are so poor that they are not worthy of the name, or for some like reason.

It is the substantive definition, or the underlying principle of democracy, that leads to its extension to other spheres than the political. Thus we speak of "social democracy," meaning a society in which the democratic virtues of equality and fraternity prevail. Liberty is of course also one of the democratic virtues. Other than democratic regimes and societies may prize liberty, but liberty for all,

11

equally, is distinctly democratic; thus a society in which distinctions are not arbitrary or hereditary and in which even "earned" distinctions are not bases for sharp class divisions but rather where an easy fraternizing prevails among the various ranks of society is generally referred to as "socially" democratic, without reference to its form of government. And an individual in any society who manifests these characteristics is spoken of as a "democratic" person.

One also hears the term *economic democracy*. Here the meaning is more ambiguous. Sometimes it refers to a society in which differences in wealth and income are relatively small. In this usage, it is the element of equality that is influential, and the usage is strictly parallel to that of the term *social democracy*. In other cases, it is the strictly political meaning of democracy that governs, and the reference is to an industrial system in which workers share in the government of the plant or enterprise.

Thus far we have been speaking as though "democracy" meant the same thing, or things, to peoples all over the earth. In fact, it is a concept, and an institution, that originated in what is known as "Western" civilization. While it has been borrowed elsewhere and is now of substantially universal use, it is often suggested that it means different things in different parts of the world. In particular, it is said that Western style democracy, or "liberal democracy," places considerable stress on individual liberty and on institutions of government designed to protect individuals against governmental arbitrariness or oppression and to see that all have equal legal opportunity to share in the selection of those who govern. On the other hand, the Communist countries also lay claim to the term *democracy*. They claim that the goals of liberty and equality are theirs as well as ours. In fact, they claim that they understand, appreciate, and indeed realize these goals to a far greater extent than we do. This difference of point of view is commonly explained by saying that they lay greater stress than we do upon equality—economic as well as political—and less upon liberty.

There is some truth in this explanation. It has been argued, however, and not only by Communists or their sympathizers, that in fact the democratic ideals of the West and of the Communist countries are identical. According to this interpretation, the difference is simply in how we view the facts. We see the lack of political and civil liberty in Communist countries, and conclude that they cannot be democratic. They, on the other hand, believe that, in the absence of substantial economic equality, political liberty is meaningless, without practical effect. Our vaunted civil liberties are ineffective as long as the few control the instruments of production. Our rule of law was aptly described by Anatole France when he spoke ironically of the majesty of the law that protected alike for prince and pauper the right to sleep under bridges. Freedom to organize in political parties that compete with each other for control of the government is perhaps an appropriate means to democratic ends under certain conditions, Communists might argue, but certainly not under the prevailing conditions of capitalism, where opinions are manipulated by the capitalist media.[16]

Clearly this way of putting the matter has much to be said for it. To an important degree, the differences between Communists and the Western world on this matter have more to do with the facts as each side perceives them than with their ultimate ideals. If we really believed that the rank-and-file Russian had as much control over his life as the rank-and-file American does, for example, we might be prepared to call their government democratic (or deny that title to ours). But a difference in the way facts are perceived may be (as in this case) vitally important. Nor is it

[16] The argument is well put by John Plamenatz in his article on democracy, in Richard McKeon, ed., *Democracy in a World of Tensions* (Chicago: University of Chicago Press, 1951).

necessarily true that differences of opinion about matters of fact are more readily overcome than are differences about values, when the former are supported by strong ideological commitments.

However, it appears to this observer that, when all is said and done, some differences in the realm of ideals remain. Communists do seem to place somewhat greater stress on equality and less on individual liberty than do liberal democrats. Yet one should beware of laying too much emphasis on this point. After all, the West itself is by no means united in its interpretation of "democracy." It is widely held that the English and English-speaking people generally, in the tradition of John Locke, put the accent on liberty; while the French, and many Continentals, follow Rousseau in giving first rank to equality.[17] Not only are there differences within the West, but also the democratic tradition is not static. It may be that at the present time it is undergoing some shift in emphasis, with equality coming to play a larger role.

Nearly all of the discussion for the last few pages has dealt with the democratic ideal, or with democracy defined by its substance rather than by its forms and procedures. By the same token, it has been dealing with that broad concept of democracy that includes more than government and politics. As has been shown, it is at least arguable that the same substantive concept of democracy will fit both West and East. A formal or procedural definition of democracy that would fit our Western-style democracy, however, clearly would rule out Communist regimes and so-called peoples' democracies. One type of definition or the other may be more useful, depending upon the use to which it is to be put. The important thing is to be aware of both types and of the relations between the two. One gives precision; the other supplies the principles for the realization of which institutions may then be more precisely defined.

[17] See George H. Sabine, "The Two Democratic Traditions," *Phil. Rev.*, 61 (1952), 451-474.

One final note. It was pointed out above that, in terms of the ideal definition, governments might be either more or less democratic. While the procedural definition has been stated in absolute terms, it too can be used as a goal or standard, as was implied in the discussion of equality of votes and freedom of voting. Thus a government in which the franchise was widely based but not universal would be less democratic, other things being equal, than one in which it was universal; and likewise if the "one person, one vote" standard was less than fully met. Or if any of various possible limitations on the effective use of the vote existed, so that "rule" by the people suffered some constraint, again one might say that such a government was less democratic than one in which that constraint did not exist, without eliminating it entirely from the category of "democratic."[18]

[18] For a fuller discussion of the problem of defining democracy and for a more precise proposed definition than seems useful for present purposes, see Felix E. Oppenheim, "Democracy—Characteristics Included and Excluded," *The Monist*, 55 (1971), 29-50.

CHAPTER II

Liberty and Equality: A Democratic Tension

"LIBERTY" and "equality" comprise the basic elements of the democratic creed. Yet these twin ideals—slogans on the emblem of democracy—are not easily reconciled. Between them, at best, a considerable tension exists. Liberty, as will appear in the next chapter, is especially congenial to the individualistic pole of democratic theory, while equality is assimilated more readily to the collectivistic pole. Moreover, each of these concepts is subject to internal tensions of its own.[1]

Liberty and equality easily went hand-in-hand when it was a question of the mass of the people being subjected to a ruling oligarchy; but, once "the people" ruled, many dilemmas presented themselves. Today examples confront us at almost every turn. In Britain, the Labour party finds itself in danger of being torn asunder by the demands of some to equalize and of others to give greater liberty to enterprisers. In the United States your liberty to contribute without limit to the campaign of your favorite candidate and his liberty to spend must contend with the ideal of equality of opportunity in the electoral race. The liberty

[1] The major political ideologies of the modern world can be categorized in terms of their positions with respect to these two ideals. All democrats favor both, but "social democrats" (and, *a fortiori*, "democratic socialists") place great (sometimes primary) emphasis upon equality, while "libertarian democrats" put liberty at the top of their value hierarchy, above equality. On the other hand, authoritarians agree in setting relatively little store upon liberty; but they are sharply divided with respect to equality. Communist authoritarians rate it at the very top, while their fascist counterparts place it at the opposite extreme (at least as far as concerns *political* equality).

16

of free association, for example in schools, clubs, and the like, confronts the egalitarian ideal of integration. And again the ideal of equal access to medical treatment finds itself in tension with the liberty of the individual to select his or her own doctor. The problems are real and concrete. No "solution," practical or theoretical, is to be found, for they reflect tensions that are inherent in society, and indeed in man. But a clear understanding of the concepts, of their variations and of their interrelations, may contribute to our ability to find viable accommodations.

1. THE MEANING OF "LIBERTY"

I shall deal first with liberty or freedom (I make no distinction between the two terms). It is a concept which stands for something so generally and widely prized that it has come to have many meanings, as persons with differing philosophical stances strive to define it so as to support their own positions. Yet the situation is by no means so confused as it is sometimes made out to be. Liberty has a central core of commonly accepted meaning from which other meanings depart by way of extensions, metaphorical applications, and the like, but without losing all contact with what remains both their point of origin and their justifying reference point.

Before going further with this discussion, I wish to emphasize that I shall not attempt to formulate and defend a precise definition of liberty.[2] But I shall try to elucidate the structure of the concept, its variations, and a type of definition that seems to me adequate *for the purposes at*

[2] For a careful attempt to develop a satisfactory definition based on a detailed critique of several prominent recent treatments of the subject, see William A. Parent, "Some Recent Work on the Concept of Liberty," *Am. Phil. Quar.*, 11 (1974), 149-167 (hereafter "Concept of Liberty"). An original and penetrating analysis of freedom, relating it to various concepts of the self may be found in Frithjof Bergmann, *On Being Free* (Notre Dame: University of Notre Dame Press, 1977), esp. Chaps. 1 and 2.

hand: namely, the meaning of liberty in the democratic ideal and its relation to its companion ideal, equality.

a. The Central Core

Liberty, said Hobbes, is "freedom from chains and prison"; or, more accurately, "the absence of external impediments to motion."[3] Here we have the root meaning of the term. Whatever extensions they may wish to make, few if any would deny that this is fundamental.[4] Some might hold, with Epictetus, that a man is as free as he feels—that is to say, he is free if he feels free. As a complete definition, this formulation has not found wide acceptance. In any case, the phenomenon of the man who feels free though confined to a prison cell is sufficiently uncommon as not to provide a basis for the major use of the term *freedom*.

Although to feel free is not enough, in normal parlance, to constitute being free, it may more plausibly be argued that to feel unfree is a necessary condition for lacking freedom or being deprived of freedom. However that may be, to feel free, I suggest, is a necessary but perhaps not a sufficient condition for being free. We enter here upon more controversial ground, for usage seems to be less than consistent in this context. I am in my study, writing, with the door closed. Unbeknownst to me, someone has locked

[3] Hobbes discusses the meaning of liberty in Chapters 14 and 24 of *Leviathan*. The quoted passage is on page 138 of the Oakeshott edition (Oxford: Basil Blackwell, 1946). See also J. Roland Pennock, "Hobbes's Confusing 'Clarity'—The Case of 'Liberty,'" in Keith C. Brown, ed., *Hobbes Studies* (Oxford: Basil Blackwell, 1965), Chap. 5. Chapter 6 of the same volume, by A. G. Wernham, takes issue with my interpretation in certain respects.

[4] Thus Benjamin Barber, who opposes what he calls "the concrete psychological-intentionalist model" to "the abstract physical-machinist model," which he identifies with Hobbes, states that " 'the absence of external impediments' is only a partial explanation of what it means to be free." Benjamin R. Barber, *Superman and Common Men* (New York: Praeger, 1971), pp. 53-54. Note that the Hobbesian definition is still the beginning point, which, however, is in itself, in this view, entirely inadequate.

18

the door from the outside. Am I free? Or a man is standing outside the door intending to shoot me if I come out. I have no desire to come out. Let us suppose that in both cases the impediment is removed before I desire to leave. Was I deprived of freedom? One might say that during that period I was not free to leave my study. But, and the line is admittedly narrow, one would hardly say either that I have been deprived of freedom or that I was unfree. In other words, freedom relates to situations in which the individual desires to act in certain ways. It refers to the absence of interference with one's ability to do what one wills.[5]

For most, then, physical freedom, the absence of physical (external) restraints upon what one wills to do, is at least a necessary condition of freedom. Few would go so far as to say it is also a sufficient condition, a complete definition. Before pursuing this matter, however, a cautionary word is in order. Discussions of liberty frequently incorporate in the definition words designed to make the liberty of one man compatible with that of others. Thus it may be said that "liberty" means "the least restraint compatible with the like liberty for all," or some such phraseology. Definitions of this kind are products of the attempt to define liberty in such a way that it will be always justifiable, always

---

[5] The distinction, which usage seems to support, between saying, in the situation described above, that one was not free to leave, while at the same time denying that one was deprived of freedom, can be explained and justified if one assumes that the speaker meant that one was not free to leave *if he wished to*. "A free man," said Hobbes, in another passage from that quoted above, "is he that in those things, which by his strength and wit he is able to do, is not hindered to do what he has a will to." *Leviathan*, Oakeshott edition, p. 137. Parent disagrees with Hobbes and with the statement in the text. ("Concept of Liberty," p. 151). His usage is more self-consistent than mine, if one does not grant my assumption of the suppressed "if he wished to," but mine seems closer to common parlance. In any case, the point is not important for my purposes, as will become evident. Moreover I believe there is virtue, for my purposes, in adhering to usage, even at some cost in terms of consistency, as long as it does not lead to serious confusion.

19

good. These attempts represent a confusion between definition and justification, between liberty and its just (or equal) distribution. Because liberty is so highly prized, the temptation to define it so that it is always good is continually present. But it can lead only to obscurity. Liberty is one thing; the right to liberty is another; likewise the circumstances under which the demand for liberty is justifiable.[6]

Returning to the main thread of the argument, the first enlargement of the Hobbesian primary definition would be to extend the idea of external impediments to include more than simply physical impediments. Threats, according to this generally accepted extension, are also incompatible with liberty. If the prison door is opened but the armed guard outside the door tells me he will shoot me if I cross the threshold, I can hardly be said to be free in the usual sense of the word (assuming that I prefer to leave). In other words, Hobbes to the contrary notwithstanding, fear and liberty are not consistent.[7] Not, at least, when the fear results from a threat deliberately aimed at preventing me from taking the action in question. If I wish to play tennis but decide not to because I fear the court will be too slippery (my son having inadvertantly left the hose

[6] Note the case where one wishes to compare polities with respect to the amount of freedom enjoyed by their citizens. Leading, as it does, to some concept of "maximizing" freedom for the polity as a whole, this requires an idea, however vague, of how to measure one man's freedom against that of another. Thus, if the government interferes with the liberty of some so that the liberty of others may be increased, it is unnecessary (and improper) to say that the liberty of the former group has not been curtailed; but liberty *on the whole* may have been increased. Where difficulty commonly arises, however, is where the liberty of some is curtailed so as to increase some other good, such as equality. Here the temptation is again to say that, since this was a justified curtailment, it was not *really* a curtailment at all. This way lies only confusion. Here, as in the text above, I depart from common usage in the interest of avoiding confusion.

[7] While Hobbes categorically states that fear and liberty are consistent, he does not himself consistently adhere to this position. See Brown, *Hobbes Studies*, Chap. 6.

20

running on it earlier in the day), one would hardly say that I am not "free" to play. But, if you threaten to turn a hose on me if I play, it might well be said that you have deprived me of freedom, made me less free.[8]

The example of the hose and the language used above suggests that freedom may be a matter of degree; that it is not an all-or-nothing proposition. Here consensus as to the meaning of "freedom" probably does not exist. Some would agree with that way of putting it, saying that threats of minor evil diminish freedom but do not eliminate it. A difficulty with this definition of the term is suggested, however, by the fact that different people will be affected differently by the same deterrent, the same threat. One will give up the idea of doing what he wished to do, while another will go ahead and risk the consequences. Can it be said that the second was freer than the first? The threat was the same; the difference was only in the reaction to it by the subject of freedom.

Another way of looking at the matter is for an impartial observer to decide what a person can reasonably be expected to resist. Thus, according to this definition of freedom, a person would be deprived of it only if he was deterred from acting on his own wishes by actions that either made it impossible for him to do what he desired or threatened him with consequences that no reasonable man could be expected to resist under the circumstances.[9]

---

[8] In short, I am suggesting that a restraint deliberately imposed upon me deprives me of liberty, while one that is accidental or incidental to some other purpose and unintended as to its effects on me is not. This position is debatable. I would say that if I am prevented from keeping an appointment by a traffic jam, I have not been deprived of liberty; but that if you, perhaps a rival applicant for the job I am seeking, deliberately block my car so as to make me miss my appointment, then I have been deprived of liberty. Even one who adopts the narrower definition, as I do, may wish to note that the broader meaning is a possible extension of the concept, to be discussed below.

[9] See Stanley I. Benn, "Freedom and Persuasion," *The Australian*

Although the discussion has been in terms of preventing a person from acting as he wishes, it should be understood to apply equally to compelling a person to act against his will. Neither logic nor usage sustain distinguishing, in this regard, between restraint and coercion. Both interfere with choice; and freedom of choice, thus far only implicit in our discussion, is a central feature of freedom.

We now have two necessary conditions of freedom: the absence of physical impediments to desired action, and the absence of threats of dire consequences, or (an alternative formulation) threats that no reasonable man could be expected to resist. The second condition suggests a third, which indeed may be classified as but a special instance of the second, although one of such importance as to merit special attention. I refer to laws, to commands of the state, backed up by its powers of enforcement. Laws that forbid or require certain actions, on pain of penalties, to that extent limit liberty. They are incompatible with liberty in the matters, and for the persons, concerned. To be sure, they may well be justified; they may be very good things. In limiting the liberty to steal, for instance, they may greatly enlarge other liberties—to own property and do with it as you will. In fact they may well result in a great increase in liberty; if, for instance, only a minority of people have any desire to steal, or (more accurately) would do so except for the fear of temporal punishment; or if the liberty lost by would-be thieves is less than that gained by themselves and others in the use of property.[10] Once more, one must be-

---

Journal of Philosophy, 45 (1967), 259-275. Parent disagrees with this view. "Concept of Liberty," p. 165.

[10] How would one make this measurement? By reference to subjective evaluations? If so, how compare them? Does one count the number of desires frustrated? Does one weight them according to their intensity? Partly this is the problem of interpersonal comparisons, a subject that is discussed below (Chap. 5). But it includes more than this; and it clearly indicates the lack of anything like precision that must attend any such comparisons and the extent to which the pos-

ware of confusing liberty with all that is good, or with the right to liberty. Insofar as my will is thwarted by a threat directed against me, by the law or even illegally, to that extent I am deprived of liberty, rightly or wrongly, for better or for worse.[11] It is important to bear in mind that a law prohibiting stealing, while it limits my liberty to steal by threatening me with punishment, likewise limits the liberty of those who might steal from me and by removing those threats thus increases my liberty on the whole.

Although laws may be considered as a kind of threat, it is better to consider them, as even Hobbes does, as obligations, amounting, in Hobbes's colorful terminology to "artificial chains."[12] If I am under obligation, by promise or otherwise, to stay at home this afternoon to take care of the children, I am not free to accept your invitation to play tennis. Obligations limit liberty. Thus whether law is considered as a threat or as an obligation, the *rule* of law, meaning thereby governance by general rules, which treat like cases alike and which apply prospectively, not punishing for acts that were not contrary to the published law when committed, make for much greater liberty on the whole than would prevail in its absence.[13]

Thus far I believe I am in step with general usage. Most people, with the allowances I have made for minor differences, would concur with the proposition that the conditions enumerated above are essential parts of the definition

---

sibility of any intelligent discussion of them depends upon a considerable degree of consensus among subjective judgments on this matter.

[11] For Parent, law does not make a person unfree—only less inclined to exercise his freedom.

[12] *Leviathan*, p. 138.

[13] This point appears to be admitted even by Hobbes, although less clearly than one would like. See Howard Warrender, *The Political Philosophy of Hobbes* (Oxford: Clarendon Press, 1960), pp. 258-261. It is to Locke that one turns for a clear and vigorous statement of this point. See John Locke, "Second Treatise of Government," *Two Treatises of Government*, ed. Laslett (Cambridge: Cambridge University Press, 1960), Sec. 57.

of liberty. Here agreement ends. Many would say that if these conditions prevail no more is required. The conditions enumerated are not only necessary but, taken together, they are also sufficient. Others would disagree.[14]

b. Possible Extensions

As in the case of the word *democracy* itself, so in the case of *liberty*, it is a constant temptation to select certain essential conditions for its existence and incorporate them in its definition. Within limits this practice is justifiable. It may focus attention upon values that might otherwise be overlooked. Reference was made above to the absence of a threat that prevents me from acting as I would as a "condition" of my freedom. It is such a "condition" because it is part of what freedom means. But suppose one says, truly, that the lack of what is essential for carrying out a certain act—the lack, that is to say, of means or power—makes it as impossible to carry out the act as would an external restraint. Here we are speaking of a "condition" of a different sort. The significant distinction is that in this case the "condition" has not been deliberately created or attached by another person for the purpose of affecting my conduct. If, I have said, you prevent me from playing tennis either by turning the hose on me (and the court) or by threatening to do so, you have deprived me of liberty. But if you

14 F. A. Hayek defends a definition of liberty essentially in agreement with the one set forth above. He defines liberty as "that condition of men in which coercion of some by others is reduced as much as is possible in society." *The Constitution of Liberty* (Chicago: University of Chicago Press, 1960), p. 11. He goes on to define "coercion" as "such control of the environment or circumstances of a person by another that, in order to avoid greater evil, he is forced to act not according to a coherent plan of his own but to serve the ends of another." *Ibid.*, pp. 20-21. Note particularly that liberty relates to control by another person and that the person coerced must act (or forbear to act) to avoid (what he judges to be) an evil. (What if the person whose acts are affected was not following a coherent plan, but was acting spontaneously?)

24

accidentally left the hose on in such a way that the water formed a pool on the court and made it unplayable, I would hardly say (on the basis of general usage) that you had deprived me of liberty. The same is true if it rains.[15]

Again, suppose I am prevented from going to the theater by threat of imprisonment. Surely my liberty has been impaired, although I do not lack the power. But if I decide not to go to the movies because it will cost more than I think it is worth to me, am I to say that I am deprived of liberty? If so, the concept takes on monstrous proportions. And if I say that lack of resources interferes with liberty only when it is absolute, the conclusion is still unsatisfactory. So I am not free to purchase a large yacht or the Empire State Building. I suppose I am not; but it would hardly occur to me to put it that way. It is intuitively more acceptable to say only that one is deprived of liberty when he lacks the means to purchase the bare necessities of life. But what constitutes a "necessity" is very vague indeed.[16]

Here we encounter the second reason for avoiding this type of definition. Not only would it be contrary to general usage, but also it would impoverish the language. Welfare, or access to the means for acquiring the necessities of

[15] Some, e.g., Parent, would deny this distinction, holding that rain, as well as someone's carelessness, might deprive me of liberty ("Concept of Liberty," p. 151). He does not discuss the question of whether the law of gravity (or, more accurately, the fact of gravitation) that prevents me from jumping over my house deprives me of liberty.

[16] A variant of the argument discussed in the text is strongly put by R. H. Tawney, as well as by many others. It is the argument that economic power is a weapon that can be, and is, used (sometimes deliberately, perhaps more often not) to limit the liberty of others. Tawney declares: "when liberty is construed realistically as implying not merely a minimum of civil and political rights, but securities that the economically weak will not be at the mercy of the economically strong, and that the control of those aspects of economic life by which all are affected will be amenable, in the last resort, to the will of all, a large measure of equality, so far from being inimical to liberty, is essential to it." R. H. Tawney, *Equality* (New York: Harcourt, Brace, 1931), p. 226.

life, is an important item in its own right and deserves to be kept apart from liberty. It is useful to be able to speak of a man who is poor but free, and of another who is rich but unfree (perhaps because serving a jail sentence). Two things equally good are not necessarily equal to each other! Welfare, like security, is both a good in its own right and a condition precedent to the most effective exercise of liberty; but it is not identical with the latter. Here again we are in danger of being misled by liberty's evaluative connotations; we are tempted to say that, because liberty without X is of little value, X must be part of its definition. *Non sequitur.*[17]

Much the same reasoning applies to other conditions without which liberty would be fruitless.[18] Education up to some (perhaps vaguely) specified level is an example. Still more difficult is the condition of psychological integrity or mental health.[19] The theory here is simply that a person whose desires are in hopeless conflict with each other or who is incapable of behaving in a fashion calculated to implement his basic needs and desires cannot use freedom effectively. Here again, it would appear, power rather than freedom is lacking; but it does no harm and may do much good to point out how closely, in this as in other cases, power and freedom are related, and how useless the latter

[17] John Rawls makes much the same distinction, saying that liberty is to be distinguished from the "worth of liberty," and that the worth of a particular liberty to a person will be influenced by his ability to take advantage of it, as affected, for example, by his means. *A Theory of Justice* (Cambridge, Mass.: Harvard University Press, 1971), p. 204f. In this paragraph and in my own definition as formulated below, I have departed marginally from the position taken in my *Liberal Democracy* (New York: Rinehart, 1950), pp. 58-63.

[18] It will be noted that I have ceased to appeal to usage as the test for definitions. The reason is simply that we have now reached the point in our discussion where consensus is lacking.

[19] Christian Bay discourses fruitfully and at length on this whole topic as it relates to freedom, under the heading of "psychological freedom." *The Structure of Freedom* (Stanford, Cal.: Stanford University Press, 1958), Chap. 4.

may be without the former.[20] Indeed, another way to define the situation just described would be to say that freedom pertains to the "self" and that the person described lacks selfhood.

A concept closely related to that of psychological freedom is that of "internal restraints." Idealist political philosophers, such as the British neo-Hegelian Bernard Bosanquet, have used this term to refer to such restraints as indolence and passion. The second of these raises the most interesting question. The argument is that when I act from passion, without deliberating, I am likely to behave in a fashion I shall later regret. Indeed it may be said that I act contrary to the interests and desires of my "better self." The idealist is likely to say my "real self." Thus the real "me" is restrained or compelled to act contrary to its will; it is deprived of liberty. Nor, the idealist would argue, is this distinction between the "I" that acts thus irrationally and my "real" self arbitrary; on the contrary, it is in accord with sound usage. We speak of a person as being "a slave to his passions," thus distinguishing between the real "him" and his passions, the latter being internal and yet not to be confused with his real self. Each of us has a concept of his own self as something relatively constant, not to be identified with the self that acts on a passing whim or in response to passion not deliberated upon and related to one's settled purposes. Rationality again enters the picture. The real me is the more rational me. (It may also be the moral me.) It is the me that seeks to bring my desires into harmony with each other and with my more permanent interests.

[20] Another way to put it would be to say that "rationality" (rather than "power") is lacking. Certainly some measure of rationality is a necessary condition of liberty as that term is being used here. As an example of a definition that incorporates both of the elements discussed above, one may cite that of Ralph Barton Perry, according to whom liberty is "the absence of external obstacles which prevent, and the presence of resources and capacities which promote, the power of any individual to realize his desires or execute his will." *Puritanism and Democracy* (New York: Vanguard Press, 1944), p. 521.

If one accepts this line of reasoning in its entirety,[21] the question inevitably arises whether, as Rousseau at one point contended, a man may be forced to be free. If a person is compelled to act against his immediate desires but in a way that he will welcome tomorrow, has he been made free, freed from "internal restraints"?

Few people would wish to go this far. Probably not even Rousseau; certainly not Bosanquet. Yet the idealist's line of reasoning underlines the important truth that freedom and rationality are related. We think of freedom as pertaining especially, if not uniquely, to rational creatures, to beings capable of taking thought before acting, of deliberating. What is to be free is a "self." The very word implies something more than an unrelated sequence of desires. Rather it implies that desires are, at least in some measure, organized around a continuing, and growing, set of purposes.

c. A Proposed Definition and Other Possible Extensions

In order to take account of the considerations just discussed, in addition to the necessary conditions previously defended, we may incorporate them in a definition of liberty as follows: "liberty is the opportunity for spontaneous and deliberate self-direction in the formation and accomplishment of one's purposes." If one accepts this wording, he is still faced with the choice of whether to interpret the word *opportunity* strictly or broadly. A strict interpretation, and one that fits neatly with what has been said up to this point, would be to say that opportunity means the absence of external control by means of threats, physical impediments, or moral or legal obligations. A broader interpretation would be to define opportunity as the presence

---

21 Even Bosanquet admits that to speak of liberty as pertaining to the "real" self is a metaphorical use of the term. He concedes that its literal meaning is the absence of external restraints, while arguing that the metaphorical meaning points to a deeper truth. *The Philosophical Theory of the State* (London: Macmillan, 1930), pp. 124-136.

of favorable conditions.[22] The stricter definition has the advantage of greater precision, of retaining significant distinctions, and of a better fit with common parlance. It would confine potential extensions of the term, beyond what is implied by "deliberate self-direction . . . ," to the role of ancillary ideas—ideas that help in the evaluation of various kinds of liberty, of various liberty-creating or liberty-hindering situations. The broader definition allows an indefinite but somewhat limited introduction of the concept of power or enablements, making the definition, in the eyes of some, more "realistic," because it would rule out many cases where "liberty" is of little value.

My own preference, as should be clear, is for the narrower definition. The broader definition lacks precision and invites confusion. But it *is* important to realize that not all liberties are of equal value. A person who follows all impulses, even when these are mutually self-defeating, who floats about in purposeless pursuit of each momentary attraction, can in a significant sense of the word be considered less free than one whose choices are controlled (by himself) in such a way that they are consistent with each other and with the achievement of his settled objectives. Note, too, that since the control comes from within—self-

[22] For a stricter and more precise, but arguably less useful, definition of liberty, see Felix E. Oppenheim, *Dimensions of Freedom* (New York: St. Martin's Press, 1961). The ambiguity of the word *opportunity* can be analyzed in another way. In a strong sense, it may mean that if I have an opportunity to do or attain something I can do or attain it if I so choose. In a weaker sense, it may mean simply that I have a certain chance of achieving it. Then the question arises whether my chance (e.g. one out of a hundred) be (a) the same as that of everyone else, or (b) the same as that of everyone else having the same skills, or (c) the same as that of everyone else who is similarly motivated and naturally endowed, or (d) the same as that of everyone else who has similar natural endowments. See A. M. Macleod, "Equality of Opportunity: Some Ambiguities in the Ideal," in Gray Dorsey, ed., *Equality and Freedom* (Dobbs Ferry, N.Y.: Oceana Publications, 1977), 3: 1077-1084.

discipline—it is compatible with our definition of liberty even if the narrower interpretation of "opportunity" is adopted. Self-discipline, it may be observed, is implied by the concept of autonomy (from the Greek word meaning "self-rule"), which is central to the concepts of both individualism and liberty.

Thus, freedom, *to be valuable*, must be accompanied by controls. These controls may be internal. They may take the form of self-control resulting from deliberation and rational choice, where "rational" includes not only means-end calculations but also a careful comparison of ends, consideration of their mutual relations, and ultimate evaluation. The youth who, after deliberating, decides to resist the impulse to experiment with heroin, for example, is almost surely contributing to his freedom in the long run. In fact, one justification for a definition of freedom that may entail giving up some immediate gratification of desire, is that the end result will be an enlargement of freedom even in the most restricted sense of the term.[23] It is easy to see then that the person with disciplined desires is more effectively free (or simply "more free," depending on one's definition) than one who lacks such self-discipline.

Suppose now that the discipline is not strictly internal, but that it is imposed by custom, tradition, by social disapproval (the mores), by the institutions of society, by legislation enacted by those over whom one has a share of control, and so on? As is evident, the examples of sources of control have been arranged in a calculated order. I do not say that

[23] It is worth noting, however, that this is only one justification. In this case health and other aspects of general welfare are probably even more importantly involved. This fact underlines an important objection to this kind of extension of the definition of freedom. While it is true that in this instance the curtailment of freedom now is *partly* in the interest of more freedom later, it is also justified, perhaps even more, by other interests. Where does one draw the line beyond which a restraint that is only marginally in the interests of freedom itself is no longer called freedom?

in any of these cases the controls in question do not constitute limitations or infringements upon liberty. I do say that in many cases they increase liberty on the whole or in the long run. It also seems clear that the fewer controls upon impulse that have been internalized, the more external controls will be required. And if they do not come from such relatively mild sources as tradition and social pressure, they will likely come in the harsher form of legislation. Only in the latter case is the restraint deliberately imposed; hence only it would interfere with liberty according to the stricter version of the definition proposed above.

Now one must look at the converse of the situations just described. Liberty has been defined initially in terms of physical impediments and threats. What are we to call restraints and compulsions that are short of these? Or, to put the matter differently, how broadly is "threat" to be interpreted? It was suggested above that it must be deliberately aimed at the person in question (or at a group of which he is a member), and that it must involve "evil consequences." Both are debatable. It may be argued, and it *is*, that fear may include fear of social disapproval. Also it may be contended that it does not matter whether or not the person or persons who influence my conduct intend to do so. If I am prevented from doing something because it is contrary to the way my neighbors behave, it can hardly be said they intend this effect. Yet some would contend that my liberty is affected. Whether or not it is considered desirable to adopt this usage (and I gave my reasons earlier for avoiding it), one can readily understand the logic of this extension of meaning.

One of the difficulties with extensions of the meaning of terms like liberty in this fashion is that they have a way of coming into conflict with other usages that may seem equally logical. The point is put clearly and succinctly by Stephen Lukes, in contrasting Marx and Durkheim. "Social constraint," he writes, "is for Marx a denial and for Durkheim a condition of human freedom and self-realization."[24] Marx, in this context at least, uses a negative definition of liberty but one that takes a broad view of what constitutes a restraint, including the unintended effects of social arrangements. Durkheim, on the other hand, is stressing man's need for social constraints to let him internalize norms that make social living possible and enjoyable, and more to the point, to provide him with the guideposts without which man becomes anomic rather than autonomous.

A final step in the progressive enlargement of the concept of freedom opens almost unlimited possibilities; but it will be dealt with quite summarily here. This step would extend the notion of restraints or hindrances to influences that are not perceived as such, perhaps not perceived at all, by the person influenced. If my desire to organize with my fellow workers in a union is thwarted by legislation making it illegal, clearly my liberty has been limited, whether or not justifiably. But if by subtle advertising techniques I am deliberately prevented from developing the desire to unionize, even though it would be to my interest to do so, has my liberty been curtailed? The example, I believe, brings out both the strength and the weakness of this position. If to thwart a desire is an infringement of liberty, is it any less so to prevent that desire from coming into being? But how is it possible to tell when a desire would have arisen had certain steps not been taken? And has my liberty also been curtailed when I am prevented from having a desire that it would not be in my interest to have? Logic unaided by judgment here seems to lead to a hopeless morass.

Yet one must not dismiss this position out of hand. In

[24] Lukes, "Alienation and Anomie," in Peter Laslett and W. G. Runciman, eds., *Philosophy, Politics, and Society*, 3rd series (Oxford: Basil Blackwell, 1967), pp. 134-156, 142. Whether the position here attributed to Marx was in fact Marx's position is immaterial to the point being made. It could quite properly have been attributed to J. S. Mill.

fact, I have incorporated it, at least in part, in my own definition by referring to individual self-direction in the *formation* of purposes. As Professor Partridge has said, "the man who has been so molded and manipulated that he always wants what his ruler or superior wants him to want is scarcely free."[25] Freedom of choice has little significance, too, in a situation where actors are unaware of the possibilities. Furthermore, without threatening me or doing anything of which I am aware, others may exercise controls that limit the choice open to me.

Several points of interest and importance emerge from these last remarks. At issue when freedom is being discussed is individual autonomy, self-rule. Autonomy can never be absolute and is seldom completely lacking. However we may define freedom, then, its spirit is inevitably a matter of degree. Hence its tendency to push beyond rigid definitions into areas that are often but vaguely delimited. Freedom also is broken up into specific freedoms and these tend to be cumulative. If many freedoms, especially many freedoms from the intrusion of the power of government, are respected, a general atmosphere is created that encourages the development and exercise of individual autonomy and choice. Moreover, the last statement implies that from the standpoint of freedom itself, some freedoms are more important than others, because in addition to their own intrinsic values they foster other freedoms. Chief among these are the traditional items of freedom of expression and belief, freedom of association, freedom of worship, freedom to choose a mate and an occupation, to live and work where we choose, freedom to spend our money as we will, to determine what books we shall read and what motion pictures we shall see, freedom from unlawful injury and arbitrary arrest, and freedom from government by those over whom we have no control.

[25] *The Encyclopedia of Philosophy*, ed. Paul Edwards (New York: Macmillan and Free Press, 1967), 3: 224.

d. Further Remarks

I have argued that liberty is a matter of degree. I have also contended that while no single definition is right, many definitions can be ruled out either because they are hopelessly vague, or because they impoverish the language by incorporating in the definition of liberty items that, though ancillary to liberty, need to be distinguished from it for clarity. Thus, though using Hobbes's definition as a starting point, I have by no means accepted it. Rather, I have attempted to illuminate the structure of liberty by considering successive enlargements, along various dimensions, of the original Hobbesian concept. Finally, while recognizing room for difference of judgment as to what definition is most useful and most nearly in accord with usage, I have suggested a definition that I think meets those tests as well as, or better than, any alternative I have been able to discover or devise.

One result of this procedure is that I have avoided mentioning certain (as it seems to me, oversimplifying) dichotomies with which the literature of freedom is strewn. Thus I have not made the distinction between "negative" and "positive" liberty central to my discussion.[26] Nor have I, despite my beginning with Hobbes, accepted the watershed type of distinction between Hobbes's "physical-mechanistic" concept of liberty and what Benjamin Barber calls the "psychological-intentional" model.[27] A somewhat similar distinction is made by Robert F. Saseen, who argues that "the freedom which is an affair of politics must be understood . . . as the ability of a person to engage in those activities which will achieve the particular excellence of his

[26] The most widely discussed use of this distinction is Sir Isaiah Berlin's "Two Concepts of Liberty," in *Four Essays on Liberty* (London: Oxford University Press, 1969), pp. 118-172. See also the Introduction to this volume for Berlin's later qualifications of the original essay.

[27] *Superman and Common Men*, pp. 40-72. See the discussion above, p. 18, n.4.

being, and in virtue of which he can exist as a man."[28] If the exposition above has achieved its purpose, it will be clear why I reject (and, I believe, avoid) the dilemma of having to define liberty either as a matter of doing as one pleases or as a matter of doing what is good for one. A person must be free to make mistakes, to do what is bad for him; and the determination of what will lead to his self-realization must be his if he is to be free.

2. THE MEANING OF "EQUALITY"

Turning from liberty to equality, we are confronted again with a term whose meaning tends to get out of hand. Curiously enough, in this case we start with a word that is defined fairly precisely. If two objects are said to be of equal weight, size, or density, for instance, we know exactly what is meant, and likewise, of course, if two men are said to be of equal height. "Equal" means "the same." But when equality is applied to human beings and their affairs generally, difficulties arise. No two men are equal in all respects, exactly alike. They are not even created equal.

But democratic equality has more to do with prescription than with description. Should individuals be made as equal as possible? Obviously they cannot be made physically or intellectually equal; but should they be made equal, or as nearly so as possible, with respect to their welfare, or the circumstances of their lives? Should the goal, in short, be equality of condition? More accurately, is that what the democratic ideal of equality means? It seems clear that it is not. Certainly this is not the way it is generally interpreted. Moreover, and more fundamentally, such an interpretation would place it squarely at odds with the other

28 "Freedom as an End of Politics," *Interpretation: A Journal of Political Philosophy*, 2 (1971), 105-125, 125. Saseen further contends that freedom "must be conceived as the ability of a person to desire, to choose, and to do what is really good, to do what in fact will enable him to realize himself." Ibid., p. 119.

democratic ideal, liberty. Equality in this sense, as has been remarked, is not natural. It could be attained, and maintained, only by suppression. For instance, either all must be compelled to save an equal share of their earnings or else a family that chooses to consume less could not be allowed to pass the savings on to their children (or anyone else) either by inheritance or by gift. Clearly no society that adheres to both of the democratic ideals of liberty and equality can define equality as equality of condition.

Another candidate is equality of opportunity. At first blush, this concept seems to provide an effective and acceptable blend of equality with liberty. It does not say that all men should have the same rewards but that they should have equal chances. Jefferson did not proclaim a right to happiness, but only to the *pursuit* of happiness—the opportunity to gain it. Far from being in conflict with liberty, this concept is closely akin to it, with the important addition of the injunction that it be equally distributed. To give one an opportunity, a chance, is to assure that he will have the liberty to pursue whatever is in question.

Appealing though it is, this concept, standing alone at least, soon runs into serious difficulties. At what point in a person's life must his opportunity be equal to that of others? If, by making use of his equal opportunities, a man soon secures the advantages of advanced education, of wealth, of station in life, and so on, and if he uses these advantages, as he can hardly avoid doing, in such a way that the opportunities open to most of his contemporaries cannot possibly equal those he now has, is that situation compatible with equality of opportunity? And what of the great advantages that his children almost necessarily acquire simply from being brought up in his family? What does society do to make the life chances of all equal under these circumstances? And should a democracy break up the family, as well as abolishing inheritance, if that is necessary to make opportunities equal? We hear much today about compensatory education for children of underprivileged families (the principle of "redress"). A strong argument can be made for it; but my concern here is not to appraise arguments; it is simply to point out the problems involved in applying the principle of equality of opportunity. Does it mean an equal opportunity to make use of such talents as one is born with? Or does it mean that society should take the steps necessary to give to the mentally and physically handicapped chances for happiness equal to those of the most gifted—insofar as this is possible?

The definition of equality as equality of opportunity leaves many questions unanswered.[29] According to certain interpretations it leans heavily in the direction of liberty and would result in great inequalities of condition. By other interpretations, it would have precisely the opposite result, greatly infringing upon liberty in order to secure a maximum of equality of condition, without which, it may be argued, opportunities cannot be equal.

Another definition, or family of closely related definitions, seeks a middle course between equality of condition and equality of opportunity—one that neither collides head on with liberty nor allows itself to be swallowed up by the latter concept. This idea derives from the Kantian notion that each person is to be treated as an end and never solely as the means to someone else's end. It may be variously expressed as the equality of rights, the equality of consideration, or as presumptive equality; but the idea of human dignity or infinite worth is central to it, whichever of these expressions is used.

[29] The ambiguities of the word *opportunity* were explored above in subsection 1b. of this chapter. The case is put more strongly, perhaps too strongly, by F. A. Hayek, who declares: "Attractive as the phrase equality of opportunity at first sounds, once the idea is extended beyond the facilities which for other reasons have to be provided by government [education, appointment to public office, and the like], it becomes a wholly illusory ideal, and any attempt concretely to realize it apt to produce a nightmare." *Law, Legislation, and Liberty*, Vol. 2, *The Mirage of Social Justice* (Chicago: University of Chicago Press, 1976), p. 85.

If we stopped here, we might seem to have a definition (I deliberately overlook the slight differences among the various formulations) that is compatible with at least one of the stricter definitions of liberty. If so, it would seem fair to presume that that is what equality means in democratic theory, since the latter holds fast to both of these ideals. But we cannot stop here, for the concept is deceptively simple; it conceals serious difficulties. If men are of equal dignity, to be given equal consideration, possessed of equal rights, to what are they entitled? Surely, they are equally entitled to be ruled by just laws, justly applied. They must not be deprived of life, or liberty, or property without justification. Different treatment must find justification in relevant differences of circumstance. But what constitutes a relevant differentiating factor? May persons with more intelligence, good will, or energy be given more votes than others? Clearly the democratic answer, by definition, is no. May citizens with superior abilities use them to gain political office and thus enhance their political power? Just as clearly the answer is yes. But suppose they use their abilities to gain wealth and they then use their wealth, by the purchase of television time and other means of advertising, to secure their own election or that of their favorite candidates? If so, has equal opportunity for some, paradoxically, denied equal opportunity for others? For this and related problems in connection with the Federal Election Campaign Act, the United States Supreme Court was forced to work out a series of uneasy compromises between the liberty of the contributors and candidates and the equality of voters.[30] This decision exemplifies the difficulty in question, as the Court's divided opinions and the unhappiness of its critics attest.

The problem just outlined is typical of a large class of cases. In general terms, it is the problem of form versus substance. In all of the three situations discussed above, in-

[30] Buckley v. Valeo, 96 S. Ct. 612 (1976).

dividuals were given formally equal opportunities. Their rights were the same; they were given equal consideration; no one was presumed to be superior or inferior. But in the last case, equal opportunities resulted in a situation where the equal voting power of some was threatened with being nullified. Formal equality (in the economic arena) led to substantive inequality, which in turn tended to defeat the purpose of formal equality.

Or take the case of the right to counsel for persons accused of crime. Is it enough that all accused persons have the right to employ counsel? That is equal liberty; but are people to be denied justice because they cannot afford counsel? In the interests of equal access to justice, it has been held in the United States that indigent persons in these circumstances should be supplied counsel at government expense. But it remains true that the rich man can hire more expensive, and presumably more competent, counsel than the state can supply. Is this an inequality that is incompatible with the democratic ideal, or is it a liberty required by that ideal?[31]

Next to the "one person, one vote" rule, one of the most important devices used in the United States to support the ideal of equality is the court-enforced principle of equal protection of the laws. This constitutional requirement is intended in the first place to ensure that laws, once enacted, are equally applied, without favoritism or partiality. More than this, and moving into much more difficult territory, it is used to see that the laws of the states do not themselves discriminate invidiously, do not treat like

[31] David Resnick has suggested that this difficulty might be avoided by providing public counsel for all persons accused of crimes or misdemeanors and limiting their right to legal counsel to lawyers thus supplied. See his "Due Process and Procedural Justice," in Pennock and Chapman, eds., *Due Process*, NOMOS XVIII (New York: New York University Press, 1977), Chap. 7. Whether such an arrangement would meet the American Constitution's provision for right to counsel is an open question.

39

cases differentially. The question of what constitutes invidious discrimination, or to put the matter in different words, of what constitutes a relevant basis for treating some people differently from others, is enormously complicated and controversial. Moreover, it again brings the democratic ideals of equality and liberty into conflict with each other.[32]

Nowhere is this conflict of ideals more evident than in the case of the struggle to eliminate discrimination on the basis of race. It is instructive to note just where and how it arises. A law that commands segregation by race (in the schools, for instance), it has been held, clearly violates the equality principle. However, a decision requiring integration may be seen by those who are opposed to integration as violating their freedom of association.[33] In practice, moreover, this is only where trouble begins. Once more, it may appear that legal equality is not enough—that the difference between legal or formal equality and substantial or "real" equality is too great. Because of the locations of people's homes, often the result of past discriminatory practices, public or private, school segregation by race may persist if there is no law requiring it. In the United States the issue raised by this kind of situation is at present hotly

[32] The matter is put even more starkly by Geoffrey Marshall, speaking of the phrase "equality under the law." He writes as follows: "In its narrowest sense it may mean that the existing machinery of law and all government facilities should be equally available to all citizens. At its widest it may imply that governments should make laws to compel every person and institution in the community to behave impartially in all their relationships with others. Tensions between equality and liberty begin at this point. . . ." "Enforcing Equality: Two Statutory Attempts," in Gray Dorsey, ed., *Equality and Freedom*, 3: 933-939, 939. He might have added, as the discussion below points out, that the term *impartiality* is also not without its difficulties. For a thorough and authoritative discussion of the whole subject of equal protection of the laws, see Laurence H. Tribe, *American Constitutional Law* (Mineola, N.Y.: Foundation Press, 1968), Chap. 16.

[33] To be sure, those who can afford to send their children to private schools may find it possible to avoid an integrated situation; but they have lost the opportunity to choose public segregated schools.

40

debated. And the reason it is so controversial is precisely because at this point the principles of liberty and equality do clearly come into conflict. If de facto segregation is combatted by requiring students to attend certain schools other than those of their choice (transporting them there by bus), that clearly interferes with their freedom to choose what school they wish to attend, which other children they wish to associate with. Their retention of the private-school option does not negate this fact. Both in practice and in theory, the issue is sharpest where white children are bused to predominantly black schools.[34]

These difficulties, as has been noted, arise primarily at the point where formal (legal) equality is abandoned as a sufficient test for democracy and substantial equality (of opportunity, at least) is sought. Alternatively, even with formal equality, if the broader concept of liberty is used, conflict once more emerges. In other words, it arises where the results of democracy according to the procedural definition are measured against the democratic ideal. In still other terms, it arises when political democracy is considered inadequate unless it achieves social democracy. As long as the test is a legal one—an equal right to vote, a vote that legally counts as equal to that of all others, a law that by its own terms applies equally to all persons—no problems arise. But, as we have seen, as soon as the law departs from formal equality, problems do appear. When it classifies persons into separate categories and treats these categories differentially, the question arises as to whether like cases are being treated alike. If the classification is rele-

[34] It may be argued that the conflict here is as much between two different liberties as it is between equality and liberty, because the demand for busing is a demand for liberty to attend an integrated school. That is true; but the fact that the liberty to attend an integrated school is demanded as a means to secure equality, or equality of opportunity, suggests that the basic conflict is between the ideals of equality and of liberty. As is suggested above, this is most sharply delineated where the liberty of blacks remains unchanged, but that of whites is invaded for the sake of achieving greater equality.

41

vant to a purpose perceived as legitimate, and if being so classified does not disadvantage a specifiable group, all may be well.[35] Thus a law that gives tax advantages to those who farm their land may be considered valid because it encourages a way of life that the society favors. One form of land use being considered socially more desirable than others, it may be given tax benefits without doing substantive injustice.[36] But a law that requires certain children to attend specified schools rather than others, as was just noted, raises more serious questions because of its impact upon their right to freedom of association.

Returning now to the main theme regarding the definition of the democratic ideal of equality, we have noted two overlapping but not identical problems, or sets of problems. One relates to the difference between equality of opportunity and equality of condition, with various midpoints between these extremes. The other has to do with the distinction between formal or legal equality and actual (substantive) equality. It is arguable that these are not so much problems as approaches, and even that they are not two approaches but one. I believe there is a distinction, although it is not of great importance. The first approach relates directly to the question of what constitutes real equality of opportunity. The second begins with identical entitlements under the law, presuming that this

[35] I say all "may" be well, with an important qualification in mind. Because of the invidious nature of classification by race, it is normally considered to violate equal treatment regardless of the justifying purpose. However, temporary segregation of prison inmates by race where necessary to avoid racial strife may be an exception.

[36] Again, a broader concept of liberty, one that included enablements, would lead to different results; for then persons whose taxes were increased to make up for the loss of public revenue resulting from the tax advantage given to farmers would be deprived of liberty. A stricter version of property rights, according to which all taxation constitutes an invasion of liberty, would lead to the same result. See Robert Nozick, *Anarchy, State, and Utopia* (New York: Basic Books, 1974), esp. pp. 167-174.

provides what equality demands, but then finds itself forced to question that presumption in the light of various factors that may render it false. Chief among these factors is (substantive) inequality of financial resources. But it may also be true that where certain identifiable groups (e.g. blacks) are viewed by many others as inferior, the very singling them out for separate treatment (as with segregated schools or other facilities), even if the treatment is equal, gives support to prejudice and so contributes to unequal (private) treatment.

At what might be called the primary political level, we settle for the legal equality of one person, one vote. We do not give the intelligent person more votes on the theory that he has more to contribute or that he is more likely to be right (nor do we give the stupid person more votes on the theory that he needs extra protection against the rapacity of his intellectual superiors). But if it is a matter of money rather than brains, we are less certain. We do allow the energetic, the able, and the lucky to earn more and to amass more wealth than their less fortunate compatriots. At critical points (the means to a fair trial, access to education), we do, in rough and ready ways, seek to limit the effects of the resulting inequalities. Interestingly enough, we distinguish between certain things that we consider rights (access to fair trial), which we enforce as a matter of right through the courts, and other things (e.g. month-long vacations) that are thought of less as moral entitlements, and which consequently are left to the vagaries of political and economic processes.

To carry this distinction even further, it is widely believed that the fundamental human equality from which this line of reasoning begins carries with it a legitimate claim for at least a minimum of welfare, simply because a given being is human. This is considered a corollary to the dignity or infinite value of the individual. If one person's life is worth as much as another's, then no one should be denied the basic necessities of life when others have them.

43

It is easy to see how this proposition is capable of almost indefinite expansion. If individuals have equal claims to life, what about equal claims to the satisfaction of all their needs, of all their desires. Of course these demands could not be satisfied without severe incursions on the liberties of some. Once again, democratic theory must seek a balance between these rival claims.

Finally, still further complexities appear. The concepts of need and of satisfaction, as touchstones for equality, have other rivals than liberty, at least by way of qualifying principles. These rivals come from within the concept of justice itself, of which equality is a major part. Chief among them is "merit," which is by no means unambiguous. In particular it may be interpreted as referring to virtue, to work, or to production, contribution to the welfare of society, or to all these factors in some indefinite manner weighed against each other. Indeed all of the elements commonly attributed to justice may be, and frequently are considered as, relevant factors in deciding when the claims of two or more persons are equal and when they are not; thus closely are the concepts of equality and justice allied. The concept of human equality, then, like that of liberty, not only comes into conflict with the opposite number of this pair of democratic ideals, but it also has its own internal tensions.

3. THE RELATIONS BETWEEN LIBERTY AND
EQUALITY REVIEWED

Much of what has been debated in this chapter could be discussed under the heading of "justice." If we had an accepted theory of democratic justice, one that provided a "just" resolution for the conflicts discussed above, the tensions pointed out would not exist in theory; and in practice that fact would at least ameliorate them. But we don't; and, as I shall argue later, it is in the nature of things that we should not, or at least that any theory which could gain general acceptance would have an internal tension of the kind I have been discussing. Utilitarians seeking the greatest happiness on the whole, or the greatest average happiness, would permit some to suffer for the (greater) benefit of others, thus violating the equality standard and perhaps the libertarian ideal as well. Nozick and Hayek would pursue liberty at the expense of equality.[37] Rawls strives for a happy medium and finds himself attacked by both egalitarians and libertarians, thus demonstrating the absence of consensus on the content of justice even among thinkers who are all professed democrats.

How far, then, are the democratic ideals of liberty and equality compatible, perhaps even mutually reinforcing, and how far are they incompatible? Let us review what has been said that bears on this question. Each of these concepts has various meanings. While each has a central, core meaning, both concepts tend to be imperialistic. They reach out for larger areas of signification. As they do so, they come into conflict each with its own core meaning and with other extensions of that core and with one or more meanings of the other term.

If liberty be defined as absence of impediments and threats (including the rule of law), and if equality be confined to formal equality, the two ideals exhibit no conflict or even tension. One must not overlook this important fact, for it is these concepts, thus defined, that constitute the essential aspects of the democratic constitution—that is, of the forms and procedures of political democracy as *technically* defined. But when the concepts are enlarged, as they tend to be in order to embrace the full meaning of the democratic *ideal*, tensions and even contradictions emerge. Thus we get definitions of liberty designed to protect liberty in the future against the liberty of the moment. Closely related to this is the conflict between the liberty to

[37] Nozick, *Anarchy, State, and Utopia*; F. A. Hayek, *The Constitution of Liberty*, and *Law, Legislation, and Liberty*, Vol. 2, *The Mirage of Social Justice*.

act impulsively and the liberty of the self, the rationalized will. Equality also has its internal conflicts, especially between equality of opportunity and equality of condition, between formal (legal) equality and substantive equality, and between equality in relation to needs and equality in relation to desert or merit.

As to the relations between the two ideals, it is clear that where liberty permits certain individuals to obtain power, whether economic or political, it immediately creates inequality of condition, whether of material goods or of status or prestige. Moreover, any such inequality is likely to be used to create even greater inequality. Similarly, the further the meaning of equality is extended beyond formal equality into the substantive area and toward equality of condition, the more it impinges upon liberty, by almost any definition of the latter term.

To all these difficulties, John Rawls attempts to provide at least a partial answer.[38] He develops a theory of "pure procedural justice." The idea is to discover a theory of just principles and then to incorporate them in a constitution. We would have done with trying to determine what would be a just result in each particular case, after the fashion of the utilitarians. No more weighing of need against productivity, of opportunity against realization, or of equality against liberty. The principles would be arranged in serial order: first, maximal equal basic liberties; then social and economic inequalities so arranged that they are both to the greatest benefit of the least advantaged and attached to offices and positions open to all.[39] The arrangement thus specified would not be accomplished by separate consideration of each case. Rather, institutions would be so constructed as to maximize the chance that each representative group would be treated in accordance with these principles.

Let us examine Rawls's scheme more closely. He distinguishes between three types of procedural justice: perfect,

[38] *A Theory of Justice.*

[39] Ibid., p. 302. The second of these he calls "the difference principle."

imperfect, and pure.[40] Perfect procedural justice would exist where there was a standard of justice independent of the procedure used to discover and apply it. Imperfect procedural justice would exist where such a standard existed but where no sure way to apply it, that is to determine what it called for in a particular case, is to be found. Jury trial is an example. Finally, pure procedural justice is the term used to describe where procedure alone is used to determine and apply the content of substantive justice, to determine what is fair in a particular case. The paradigm case is that of gambling. Now Rawls appears to believe that it is possible to construct a set of political institutions the operation (and therefore the outcomes) of which constitute pure procedural justice. He says that "to apply the notion of pure procedural justice to distributive shares it is necessary to set up and to administer impartially a just system of institutions. Only against the background of a just basic structure, including a just political constitution and a just arrangement of economic and social institutions, can one say that the requisite just procedure exists."[41] Again he declares that "the role of the principle of fair opportunity is to *insure* [my italics] that the system of cooperation is one of pure procedural justice."[42] The practical advantage of such a system is obvious, because it is by this means that it would no longer be necessary, in meeting the demands of justice, "to keep track of the endless variety of circumstances and the changing relative positions of particular persons."[43] Now if Rawls were willing to accept some system of government, e.g., representative government with majority rule subject to certain restrictions to protect fundamental liberties, as one the outcomes of which would constitute the very definition of fairness, he could properly claim that this system was indeed one of "pure procedural justice." But he avoids making that claim. He seems to go to the brink of

[40] Ibid., pp. 84-86.
[41] Ibid., pp. 86-87.
[42] Ibid., p. 87.
[43] Loc. cit.

47

making it and then retreat. He is not satisfied, for example, to trust to the results of a particular electoral and legislative system. Legislators, he insists, must act justly. It is the ("external") standard of justice the legislators should follow rather than what the majority of their constituents seem to desire.[44] Note also the following passage:

> Suppose that law and government act effectively to keep markets competitive, resources fully employed, property and wealth (especially if private ownership of the means of production is allowed) widely distributed by the appropriate forms of taxation, or whatever, and to guarantee a reasonable social minimum. Assume also that there is fair equality of opportunity underwritten by education for all; and that the other equal liberties are secured.[45]

It would seem that in directing legislators to follow his principles of justice, Rawls has pushed them into a mare's nest. It is far from clear that their task would involve significantly less weighing of imponderables and complex and necessarily indeterminate calculations of consequences than would be required of a legislature acting on utilitarian principles. Yet the claim of greater simplicity is one of Rawls's arguments that his system is likely to be acceptable and stable. What is a "reasonable social minimum"? How can it be determined with any assurance when the point is reached where a further attempt to raise that minimum would not lower the expectations of some of those who are better off? To be sure, such a lowering is permitted by Rawls if "the basic structure is unjust."[46] (Incidentally, is there no limit to this process, no consideration of contracts or expectations otherwise established?)

But this determination too is one that may not be easily made. Rawls's legislators, in accordance with his priority principles, are to seek equal basic liberties before

44 Ibid., p. 361.   45 Ibid., p. 87.
46 Ibid., p. 79.

pursuing substantive equality, but as to how far equality of opportunity (one of his "basic liberties") requires compensation for innate inequality he is unclear. This is a principle, he says, that has prima facie validity; it must be weighed "against the principle to improve the average standard of life."[47] (Why the "average standard of life"? Surely this must be a slip, for a few lines later he says that the difference principle would allocate educational resources to the least favored—meaning, in this instance, the mentally least favored—and that spending more on the better endowed would be permissible only if it improved the long-term prospects of the least favored.) In any case it appears that we are here confronted with a most difficult problem of calculation of probable consequences, and perhaps also one of weighing one principle against another.

Although the case of compensatory education ("redress") may appear to be especially difficult, it is not essentially different with respect to our present concerns from every legislative act affecting distribution. Especially is this true regarding who constitute the "least advantaged" class. Rawls tries more than one definition of this class and concludes that either of them, or some combination of them, "will serve well enough."[48] But he seems in this passage, which deals solely with economic welfare, to overlook the fact that elsewhere he insists that "social welfare," including one's prestige and self-esteem, is equally important, or certainly at least also to be taken into account, in determining one's total welfare.[49] While social and economic welfare certainly are not unrelated it would fly in the face of known facts to assume that they necessarily varied in like fashion. And what, one wonders, of health—surely an important determinant of psychic welfare? In a just society, how much should be spent on kidney dialysis? If the difference principle provides an answer by any means other than

---

[47] Ibid., p. 101.   [48] Ibid., p. 98.

[49] Ibid., pp. 440ff.

the rough and ready guesswork current today, it escapes me. Yet, here as elsewhere in the examples I have been discussing, the problem of tension between liberty and equality is just beneath the surface. Greater equality can be obtained in many cases only by limiting the liberty of many to carry out their "life plans." The tension remains.

In short, I have been arguing that, contrary to Rawls's opinion, ease and certainty of application does not provide a reason for adopting his theory of justice, especially the difference principle. I concentrated upon this argument simply because I believe little attention has been given to it, though it is a point of which Rawls makes considerable use. But I do not wish to leave the subject of Rawls without paying some attention to his substantive arguments for his theory. Assuming that, despite his apparent claim, his theory is not one of "pure procedural justice" but rather one of "imperfect procedural justice,"[50] is it nonetheless one that commends itself to our intuitive ideas, or one that would do so on reflection? So much has been said on this subject that it is unlikely I shall be able to add anything new. Nevertheless, I should like to point to certain difficulties that seem serious to me. Why should legislators be expected to follow the principle of always insisting on helping the least advantaged first? And, for that matter, why would the rational man in the original position accept this rule? One can look at this question in various ways. Sen has dealt with it neatly and logically, showing that the difference principle is concerned with changes in levels of welfare only, not with changes in the differences between various categories.[51] Others point out that just as

[50] At certain points he seems to admit as much—as when he states that we should "recognize unjust laws as binding provided that they do not exceed certain limits of injustice." Ibid., p. 351. Clearly he is here applying an "external" standard of justice.

[51] A. K. Sen, "Rawls versus Bentham: An Axiomatic Examination of the Pure Distribution Problem," in Norman Daniels, ed., *Reading Rawls* (New York: Basic Books, 1975), Chap. 12.

50

utilitarianism has its hard cases, so does Rawls. Is it sensible to deny a large increase in welfare to most groups in society because it will not result in even a slight increase in the welfare of the least advantaged?

I should like to approach the question from a slightly different point of view. Why is it rational for the man in the original position to accept the maximin rule? Rawls acknowledges that it would not generally be a suitable guide for choices under uncertainty.[52] However, he believes that certain features of situations make it plausible and that these features in fact characterize the original position as he has defined it. The first of these is that "the veil of ignorance excludes all but the vaguest knowledge of likelihoods."[53] But is it unreasonable to suppose that a person in the original position would envisage the likelihood of numerous gradations of welfare in society and further to assume that the chances of his being in the lowest of these would be relatively small? It seems to me not. But in any case, let me reinforce my position by suggesting that this person (and of course all the others in his position, being equally rational) might adopt a principle of justice (neither Rawlsian nor utilitarian) that all should be guaranteed "the basic necessities of life." In this case, surely, Rawls's first special feature would not prevail.

Rawls's second feature suggesting, or making plausible, the maximin rule is that "the person choosing has a conception of the good such that he cares very little, if anything, for what he might gain above the minimum" guar-

[52] *A Theory of Justice*, p. 53. Roughly speaking, Rawls's principles of justice are conceived as those principles that rational men would agree to for the governance of their society if they were ignorant of their personal talents, wants, and ideals, i.e. in the "original position," "behind the veil of ignorance." The "maximin rule" calls for seeking the best possible worst likely condition as the goal of principles of justice. That is to say, it assumes that persons in the original position would seek above all to protect themselves against bad consequences: they would "play it safe."

[53] Ibid., p. 155.

51

anteed by the maximin rule.[54] This feature flows, he argues, from the principle of diminishing utility and, one must assume, from the belief that the minimum will be considerably above what I have described as providing for "the basic necessities of life." The latter assumption, not being stated, is not supported. Moreover, it would seem to me that it might be doubted. However that may be, Rawls states that "in justice as fairness the parties do not know their conception of the good."[55] How then can they know that they will care very little for increments of welfare above the presumed minimum? (I shall argue presently that they would be likely to care a good deal.) Lastly on this point, Rawls argues that the priority of liberty, which he argues for elsewhere and which for the moment I am not disputing, would be jeopardized if one gave up the maximin rule for the sake of greater economic and social advantages.[56] But it is not clear why striving for greater gains need be at the expense of liberty. In fact, what might be demanded would be the liberty to strive for greater gains. Granted that the liberty whose priority Rawls is concerned to maintain is political and civil liberty, it is still not obvious why these would be threatened by striving for economic and social advantages unless all economic and social differences are thought to impinge upon political or civil liberty. But since Rawls does not believe in absolute equality of condition, that is clearly not what he means.

Finally, the third of the special features is that the rejected alternative theories of justice have unacceptable outcomes.[57] Here as elsewhere Rawls seems to consider utilitarianism as the only likely alternative. But again why cannot one simply postulate principles of justice that guarantee both basic liberties and basic necessities? Surely one can "buy" parts of Rawls's package without taking the whole thing! The resulting theory may be less neat; it may

[54] Ibid., p. 154.
[56] Ibid., p. 156.
[55] Ibid., p. 155.
[57] Ibid., p. 156.

leave much more to intuition or to social conventions growing at least partly out of intuitions; but it may be the best
we can do.

Having substituted "basicmin" for maximin, let me proceed to another of Rawls's assumptions, this time the assumption that rational men are not envious, not interested
in relative standings.[58] We are involved here with a matter
of degree. Rawls does not seem to contend that rational
men would be totally devoid of envy. I, on the other hand,
do not argue that envy would be a consuming passion.
Clearly the rational man in the original position would not
wish to adopt a principle that would be destructive of society and of each other. But it does not follow that he
must adopt principles of justice that give no heed to relative as well as absolute welfare. To recognize some claim
by laborers with differing degrees of skill to maintain
something like their traditional wage differentials does not,
I think, conflict with any principle that the person in the
original position need reject. Rawls's contention that concern for relative standing, whether economic or social, is
destructive of cooperative inclinations and of the possibility of social union[59] seems to me to fly in the face of well-
known facts. The desire to excel, to surpass one's fellows,
need not be antisocial. All members of a golf club are not
at each other's throats because they have a system of handicaps (which publicizes relative differences) or because they
have intraclub competition in the form of a tournament.
At a more serious level the same sort of thing may be said
of the members of the executive staff of a corporation.

Further, it may well be that the competitive spirit, the
desire not just to make a high score but to score higher
than Jones, plays an important role in increasing total
production. In fact it may be that the desire to "keep up
with the Joneses" makes us all better off. And what is irrational about the man behind the veil of ignorance feel-

[58] Ibid., p. 144.   [59] Ibid., pp. 545-546.

ing that it is proper for men who work hard to receive a greater reward than those of equal talents who loaf—and this without regard to whether the least advantaged are helped? But here I am unsure of Rawls's meaning. Perhaps he insists only that the production of the hard-working group should benefit the "life chances" of the least advantaged, and all others, meaning that they can share in the benefits if they work as hard as the first group. Even here we have the problem of whether hard work is a matter of merit or of glands.

If then rational men behind the veil of ignorance would be concerned about relative as well as absolute welfare, what follows? In the first place, this would strengthen the argument against the maximin principle, as was argued above, because it weakens the second of the special assumptions supporting maximin. As to the priority of liberty being reinforced by the rapid onset of diminishing returns from increased amounts of social and economic welfare, as Rawls contends, two points may be noted. If people seek relative advantages, at the very least the returns from increased welfare for a given group and not for the whole diminish less rapidly than they otherwise would, because the group enjoys an improvement in its relative as well as in its absolute position. Possibly, then, what would be reinforced would not be the priority of the political and civil liberties that Rawls has in mind when he speaks of the priority of liberty but rather the liberty to compete in the marketplace.

The second point, I confess, confuses me even more. If the rational man does tend to believe, with Aristotle, that a just distribution entails relative equality, the treatment of unequals unequally, what results will he envisage from a legislature charged with enforcing that kind of justice? In addition to all the complexities involved in the calculation of what justice called for, we now have a large and highly intractable subjective element to take into account—or at

54

least an element so vaguely defined that the room for subjective variations in judgment is large indeed. One can
foresee each group struggling for legislation designed to insure, or obtain, its (relatively) just position. Since the
effect on certain groups would be both more obvious and
more keenly felt than the effect on others, many of them
would be successful. The net result might well be chaotic,
inefficient, and destructive of valued (though not highest-
order) liberties. Does this mean that the man in the original position, foreseeing all this, would after all reject the
inclusion of relative equality as part of the concept of
justice? If so, he must go back on the reasoning of the last
several paragraphs. Otherwise, it appears that he would be
forced to give up the whole enterprise of finding a neat
theory of justice and to accept one that relies more on the
weighing of need against effort against production of what
is socially useful (as measured partly by what is demanded)
against the goods of cooperative activity and social union.
But surely this does little to alleviate the tension between
liberty and equality.

Incidentally, the problem of envy and of relative equality bedevils Rawls again when it comes to the discussion of
his system's stability. Even apart from envy, as long as
some (perhaps most) demand the freedom to make the
most of their talents and to be rewarded for their efforts,
while some also demand that their opportunities shall be
equal to those of all others, tension will exist. Particularly
is this true if one takes account of man's desire for precedence. One does not have to be a Hobbesian to see here a
force that is in sharp conflict with the drive for equality.
Tocqueville saw the same problem from the opposite side
when he declared: "[D]emocratic communities have a natural taste for freedom; left to themselves, they will seek it,
cherish it, and view any privation of it with regret. But for
equality their passion is ardent, insatiable, incessant, in-
vincible; they call for equality in freedom; and if they can-

55

not obtain that, they call for equality in slavery."[60] Finally, we may note with Aristotle that those who agree that men should be treated equally may yet disagree as to whether they should be treated with absolute equality or according to merit. As he put it, "[I]nferiors become revolutionaries in order to be equals, and equals in order to be superiors."[61]

One other proposal for solving the problem of the tension between liberty and equality, or the problem of "social justice," deserves attention. I refer to the work of F. A. Hayek. He argues at length that the very concept of social justice is meaningless. "Justice," he says, is "an attribute of human conduct."[62] A society cannot be just or unjust. Tensions, quarrels, disputes over what constitutes a just distribution of life's goods are inevitable if liberty is limited in the interest of equality. Much more than Rawls, Hayek reduces the pursuit of justice to a procedure. Rather, since he would not give society the appellation of either "just" or "unjust," he substitutes for a procedure designed to secure justice one designed, in the only way compatible with freedom, he argues, to maximize the opportunity for each individual to pursue his own interests on the basis of his knowledge and in the light of his understanding of his interests. Any other course, Hayek believes, leads to totalitarianism.[63] In short, his resolution of the problem is to confine government to a minimum, with the great majority of social arrangements being a product of "spontaneous order."[64] Impersonal (frequently market) determinations are substituted for personal (governmental) decisions. Like the physical facts that prevent us from jumping over the moon, these circumstances would not be seen as inter-

[60] Alexis de Tocqueville, *Democracy in America*, ed. Phillips Bradley (New York: Knopf, 1945), 2:97.

[61] *The Politics of Aristotle*, trans. with an introduction by Ernest Barker (Oxford: Clarendon Press, 1946), v, ii, 3.

[62] *Law, Legislation and Liberty*, 2:30.

[63] Ibid., pp. 82-83.

[64] Ibid., passim, and vol. 1 of the same work.

fering with liberty. In the great society, our ignorance of the infinitude of facts required to calculate the consequences of legislation designed to secure "social justice," together with our ignorance of the ends of each individual, makes any other approach to the problem self-defeating.

Although Hayek's theory entails no tension between liberty and equality, he recognizes that it is far removed from most people's intuitions about justice. Only if they could be persuaded to accept his theory would tension be eliminated in practice. Yet he is convinced that the current misconception, as he deems it, is based upon a fallacy. He recognizes that prevalent ideas of justice are appropriate to small, face-to-face groups, like the family. Here the requisite amount of information is both obtainable and encompassable by the human mind—at least within tolerable limits. In the great society it is not so. Hence the same principles do not apply.[65]

Here, as with Rawls, it seems to me that Hayek is expecting the impossible of human nature. He overlooks its ambivalence. In this case we can even identify the source—or part of it—of this ambivalence. It lies precisely in the fact that men are members at once of very small societies and of larger ones. But societies are not divided into just two sharply distinguishable kinds. The societies of which we are members range from family to humanity, with countless groupings of intermediate size. As the love and sympathy that gives force to our concern for equality, at least as it affects others than ourselves, is gradually attenuated in larger and larger circles of human groupings, so the more self-regarding concern for liberty tends to take command. To be sure, our anxiety not to be dominated by those whose luck or ability brings them to positions of wealth and power may make us espouse the cause of equality to an important degree, but the fact of the opposition, the tension, the human ambivalence, remains.

[65] Ibid., 2:88.

Whether or not Hayek's vision of the best society possible (he would never be a Utopian) is sound, like Rawls's theory of justice it encounters hard facts of human psychology that make it unattainable—or so it seems to me.

A kernel of truth in Hayek's theory remains. The more we expand the role and scope of governmental activities, the more we invite threatening tension between the demands for liberty and equality. Especially is this true to the extent that we seek to achieve equality of condition at the expense of liberty beyond the point where a substantial consensus to this application of social justice has developed.

Further light will be shed upon the tensions between liberty and equality by the next chapter, which deals with a similar and partly overlapping set of tensions, that between individualism and collectivism. Let this much, however, be observed here: the differences in analysis and appraisal of these tensions manifested in the works of various writers often are dictated by differing views of the facts. Frequently the facts in question have to do with the nature of man, with human nature, as we have just seen to be the case with Rawls and Hayek. They tend, not surprisingly, to be part of whole mind-sets, or ideologies, that dictate the aspects of human nature each will stress. Thus a Rousseau will place a high value upon equality, especially social equality, because he believes it is essential for the respect for persons and for the moral freedom postulated by the democratic ideal. On the other hand, a Tocqueville will see that same equality as undermining freedom, because it leads the mass of men to resent, and therefore to oppose, those inequalities which differences in abilities and enterprise tend to create. At issue here, in large measure, are beliefs about the extent to which inequalities in talent and motivation are inescapable.

58

CHAPTER III

Individualism and Collectivism:
An Additional Tension

1. INTRODUCTORY REMARKS

THIS chapter is devoted to an exploration of what may be referred to (with considerable oversimplification) as the individualist-collectivist axis in democratic theory. In fact, we are dealing here with two families of theories rather than with two distinct theories. Differences among members of the families cannot in all cases be described in terms of being more or less extreme, closer to or farther from the other family. Each member, however, generally can be thought of as susceptible to variations in degree with respect to its distance from members of the opposing family. This situation creates some major tensions within the body of theories referred to collectively as democratic theory: as in the case of liberty and equality, some will be internal to each family of theories, while others will cross the family lines.

These (and other) tensions within democratic political theory largely reflect man's tensions: between desire or interest on the one hand and duty or obligation on the other; between belief in equality and the demand for differential reward, status, and prestige; between the liking for privacy and the enjoyment of collective activity; between autonomous man and heteronomous man; and between selfishness and altruism. As different theorists feel greater awareness of one or the other of these pairs of opposites, their theories tend to vary accordingly.[1]

[1] Like most democratic theorists, I am dealing with man as we know

59

Throughout the history of political theorizing, the individualist-collectivist tension[2] has made itself evident, largely as an alternation from period to period but sometimes as a distinguishing mark of contemporaneous cultures. Thus some early-Greek thought, as manifested for instance by Democritus, was atomistic; and ideas smacking of individualism carried over into political theory not only in the pre-Platonic period but even during Plato's lifetime.[3] With Plato, and to an important extent with Aristotle as well, the pendulum swung to the opposite pole. The collectivity, the *polis*, tended to replace the individual as the starting point for political analysis. This collectivistic period, if it can be called that, was short-lived, however. Periclean democracy itself had a distinctly individualistic cast. Note the statement attributed to Pericles by Thucydides: "The freedom which we enjoy in our government extends also to our ordinary life. There, far from exercising a jealous surveillance over each other, we do not feel called upon to be angry with our neighbour for doing what he likes, or even to indulge in those injurious looks. . . ."[4] The Stoic and (especially) Epicurean philoso-

---

him and as he has been known throughout recorded history. Marx, and others, would argue that man's nature can be (and will be) changed in such a way that these tensions will be eliminated. For the most part I shall assume throughout this book that men are, by and large, ambivalent in the ways I have described, while I discuss and try to do justice, at appropriate places, to those who make a contrary assumption.

[2] I speak of it here in the singular as it is commonly perceived.

[3] See Eric A. Havelock, *The Liberal Temper of Greek Politics* (New Haven: Yale University Press, 1957), Chap. 13. And, more specifically, note Aristotle's criticism of the Sophist Lycophron. Contrasting his own position, that the state should devote itself to the development of goodness, he declares that otherwise "law becomes a mere covenant— or (in the phrase of the Sophist Lycophron) 'a guarantor of men's rights against one another.'" *Politics*, Bk. III, Sec. 8, 1280b.

[4] Thucydides, *History of the Peloponnesian War*, trans. Richard Crawley (New York: Dutton, 1910), p. 122.

phies, which soon came to prevail, were markedly of this order.

In due course, however, yet another, more prolonged swing toward collectivism manifested itself. Despite the relatively individualistic bias of the Hebraic and Christian traditions, the organized Church, combined with the great need for security so characteristic of European life in the Middle Ages, gave strong support to organic and collectivistic theories of politics.[5] Some modern writers may have exaggerated the organic aspect of medieval political thought, and the organic analogies of John of Salisbury and others may have been less literally intended than they have often been taken to be; yet clearly "individualism" would be a singularly inapt term for most of the political thought of this long period of Western history.[6] And post-Reformation political theory did constitute a sharp break from what had preceded it. "The Great Chain of Being," celebrated by Arthur O. Lovejoy, and the radical individualism of Thomas Hobbes and his successors respectively typify the opposing philosophies. On the Continent, the individualistic political implications were generally not accepted in so extreme a form as in England. To some extent Montesquieu, and more clearly Rousseau, stand witness for

[5] "Organic" theories treat the state as an organism, the parts of which are of value only as they serve the whole. "Collectivist" theories hold that the state has a nature and a value neither of which is reducible to the nature or value of its parts. All organic theories of the state are collectivistic, as I am defining that term, but not all collectivist theories are organic.

[6] While "collectivism" is not normally applied to this genre of political thought either, I believe the word can properly include it, because of the term's emphasis on the whole (and various partial wholes), or collectivity. To be sure, medieval political thought was not completely organic. As Ewart Lewis wrote, "Elements of the theory we call organic can form, and have formed, stable compounds with elements from individualistic theory. Medieval political thought was such a compound." *Medieval Political Ideas* (New York: Knopf, 1954), 1:193.

this proposition. And for the nineteenth and twentieth centuries one can make a fairly strong case for the contention that east of the Rhine collectivist philosophies found more fertile soil than in Western Europe or America.[7]

In the modern era at least, democratic theory got its start as an individualistic doctrine. One need think only of the Levellers and of Locke to appreciate this.[8] The rights of the individual, especially to political liberty, were being asserted as against the claims of rulers, based not only upon elitist beliefs but also upon supporting organismic philosophies that were extremely antiindividualistic in the degree of their subordination of the individual to the whole. Historically, then, democratic theory is associated with individualistic theory. Nor would it appear that the association is only historical and accidental. Its ideal of liberty relates to the individual; and the means taken to secure it, the franchise backed up by a series of individual rights, likewise reflects an individualistic philosophy. And, on the other side, until quite recently, collectivism has been associated with totalitarianism or some other form of antidemocratic theory.

Today the situation is radically changed. "Liberal democracy," or "pluralistic democracy," is under attack by critics who espouse "collectivism" or "holism." They attack it for its individualism; but they do not normally attack democracy itself. They usually claim to be attacking one (spurious) version of democracy in behalf of the proper ideal of democratic government and society. "Liberal," for these critics, has become a form of denigration;

[7] Note Sir Ernest Barker's somewhat lyrical account in his "The Breakdown of Democracy," *The Contemporary Review*, 145 (1934), 18-31, 19.

[8] Cf. Col. Rainborough's proclamation that "every man that is to live under a government ought first by his own consent to put himself under that government." A.S.P. Woodhouse, ed., *Puritanism and Liberty*, p. 53.

and likewise "pluralistic." Both terms are thought to support a theory of democracy that is too much concerned with private interests and not enough with public interests. (At the same time, pluralistic democracy is also under attack by the more extreme individualists.)

This conflict about democratic theory provides the background for the present discussion. It is true that although democracy is in one sense profoundly individualistic, democratic theorists at least as far back as Rousseau accommodated it to a much more collectivistic outlook. Indeed, I contend, just as man is both self-seeking and altruistic, so democracy has its collectivistic aspect. To this extent, at least, the critics are right. The aim of this chapter is to sort out various meanings of the concepts in question (dealing with them separately where the differences are relevant to this discussion), to clarify the issues and their implications for democratic theory, to find the strengths and weaknesses of each position, to point out misunderstandings where they exist, and to discover the extent to which residual differences arise out of differing empirical assumptions and the extent to which they are evaluational (recognizing that this dichotomy may be less than absolute). My own position is based upon the belief that, at their extremes, both individualism and collectivism are one-sided views, and that to choose either extreme is neither necessary nor correct.[9]

[9] I say "individualism" instead of "atomism" because it more readily admits of differences in degree. Thus I can speak of "radical individualism" and also of various forms of modified individualism. "Atomism" tends rather to suggest an all-or-nothing position. For theories toward the other end of the spectrum, I generally use "collectivism" (in spite of the fact that it suggests "socialism," which it does not necessarily imply) instead of "organicism," which is too restricted, or "holism," which admits less of degree than does "collectivism." No terminological choice is entirely satisfactory. "Collectivism," suggesting, as it may, a mere collection of discrete individuals—certainly not appropriate for the holist position—must be understood here in a rather special sense. Not all antiindividualists are holists,

Some idea of how large a territory the term *individualism* covers may be gained from the fact that Stephen Lukes has distinguished eleven meanings of that term.[10] He lists the belief in the dignity of man, in autonomy, in privacy, and in the abstract individual, each as a brand of individualism; and to these he adds "political individualism," "economic individualism," "religious individualism" "ethical individualism," "epistemological individualism," and "methodological individualism." Not all of these are of direct relevance to democratic theory, and of those that are, some, such as the belief in the dignity of man and the belief in autonomy, generally appear in combination, and may be shared by collectivists. Other important distinctions remain to be taken account of.

One can also distinguish varieties and degrees of collectivism.[11] For the most part, I shall let them appear as the discussion proceeds. It is well to note now, however, the major watershed between organic and hierarchical col-

---

most certainly, while some antiholists shy away from the designation "individualist."

[10] Lukes, *Individualism*.

[11] Today's critics of democratic individualism are generally more concerned with what they are criticizing than with making clear their own position, in particular whether their antiindividualism is in some sense properly called collectivism. Today's antiindividualists, however, are generally inclined to assume a somewhat Marxist position, with whatever collectivist aspects that position entails. A clear example is C. B. Macpherson. See his *Democratic Theory: Essays in Retrieval* (Oxford: Clarendon Press, 1973) and *The Life and Times of Liberal Democracy*, Oxford: Oxford University Press, 1977). A more difficult case is that of Robert Paul Wolff. From one point of view he is an individualist, as his essay *In Defense of Anarchism* (New York: Harper & Row, Harper Torchbooks, 1970) indicates. But at the same time the communal nature of his anarchistic theory, especially his insistence that community is an end in itself, marks him as at least having much in common with those who are here denominated collectivists. He is, in short, a political individualist and a social collectivist; in other words a communistic or communitarian anarchist. See his *The Poverty of Liberalism* (Boston: Beacon Press, 1968), esp. Chap. 5.

lectivist theories on the one hand, for which the names of Plato and Hegel may stand as examples (and as indication that collectivist theories often are not democratic theories), and the more egalitarian theories on the other hand, of which much is heard today. Since the collectivist democratic theories do not appear at the extreme collectivist end of the spectrum we are discussing, it is more difficult to suggest names of theorists that will not occasion controversy as to their classification. Taking this risk, one may name Rousseau and Marx. Many modern writers who are by no means Marxists, but who have Marxist leanings, would appear, if only by their denunciation of individualism, to belong in this general category.[12]

2. The Individual versus the Whole, as Starting Point for Analysis

A substantial portion of the ongoing controversy between individualists and collectivists in democratic theory has to do with what is the appropriate starting point for analysis. Sometimes the argument is purely methodological, having to do with what is the best way to explain or to achieve understanding; at other times it is more fundamental, relating to the nature of reality, to ontology. In the latter case, the individualist position verges on psychological reductionism. Often the two positions are not sharply distinguished by the debaters themselves and they will be discussed together in this section.[13]

[12] In short, to treat the different meanings of each concept as though they represent distinct positions along a single continuum is indeed an oversimplification, as will become clear as the exposition unfolds. Yet, for present purposes, I believe that this procedure is heuristically helpful and philosophically harmless. The extremes of the spectrum could be expressed as "atomism" and "holism," which at appropriate points I shall designate "radical individualism" and "radical collectivism," respectively.

[13] Substantial collections of materials embodying this controversy are to be found in Patrick Gardiner, ed., *Theories of History* (Glen-

a. *"Dispositions" and "Reductionism"*

The individualist holds that all social behavior can be reduced to individual behavior in the sense that it can be explained in terms of the motivations or "dispositions" of individuals. "Every complex social situation, institution or event," writes a leading protagonist of this position," is a result of a particular configuration of individuals, their dispositions, situations, beliefs, and physical resources and environment."[14] Further, it may be argued, insofar as we have true explanations of either social or individual behavior, they must be cast in terms of general propositions about individual psychology. (This argument for the ultimate reducibility of all social and political theory to psychology is made by John Stuart Mill and, today, by a leading sociologist, George Homans.) Individuals, it is contended, respond to rewards, whether of a "spiritual," "psychic," or "materialistic" variety. They may conform to the rules of institutions, for instance, because, in one way or another—perhaps by the approval of their fellows—they are rewarded for so doing or punished for acting in contrary fashion.[15] "In the social sciences," says Homans,

---

coe, Ill.: Free Press, 1959); John O'Neill, ed., *Modes of Individualism and Collectivism* (London: Heinemann, 1973); and Herbert Feigl and May Brodbeck, eds., *Readings in the Philosophy of Science* (New York: Appleton-Century-Crofts, 1953). For an excellent summary and evaluation, see W. H. Dray in *The Encyclopedia of Philosophy*, 4:53-58. Much of the controversy is not relevant to our concern and is omitted from this discussion—for example, the whole question of what constitutes an explanation. For an excellent summary and critique of the controversy in this area, see Georg Henrik von Wright, *Explanation and Understanding* (Ithaca: Cornell University Press, 1971).

[14] J.W.N. Watkins, "Historical Explanation in the Social Sciences," in Gardiner, ed., *Theories of History*, pp. 503-514, 505. See also Watkins, "Ideal Types and Historical Explanation," in Feigl and Brodbeck, eds., *Readings in the Philosophy of Science*, pp. 723-743.

[15] See George C. Homans, *The Nature of Social Science* (New York: Harcourt, Brace and World, 1970), passim, esp. Chap. 2. For Mill, see *A System of Logic* (London: Longmans, 1868), Bk. VI, Chap. 6.

"our only general propositions are propositions about individual behavior."[16] (By "general," Homans means *completely* general, not confined to any particular time, place, culture, or society.)

The opposing position denies that all social behavior can be so reduced. This proposition is about all that the critics of this kind of individualism (not all properly called holists or even collectivists) have in common. It will aid our understanding of the relations between individualism and collectivism to examine several lines of antiindividualist criticism with respect to methodology and causal starting points.

The antiindividualist may assert that it is possible to discover laws or tendencies of society which are not explicable in terms of individual motivations or dispositions. It should be observed that if the laws or tendencies in question are of a purely statistical nature, that is to say regularities which are presumably determined by the random behavior of many individuals, as for instance with such scientific laws as Boyle's law, they in no way contradict individualism. They do not represent, or have not been shown to represent, a characteristic of the collectivity as such. They are merely summations of individual actions, taken in sufficient numbers for the law of averages to apply. It is true that they do not represent a reduction to individual actions in the sense that the latter are explained by reference to certain motivations or dispositions. Possibly such an explanation could be advanced; possibly it could not. But if it could not, the individualist would argue that it is simply because we do not have enough facts. It might indeed be inconceivable that we could ever assemble all the necessary facts. He would contend, however, that *if we did have them* a reductivist explanation would in principle be possible, although it might be very complicated. Further, an average is a function of the individual units

16 Homans, *The Nature of Social Science*, p. 103.

of which it is composed; they impose their restrictions upon *it*, rather than the reverse.

b. Heuristic Devices and "Functionalism"

Another line sometimes advanced against the individualist is to support the use of the holistic approach as a purely heuristic device. It may be argued, for instance, that, just as it is much more useful for social science to examine the needs of the whole person and to relate his behavior to those needs than it is to attempt to explain his needs in terms of the chemistry or physics of the individual cells, so state and society have needs that serve better to explain political and social behavior than do the known dispositions of individuals. But note that already the argument has gone beyond a heuristic device. It speaks of "explanation." Without becoming involved in a far-reaching discussion of the nature of explanation, the flaw in this argument can be made apparent. The example, it will be noted, relies upon an analogy between a person and a state or society. The story is told of an AID project in an underdeveloped country to eliminate the traditional market system, which involved long walks by peasants carrying heavy burdens and much "waste" of time, in favor of a system that was much more "efficient." But the peasants were unhappy with it and the experiment was a failure, although it would have made them economically better off had they taken advantage of it. Apparently, the old system satisfied a need for socializing that was not met by the new, more "efficient" system. For most purposes this is a perfectly satisfactory explanation. But if one moves to the societal level and tries to locate a need of the society (as distinct from the individuals who make it up) that accounts for the success of the old market system, one is baffled. It was the individuals who felt the need.

Or one might begin at the other end, selecting a social "need" and finding it being fulfilled. It might be argued, for instance, that in every polity a need exists for most people to obey the law voluntarily—a need that is generally fulfilled. But one is immediately struck by the fact that states differ markedly in the degree to which, for example, citizens report their incomes for taxation purposes; and the evidence does not suggest that this behavior reflects the relative need of the respective governments— probably quite the contrary. The world today badly needs a decline in the rate of population growth, yet not only is it slow in coming, but it appears to occur least where it is needed most. Both in the case of taxation and in that of population, one is driven to examine the motivations of individuals for a satisfactory explanation. Note that proposals for trying to change either situation do not follow the line of seeking somehow to change the social need, however it might be done. Rather they seek to motivate individuals to alter their conduct, or to alter the conditions that determine the means by which present motivations may be effectuated. This is precisely because individuals do not bear the same relation to the polity as organs do to the body or the person. They have not been genetically programmed or even psychologically conditioned to act always in ways that are most "functional" for the body politic.

To return to the population analogy, certain species of birds have apparently been so programmed that they lay more eggs when conditions are favorable for their species or when their numbers are dwindling, and fewer when the opposite conditions prevail. (In many if not most instances of bird and animal population control the governing factor seems to be space.) Alas, it is not so with humankind. Their actions appear to respond to, and so must be explained in terms of, individual motivations and dispositions. Of course, they may be influenced by feedback they receive from society at large; but there appears to be nothing automatic or assured about it, and the effect of any feedback, once more, is in terms of individual motivations and dispositions. It is not meant to imply, to be sure, that the latter need vary greatly from one individual to the

69

ual wills (although possibly in some sense imminent in society), some "cunning of Reason," in ways not explained somehow directs their blind activities to its foreordained end. Hegel of course made this assumption. Without it individualism takes over; the market provides a perfect example of individual actions that achieve results never contemplated by any of the participants. So much so that Adam Smith coined the phrase the "Unseen Hand" to describe, but by no means to explain or account for, the effect! The political market operates less smoothly, but Lindblom's "partisan mutual adjustment" is again a process by which individualistic rationality achieves a social rationality beyond the intentions or anticipations of the participants.[17] The point to be noted is that the individualistic method, *as qualified below*, suffices: it explains what man has thus far been able to explain; while the holistic approach ends in mystery, or perhaps more fairly stated, in a worldview quite contrary to the procedures that have led to man's great scientific accomplishments.[18]

Perhaps the commonest form of ontological holism is based upon the contention that systems—by virtue of being systems— have laws or tendencies of their own and that social wholes may act as causes. This position differs from Hegel's in that it does not postulate any extrinsic cause. It is argued that in some way the whole shapes the part. But of course, the individualist does not for a moment deny that the individual is affected by being part of the whole and that in this sense he is what he is because of the whole of which he is a part. The behavior of individuals may be

[17] Charles E. Lindblom, *The Intelligence of Democracy* (New York: Free Press, 1965).

[18] The methodological holist may claim with Marx that the methods of natural science are not applicable to the study of man, or at least not to the study of society; that for this objective a wholly different kind of science is required. The individualist replies that this is all conjectural, since no laws of history or society have yet been discovered.

influenced by their conception of the whole, by their loyalty to it, and by their ideals of what it should be like or what they would prefer it to be like.[19]

d. Institutionalism

Moreover, and this is an important point for the collectivist or holist to recall, the individual may belong to many wholes and he will behave differently depending upon which whole he conceives of himself as being a part of at the time of his action. My behavior in general may be influenced by the fact that I think of myself as belonging to a particular religious community. Or, again, in certain contexts, where that role is not brought to the forefront of my consciousness, I may even behave in ways that seem hardly compatible with that office. The various roles that guide my behavior are united by a single, common "I" that plays them.

This idea of individual behavior as affected by roles, by institutions, and by concepts of the particular society of which the individual is a part calls for further treatment. It is one of the important points upon which collectivists insist. But one does not have to be a holist to support it, although he may count himself an antiindividualist. Writers who would not number themselves among the holists, notably Maurice Mandelbaum, would also insist that the fact that individual behavior is influenced by these institutional or societal factors is incompatible with holding that

---

[19] A parallel argument is made by the organismic biologists, who contend that the whole (organism) determines the nature and function of the part, acting as a causal unit. At least one critic contends that the most they have been able to give evidence for is not that the whole determines the part, but that "The concept of the whole determines the concept of the part." Morton Beckner, *The Biological Way of Thought* (New York: Columbia University Press, 1959), p. 188. The application of this analysis to the problem of social science methodology would be that the concepts of whole and part would continue to be concepts in individual minds. Abstractions, such as "society," must not be reified.

all social behavior is reducible to individuals and their dispositions. The individual, they would argue, is not autonomous; he is governed in part by duties imposed upon him by the institutions of society, by the roles in which he is cast. And the social unit has a continuity that outlives the particular individuals that, at any given time, make it up.[20]

Mandelbaum's ultimate position midway between individualists and collectivists is akin to my own. Yet it seems to be closer to that of individualism than he admits. I know of no individualist who denies that men are influenced by ideas "imposed" from without, as well as those not "imposed." No one who admits the most obvious facts of family life could take such a position. Our ideas of how we should behave are of course influenced, to say the least, by what we are taught in the home. Families may bear marked distinguishing characteristics for generations. Whether this fact is genetically or culturally determined or both is immaterial in the present context. Moreover, families are perceived as social units that outlive their individual members. If belief that the Adamses, the Roosevelts, or the Kennedys

---

[20] See Maurice Mandelbaum, *History, Man, and Reason* (Baltimore: Johns Hopkins University Press, 1971), 252-254. See also his outstanding article, "Societal Facts," in Gardiner, *Theories of History*, pp. 476-488. Mandelbaum goes on to distinguish his position from that of Durkheim and of organicists generally by contending that not all social behavior can be explained in these terms and that it must be explained in part by "inherited capacities which are not themselves explicable in social terms," *History, Man, and Reason*, p. 254. Mandelbaum's position (without reference to him) has been made the basis for a call to political scientists to return to the study of institutions, while avoiding formalism. Studies of political behavior, it is argued, are completely inadequate apart from the institutional norms that guide that behavior. Moreover, this approach, it is said (with great merit, it appears to me) , "provides an opportunity for reintegrating the empirical study of politics with the analysis of political values. . . ." For, it is suggested, "political values are meaningless if they cannot be institutionalized; [and] institutions cannot be defined exhaustively in factual terms." See Nevil Johnson, "The Place of Institutions in the Study of Politics," *Political Studies*, 23 (1975), 271-283, 280.

were characterized by traits that tended to mark them apart and to be handed down from one generation to another marks one as not an individualist, then probably no serious thinker could be so classified.

In fairness to the "institutionalists," of whom I have cited Mandelbaum as a prime example, one should deal not only with the influence of a particular family tradition, but with the influence of the institution of the family. Thus, if, at a particular time and place, that institution includes the ideas that a woman's place is in the home and that the man of the house should be the breadwinner, this too affects behavior. One may call such concepts "ideas," as I have done, or "roles" and therefore parts of "institutions." The impact is the same. They are ideas more or less permanently implanted in a society, that is to say in the members of that society, and handed down from generation to generation. Some individualists may have overlooked this important fact, but it is difficult to think of contemporary scholars doing so. They are concerned first to deny that these concepts reside anywhere but in the minds of individuals. Further, they are concerned to assert two important propositions. The first is that in accepting their roles and acting in accordance with dictates of these roles, individuals are responding to well-known, even commonplace, laws of individual psychology. The second, crucial for democratic theory, is that individuals do not always accept their roles and act accordingly. They may modify them or act contrary to them. To this extent they *are* autonomous. This is how institutions change—like the institution of the family and the idea that a woman's place is in the home.

It is clear that any particular individual may be greatly affected by the roles in which he is cast, by traditions and by institutions; and so, likewise, for all the individuals in a society. The question can then be raised whether a role or an institution can always be explained in terms of, or reduced to, the acts and dispositions of individuals. Fortunately, it seems unnecessary for our purposes to deal with this problem. Even if institutions, like the environment, must be treated as independent variables exerting an influence on the nature and behavior of individuals, the individual may remain also an independent variable. He is not thereby reduced to an "organ" of society, completely under its control. As Mandelbaum, a critic of individualists and one who insists on the autonomy of such "societal facts" as roles and institutions, points out, it is the human individual who learns the duties imposed upon him by institutions. This individual must have the innate capacity to learn in order to be influenced in this way. Even Pavlov considered it necessary to assume the unconditioned reflexes of purpose, of freedom, and of slavery. And, perhaps more to the point, self-esteem and approbativeness seem absolutely essential to the training of children, that is to their "social conditioning"; likewise with sympathy. In short, "in order to understand the nature of human beings in any society whatsoever, we need a science of psychology which is independent of sociology. . . . "a point which Comte, Hegel, and Marx all denied."[21] The individualist's insistence on the existence of certain fundamental human characteristics ("human nature") and his complementary desire to avoid the reification of society and the attribution to it of a "group mind" that controls the minds of individuals is not incompatible with allowing to institutions a certain independence and irreducibility (leaving the latter question open).

In speaking of institutions, roles, and concepts of the whole, one has not exhausted the influences that help shape the individual and his wants and preferences. Beliefs and practices, moral and otherwise, handed down from generation, are likewise important. Michael Oakeshott puts it this way. "This so-called 'social inheritance' is an accumulation of human understandings and is composed of the moral and prudential achievements of numberless individuals expressed in terms of the rules and conditions which

[21] Ibid., pp. 240-254. The quotation is from page 254.

75

specify a multiplicity of particular practices." He goes on to insist that "none but an individual initiate can either use it or educate others in its use." And, a paragraph later, he asserts that "[t]here can be no social consciousness which is not the consciousness of a *socius*; that is, of a particular agent understanding himself to be associated with others in recognizing the conditions of some specific practice."[22]

Collectivists sometimes accuse the individualist of opening the door to an infinite regress; for, the argument runs, individuals are themselves created by society and are constantly being created by it. Here the collectivist position owes much to the work of George Herbert Mead.[23] His contention, elaborated in great detail and now widely accepted, is that the self is not born but made, made by the individual's life in association with others. Development of an individual into a self is a kind of bootstraps operation—at least so it must have been in the early days, before the invention of language and before any real "selves" existed. The first sound or gesture that is perceived by an individual other than the one initiating it, which is interpreted by the "receiver" as having a meaning intended for him by the "sender," initiates the process. An awareness of "self" as contrasted with "other" is now emerging. Individuals develop selves; and yet "selves can only exist in definite relationships to other selves."[24]

[22] Oakeshott, *On Human Conduct* (Oxford: Clarendon Press, 1975), pp. 86-87, and 88. The social consciousness, as he neatly puts it, is "a collected, not a 'collective' achievement." Ibid., p. 87.

[23] The idea was not original with Mead. It was developed by Hegel, although cast in metaphysical terminology difficult to grasp and apparently implying more than is essential to the position taken in the text above. See *The Phenomenology of Mind*, trans. J. B. Bailie (New York: Harper & Row, Harper Torchbooks, 1967), pp. 217-227. For a lucid discussion of Hegel's position, see Judith N. Shklar, *Freedom and Independence* (Cambridge: Cambridge University Press, 1976), pp. 26-30.

[24] Mead, *Mind, Self, and Society*, ed. with an introduction by Charles W. Morris (Chicago: University of Chicago Press, 1934), pp. 154-164. The quotation is from p. 164.

Mead goes on to say, "No hard-and-fast line can be drawn between our own selves and the selves of others, since our own selves exist and enter into our experience only insofar as the selves of others exist and enter as such into our experience also."[25] Mead's own argument seems here to be verging dangerously upon the infinite-regress trap. Evidently at some point the concept of self, or some dim precursor thereof, first emerged in the mind of an individual. By definition it includes the concept of another self. Note that what it includes is the *concept* of another self. It does not follow that "no hard-and-fast line can be drawn between our own selves and the selves of others." On the contrary, just such a line seems to be an intrinsic part of the very idea of self. Mead speaks of our "selves" as entering into "our" experience. Whose experience? Clearly, Mead is distinguishing the self from an experiencing entity, the individual. Regardless of how this individual came to be what he is, regardless of the extent or nature of the influence of society or institutions upon him (and his self), *he* is the experiencing unit. This Mead does not deny. Thus the individual remains in a fundamental sense a distinct and basic unit, necessarily presupposed even by the collectivist mode of analysis.

The same point is put somewhat differently by Gibson Winter. He contends that Mead underemphasizes the "I," tending to subsume it in the "Me" (the social self). "The significance of sign, gesture, and symbol," he argues, "need not be underplayed in order to achieve the balance of in-

---

[25] Ibid., p. 164. For a discussion of the theory of the self that accords with Mead's account and extends its political implications, see Roberto Mangabeira Unger, *Knowledge and Politics* (New York: Free Press, 1975), Chap. 5. The following passage indicates the direction and mood of his thought. "Community is held together by an allegiance to common purposes. The more these shared ends express the nature of humanity rather than simply the preferences of particular individuals and groups, the more would one's acceptance of them become an affirmation of one's own nature. . . . The conflict between the demands of individuality and of sociability would disappear." P. 220.

77

teriority and exteriority in the emergence of mind, self, and society." And again, "Sociality is not a product of external forces or so-called interaction; rather, interaction, communication, and the emergence of complex social structures are *derived* typifications of the essential sociality of man."[26]

Thus far it would appear nothing has been asserted that the individualist *need* deny (although, as will appear later, some individualists might in fact take issue). Indeed, most modern individualists assert similar propositions. That rugged individualist Ludwig von Mises, for instance, freely admits that man is what he is because of society, and, more specifically, because of that social phenomenon, speech. Explanation of human behavior and of the self must, indeed, take interaction into account and perhaps even "begin with it"; but by beginning with the collective units, he argues, one encounters an insurmountable obstacle. This obstacle arises from the fact that the individual normally belongs to various collective entities. Actions are performed by individuals; and explanations of these actions performed by individuals who belong to more than one group present problems that can be solved only by referring back to the individual as a starting point. "The ultimate goal of human action is always the satisfaction of the acting man's desire."[27]

Now what will be the collectivist's reaction to this statement? He is likely to acknowledge the point but claim that it is trivial, because, he will say, the acting man's desire is a mere reflection of what society has made the acting man

[26] Winter, *Elements for a Social Ethic* (New York: Macmillan, 1966), Chap. 4. The quotations are at pages 98 and 99, respectively. The significance of the last statement goes beyond the question of methodology and will be discussed later on in this chapter.

[27] Mises, *Human Action* (London: Hodge, 1949), pp. 41ff. The quotation is at page 14. Mises is referred to above as a rugged individualist. However, he is not an extreme methodological individualist, his individualism being more of the substantive variety. At one point he states that at present he sees no alternative to methodological dualism: no way to reduce human action wholly either to the realm of the external or to that of the internal. Ibid., pp. 16ff.

to be. Thus we are faced with a chicken-and-egg problem. If one is seeking explanations of social phenomena, where is the best place to begin? Is inflation to be explained in terms of individual dispositions (e.g. to seek "free rides," hoping to enjoy the benefits of rising income while someone else pays the cost); institutions (e.g. democracy, because it makes those who determine policy responsive to people disposed to be "free riders," which, perhaps, is nearly everyone); or the society as a whole (because it has socialized people to be "free riders" when they can, rather than willingly pitching in to bear a fair share of the burden)? From a methodological point of view, this example might suggest that the social scientist would do well to keep an open mind and to use whichever method seemed most useful for the purpose at hand. Nor is there any reason why the democratic theorist may not adopt this compromise position, as many do.[28]

In fact, the controversy over starting points has led each side to moderate its extreme claims. We have noted also the development of a possible third position, institutionalism. Nothing has been established that finally collapses the position of either the moderate individualist or the moderate collectivist.[29] Whether *all* social phenomena can

[28] Ernest Gellner, "Holism versus Individualism in History and Sociology," in Gardiner, *Theories of History*, p. 509. For further indication that the argument over starting points involves little direct opposition, see ibid., p. 515; Watkins, in Gardiner, op. cit., p. 506; and W. H. Dray, in *The Encyclopedia of Philosophy*, 4:53-58.

[29] Stephen Lukes argues that for (methodological) individualism to provide useful explanations it must be defined in such a way as to make it both harmless and pointless. Or rather, he contends, it would no longer be appropriate to call it individualism. At the same time, he concedes that one who does not accept "holism" or "historicism" is not necessarily a (methodological) individualist. (In this respect his position is similar to that of Mandelbaum.) I would suggest that denial of "holism" or "historicism" is precisely what most individualists are concerned to accomplish; and it may well be that they would give up nothing they believed in to adopt the position suggested in the text above and call themselves methodological dualists. See Lukes, *Individualism*, Chap. 17.

be explained in terms of individual dispositions is open to question; but in any case, reference to certain "societal" (institutional) facts as partial determinants in no way entails the elements of collectivism—such as the assumption of a collective mind or will, independent of individuals—to which the individualists take exception. On the other side, most collectivists today are content to argue that understanding social phenomena is facilitated if we try to find generalizations about social behavior without regard to their reducibility to individual dispositions and if we recognize that individuals, to a large extent, are what they are because of their associations with other individuals in society and their inherited traditions.

In the attempt to show that the dialectic of scholarly discussion has today brought most individualists and most collectivists close together on this matter of starting points, it would be a mistake to give the impression that historically the gap has not been much wider or even that today examples of writers who are far apart on this matter could not be found. Although the position outlined above is not incompatible with what I think is essential to individualism, its recognition of the importance of the social context goes much beyond what Hobbes or even Locke had in mind. Emile Durkheim attacked the utilitarians vehemently and not least because of their use of the individual as the great starting point for social analysis. For his part, one must always begin with society and look for social and institutional laws and causes to account for even such apparently individualistic behavior as suicide. He admitted that some nucleus of individual human nature was always there, but he insisted it was so acted upon and formed by society that at most it could be only a very indirect explanation of social or even individual phenomena.[30] On the other hand, George Homans, a contemporary sociologist, contends, as we have seen, that there will be no true

[30] See Robert A. Nisbet, *The Sociological Tradition* (New York: Basic Books, 1966), pp. 82-97.

science of society until all behavior has been explained in terms of the laws of individual psychology.

As even more extreme polarization appears between a man like Homans and one like Hegel, who insists that it is possible to discover a mysterious force in the world in terms of which historical and sociological phenomena can be explained. Between this collectivist approach and that of any individualist like Hegel the difference is indeed substantial, although even a historicist collectivist might support democracy, not as an ideal but as the best practicable form of government under prevailing conditions.

In concluding this discussion of individualism and collectivism as starting points for analysis, in which the emphasis has been heavily on the extent of theoretical convergence, it should be recalled that this comprises only one aspect of the individualist-collectivist tension. I believe that from the standpoint of democratic theory it is less important than much of the literature would suggest. I turn now to another phase of individualism-collectivism.

3. The Nature of Man

Since the individualist takes man, the individual man, as the starting point for analysis, not surprisingly he has a good deal to say man's nature. What he has to say can be conveniently classified under the headings "autonomy and dignity" and "psychological attributes." But of course the collectivist does not ignore the individual; and what he says about him sometimes even coincides with the individualist's position. I shall try to bring out the agreements and disagreements in the discussion that follows, presenting a fuller account of the collectivist's position in the ensuing section.

a. Autonomy and Dignity

In discussing the nature of man, the individualist often stresses man's uniqueness; and in seeking what renders him

81

unique, historically he has fastened upon man's reasoning power, pointing out that at least the higher forms of rationality, especially the ability to think in terms of abstract concepts and general propositions, seem peculiar to man. That the ability to think abstractly is dependent upon the development of language, a societal product, does not alter the fact that only human beings develop this ability. Democratic collectivists do not appear to disagree with individualists on this point. Such tension as exists is purely a matter of greater emphasis upon it by individualists.

Fully as distinctive of man as his reasoning power, and probably more significant for present purposes, is his moral sense of duty and of justice. Here again is a proposition, of great importance for democratic theory, on which most individualists and collectivists agree. Man's moral sense immediately marks him as a social creature and takes him beyond the reach of his own person—possibly beyond his own self, depending on one's definition of that term. In any case, it involves an awareness of the distinction between self and others and of the fact of their common concerns as well. In fact, it is self-awareness, self-consciousness, that some would insist is man's *most* distinguishing feature. A contemporary philosopher of individualism, David L. Miller, relates his brand of individualism to self-consciousness. After declaring that "the individual—not the community, not public opinion, not external environmental forces—is the source of new ideas that enable society to make changes for the achievement of ideals that in the short run at least are fairly explicitly stated," he continues, "only human beings have selves and are persons. The basic requirement of being a self is that a person (or a self) be an object to himself: a self must be able to conceive of itself, to 'look' at itself as it looks at objects. It must be self-conscious." He also argues that the desire for significance or self-esteem is the one culture-free and universal element of "human nature." Yet, at the same time, he insists that "we should not be misled into believing that the self as a present entity motivates. Rather, the individual's conception of what he may and can *become* serves as a stimulus to becoming that self; one's ideals, so to speak, motivate the self, and the normal person's ideal is, in fact, a more worthy image of his self that he tries to achieve."[31]

Nothing in Miller's individualism denies that the individual owes his specific character to life in society; and von Mises, it will be recalled, definitely affirmed that proposition. The autonomy most individualists postulate, especially democratic individualists, including Bentham, does not imply complete isolation. What the individualist must hold (as far as autonomy is concerned) is simply that the individual, *as he is at present,* regardless of how he came to be what he is, forms the ultimate unit of society; and that this unit is self-conscious and capable of acting rationally and deliberately, as contrasted with reacting to external impulses blindly, unself-consciously, and without power of control. It need not deny the power of tradition and institutions to mold and influence him. This position will here be denominated Basic Individualism, to distinguish it from more extreme forms of individualism. No more is required for democratic theory. (But, as will appear, some more extreme individualists insist on greater constancy of human nature than is implied above.)

For the individualist nothing is valuable save as it has value for some human being. In this connection, the terms *autonomy* and *dignity* constantly recur. Each serves both as a reason why men should be treated as of the highest value and as a guide to what that treatment requires.

Thus, as to autonomy, the individualist stresses that decisions, choices, are made within the individual mind. This is not to deny, *pace* B. F. Skinner,[32] that these events are caused; but it is to focus attention upon the point at which

---

[31] Miller, *Individualism: Personal Achievement and the Open Society* (Austin: University of Texas Press, 1967), pp. 3, 15, 172.

[32] See his *Beyond Freedom and Dignity* (New York: Knopf, 1971), esp. Chaps. 1-2.

they occur and upon the (deliberative) process they involve. It is to say that this process of rational deliberation, as opposed to impulsive, reflexive, or irresponsible, unthinking action, ought to be encouraged, and that to respect man's autonomy is essential for this purpose.

Turning for the moment from *autonomy* to *dignity*, this term encompasses more than the belief that the individual is the center of value in the sense that the valuing experience takes place in his consciousness. It is, as Abraham Edel has put it, an "ethical construct."[33] This construct is implied by the valuations we place upon liberty and equality, by our efforts to remove individual discriminations and human exploitation, by our solicitude to preserve the individual from being overpowered and crushed by organized society, and by our concern for privacy.[34] In short, persons who share the value judgments just referred to are, by the very fact of making them, ascribing to each individual a value of the highest order. *Dignity* is the term used to sum up the attributes, the entitlements, that these and similar judgments ascribe to men as men.

Dignity is further derived from characteristics essential to the whole moral enterprise, from the ability to make value judgments and judgments of right and wrong. One of these characteristics is the ability to be self-determining (autonomous), to think and to act rationally and to carry out decisions without undue reliance upon others. Also involved, as Downie and Telfer point out, is the ability to adopt rules that one holds to be binding upon oneself and all other rational beings, and the ability to experience a

[33] "Humanist Ethics and the Meaning of Human Dignity," in Paul Kurtz, ed., *Moral Problems in Contemporary Society* (Englewood Cliffs, N.J.: Prentice-Hall, 1969), pp. 227-240, 239.

[34] See further Kurtz, p. 240; also R. S. Downie and Elizabeth Telfer, *Respect for Persons* (London: Allen & Unwin, 1969), from which also the sentence in the text following borrows. On our concern for privacy, see Pennock and Chapman, eds., *Privacy*, NOMOS XIV (New York: Aldine, 1971), Chap. 11, for anthropological evidence in support of the universality of this concern.

wide range of emotions. When the individualist speaks of human dignity, then, he refers to a quality implied by widely held value judgments and by characteristics essential to morality itself. For the latter reason especially, he attaches supreme value to it.

Here, as at numerous other points, it is clear that the distinction between individualist and collectivist, especially if nondemocratic extremists are barred from the comparison, can easily be overdrawn. One can make this point without getting into the controversy about the nature of free will and self-determination. Yves Simon remarked that "autonomy is nothing but the climax of a process of interiorizing the law."[35] In other words, the apparently self-willed act of the individual is really in response to a socially conditioned disposition. The individualist stresses the willed action; the collectivist the conditioning. Many occupy a middle ground.

To the individualist, however, this distinction is all-important: when an individual acts "autonomously," he acts with a feeling of freedom and in the absence of coercion, regardless of the original source of his disposition to behave in that manner. The law may have become part of his self, but it is *his* self that acts, and acts freely, that freely wills to act. The distinction between action of this kind and action taken at gunpoint, whether or not we call the latter "willed," is plain enough. (We all, on occasion, find ourselves forced to act "against our will," as when coerced by threat of death, injury, or overwhelming deprivation.)

However, a caveat: the interiorized law to which Simon referred must not have been the product of irresistible coercion or Skinnerian conditioning. It must have left the individual autonomous, in the sense in which I have been using that word. It is precisely such matters that many collectivists are concerned about. And so are individualists.

[35] Simon, *Freedom and Community* (New York: Fordham University Press, 1968), p. 27.

But they may differ as to the facts. Marcuse sees conditioning and destruction of individual volition where most individualists do not. He sees the individual in our society as conditioned by a monolithic front of media, schools, and parental influences, such that little if any freedom of judgment is possible. Most individualists, on the other hand, see sufficient differences among opinion-molding forces, enough development of critical abilities and tendencies, and sufficient impact on opinion of varieties of experience and varieties of individual ways of thinking (from whatever cause) that individual autonomy seems to them a very real and important fact of life.

For the individualist, then, the distinction between actions that are "willed" and those that are taken "against our will" or even automatically and without deliberation is of great significance; nor is its importance gainsaid by the fact that it is a matter of degree. Autonomy, responsibility, and freedom are all matters of degree. We acknowledge powerful community pressure as a limitation on autonomy and as a mitigation of responsibility for acts performed under pressure.

The characteristics of autonomy, like those of dignity, are the features that make man a moral being, a being that makes "ought" judgments about his own conduct and that of others and (generally) strives to conform to them. The individual not only thinks, chooses, and acts; he holds himself and is held by others morally responsible for his acts, especially for their effects upon others.[36] Of no other known natural entity can these things be said. Not only do most men (one is tempted to say all "normal" men) make the judgment that these facts entitle men, persons, to supreme value and respect; in fact, it would come close to being a logical contradiction for man, the only moralizing creature, to deny to his fellow men supreme moral worth.

[36] See A.J.M. Milne, *Freedom and Rights* (New York: Humanities Press, 1968), p. 191.

From the value placed upon autonomy and its role in making a man a moral being, it follows that the preferences of the individual, *other things being equal*, should be honored. To say that a person has value but that his preferences do not would be, if not self-contradictory, at least absurd, for a person's preferences comprise an essential part of what he is. The burden of proof is upon him who would deny one man's preference, except out of respect for the preference or interest of another man.[37] (To this extent, equality as well as liberty is implied.) Thus the concepts of human dignity and autonomy entail heavy emphasis upon individual liberty. The individual should be free, *other things being equal*, to make his own decisions, determine his own actions, seek the satisfaction of his own wants and desires, pursue his own ideals, and respond to his own moral imperatives. Dignity and servitude are incompatible.[38]

Many individualists hold that the individual should be permitted, other things being equal, to satisfy his desires for the sake of present satisfaction, and also—most importantly—because the act of choice and the varieties of experience to which choice may give rise develop men's capacities, enable him to enlarge his physical, intellectual, emotional and moral horizons, and contribute to a richer, more varied society, all of which they value highly. This line is taken both by liberal individualists of the modified

[37] To be sure, the value of a preference might be negated if its realization would seriously damage the autonomy or dignity of the preferring individual. As will be pointed out more fully below, however, the individualist democrat would hold that, save in the most extreme cases, the individual should himself be the final judge on this point. To say that the individual's preferences are to be valued does not, of course, mean that they may not be overridden by other values.

[38] Insofar as the concept of human dignity is a construct derived from the value we place on liberty, the argument above is circular. That valuation, however, was only one of four or five of the implications upon which the construct was based, the most decisive of which was the nature of the moral enterprise itself.

utilitarian type, among whom John Stuart Mill is preeminent, and by democratic idealists, like T. H. Green.[39]

For their part, collectivists, while focusing upon the societal origins and destiny of the individual, need not deny either the existence or the value of a significant degree of individual autonomy or the concept of human dignity. Nor do such democratic theorists as can be denominated collectivists appear to do so. Take, for instance, Rousseau. His collectivistic leanings are well known, yet no one is more insistent than he upon the possibility of individual autonomy. The same can be said of Marx, a clearer example of collectivism. For him, unalienated man, who has been fully transformed into communitarian man, *is* autonomous; and only such a man, he believes, can achieve autonomy. However, individualists may dispute the *possibility* of both of these propositions. Indeed here is where lies much of the dispute between individualist theorists and such democratic collectivists as Marx. All affirm that in a truly democratic society men must be autonomous. Thus far they are in agreement. They also agree that nothing in the nature of man makes autonomy impossible. Where they often differ is with respect to the collectivists' belief that man's nature is such that he can be at once autonomous and an integral part of a community *to a greater extent than he is (or can be?) in a liberal ("bourgeois") democracy.* Marx, at least, believed this to be true. For Rousseau it was more

[39] Another form of individualism, existentialism, deserves mention. While the classical individualist builds his case upon certain ideas about human nature—not precisely the same in each case—the existentialist denies there is a human nature. With Sartre, he proclaims that "man is nothing other than he makes himself." This proposition amounts to at least as strong a demand for individual autonomy, and the political implications that go with that demand, as anything set forth by the more orthodox individualists. For a good brief analysis of the ethical implications of existentialism, see John Wild, "Authentic Experience," *Ethics*, 75 (1965), 227-239. Sartre himself, despite what appear to be the clear individualistic implications of existentialism, has managed to be a supporter of Communism.

doubtful; and, in any case, he appears to despair of the attainability of his ideal society, and certainly of its permanence.[40]

b. Psychological Attributes

The individualist, however, is likely to ascribe more to man than uniqueness and to assert man's autonomy in a stronger sense than does the collectivist. He may also insist that men have certain basic needs, psychological as well as physical, that are fixed and immutable. He may say that they are inborn; on the other hand, he may admit that they develop only in society, and so in this sense are social products, but that nonetheless they are alike and unchangeable in all men. (Even Rousseau includes among man's natural characteristics the desire for self-preservation, compassion, and the faculty for self-improvement.[41]) As to the nature of these basic traits, persons classified as individualists differ widely among themselves. Hobbes, for instance, sees man as extremely self-centered, as generally desiring his own preservation and advancement above all else. But Hobbes, of course, was not a democrat. Others would insist, with Bentham and the utilitarians generally, that man seeks first of all to maximize his own pleasure and to minimize his pain, pleasure and pain in Bentham's words being man's "two sovereign masters."[42]

Even this position allows a great deal of variation as to

[40] The relevant views of both men are scattered at various points throughout their works. For Marx, see Bertell Ollman, *Alienation* (Cambridge: Cambridge University Press, 1971), Chaps. 9 and 14, esp. pp. 84 and 107; Shlomo Avineri, *The Social and Political Thought of Karl Marx* (Cambridge: Cambridge University Press, 1967), pp. 33-35; and Kenneth A. Megill, "The Community in Marx's Philosophy," *Philosophy and Phenomenological Research*, 30 (1970), 382-395. For Rousseau, see John Plamenatz, *Man and Society* (New York: McGraw-Hill, 1963), vol. 1, Chap. 10.

[41] Rousseau, "A Discourse on the Origin of Inequality," *The Social Contract and Discourses, trans. Cole* (London: Dent, 1923), pp. 197, 185.

[42] Bentham, *An Introduction to the Principles of Morals and Legislation*, ed. Wheelwright (Garden City, N.Y.: Doubleday, 1935), p. 7.

what men find pleasurable. At one extreme are those who insist that material needs and comforts top the list. Some would place high priority on self-esteem; and many argue that men seek power, status, and social acceptance. Even among that trilogy, one may note considerable tension, for the ways of obtaining social acceptance are numerous; they vary with the circumstances, with the culture, and may run contrary to the ordinary manifestations of power-seeking.

Another form of individualism is described (but by no means favored) by Alexis de Tocqueville. "Individualism," he wrote, "is a mature and calm feeling, which disposes each member of the community to sever himself from the mass of his fellows and to draw apart with his family and his friends, so that after he has thus formed a little circle of his own, he willingly leaves society at large to itself. . . . Individualism," he continues, "is of democratic origin, and it threatens to spread in the same ratio as the equality of condition."[43] Tocqueville was not asserting that it was man's inescapable nature to behave in this fashion, but he did ascribe it to democracy. For collectivists, this kind of behavior represents the "privatism" they so strongly criticize. It is of course in no way logically essential to the individualist position, but the fact that, as Tocqueville discerned, it is characteristic of some individualists and obviously an attitude properly called "individualistic," contributes to collectivists' antipathy toward the individualistic approach.

At the opposite extreme from those who stress the egoistic motivations are those who emphasize sympathy, the need for belonging, and sociability. Here we may move from the individualistic end of the spectrum toward collectivism, while remaining within a basically individualistic framework. Although Bentham did not stress these motivations, it is characteristic—some would say a weakness—of his theory that it can be expected to cover almost anything,

---

[43] *Democracy in America*, trans. Reeve, p. 98.

including such theories as those just mentioned. Moreover, John Stuart Mill went further still, admitting the existence and force of such motives as benevolence, sociability, and a sense of virtue. He reconciled this position with utilitarian hedonism by arguing that the individual may be motivated by the pleasantness or unpleasantness of his *present* ideas, whatever they may be.[44]

Further, an individualist need not be a hedonist, or for that matter any kind of utilitarian, as the example of Kant makes clear. He may admit such nonhedonistic motivations as the desire for honors, or to be honorable, and the sense of duty and the sense of justice.

One further point under this heading. Individualists generally believe in the variousness of human nature—that human beings are highly differentiated. And, like John Stuart Mill, they believe that the more liberty they are allowed the more this differentiation will develop. Collectivists, insisting that man is a product of society, often (but not necessarily) stress similarities more than differences.

A sketch of the collectivist view of human nature can be derived from the preceding discussion of individualism. It needs to be filled out. Collectivists hold that man needs society to develop his full potentialities, to satisfy his "need for belonging," and even to enable him to become fully autonomous. Some sociologists upon whom modern collectivists lean heavily go further and maintain that the individual is almost completely the product of society. Emile Durkheim, as was noted above, declared that the great error of the utilitarians was in deducing society from the individual. "Collective life," he remarks, "is not born from individual life, but it is, on the contrary, the second which is born from the first."[45] And at another point, he declares that

---

[44] "Utilitarianism," Chaps. 3-4, in *Utilitarianism, Liberty, and Representative Government* (New York: Dutton, 1926).

[45] Durkheim, *The Division of Labor in Society*, trans. Simpson (Glencoe, Ill.: Free Press, 1947), pp. 279.

91

The major part of our states of conscience . . . come
. . . not from the psychological nature of man in general,
but from the manner in which men once associated mutually affect one another, according as they are more or
less numerous, more or less close. . . . Individual constitutions are only remote conditions, not determinate
causes.[46]

It will be observed that Durkheim's theory of human
nature is closely related to his theory of starting points. So
far as individualism connotes an idea of human nature that
is egoistic, self-seeking, he would have none of it. Rather,
he is concerned to argue that altruism is as primordial as
egoism. The importance of a variety of social roles and
of that fundamental cultural product, language, is also
stressed. Yet he does not deny that men seek to realize their
interests, including decidedly self-related interests. He does
deny that their doing so is what holds society together, a
function he attributes to moral sentiments; but this is
quite a different—and much milder—proposition than one
that would apply to all behavior in society.[47] He also insists that man's nature changes throughout history and
that "in more advanced societies his nature is, in large part,
to be an organ of society."[48] At the latter point, in terms
of democratic theory, he is verging on dangerous territory.

While opposing individualism, Durkheim looked with
favor upon individuality, which he found to be increasingly a feature of modern society. In fact, he urged that
modern society develop a set of values and beliefs which
stress the dignity and worth of the individual and the ideal
of self-development. His concern is chiefly to argue that
this development could not be logically deduced from the
nature of man himself.[49]

[46] Ibid., p. 350.   [47] Ibid., pp. 196 and 279ff.
[48] Ibid., p. 403.
[49] For a good brief of Durkheim's theories, see his *Selected Writings*,
ed. and trans. Anthony Giddens (Cambridge: Cambridge University
Press, 1972), pp. 1-50, esp. 1-15.

The work of the early pluralist and historian of political thought, Otto von Gierke, exhibits a similar but slightly different aspect of collectivism, or at least of antiindividualism. His concern was to substantiate the "reality" of group entities, and particularly of the community. He wrote:

> If we could think ourselves free of any connection with any particular nation and state, a religious community and church, a professional association, a family and unions and associations of many sorts, we would not recognize ourselves in the pitiable remnant that would remain.[50]

One of the areas in which individualists and collectivists differ most relates to their empirical assumptions about the nature of man's basic desires and drives, if indeed he has any such immutable motivations. Yet, among the classical theorists of democracy, it is difficult to find one who either believed in the complete plasticity of human nature or believed that man was by nature primarily more concerned with the welfare of society than with his own. Rousseau is the most likely candidate, but even he is an ambiguous one. He did believe, as has been noted, in certain basic human traits; and he also believed that self-love and self-preservation came before all else. Yet from this point on man could develop in any of various directions, for better or for worse. In *Émile*, great artifice is required to enable a boy to develop "naturally." And countless passages throughout Rousseau's works demonstrate his belief that man can be so educated (some would say "brainwashed")

---

[50] Gierke, from *Das Wesen der Menschlichen Verbande*, as translated and quoted in Sobei Mogi, *Otto von Gierke* (London: King, 1932), p. 120. The passage invites comparison with a statement by Nevil Johnson, the institutionalist referred to earlier (note 20). He remarked that "the isolated individual, released from the ties of institutions, is a figment of the imagination." "The Place of Institutions in the Study of Politics," p. 278.

as to place love of country and devotion to the General Will above all else.[51]

Yet all of this remains for Rousseau a theoretical and highly unlikely possibility. Even in the *Social Contract*, where he was laying out what one must understand to be his ideal form of government, many provisions and many cautionary words make it clear that he felt it necessary to guard at every turn against man's inherent tendency to prefer his private interest to the public welfare. This recognition led him to insist that the assembly should never be called upon to pass upon any but the most general questions, so that individual members would not be tempted by the opportunity to obtain special benefits for themselves. The ban on groups was similarly motivated, as was the prohibition of discussion preceding a vote. Likewise the famous passage about the canceling out of the pluses and minuses has direct reference to the need for practical devices to prevent individual and partial interests from prevailing over the public interest.

Many modern writers take a more optimistic view. Some stress the malleability of human nature, as in the following statement: "Once we get much beyond the physiological or neurological base of behavior, human nature spreads out as far as we can see."[52] Others list basic characteristics that lay considerable emphasis upon the social side of man's nature.[53] In either case, they often hold that men who place the highest value upon society are happier than those who

[51] See Rousseau, "Discourse on Political Economy," pp. 262-264, and *Émile*, trans. Foxley (London: Dent, n.d.).

[52] Bernard Berelson and Gary A. Steiner, *Human Behavior* (New York: Harcourt, Brace and World, 1964), p. 667.

[53] For instance, A. H. Maslow, *Motivation and Personality* (New York: Harper & Row, 1954), Chap. 5; and James C. Davies, *Human Nature in Politics* (New York: Wiley, 1963). For various other listings of man's basic characteristics, see Amitai Etzioni, "Basic Human Needs, Alienation and Inauthenticity," *Amer. Sociological Rev.*, 33 (1968), 870-884; Carl Joachim Friedrich, *Man and His Government* (New York: McGraw-Hill, 1963), p. 46; J. R. Lucas, *The Principles of Politics* (Oxford: Clarendon Press, 1966), p. 2.

live a more competitive and self-serving life, such as the individualist tends to postulate. Moreover, they often assert that man's social nature drives him increasingly toward a highly integrated society—or at least that it *would* do so, if we could rid ourselves of our individualistic institutions and ideas. Here, then, with respect to their theories of human nature individualists and collectivists tend to differ rather sharply; albeit a considerable range of difference also exists within each group, as between Bentham and J. S. Mill or between Hegel and Marx.

4. The Nature of the Collectivity

For a full appreciation of the differences between individualists and collectivists, one needs to consider also what they have to say about the collectivity. For the individualist, little needs to be added to what has already been said. The collectivity is a collection of individuals. To be sure, it is not just any old collection, but one held together by self-interest, sympathy, common beliefs and values, and even loyalty and altruism, the relative weights of these elements varying with the theorist in question. Collectivists, too, differ among themselves; and some are hard to classify. Thus Rousseau and even Marx have been called individualists by some. Both will be treated as on the collectivistic part of the spectrum here, but with Marx farther in that direction than Rousseau. The British neo-Hegelians fall in the same category, although their political views are very different, especially from those of Marx. In spite of all this variation, some generalizations are possible.

The collectivist is not the logical opposite of the individualist. He holds that the collectivity (group, community, state, or other) is of great value. He may say it is of "supreme" value, "in and for itself," "for its own sake," or some similar locution. But he can hardly say that it is valuable without reference to individuals.[54] It may be said

[54] Perhaps Plato comes close to this in the famous passage where

that the individual must "lose himself to find himself," that is to say, lose himself to others or lose himself in the whole (better, "to the concept of the whole"); but the ultimate outcome is that he finds *himself*. The "self" he finds may be very different from that with which he began. It may be greatly enlarged; it may be as concerned, or even more concerned, about the welfare of others as about the individual to whom it is uniquely attached. But that unique attachment remains; the individual identifies with his "self."

However that may be, the idea of the whole, for the collectivist, is a powerful motivating force. Even that statement does less than justice to a phenomenon which underlies certain "group mind" theories. As Peter Strawson points out, some groups of people do act "as one." They may make no reference to individual persons at all. The "we" in "we lost the game" is a plural without a singular. A part of such a whole, such as "the pitcher," may be thought of as only a part, rather than as an individual person. Strawson goes on to suggest, however—persuasively, it would seem— that the concept of an individual person would be impossible if we regularly thought of the community in these terms, if the spokesman of a group, for instance, was thought of not as its mouthpiece but as its mouth.[55]

Actually, it seems doubtful that individual players often so lose themselves in the team that it, rather than they, becomes the "individual" in their minds. The "we" in "we won" refers to what Mandelbaum would call a "societal fact," an institution, whether it be "Swarthmore College" or "the Dodgers."[56] And the person who says "we won,"

---

he says that if one were painting a statue, he should not paint the eyes crimson, though that is a beautiful color, because it is not appropriate for eyes. The question, he says, is "whether . . . we make the whole beautiful." *Republic*, p. 420 (Cornford translation). But one should not base too much on a simile.

[55] P. H. Strawson, *Individuals* (London: Methuen, 1965), pp. 112-114.
[56] "Societal Facts," in Gardiner, *Theories of History*, pp. 476-488.

whether he was a member of the team or merely a rooter, no matter how much he identifies for the moment with some ideal entity (whether group or institution), is well aware that in other contexts his spoken "we" would have a different referent. (This takes us back to Mises's point that the individual cannot be thought of as simply a part of a collectivity, because he is a part of many collectivities, no one of which exhausts his individuality.)

The use made by some collectivists of the social origins of the self and of self-consciousness may be illustrated by the work of F. H. Bradley. Individuals exclusive of other selves, he says, do not exist. "[W]hat we call an individual man is what he is because of and by virtue of community." Communities "are thus not mere names but something real. . . ."[57] And again, "The 'individual' man, the man into whose essence his community with others does not enter, who does not include relations to others in his very being, is, we say, a fiction. . . ."[58] Such a "mere individual" is indeed "a delusion of theory."[59] If a person introspects carefully, he will discover that all of his desires are part of a whole and that his self-realization depends upon his identification with that whole. This whole, it would be fair to say, is for Bradley the supreme value. But at the same time one must recognize that for Bradley the individual *is* (potentially) this whole. "The self to be realized is not the self as a collection of particulars, is not the universal as all the states of a certain feeling; and . . . it is not again an abstract universal, as the form of duty; . . . neither are in harmony with life, with the moral consciousness, or with themselves; . . . when man is identified with, and wills, and realizes a concrete universal, a real totality, then first does it find itself, is satisfied, self-determined and free, 'the free will that wills itself as the free will.' "[60]

[57] F. H. Bradley, *Ethical Studies*, 2nd ed. (Oxford: Clarendon Press, 1927), p. 166.

[58] Ibid., p. 168. [59] Ibid., p. 174.

[60] Ibid., p. 81.

If it is possible to pinpoint at any one place the philo-sophical difference between the individualist and the type of metaphysical collectivist represented by Bradley, that place is to be found in this quasi-mystical concept of the concrete universal. It permits the collectivist to say that the individual can and should become so identified with society that "the individual's consciousness of himself is inseparable from the knowing himself as an organ of the whole," to the extent that "the residuum falls more and more into the background, so that he thinks of it, if at all, not as himself, but as an idle appendage."[61] As we have seen, some individualists, although certainly not all, recog-nize that the individual is in large measure a social prod-uct, and also that he will be morally better if his self is enlarged to include that of others, possibly of all others; but he balks at the collectivists' apparent contempt for the individual as he now is, and at his glossing over the importance—indeed, the necessity, as the individualist sees it—of the individual making his own choices, planning his own life. (Note the blending of factual and moral judg-ments that underlies this difference of opinion.)

Many collectivists formulate their view in terms of the aphorism, "The whole is greater than the sum of its parts." As it stands, the statement is highly ambiguous. Ac-cording to one possible interpretation, it is little more than a truism: that the parts lose some of their value if they are separated from the whole. Few would deny that each per-son would be a poorer, less valuable person if he were snatched out of society in general; or that he would be poorer, at least for the time being, if he were transplanted from his own society to one alien to him. Yet, though few may deny these propositions, many might overlook or mini-mize them; and it is an important virtue of democratic col-lectivist theory that it checks this tendency.

Another formulation of the collectivist position is to the

61 Ibid., p. 183.

effect that the whole, in particular the state, is more "real" than its members, who achieve "reality" only in and through it. It will be recalled that Gierke used language to this effect. Likewise Bradley: "Man is a social being; he is real only because he is social, and can realize himself only because it is as social that he realizes himself."[62] Again, if such statements mean only that an individual who is a member of a state is more what we consider a human being than is a wolf-man, a person who somehow grew up apart from other persons, who presumably has not even developed the faculty of speech, no one would disagree. More generally, they doubtless mean that man realizes his potential, developed ("real") self only in an organized society. It is not clear that they mean any more than this; and yet, stated in this way, the position is not at odds with Basic Individualism, although it adds something that the latter does not imply.

Still a slightly different interpretation, taken this time from critics of collectivism and suggested by statements to the effect that the state is the "highest end," or an "end in itself," is that the collectivist would "sacrifice" the individual to the state. If the former means only that individuals ought to take account of the welfare of others and thus, in an extreme situation, even risk their lives to preserve institutions that will benefit others, even those who are yet unborn, it is a view held by all but the most extreme individualists.

If making the state the "highest end" is merely another way of expressing a nonegoistic principle of morality, making the state "highest" because it is most inclusive, we have here no absolute conflict between collectivists and individualists (except for pure egoists, like Hobbes). But, just as collectivists believe that individualists neglect man's social nature, so calling the state the highest end makes individualists bridle, for two reasons. In the first place, it may con-

[62] Ibid., p. 174.

note that the state must be valued in and of itself and apart from its support of any human values. It is difficult to be certain that any collectivist takes this view (certainly most do not), but if he does the conflict with the individualist is irresolvable at that point. Also, individualists fear that the collectivist is denying the right of individual conscience, and, even more, that the state (finding expression through its government) may be wrong. Again the individualists' fear is probably mistaken, What is true is that collectivists sometimes, in speaking of *the state*, and meaning the *ideal* state, encourage misunderstanding. By definition the ideal state would do nothing counter to the rights of any individual. The residual tension between the two positions in this regard relates to the degree of presumed validity that the individual should grant to the commands of the government. For the individualist it may be minimal, perhaps nonexistent; for the collectivist it may be very considerable, approaching absolute: yet (today especially) most individualists and most collectivists will be found closer to the center than to either extreme.

Now, let us examine the question of what is meant by saying that the state is an end in itself. The state serves so many human needs and (at its best) ideals that its citizens come, rightly, to view it as an end. We value that which produces or increases values—like liberty, or safety, or welfare. But the state may be valued not solely because it produces things we value, but also because its members enjoy participation in it, take pride in its accomplishments, find fulfillment in its achievements, and are enriched by its glory.

So far so good, and no individualist need take exception. He will want, however, to insist that the state still is an end of *man, for* man, and is subject to judgment by man's standards. Otherwise we may be led into the trap of saying "My country, may it always be right; but my country, right or wrong!"

In this latter connection two further points are in order.

First, when idealist philosophers, most of whom are properly classified as collectivists, speak of the "state," they mean "a living whole, not the mere legal and political fabric, but the complex of lives and activities, considered as the body of which that is the framework."[63] Moreover, like Plato, he is likely to be thinking of an ideal state, in which the good of the individual and the good of the state are merged; hence no question of priority can arise. For his part, the individualist believes that reasoning from models of perfection is likely to be misleading and that to identify the state with organized society may also be misleading when the subject under discussion is forms of government.

A second difference between what collectivists often mean and what individualists tend to mean has been lurking in the shadows. The collectivist usually means that the collectivity is valuable in some way not translatable into benefit, advantage, or enjoyment by individuals as they are. The clue to this meaning may be found in the collectivist's concepts of individuality and of development. Individuality, for the collectivist, implies more than separateness or exclusiveness; it implies also a unity arising out of the integration of differences. Development, too, is important. We value some individuals more highly than others, says the collectivist; we say it is better that a man develop speech, intelligence, sympathy, and so on and so forth, than that he remain like an infant; and it is better that he maximize these and other capacities than that he become a vegetable. We contrast both infant and vegetable-man with "true" man, "real" man, "man-as-he-ought-to-be," or "developed" man, and place a higher value on the second type, by whatever name. This projection, this contrast, with inescapable ideas of degrees, implies a series, possibly an infinite series; certainly a series the final term of which one never expects to see. It might be argued, then,

[63] Bernard Bosanquet, *The Principle of Individuality and Value* (London: Macmillan, 1927), p. 311, n.

101

that by implication we envisage something more real than reality as we know it. For a full-fledged collectivism one need add only the notion (but it is no insignificant addition) that the state itself (considered as the whole of society, politically organized) is a kind of individual (unity in diversity) and one without which the kind of development we have been suggesting could not get far, and which embodies within it both the facilitating structures and the motivating ideas and ideals that maximize development.

In justice to the collectivist, these ideas of unity and of development as basic to value need further explanation. A typical nineteenth-century exemplar of this type of thought—and one who considered himself a democrat— was Bernard Bosanquet. Bosanquet was a philosophical idealist in the Platonic tradition and a neo-Hegelian. For him all value was relative to persons, but *person* was a far more inclusive term than the finite bearer of consciousness commonly known as such. The state of consciousness of an intelligent being is not confined to itself. Its object is not a mere means to its character but is "a partial apprehension by consciousness of its own nature."[64] Following T. H. Green, Bosanquet argues that the individualist position, carried to its logical extreme, would make not every individual but every pleasure the unit of value. Moving in the opposite direction, Bosanquet argues that the "real," "true" person, or individual, must be that whole, that concrete universal, toward which all are tending, which is all-inclusive—not, indeed, the state but the universe. If one denies that the basic unit is an individual experience but attributes greater importance, value, reality, as the individualists do, to the unity of the individual, "how can he deny his unity with the further stages in individuality?" "There seems no reason for drawing a line at which the continuity is to break off, and prima facie the inference is to a unitary perfection lying in the complete individuality of the universe

[64] Ibid., p. 306.

as a conscious being, which is the ultimate value and stand-ard of value."[65]

5. IMPLICATIONS FOR DEMOCRACY

I shall now discuss the implications for democratic theory of individualism and collectivism in a more unified fashion than has been done above. The democratic individualist, to begin with, tends to place a high value on the freedom of the individual to do as he pleases (compatibly of course with liberty for all and with justice). He believes in liberty in this sense and in the diversity and the personal develop-ment to which he believes it leads. He is suspicious of au-thority and may even lean toward anarchism. Individualists vary a great deal as to the amount of state "intervention" they approve of; but for them the effect of proposed state regulation on individual liberty, in their sense of that term, is always an important criterion.

Individualists often say—perhaps only carelessly—that each individual knows his own interest best. "Only the wearer," the saying goes, "knows where the shoe pinches." But the argument as thus stated overlooks an important distinction. Granted that only the wearer can feel, and therefore locate, the pinch, perhaps someone else could have predicted better than he that that particular shoe would pinch that foot. Democracy gives each voter an op-portunity to say when and where he is "hurting," and to

[65] Ibid., p. 309. Reference to the work of Roberto Unger, briefly alluded to in connection with the discussion above of Mead's theory of the self, is pertinent here. Like Bosanquet, Unger holds to the view that the individual is concrete in his bodily reference and (poten-tially) universal in his kinship with the universal elements in human nature as it develops. Resolution of this tension is to be found in the idea of concrete universality—the capacity to put one's particular work in the service of a universal ideal. Whether this ideal is attainable is a matter about which he professes ignorance. *Knowledge and Poli-tics*, pp. 222-231.

say it in a way that will be heard. The importance of this fact must not be minimized. But can the average voter go beyond this point? Can he use his political power to obtain a better fit? Or will he, feeling, let us say, the pinch of higher prices, insist on a remedy that will make matters worse? In short, can he calculate the consequences of alternative policies or judge the qualities of rival leaders well enough to bring about a better state of affairs for himself?

The voter's ability to calculate consequences might affect the difference between individualist and collectivist in any of several ways. It might have no relevant effect, for it does not appear that the collectivist, as such, is compelled to differ with the individualist's assumption. Assuming, however, that he does, it might lead him to support some form of nondemocratic elitism, like aristocracy. Short of that it might lead him to favor an elitist form of democracy, educational qualifications for office-holding, more use of delegated authority, and so on. Finally, the collectivist might insist that many heads are better than one, that group decisions are superior to those taken by individuals and thus that majoritarian institutions can be counted on to make sound calculations. Here it might seem—and indeed it might *be*—that the individualist would come out at the same place; however, he would probably tend to submit fewer questions to political determination, reserving a larger sphere for individual autonomy.

Today it is increasingly apparent that to know the remedy and to be able to calculate the likely consequences of possible public policies is not enough. It may be quite evident that the use of monopoly power, whether of capital or of labor, is against the public interest. At the same time, it may be in the interest of each particular group to use its power to the limit, in the belief (probably accurate) that if it does not do so other groups almost surely will; the group in question would then have to share the cost of other monopolies while gaining none of the benefits. This

104

is a prisoner's-dilemma situation that undoubtedly carries with it a serious challenge to democratic institutions. It arises from individualistic, i.e. self-regarding, behavior. It could be avoided if men would act in Kantian fashion— that is, if they would act only according to rules they would wish everyone to follow; and if necessary enact laws to enforce such behavior.[66] It is painfully evident that individuals, in general, are not behaving that way today. A collectivist theory can be helpful in this regard only if it can propose institutional devices or other measures which will alter that behavior. Marx's answer would be to abolish the capitalist system, to eliminate the people's opportunity and desire to benefit themselves at the expense of others. Two vital questions remain unresolved. Can opportunities for individuals or groups to pursue their own benefit be eliminated within a democratic framework? It is difficult to see how, although they may be limited. And one cannot help suspecting that the problem is directly reflected in the failure of democratic regimes to develop wherever capitalism was eliminated. Marx, to be sure, believed that the *desire* to put self-regard ahead of concern for the whole would be eliminated once the injustices of capitalism were removed. Here again is a basic disagreement over the fact (about human nature) that goes to the heart of the issues

[66] Rousseau's solution—or part of it—was to insure that only questions of complete generality should be submitted for determination by the General Will. He made no attempt to show how this could be accomplished in a large and complex society, because he did not believe democracy could survive in such a society. In our own day, Theodore J. Lowi would rely heavily upon the same principle. He would have the Supreme Court revive the rule against delegating legislative authority (especially to interest groups) and, where delegation to administrative agencies is unavoidable, require its exercise by formal rule. Lowi, *The End of Liberalism* (New York: Norton, 1969), pp. 297-303. If such a (literally) reactionary proposal were to be adopted, it might do some good, but hardly in the proportions called for by the challenge referred to above. Lowi has defended and elaborated his position in *The Politics of Disorder* (New York: Basic Books, 1971). See especially Chap. 8.

between individualist and collectivist democrat. Until a noncapitalistic society succeeds in creating the "new man," the issue must remain unresolved; but each year that passes without clear evidence the goal is being achieved throws increasing doubt upon its possibility.

A further point suggested by the "only the wearer . . ." saying calls for attention. Does the individual know his *interest* best? That he best knows his own desires is little more than tautological: but that he knows what will satisfy them is another matter. Will he like what he wants when he gets it? That is the question. Moreover, one may distinguish, with Plato, Rousseau, Marx, and many others, between real or natural desires and artificial desires, the latter tending to lead to frustration and unhappiness rather than to happiness.

As the example of Plato suggests, beliefs of this kind may easily lead to an antidemocratic position. In a moderate form, however, they may accord with an elitist version of democratic theory, one that retains ultimate popular control of policy, while giving substantial powers to elective officials and their appointees. Or the democratic collectivist may take another line: he may hold that if the average individual is subjected to certain experiences (training, education, indoctrination, or perhaps simply undirected acculturation to a particular form of society), he will develop desires he would not otherwise have felt, the satisfaction of which would give him far greater happiness or fulfillment or "realization" or "actualization" than would otherwise have been possible for him. Rousseau took the latter line. Whether he did so successfully is another question.[67] Any theory that depends upon education necessarily takes on a hortatory flavor. As with Plato and Rousseau, it may be forced to rely upon a great Law-giver to initiate the system. It may also, as with Plato and arguably with Rousseau, rely

[67] Thus it would appear that not all "artificial" desires (if by this is meant those which must be cultivated) are bad.

upon indoctrination and censorship, thus abandoning the liberal aspect of liberal democracy.[68]

In yet another way, liberal democrats feel threatened by the collectivist philosophy. The most extreme of these doctrines appear to derive the worth and meaning of the individual from the political whole of which he is a part (an "organ," as it is frequently put). Thus key values, as well as individual behavior, are determined by the whole, rather than the other way around. This version of the theory appears to threaten individual autonomy and, with it, democracy. This threat is made good in totalitarian theory, a vulgarized form of collectivist theory.

Special attention is due the position of Marx. He believed that individual autonomy was the ideal and that it was achievable. But he also believed that man was a creature of the society in which he lived. More frequently than not, he thought, this society produced "false consciousness," a condition in which men were deceived as to their real interests. Only after a class society was somehow eliminated could truly social and autonomous man, aware of his real interests, come into being. This points to a weakness in collectivist democratic theory. (Of course that does not mean that collectivist theory is necessarily false; only that, if it is true, democratic theory may be less plausible than would otherwise be the case.) For Marx, as long as classes prevail democracy is little more than a stratagem. He relies upon the vanguard of the proletariat to effectuate the revolutionary change without which true democracy is impossible. But if men are so easily fooled (made victims of "false consciousness") in non-Communist societies, how much can one rely on their autonomous ability to know their own interests in a Communist society, where inevitably some would be in positions of greater influence than others?

[68] For passages from Rousseau and from commentators on his relating to this issue, see Guy H. Dodge, *Jean-Jacques Rousseau: Authoritarian Libertarian?* (Lexington, Mass.; Heath, 1971).

Closely related to the individual's knowledge of his interests is the proposition that regardless of who knows best what is in the interest of Joe Doakes, he himself is the one who can best be trusted to promote and defend it. Intelligence and good will do not necessarily go together. While individualists (such as James Mill) have been especially insistent upon this point, it is not a position that collectivists are logically forced to deny. Nor do all of them do so. It is true, however, that both the idea of allowing each individual to judge for himself and the idea of providing him a weapon (the ballot) with which to enforce his judgment are expressions of individualistic self-reliance that fit much more congenially with the individualist attitude than with that of the collectivist, just as the stress on man's malleability and on his other-regarding ideals and interests come naturally to the collectivist, while a tendency to emphasize man's unalterably selfish and materialistic desires as dominating is more commonly an individualist trait.

Put differently, the last point means that the democratic collectivist tends to deplore the *self*-interested tone of the propositions just discussed. For him democratic institutions are important less to protect and advance the interests of the individual than to encourage the individual to think and act in terms of the whole and its interests. For him, then, the important empirical question is What institutions will have this effect? Many collectivists today tend to follow Rousseau's lead in believing that direct participation in relatively small groups provides the key to this desideratum. In any case, although in the absence of consensus voting may be the necessary final stage of the decision-making process, the emphasis for the collectivist should be strongly on group deliberation.

Why does collectivism appear somewhat inhospitable to the democratic ideal or at least to institutions widely thought essential to the realization of that ideal? At least three reasons may be suggested. First, one who would bend all efforts to the development of a political whole that absorbs all individuality into itself might well hesitate to entrust this operation equally to all men. He would, on the contrary, be strongly tempted to give authority to those who, like himself, could see that end most clearly and who were best equipped to determine how it could be achieved. And he might well find that the operation of the democratic suffrage did not work this way. One thinks of Plato or of Herbert Marcuse.[69] We have here the exact opposite of the individualist's belief that the individual is the best guardian of his own interests. To trust the individual to protect his own interest is one thing; to trust him to protect and advance those of that remote entity, the state, may be thought to be quite another.

The second reason grows out of the collectivist's distinction between "real" and "artificial" desires. As was hinted earlier, that distinction soon runs into difficulties. The idea, of course, is that the former are good and the latter bad. But surely not all natural desires—e.g. the desire of a big boy to bully a smaller one or of any child to pull a cat's tail—are good. Nor can it be said that all artificial desires, if by that is meant those which must in some way be taught or created, are good. And if the distinction intended is simply that between good and bad desires, surely the question for political theory is whether the determination of what is good and what is bad is to be made democratically, undemocratically, or by each person for himself as far as it affects only himself. It is easy to see why the collectivist is here tempted to opt for a less than democratic solution.

At this point the contemporary collectivist may say that artificial desires are typically created by advertising. To eliminate that, and other inducements to self-interested desire, he is likely to recommend either drastic modification or total abolition of the competitive, free enterprise economy and the substitution of one that appeals to, and generates, cooperative rather than competitive attitudes.

<hr />

[69] Robert Paul Wolff, Barrington Moore, Jr., and Herbert Marcuse, *A Critique of Pure Tolerance* (Boston: Beacon Press, 1969), p. 106.

This proposal raises a completely different set of issues from those we have been discussing; the argument is properly directed not against a particular political theory but rather against a particular economic theory.

Moreover, in a democratic collectivist society the question would still arise whether the individual should be allowed to choose between satisfying his real and his artificial desires. Would a majority say that he should not? *Should* a majority say that he should not, and compel adherence to their judgment? If competition were to be given a less important role in the management of the economy, would that assure that *social* competitiveness would diminish? Or would it work in precisely the opposite direction—people seeking to enhance their image, their power, or their self-esteem by achieving political rather than economic superiority? And, more than incidentally, might that in turn lead back to economic superiority measured in terms of perquisites and privileges if not in ordinary income? Here we come once more to different (factual) beliefs about human nature. The collectivist can escape elitism at this point only if he believes social competitiveness and other false values can be eliminated by abolishing the economic competitiveness inherent in a market economy. (Note, too, that this competitiveness is inherent in a *market* economy, whether or not it is capitalistic.)

The third reason for the collectivist's tendency toward elitism is that he cannot accept the high valuation placed upon the individual *as he is at any given time and place*, which is the heart of individualistic democratic theory. He finds such a position impossible to accept, because the actual individual is vastly different from, and inferior to, the "real" individual, the goal of development, or self-realization. Moreover, it is tempting, if not actually essential, for the collectivist to see the ideal whole as composed of individuals of different grades of value; and, if so, why should not these differences be reflected in the allocation of political power? This most extreme, this "radical" collectivism

110

appears incompatible with the equalitarian ideal of democracy. The continuum that runs from radical individualism to radical collectivism overruns the spectrum of democratic theories.

Against the general charges of elitism, in addition to what has already been said, the collectivist has at least two lines of defense. Unlike Plato, he may believe that in a well-ordered society individual differences in ability will be slight. The nearer people are to equality of knowledge, intelligence, and virtue, the less is the temptation to qualify or eliminate democracy in favor of some aristocratic form of rule. A further belief (already referred to) on which collectivists frequently rely is that the process of collective action, participation, and emotional involvement in public affairs will tend to divert the individual from private interests and increase his commitment to the public welfare and to justice, to the General Will, to use Rousseau's term. It is indeed this line of reasoning that makes it easier for Rousseau to lean toward a collectivist philosophy, while remaining a democrat. Though this was Rousseau's ideal, one must not overlook the fact that he was extremely pessimistic about the possibility of attaining it. It was also Marx's ideal; and unlike Rousseau, he was confident it was attainable. "When the laborer cooperates systematically with others, he strips off the fetters of his individuality," Marx declared, "and develops the capabilities of his species."[70] Unfortunately no support for this statement of faith is to be found in the passage from which it is quoted, unless it be the assertion that cooperation "excites emulation between individuals and raises their animal spirits."[71]

Finally, on this point, it would be possible for even a

[70] Karl Marx, *Capital*, trans. from 3rd German ed. by Moore and Aveling, ed. Friedrich Engels, revised and simplified according to 4th German ed. by Untermann (New York: Modern Library, 1906), p. 361.
[71] Ibid. The subject of participation will be treated more fully in Chap. 11.

111

radical collectivist to support democratic institutions at present, on the theory that under prevailing circumstances anything else would be worse. He might believe that the only alternative would be a vicious tyranny. Thus even Plato compromised his aristocracy with democratic elements when he sought to recommend the best practicable form of government. But the radical collectivist would have great difficulty subscribing to the belief in representative democracy as, in Mill's words, "the ideally best form of government."[72]

Throughout this section and elsewhere in this chapter, it has been frequently argued that democratic individualists and democratic collectivists differ more in degree than in kind, and that these differences relate especially to their beliefs about human nature, an empirical matter of an especially complicated kind, where one's values are likely to color his view of the facts. The latter tend to be critical, however, as is brought out by the position of J. S. Mill. While Mill admitted that men "are not governed in *all* their actions by their worldly interests," he at the same time insisted this was a less serious objection to the theory of his father and of Bentham than it might seem. And the reason for this was that "in *politics* we are for the most part concerned with the conduct, not of individual persons, but either of a series of persons (as a succession of kings), or a body or mass of persons, as a nation, an aristocracy, or a representative assembly. And whatever is true of a large majority of mankind, may without much error be taken for true of any succession of persons considered as a whole, or of any collection of persons in which the act of the majority becomes the act of the whole body."[73]

To what extent democratic collectivists would agree with the proposition that people in the mass tend to be governed

[72] Mill applied this phrase to representative government, although not necessarily to one that was completely democratic.

[73] John Stuart Mill, *A System of Logic*, Bk. VI, Chap. 8, p. 480 (emphasis added).

by their worldly interests hardly admits of generalization. One may, however, hazard this proposition: collectivists are more inclined to assert that men have the capacity, and the tendency *under favorable conditions* (very different from those that prevail today), to behave politically in other-regarding fashion than they are inclined to ascribe such behavior to the mass of men at the time of their writing.

6. FURTHER CRITICISMS OF COLLECTIVISM

Collectivism has much of value to contribute to democratic theory, as has already been made clear. It is also subject to certain valid criticisms, some of which remain to be expounded. If it takes a democratic form, collectivism may be elitist, stressing the superior wisdom of leaders and administrators, and relying heavily upon the state to "socialize" its members in the right directions, or it may emphasize the values of participation, consensus, and solidarity. Democratic collectivists today generally take the latter line.

In stressing the virtues of community, the collectivist often plays rather fast and loose with the terms *community* and *state*. A community (*Gemeinschaft*) may be a very good thing, although the individualist would point out that it may also be smothering, conducive to conformity, and the enemy of initiative and change. More than this, however, it would be a great mistake to assume that the polity and community, especially in our modern heterogeneous and dynamic societies, will be even approximately coterminous. The virtues of community cannot, then, be automatically ascribed to society (*Gesellschaft*) or to the state. In fact, one might cast the situation in the form of a dilemma: if state and community are coterminous, the dangers of conformism and stasis are great; and, on the other hand, if the state is not a true community but tries to make itself one, or at least to act like one, the dangers of

113

tyranny, whether of a majority (if the state is democratic) or of a minority (if it is not democratic) are likewise accentuated. Consensus without powerful repression, in any sizable community, appears to be a will-o'-the-wisp.

Further along this line of criticism, the assumption that greatly increased popular participation is compatible with retention of a democratic, moderate temper, and with the attainment of consensus, is highly questionable. In a face-to-face group and perhaps in any true community, ample discussion and active participation by the rank-and-file may indeed lead to agreement. Experience with the larger, looser organization of the state, however, where the common tie of loyalty and mutual interest is weakened by number, distance, and the competing claims of other groups, lends little support to the collectivist's hopes. Again the jump from community to polity appears to have led him astray.

Once more the differences here between individualist and collectivist depend more upon differing factual assumptions than upon contrary evaluations; for most Western collectivists today do not cherish conformism, or stasis, or tyranny; nor do they wish to be confronted with a choice between activism and consensus. On the contrary, they assume the possibility of developing a degree of public spirit, of concern for the public welfare, that is seldom found in a generalized and sustained form. It should be observed how few give all their wealth to the poor, even when they know they are dying. They may "sacrifice" something for those who are near and dear to them (those whose "selves" have really become part of their own "selves"); but how many people voluntarily leave their fortunes, or any part thereof, to the state or even to their local community? The factual assumptions of the collectivist in this instance appear to be unrealistically optimistic.

The collectivist may argue that it would be a mistake to expect such altruistic behavior as was just referred to among persons brought up in a competitive, individualistic society; but they believe that it can be made characteristic of a reformed society. Such an argument cannot be disproved, but one can however, point out it is not just in bourgeois societies that men have been at best only modestly public spirited. Rather this description seems to fit virtually all known human societies that have long survived. Also, the attempts made to create a "new man," in such countries as the USSR, Cuba, and China, do not appear to be succeeding in that endeavor. It may not be so much that man is inherently selfish (although that too may be true) as that he finds it impossible to identify with such a large and impersonal body as the Great Society.

7. CONCLUDING REMARKS

Throughout the discussion of these two families of theories we have found sharp differences at the extremes and marked convergences at many other points. Clearly, neither individualists nor collectivists of necessity adopt a democratic theory; and equally clearly, both are capable of doing so. When a democratic theory *is* adopted, the convergence sometimes results from successive concessions to the other side (as is especially true of the controversy over methodology and starting points for causal analysis). At other times it grows out of an agreement on political institutions that is based upon quite different underlying philosophies. In the latter case the tension in democratic theory remains. Further, each side often suspects the other of harboring values and supporting institutions that it abhors.

Both individualists and collectivists, when they criticize each other's views of the facts, tend to be thinking of the most extreme versions of their opponents' theories. In general, their extreme positions are incompatible not only with each other but also with any viable form of democratic theory. For instance, the belief that man is completely self-seeking and unconcerned with the welfare of others is at best barely compatible with democratic theory.

115

Hobbes is the leading exemplar of this position; and for him democracy was the least desirable form of government. On the opposite side, we have the view that human beings vary so greatly in their intelligence, their understanding of their own wants and needs, and of how best to satisfy them, that their interests would be better served if their rulers were selected from among the wise, by some method that gave little or no control to the great majority of the people. It hardly needs to be said that such a belief, exemplified in Plato's *Republic*, is a form of collectivism that is incompatible with democracy.

However, individualistic and collectivistic theories that are in fact mutually opposed in their assumptions about human nature may both be democratic. The tension in these cases is between two different types of democratic theory, as between that of James Mill and that of Jean-Jacques Rousseau or Emile Durkheim, or between Hayek or Mises on the one hand, and Robert Paul Wolff on the other. Though they disagree as to significant facts, both positions are compatible with democracy; both, that is to say, are examples of democratic theory, although they may lead to differing prescriptions as to democratic policies and institutions.

The tension exists within the thought of individual theorists of democracy as well as between them. This tension derives less from incompatible beliefs that the theorist is trying to reconcile or hold in some sort of equilibrium than it does from a polarity, or at least a tension, that the theorist holds to be characteristic of human nature. Many democratic (as well as other) theorists hold that man is inherently ambivalent. He desires *both* privacy and community, and both are essential to his development. Although this particular tension, or contradiction, is the most directly related to individualism and collectivism, others are also relevant: that between the pleasures of cooperative activity and the desire for competition and precedence; or that between the desire for security and the longing for adventure and new experience; or that between altruism or duty and self-interest. A tight community is favorable to the former of each of these pairs of alternatives but unfavorable to the latter.

Historically, collectivism has generally been associated with conservative doctrines. One thinks of Plato, of the bulk of medieval theory, of Burke, and of Hegel. In contrast, we owe the great impetuses for change, for individual liberty, for reform, and even for revolution, in the modern era, to the doctrines of individualism. Names that stand out in this connection include Lilburne, Locke, Bentham, and the two Mills. Yet today most revolutionaries and also more moderate critics of the status quo adhere to a collectivist philosophy and violently attack individualism. How does this come about?

In the first place, one must admit to the existence of certain exceptions to my generalization. Certainly not all individualists have been reformers. One need mention only Hobbes to make this point. On the other hand, Rousseau, who was at least as much of a collectivist as an individualist, attacked the existing political order, and is widely credited with having indirectly influenced the French Revolution. Note also the great revolutionary and collectivist Karl Marx, although he too, had an individualistic strain.

Possibly it is only that those who desire change adopt a philosophical position opposed to that which prevails at any given time. Those who wish to bring about drastic, revolutionary transformations generally will find that they need an ideological weapon, more specifically that they need to attack the philosophical rationale underlying the existing regime. Yet there is more to it than this. A collectivist theory, with its emphasis upon solidarity of the whole, upon a society with a strong set of common beliefs and loyalties, is hardly conducive to dynamism and change, unless one believes, as many of today's collectivists do believe, that the prevailing system is radically wrong and

117

must be replaced, lock, stock, and barrel. In other words, such a theory tends to be either conservative or revolutionary. And, one may hazard the opinion, well supported by history, that success, when it is revolutionary, will be followed by a new conformism and conservatism. Individualism, on the other hand, with its emphasis upon the creative role of individual difference and dissent, may be used for either reformist or revolutionary goals, as the situation appears to warrant. To be sure, its doctrine of individual rights may also be used to defend the status quo, although not to the exclusion of those who would use it to bring about change.

A final point along this line of thought: insofar as individualism is of the materialistic brand, insofar, that is to say, as it stresses personal benefit of a material kind as a major motivating factor, it relies upon, and gives impetus to, all the dynamic forces of a technological society. Conversely, the collectivist critics of such a society, if they are consistent, must be willing to settle for one in which the long-run forces making for change are weaker and those supporting the status quo are stronger. And perhaps the evils attendant upon materialism and technology are such as to justify that choice. My purpose is simply to point out certain of the probable consequences of this brand of collectivism to those who think of it primarily as a revolutionary doctrine. It may lead to greater justice; and some may hold justice to be more important than liberty; but if liberty declines, will justice long survive? And in the long run the effects of this brand of collectivism are likely to be conservative rather than dynamic.

Returning to the main line of the argument, it may be remarked that each side risks underrating the values the other stresses. The individualist may emphasize liberty, equality of opportunity, privacy, and competition, at the expense of substantive equality, cooperation, and community, while the socialist collectivist commits the opposite errors. More than this, however, the collectivist appears to make the intellectual mistake of confusing community with polity, with the potential consequences sketched above.

One final criticism of modern collectivism: if man is wholly a creature of society, if his nature is completely plastic, what basis have we for criticizing the ideals and practices of any society? We might say its ideals and practices are at odds with each other; but then which should be changed? We might say the Soviet or the Maoist man has been molded by indoctrination and "brainwashing," but who is to say this is not for the better? Must we, with the late Justice Holmes, conclude that that nation is right which can lick all the rest?

Man's motivations are not exhausted by the dichotomy between self-seeking and altruism; nor could we deduce his character either from the alleged fact that he was born with a fixed nature or from the alleged fact that he has been completely molded by society. Either way, he develops ideals. Truth, integrity, respect for persons, and equality of rights, as well as compassion, are values men come to cherish, goals they come to pursue, with varying degrees of commitment and, in the case of equality of rights, with some variations in meaning the world over. These indeed become "ends in themselves": they are cherished for their own sakes, not as the means to further ends. As one man has put it, "The conflict between society and the individual is resolved only by transcending both, by surmounting the vacillations of egoism and altruism and rising to the objectivity of idealized endeavor."[74]

[74] Matthew Lipman, "Some Aspects of Simmel's Conception of the Individual," in George Simmel, *Essays on Sociology, Philosophy, and Aesthetics*, ed. Kurt H. Wolff (New York: Harper & Row, 1965), pp. 119-183, 134. The point is elaborated at much greater length by William Ernest Hocking, *Man and the State* (New Haven: Yale University Press, 1926), esp. Chaps. 12, 13, 22, 27. In almost Hobbesian manner Hocking begins his study with the proposition that man seeks power above all else. He soon learns, however, says Hocking, that the direct pursuit of power by means of force is self-defeating. Cooperation adds tremendously to his effectiveness. But even this is not the

But not only does the recognition of these common human ends remind us that man is something other than simply selfish or simply altruistic; it also reminds us that man has many ends, many ideals. He is not only ambivalent, as I have been arguing; he is highly pluralistic. And while he is malleable to an important degree, he remains incorrigibly manifold in his motivations and pursuits. A political theory based upon the assumption that man's nature is in any sense monistic—or that it can be made so—does violence to the facts and must suffer the consequences. The same is true, I believe, of a theory that assumes man is completely malleable, overlooking the competing tendencies that seem always, though in variant degrees, to be present.

---

final answer, for it is by the pursuit of ideals—ideals that will command the strenuous and enduring support of other men—that man attains his fullest satisfaction and self-realization.

CHAPTER IV

Justificatory Democratic Theory

FOLLOWING the Second World War, it became common-place to say that democracy had become the universally accepted political ideal. In countries where Communist parties were in power, to be sure, the day of its realization was deliberately postponed, and part of the prevailing creed was that real democracy could not exist under capitalism, or even in a world in which capitalism remained a powerful force. And in the Third World, lack of democratic requisites frequently prevented democracy's attainment, maintenance, or at the very least its satisfactory operation. But among the politically aware, barring the power-holders in the few remaining traditional regimes, democracy was generally recognized, in John Stuart Mill's phrase, as "the ideally best form of government." Moreover, social democracy, "the democratic way of life," championed especially in the Communist and Socialist countries, and increasingly the actual practice in the West, likewise achieved almost universal acceptance as a "good thing."

Today the bloom is off the rose. It would no longer do to say that democratic aspirations—or any particular political aspiration—generally prevails. In the older democracies, one finds widespread discontent, disillusionment, "alienation." Perhaps this is no more than the normal reaction to a wave of somewhat unrealistic optimism. Something of the same sort set in during the thirties, after the honeymoon period that followed the First World War had run its course and the world had turned out to be less safe for democracy than had been widely hoped. Even if this interpretation is correct, it is not necessarily reassuring. Disillusionment with an ideal is hardly a healthy state of affairs for

121

that ideal. It is true that much of the criticism of democracy heard today is *in the name of* the ideal. It claims only that democratic institutions are not working democratically. But of course we have heard before that the remedy for the ills of democracy is more democracy—initiative and referendum, recall, direct election of judges, and the like. It may have been true then, and it may still be true, that we only need to push the ideal to its logical conclusion, whatever that may be. But the second time around, disillusionment inevitably cuts deeper. It is also true that much of the disaffection with democracy today stems from conditions not inherent in democracy itself—the economic system, science and technology, and the prevailing scheme of values. Often the charge seems to be that democracy has not solved the problems of the technocratic age, without acknowledgment that no other form of government has solved them either. Just possibly it is not the form of government that is at fault.

However that may be—and I have here opened up a larger set of problems than I shall attempt to cope with in this book—it does suggest the importance of reexamining the justification for the democratic ideal. Is it something to which all should aspire, for which all should strive, which all should practice as far as conditions permit, even though those conditions may severely limit its realization?[1] It is, ac-

[1] It is true that most critics of contemporary democratic institutions attack the practice rather than the ideals of democracy. But many seem willing to suppress one ideal in order to maximize the other, and some give more than a hint of willingness to depart from both liberty and equality at least as those terms have been defined in this book. Note for instance the elitist as well as antiliberal overtones of the work of Herbert Marcuse, as illustrated in his essay "Repressive Tolerance," in Wolff, Moore, and Marcuse, *A Critique of Pure Tolerance*, pp. 81-117. For a criticism of equality, see J. R. Lucas, "Against Equality," *Philosophy*, 40 (1965), 296-307, and his "Against Equality Again," *Philosophy*, 52 (1977), 255-280. Moreover, quite apart from any contemporary attacks upon democratic ideals, it is important on Millean grounds to articulate the arguments in support of those ideals.

cordingly, justificatory democratic theory to which the present chapter will be devoted.

1. The Development of Modern Democratic Doctrine

a. Background

Until relatively modern times, democratic theory was almost nonexistent, as was democratic practice (with the partial exception of certain city-states). Was the lack of theory responsible for the absence of practice? Or was it the reverse? It seems more plausible that neither is the case. The conditions for democracy (the subject of Chapter Six) did not exist. In general, the great political theorists of the ancient and medieval worlds took for granted conditions (such as prevailed in their times) that were unfavorable to the successful functioning of large-scale democratic institutions. Or, as in much of the Middle Ages, they saw populaces too ignorant and lacking in the means for communication essential to conjoint action to be self-governing. They also saw, as in much of the Middle Ages, such political instability, such disorder, as to require domination by the militarily powerful as the condition for any community's survival. The other side of the coin is that as conditions favorable to popular government developed, so also did more thinkers draw democratic conclusions from humanistic values latent in the Western tradition since almost the earliest times.

As conditions changed, as gunpowder and the printing press added to the power of the common man while enabling the growth of popular knowledge and common culture throughout large territories, these facts found reflection both in the realities of political life and in the ideals of philosophers. We need not review the steps by which theories of popular compacts and of natural rights grew and eventually prevailed in Western Europe and in the areas colonized by it. The parallel developments of the Commercial and Industrial Revolutions on the one hand,

123

and of democratic ideals and practices on the other, is surely not accidental. Within a relatively short period, it was the defenders of authoritarian regimes who were on the defensive. Among these Thomas Hobbes was by all odds the foremost; and it is notable that Hobbes's defense of absolute government accepted the theory that all men are equally entitled to liberty, and built on the theory that, at least initially, government must be based upon consent.

b. Seventeenth-Century Theories

A survey of the modern development of democratic doctrine provides a valuable prelude to a more analytical approach to the problem of democratic ideals and institutions. We need not speculate here about the causes for the rise of individualism and the concomitant withering of the erstwhile dominant organic modes of thought that characterized the sixteenth and subsequent centuries in Western Europe. Considering the individualistic roots of democratic theory, it is not surprising that the strengthening of the human ego, the burgeoning of individualistic doctrines both theological and secular, brought with them the growth of democratic philosophies.

In sixteenth-century France, Hugenot resistance to intolerant Catholic rulers had already given rise to doctrines of man's natural right to liberty from oppressive rule. In seventeenth-century England, secular issues came to the fore as rising classes of merchants and artisans struggled against the arbitrary rule of the Stuarts. Among the many political theories that emerged from this contention, ranging from the communism of Winstanley and his "Diggers" to the conservative constitutionalism of the Presbyterians, the most profoundly democratic was that of the Levellers, led by John Lilburne. Contrary to the suggestion of the tag that became attached to them, their belief in equality related to matters of rights, including suffrage, but not including the distribution of wealth or income. Their concern was to insist that economic differences, like differences of birth, should not extend to men's equal right to political liberty. Their theories were not extensively elaborated; and their demands for political equality tended to be based either upon Scripture or upon assumed self-evident truths. "Right reason" or "the light of nature" made it evident to all who would look with unprejudiced eyes that some were not born to rule and others to be subjects, but rather that no man should be subjected to the will of another save by his own consent. Rational men would give such consent, but only to a government that recognized the equal rights of all, including the right to the franchise.

Out of the same milieu came Milton's classic reasoned denunciation of censorship and defense of freedom of the press, as well as John Locke's equally famous *Letters* in defense of religious toleration. These ideas of course have become part and parcel of the liberal democratic creed. For our purposes, however, Locke's second *Treatise of Civil Government* is of primary interest and importance. His theory had much in common with that of Hobbes as well as with that of the Levellers. They all began with the individual, assuming that his preservation, his liberty to exercise his talents, and his right to be governed by a regime to which he consented were fundamental. If Hobbes assumed, unlike the others, that this consent, once given, amounted to an almost irrevocable carte blanche to the governors, it was only because he judged that if men used their reason, they would see it was to their advantage to have it that way. His position grew not so much out of any undervaluation of liberty and moral equality as from his belief that all other values depended upon security and that the price of security, man being as he was, was very high. Locke was a better sociologist than Hobbes. He saw that the fabric of society is not so fragile as to disintegrate once absolutism is qualified. Indeed, in the extreme, he rightly argued, even a political revolution need not rend it. Individual rights of person and property would probably be observed with considerable regularity even in the ab-

125

sence of government (i.e., in a "state of nature"); certainly they would not be destroyed during the temporary hiatus in law and order that characterizes a political revolution. The English Civil War itself had proved that point, if proof were needed.

If we were to ask Locke why all men should be equally entitled to a natural right to liberty in accordance with which no man could be placed under the dominion of any other man save by his own consent, his answer would be not unlike one we shall encounter when we come to consider contemporary theories. In essence, it is Why not? Why should it be assumed that some men were born to rule over others, since all had been given by their Creator the use of the same senses and the same rational capacity. He did not argue that men were all alike or deny that their reasoning powers differed; but he did contend that all men shared a kind of reason enabling them to see, for instance, that they should not harm one another and that unless their own preservation were endangered, they should seek the welfare of others along with their own.

c. The Utilitarians

A century later in England, Jeremy Bentham, followed by James Mill and his son, John Stuart Mill, dropping all reference to states of nature, natural rights, and social or governmental contracts, pursued a utilitarian line of reasoning that had been adumbrated by Hobbes and that also played an important part in Locke's philosophy, although it was muted in his political theory. Bentham's thought was rigorously individualistic, at least in its starting point. The single test for right and the good was the interest of the individual, or the happiness to which satisfaction of that interest, by definition, gave rise. "Interest," for Bentham, was simply that whose satisfaction produced happiness. But does each man know his own interest? The utilitarians said yes. At least they affirmed the proposition that men are generally better off it they can hold their governors accountable to them. What men might lack in understanding, the utilitarians held, was more than made up for by their self-interest in resisting exploitation and tyranny. Government by others, not subject to the elective check, would develop "sinister interests" against which the unenfranchised would be defenseless. Critics tend to overlook the latter step in the utilitarians' reasoning, which is just as central as their confidence that men know their own interest best. In short, utilitarians say, "Even if rulers know my interest better than I do, will they protect and pursue it?"

If each individual's interest (or happiness) should be maximized, how should this objective be attained? Clearly, in the light of the reasoning just outlined, the answer was to allow public policy to be determined by popular vote, thus, as we say today, "aggregating" the individual interests. If there were conflicts of interest, "each should count for one and none for more than one"—in other words, "one person, one vote." This equality of right, which Bentham supported without calling it a right, involved reliance upon interpersonal comparisons as well as upon the belief in men's equal claim to happiness. The possibility of interpersonal comparisons, Bentham recognized, could not be proved. Yet he felt that no political reasoning could do without it; and moreover, while not susceptible of proof, it was so probable as to be as soundly based as the law of probability. As for the equality principle, with the utilitarians as with most individualists, the assumption is that the rational man is so set apart from other creatures as to be in a very special category, that he alone has the capacity to make moral judgments and behave morally. This unique capacity, the utilitarians argued, gives the individual such dignity, such supreme worth, that no assumption other than moral equality makes sense.

d. Rousseau

This line of reasoning was accepted by John Stuart Mill as well as by his father and by Bentham, but he supplemented it with an important additional argument. However, before dealing with Mill, it will be best to refer to the views of the greatest political philosopher of the Continental democratic tradition, Jean-Jacques Rousseau. His thought is too complex for brief summary. But, as a prelude to the analytical discussion of justificatory democratic theory, it will be useful to note some elements of his reasoning in support of the democratic ideal.

Rousseau, like Hobbes, began his analysis from the extreme point of radical individualism and proceeded to a conclusion that seems at times almost to lose sight of the individual. But the reasoning by which he negotiated this transition was very different. In one important respect, Rousseau was more anthropologically and psychologically sound than his great predecessors in the contractual school of thought. All three reasoned from the nature of man and from assumptions about how man would behave in the absence of government. Their "history," their descriptions of a "state of nature," were never intended literally, but were the conventional mode of discussing human nature and its political consequences. For Hobbes and for Locke, that nature was given; and it was discovered by introspection and by observation of others, and to some extent deduced from history. But Rousseau insisted on attributing to society certain traits which his predecessors had attributed to human nature. In seeking the state of nature, they had not gone far enough back, as he put it. The really natural man was far more primitive and more malleable. Concerned primarily with self-preservation, he was also characterized by sympathy and the faculty for self-improvement. The latter is particularly important, being dependent upon another aspect of man that, for Rousseau, was fundamental: the "quality of free-agency," or autonomy.[2] While Rousseau insisted upon the plasticity of human nature and accordingly laid great stress upon the importance of education,

[2] "A Discourse on the Origin of Inequality," in Rousseau, *The Social Contract and Discourses*, p. 184.

one of education's main objectives for the democratic citizen should be to develop personal independence, or autonomy. Here then is an important limitation to Rousseau's collectivism. In this fundamental sense he remained an individualist. Men were to be trained to be patriotic, to be devoted and loyal to the state, to follow the General Will or pursue the general welfare; but these things they should do not as conformists or automatons, but as free-willing, autonomous citizens.

The most important new element Rousseau added to democratic theory was his conviction that men could develop the qualities essential for their greatest happiness only by active participation in the government of their society. For him, the exercise of political power was not only a citizen's way to protect himself against the abuse of power by others, and not only the means by which (private) interests were aggregated, it was also the means by which a citizen, through the exercise of his sympathetic imagination, broadened his interests and made them harmonious with those of his fellow-citizens. Sympathetic though he was, natural man became, as we say, "involved" with the welfare of others only by active participation in their common government. Rousseau felt partly that the state must be democratically organized because this was a natural "trade-off" for that individual liberty (which is men's crowning glory) in a state of nature (for which we may read "state of anarchy"). But another and more distinctive side of Rousseau declared that this was no mere "trade-off" or *pis aller*; rather it was an opportunity for bringing out the best in man's nature, enabling him to reach his highest potential. Only in such a society could he achieve the greatest happiness of which he was capable.

Clearly then for Rousseau as for Locke (and Hobbes) the dignity or value of each individual was primary, and both civil and political liberty and political equality were corollary values of the greatest importance. A highly participatory democracy was the essential means for the realization

129

of these values for the same reasons that were at least implicit in Locke—that is to say, it was essential to the liberty of the individual and to his equal right to control his own destiny—and also because participation had beneficial effects on the participant, as well on the conduct of government. It is the latter, the developmental argument, that constitutes Rousseau's distinctive contribution to the case for democracy as a form of government.

This contribution of Rousseau was taken up by the German idealist philosophers and was given what is perhaps its most eloquent statement by Baron von Humboldt. He wrote as follows:

> The true end of man, or that which is prescribed by the eternal and immutable dictates of reason, and not suggested by vague and transient desires, is the highest and most harmonious development of his powers to a complete and consistent whole. Freedom is the first and indispensable condition which the possibility of such a development presupposes. . . .[3]

This is the "important additional argument," referred to above, by which John Stuart Mill supplemented the case for democracy that had been erected by his father and Jeremy Bentham. It was his answer to the argument of Macaulay and other critics that the utilitarians relied on a false hedonism and, even more to the point, that they too easily assumed people were the best guardians of their own interests.

2. Justification of Democratic Ideals: An Analytical View

a. Preliminary Remarks

Enough has been said in this survey of the modern development of democratic doctrines to furnish a serviceable

---

[3] Wilhelm von Humboldt, *The Limits of State Action*, ed. J. W. Burrow (Cambridge: Cambridge University Press, 1969), p. 16.

130

foundation for a contemporary analysis of the justification for democratic government. First, some words of caution. When we speak of justifying democracy, we are talking about the reasons that make it desirable, indeed about the reasons that may make it the "ideally best form of government." But the ideally best form of government is not necessarily the best form of government for any particular time and place. Just as Plato and Aristotle had their second-best forms of government, so may the democrat. The difference is that Plato and Aristotle may not have believed any conditions existed or were likely to exist that would make their ideals feasible, while the democrat normally believes such conditions do exist in many places and may, in time, be established where they are now lacking. Our present concern is with the justification of democratic ideals and with support for the belief that a democratic form of government may, under favorable conditions, achieve those ideals to a reasonable degree.

Further, this selective survey of political theorizing about the best form of government has been used not only to provide a basis for an analytical approach to the subject but also to show that attachment to democratic ideals tends to develop whenever and wherever conditions are favorable. It has not been meant to imply, however, that the theories discussed were necessarily representative of their time and circumstance. In particular, except for reference to fascist and communist doctrines, no attention has been payed here to numerous theorists, especially in the years since the French Revolution, who have taken a strong antidemocratic stand. Saying, then, that circumstances favorable to democracy tend to call forth philosophical defenses of it as the best form of government does not for a moment suggest that all political philosophers in such times believe in democracy.

I believe it could be effectively argued, however, that today most of the countries in which circumstances favorable to democracy obtain do in fact have governments that are, broadly speaking, democratic. A strong case could also be made that no countries in which the requisites for democratic government can fairly be said to exist have operated for extended periods under nondemocratic regimes. Obviously neither of these propositions could be sustained until agreement had been reached as to what constitutes democratic requisites, after which a country-by-country survey of the facts would have to be conducted, a project that will not be undertaken here.

The remainder of this chapter provides a justification for the democratic ideals of liberty and equality, and then discusses the implementation of these ideals and argues that, granted the existence of certain necessary conditions, formal (or procedural) democracy is by all odds more likely to approach these ideals than is any other form of government.[4]

b. The Case for Liberty

The case for liberty as a basic ideal for the form of government, for its operation, and also for all other aspects of social life can be initiated from any of various starting points.[5] It is well here to begin on ground laid in previous chapters. If one accepts the notion that regardless of differences among them, individual human beings should be accorded a dignity, granted a worth, and permitted a moral autonomy and an opportunity for self-development that

---

[4] The subject of requisites for democracy will be discussed in Chapter 6.

[5] To be sure, as appeared in Chapter Two, men do not agree what "liberty" is. But, as was contended there, the term has a core meaning upon which substantial agreement obtains. Moreover, while men may differ as to how far and in exactly what directions that core should be enlarged, these issues are frequently more definitional than substantive. Often it is agreed that a proposed extension represents something of great value even when, for any of a variety of reasons, many would contend it is best considered under some other heading than "liberty." Hence the enterprise of this section is not rendered nugatory by definitional problems.

sets each apart from the rest of nature, then one is committed to placing a high value on the individual's freedom. "To be free to choose and not to be chosen for" is, as Sir Isaiah Berlin remarks, "an inalienable ingredient in what makes human beings human."[6] Another English writer puts it this way.

> Freedom is a necessary condition of rationality, of action, of achievement. Not to be free is to be frustrated, impotent, futile. To be free is to be able to shape the future, to be able to translate one's ideals into reality, to actualize one's potentialities as a person. Not to be free is not to be responsible, not to be able to be responsive, not to be human. Freedom is a good, if anything is.[7]

To say that liberty is essential for moral autonomy, as by definition it is, and even to go on to say that it is also essential for self-actualization, the development of one's potentialities, is not to say *how much* liberty is required for these purposes. Once a person is freed from chains and prisons, assuming also that he is psychologically capable of rational and independent action, he is possessed of at least a modicum of moral autonomy. But the freedom of a man who can act only in accordance with what he believes to be moral on pain of some severe deprivation is seriously qualified. Freedom is indeed a matter of degree. The considerations urged above support not just a bare minimum of freedom; they support the proposition that freedom should be one of the main objectives of a social and political system, what John Rawls refers to as a "primary social good."[8]

[6] *Four Essays on Liberty*, p. lx.

[7] J. R. Lucas, *The Principles of Politics* (Oxford: Clarendon Press, 1966), p. 144.

[8] Rawls, *A Theory of Justice*, p. 62. "Freedom," or "liberty," as used here, must be understood in terms of the concept as defined earlier (p. 28). Even as thus defined it is of course true that "liberty" is composed of, or results from, many "liberties." They may conflict with each other. It is not just a question then of giving priority to liberty. Certain liberties or freedoms must be given priority over others. Since

133

Mill made it one of the foundations of his case for representative government as the ideally best form of government that the opportunity and responsibility for participating in the political process would encourage citizens to think beyond their own narrow concerns, to broaden their moral horizons by giving some thought to the general welfare, to acquaint themselves with the facts relevant to public policy, and to exert and develop their minds by considering the probable consequences of various alternatives before them. Much later, John Dewey made substantially the same point. He wrote:

> Full education comes only when there is a responsible share on the part of each person, in proportion to capacity, in shaping the aims and policies of the social groups to which he belongs. This fact fixes the significance of democracy. . . . It is but a name for the fact that human nature is developed only when its elements take part in directing things which are common, things for the sake of which men and women form groups. . . .[9]

Today these arguments may seem to be based on a highly idealized version, not to say vision, of the average citizen's role. Yet it would be a mistake to discount it entirely. One must consider the alternative. If the individual has no recognized right, and therefore presumably little power, to affect public policy, in most cases he will give it no thought at all, or at least not think about it responsibly. Is this not the greater evil?

Doubtless one should not jump too quickly to this conclusion. A recent writer finds "something morally and intellectually corrupting about a regular invitation to register one's preferences between alternatives whose merits

---

the political and civil liberties are the key to so many others, in fact liberties without which all others may be lost, it is these democratic freedoms to which priority should attach.

[9] Dewey, *Reconstruction in Philosophy*, enlarged edition (Boston: Beacon Press, 1966), p. 209.

and demerits one has neither time nor competence to investigate, and which, in a party system, are as likely as not obscurely stated, nonexclusive and nonexhaustive."[10] Probably so. But it is less corrupting and certainly less degrading than being told he has no say about things that are manifestly his concern, no equal right to share in shaping the laws by which he is to be governed. People who are publicly proclaimed to be inferior, as by being denied the vote, will be generally regarded as inferior, will find their rights ignored, and will either wind up considering themselves inferior and losing all self-esteem, or will become rebels.

Mill speaks in terms of the vote; and when we think of electoral behavior as revealed by the extensive research conducted in this field during the last generation, it is easy to give his contention low marks. But one must think of all that the ballot entails. Pressure groups of all sorts, public-interest organizations, voluntary associations from churches to trade unions that take an interest in political affairs, multiply the opportunities for citizens to think about, to become educated about, and to exert influence on public policy. In spite of the thousands of such organizations in the United States, for instance, the proportion of the electorate that belongs to organizations with any significant political orientation is less than half, perhaps less than a quarter of the total, and the number who actively participate is even smaller. What must not be forgotten, however, is the clear fact that in view of the notoriously hostile attitude of nondemocratic regimes toward voluntary organizations in general and especially toward those with any political tinge, these numbers would be far smaller in the absence of democracy.

[10] N.M.L. Nathan, "On the Justification of Democracy," *The Monist*, 55 (1971), 88-120, 112. A counterargument similar to the one set forth below is developed by Ramon Lemos, in "A Moral Argument for Democracy," *Social Theory and Practice*, 4 (1976), 57-79. See especially pp. 62 and 73.

On the matter of group membership and its relation to the highly significant variable of subjective competence, Almond and Verba have provided us with interesting information.[11] The percentages of respondents who report membership in some organization are as follows for the five countries studied: United States, 57%; Great Britain, 47%; Germany, 44%; Italy, 30%; and Mexico, 24%.[12] Of those reporting organizational membership, generally about 40% believe that an organization to which they belong is involved in political affairs.[13] Uniformly throughout the five countries studied, members of organizations whose members believe them to be involved in politics score higher on the subjective-competence scale than do members of organizations that do not qualify as "political" by this test, while even the latter group scores notably higher than do those who report no organizational membership.[14]

To be sure, these figures tell us nothing about causal relations. Whether citizens' political self-confidence results from their group membership or the other way about is not revealed. One can rely only on the commonsense judgment that participation in the organization must be at least partly responsible for the feeling of competence.[15] Nor is

[11] By "subjective competence" they mean citizens' perception of themselves as able to affect governmental decisions. Gabriel A. Almond and Sidney Verba, *The Civic Culture: Political Attitudes and Democracy in Five Nations* (Princeton, N.J.: Princeton University Press, 1963), p. 181.

[12] Ibid., p. 304.

[13] Ibid., p. 306. This fact must be taken into account to explain the statement above about the number of Americans who belong to organizations of the kind under discussion. (In Mexico the figure is only 20 percent.)

[14] Ibid., p. 308. Averaging the results for the five countries, 71 percent of the members of political organizations received the highest scores on the subjective-competence scale. The percentages for the nonpolitical and nonmembership groups, respectively, were 57 and 43.

[15] It should be noted, too, that in the absence of politically involved organizations their potential members would be deprived of opportu-

the feeling of competence the same thing Mill was talking about. Certain facts from the Almond and Verba survey do bear upon the latter. First, those who rate high on the subjective-compentence scale have a much higher rate of exposure to political communications (and so, presumably, to relevant, though doubtless incomplete and biased, information) than do those further down on the scale. They also engage in political discussion to a far greater extent. Finally, this group takes much greater pride in its governmental and political system.[16] This last point comes closest to Mill's contention that political participation broadens the moral horizons of the citizen, for what it measures would not seem to be related to self-interest narrowly conceived and is at least presumptively related to concern for the whole.

Returning to the point that freedom is valuable because people value it and are frustrated without it, we must recognize that by no means all people want freedom all the time. In part, this fact is taken care of by the definition offered earlier, which recognizes that freedom requires restraints, that little freedoms must often be sacrificed for greater ones, present ones for future ones, and so on. But it must also be acknowledged—who would deny it?—that, important though it is, freedom is only one of man's basic needs. Some are even more basic: for instance, a reasonable degree of safety and the satisfaction of physiological needs. Also high among man's basic needs are his need for love and for the feeling of belonging to a group, and his need for self-esteem and for the esteem of others. A. H. Maslow, a leading psychologist and student of human motivation, argues that the basic needs can be ranked according to

nities to utilize their political competence and to satisfy their desires to participate politically in this way.

[16] Ibid., pp. 238, 240, 248. Regarding the last point, Italy is a partial exception, where those in the middle group with respect to subjective competence feel more pride in their governmental and political system than either the high or the low groups.

their temporal priority. First the physiological needs must be satisfied, then the safety needs, followed in turn by the need for self-esteem and for the esteem of others. Only after these have been met in reasonable degree does the need for self-actualization present itself. But at that point this need becomes powerful. And for its satisaction liberty is a sine qua non, liberty that must include the freedom for self-expression, and freedom to seek information, and the freedom to do as one wishes within reasonable limits.[17] Maslow's theory is not universally accepted among psychologists, but at the very least it suggests in a general way how liberty can be of prime importance, a primary value, and yet not be a major concern of men under all conditions. Other needs must be satisfied first, because until they are, liberty will be of little use. Moreover, people who have come to love and demand, and perhaps enjoy, liberty may become so frustrated, so deprived, that they will gladly give it up in return for security, for release from over-powering tension.

Granted favorable conditions though, people demand freedom not just because they want what they want but because it lets them develop their capacities, choose which of their potentialities they will develop most fully, and attain the particular balance of activities that best suits their individualities.[18] They can approach the human goal of

[17] Maslow, *Motivation and Personality*, Chap. 5. James C. Davies, modifying Maslow, lists the basic needs in the following order: physical needs; social, affectional or love needs; self-esteem or dignity or equality needs; and self-actualization needs. See his "Priority of Human Needs and Stages of Political Development," in Pennock and Chapman, eds., *Human Nature in Politics*, NOMOS XVII (New York: New York University Press, 1977), Chap. 6.

[18] C. B. Macpherson distinguishes between man as consumer of utilities and man as exerter of powers or capacities, noting that Mill added the second dimension to the narrower doctrine of the earlier utilitarians. He considers the result "an uneasy compromise between the two views of man's essence, and, correspondingly, an unsure mixture of the two maximizing claims made for the liberal-democratic society." *Democratic Theory*, pp. 4-5. In other words, he sees this theo-

happy and harmonious self-fulfillment only if they are free to experiment. The evidence as to what provides the most harmonious and satisfying balance of our conflicting desires is subjective, capable of being finally appraised by ourselves alone.[19] Furthermore, the making of this appraisal and the acts of choice that follow it are themselves vital elements in a satisfying life. It is also characteristic of what is most distinctively human about man. One cannot do better than to quote Mill on this point. He writes: "He who chooses his plan for himself, employs all his faculties. He must use observation to see, reasoning and judgment to foresee, activity to gather materials for decision, discrimination to decide, and when he has decided, firmness and self-control to hold to his deliberate decision."[20]

c. Collectivist Views on Liberty

Much more could be said in praise of the democratic ideal of liberty. It hardly seems necessary.[21] However, since liberty, at least in its usual connotation, is a peculiarly individualistic value, it is appropriate to ask what collectivists have to say about the matter; does the position taken here rest upon individualist propositions the collectivist would deny? In large measure, the answer is no, but the

---

retical mixture in conventional democratic theory as a weakness. An important argument of my book, on the other hand, is that the mixture is part of democracy's strength. Man's nature is to want *both* to consume *and* to create. To build a theory on a contrary assumption would be to build upon a false foundation.

[19] In one sense, no appraisal is "final." You may rightly judge my self-satisfaction to be unjustified, mistaken. But, a person is diminished who is forced to accept someone else's appraisal and to act accordingly.

[20] John Stuart Mill, "On Liberty," in *Utilitarianism, Liberty and Representative Government*, p. 117.

[21] Writings on the subject are legion. I have discussed the subject in compressed form, though much more fully than here, and with considerable bibliographical material, in *Liberal Democracy*, Chap. 4. The paragraph above draws heavily upon material from that chapter.

collectivist position cannot be dismissed summarily and must be considered in some detail.

In general, as far as concerns liberty, modern collectivists are more concerned to assert certain other propositions than to deny those of the individualist. They wish to assert the value of the collectivity and of collective action. This is not necessarily to say that the individual should be *forced* into "togetherness," nor is it to deny the value of privacy or of free choice. They believe that the individual who chooses to expand the "public" area of his life, to pursue goods cooperatively and in common, will find greater satisfaction and self-actualization than the one who chooses to place greater stress upon self-reliance and tends to retreat within the domain of his own family or other small group. They also stress the influence of the collectivity on the individual, arguing, as did Gierke, that if all the products of society were removed from an individual's personality only a miserable remnant would remain. But this point can be fully granted without diminishing the importance of providing conditions for the individual's further satisfaction, development, actualization, or "realization," from whatever source. Finally, the collectivist places high value on benevolence, on man's concern, or what (he would contend) ought to be his concern for his fellow man and for future generations. With this, too, the kind of individualism underlying the basic case for liberty has no quarrel.[22]

Taking the specific example of Hegel, it appears even more clearly that liberty was for him of supreme value. For him Reason and Freedom were in some uses synonymous, and he frequently spoke of the great moving Idea of history

[22] Even fascists, who often adopted a collectivist philosophy, were less concerned to deny the value of liberty (although they would be careful to distinguish it from "license") than they were to have it unequally distributed. In other words, their attack was more upon equality than upon liberty, although they certainly downgraded liberty as compared to security, order, and community.

as the Idea of Freedom. Nor was this, for him, such a vague abstraction as to have no application to the practical world. "As a general principle," he wrote, speaking of ancient Athens, "the democratic constitution affords the widest scope for the development of great political characters; for it excels all others in virtue of the fact that it not only *allows of* the display of their powers on the part of individuals, but *summons* them to use those powers for the general weal."[23] John Stuart Mill could not have put it more eloquently! To spell it out even more clearly, in the following paragraph he praises Athens for its "vital freedom."[24]

Yet members of this general school of thought (with whom, incidentally, Hegel would agree) argue that the kind of liberty and individuality glorified by Mill are in fact threats to the integrity and health of the personality, citing in their support Durkheim's studies showing that "where the intensity of the collective life of a community diminishes—as their 'freedom' in the Millean sense, increases, therefore—the rate of suicide rises."[25] On this line of argument two comments are in order. First, the ideal of liberty being supported here, as has been pointed out, is not Millean. It is a modification in the idealist, or collectivist, direction of Mill's concept. Second, and more importantly, one must recall the distinction made in the preceding chapter between the state and the community. It is in communities *within* the state, not least in the family, that the conditions for psychological health Durkheim de-

23 Hegel, *The Philosophy of History*, trans. J. Sebree, rev. ed. (New York: Wiley, 1900), p. 260.

24 Reference to Athens naturally suggests the name of Plato. To indulge in understatement, he was obviously one collectivist for whom neither individualism nor liberty ranked high in the hierarchy of values. The same could be said of many others who lived before the day when the individual emerged from the chrysalis of the tribe.

25 See Robert Paul Wolff, "Beyond Tolerance," in Wolff, Moore, and Marcuse, *A Critique of Pure Tolerance*, pp. 3-52. The relevant section is at pages 23-38 and the specific reference to Durkheim is at pages 32-33.

scribes are to be found. Their importance does not diminish the importance for the political realm of the democratic ideal of liberty as defined in Chapter Two.

Contemporary antiindividualist theorists often advance a position they refer to as "intentionalism." Their concern is with the quality of life and, with respect to liberty, they stress the point that the absence of restraints is no guarantee liberty will be used well, either for the individual or for society as a whole. One might say that for them absence of restraint is a necessary but not a sufficient condition for liberty. However, in certain cases they would go beyond this and argue that restraints are better than the alternative, especially if the alternative is something—whether an educational policy or whatnot—which would lead to creative thinking and action rather than a mechanical exercise of choice among superficialities. It seems the definition adopted in Chapter Two, with its stress on the development of purpose rather than aimless choosing, is not subject to this line of criticism; but it is well to point out that the definition was a deliberate modification of the purely individualistic theory of liberty by the injection of what might properly be called an "intentionalist" approach.[26]

---

[26] For a good statement of the position outlined in this paragraph, see Benjamin R. Barber, *Superman and Common Men* (New York: Praeger, 1971), pp. 37-97. Two paragraphs from this little book (not consecutive in the book) will help give the flavor of this point of view. They read as follows: "A full account of what tolerance betokens reveals, finally, a picture of the nature of political life that is partial and flawed. Men, in this portrayal, appear as self-interested, self-sufficient creatures who have invented politics to reconcile their differences and accommodate their interests, and who therefore demand that for every encroachment of their interests or of the freedom by which those interests are thought to be guaranteed there be a corresponding justification. Seen from this perspective, morality is confined to judgments of utility—a calculation of lesser evils whose aim is the maximum extension of Self at minimum cost and risk. Tolerance is merely an instance of this form of calculation."

"The politics which concerns itself with the good life, which is grounded in man's inadequacy as a solitary being, and which aims at virtue rather than at mechanistic freedom may not find much room

d. The Case for Equality

With equality, again, as in the case of liberty, the explication of the concept in its various applications in Chapter Two has already gone some of the way toward justification of the concept as an ideal. Let us begin with formal equality, the simple proposition that likes should be treated alike. So simple it is, so inescapable, that little needs to be said in its justification. The practical reason, or whatever we choose to call that by which we reason about such matters, finds this proposition as axiomatic as that two things equal to the same thing are equal to each other. At the very least, this notion of the like treatment of like cases is implied by engaging in ethical discourse. The very essence of the enterprise of such discourse is commitment to the principle of impartiality, which is what the equal treatment of equals is all about. One could also approach the matter from the standpoint of linguistic analysis. In that case, the key word in this context is *justice*. An ideal society must certainly be a just society; and justice, whatever else it may mean, surely means impartiality, the like treatment of like cases.

Now this purely formal concept is often said to be vacuous.[27] No two cases, no two persons, are exactly alike;

for, or be particularly interested in, tolerance. It may perceive in privacy an arena for greed, in individuality the specter of loneliness and alienation, and in negative freedom a rejection of the bonds of human commonality. Its aim will be less to defend the rights of its subjects than to transform subjects into citizens." Ibid., pp. 96-97.

Are these paragraphs intended simply as moral exhortation or do they have institutional implications? From the standpoint of democratic theory, it is a crucial question left unanswered by Barber as well as by others who express this line of argument. The denigration of tolerance arouses fears that are intensified by talk of giving priority to the transformation of subjects into citizens over the defense of rights. Who is to decide and what means are to be used? The words may be spoken by a democrat (as in this case they certainly are), but the ideas are reminiscent of a Maoist philosophy and of the means to which that has led.

[27] See, for example, David Lyons, "The Weakness of Formal Equality," *Ethics*, 76 (1966), 146-148.

143

therefore it is always a question of whether the differences are relevant for the purpose in question. So runs the argument. But, accepting this line of reasoning, what follows? In the light of history, of human experience, one thing seems clear: pains will have to be taken, machinery will have to be established to ensure that these judgments of relevance (and of what follows from them) are made impartially, in the light of the fullest possible information, and after deliberate consideration of all arguments adduced on one side or another. Man being what he is, partial to his own interests and those of his friends, and limited in his ability to acquire and consider for judgment a vast amount of factual information, it is clear that to constitute the government of a society so as to achieve the maximum possible correspondence between its laws and their administration on the one hand, and justice on the other, will be no mean feat! Specifically, nearly all of the machinery and constitutional provisions of a modern constitutional democracy are aimed at precisely this objective. Thus, even if we accept the ideal of equality only in its most formal, allegedly "vacuous" sense, the sense implicit in moral reasoning, we have accepted a principle that provides a powerful justification for democratic institutions. Conceivably, we have accepted all that is necessary to justify the democratic political ideal.[28]

Marxists, to be sure, would mount two lines of attack against this constitutionalist argument. First, they would argue that the constitutional machinery of Western democracies, far from preventing injustice, perpetuates it; and, second, they would contend that if the capitalist roots of present injustices were eliminated, formal judicial procedures would not be required to see that justice is done. If

[28] From one point of view, this paragraph's argument belongs in the following section, which deals with the *implementation* (in political institutions) of the democratic ideal. But it is also integrally related to the defense of the ideal of equality, because it answers an attack on one version of the ideal.

the first argument means that constitutionalism, as practiced in this country, for instance, does no more than maintain the status quo, it is demonstrably false. If inequality
of income is thought to indicate an injustice, as Marxists
think, it is clear that the record in this country shows
marked improvement. For example, the percentage of aggregate income going to the lowest fifth of families in 1950
was 4.5 percent. By 1976, this percentage had risen to 5.4, a
20 percent increase. Again, in 1959, 22.5 percent of our
population was below the poverty line, while the percentage for 1976 was 11.8 percent, only slightly more than half
of the earlier level.[29]

The claim that the abolition of capitalism would render
superfluous the machinery of constitutionalism, that a
"new man" would be created, one who always behaved
justly, or at least who, when in a position of authority, always saw that justice was done, is unsupported by evidence,
and goes contrary to common experience of human nature.
Moreover, one regime after another has eliminated capitalism and has tried to create the "new man," to eliminate
suppression, and to socialize man in such a way that differential material incentives would not have to be resorted
to, all without success.

But we can go further than this. It appears there is an
initial presumption in favor of equality of treatment just as
there is an initial presumption in favor of liberty in the
basic sense of noninterference. Both interference and discrimination have to justify themselves.[30] In the case of
equality, the alternative to equal treatment is unequal
treatment. But what is that? Inequality is not a standard but
the denial of a standard. Equal treatment is precise; unequal
treatment is indefinite, vague. For this reason, procedurally
at least, one can make a strong argument for beginning
with the assumption of equality and proceeding from there

[29] *Statistical Abstract of the United States* (Washington, D.C.: GPO,
1977), pp. 443, 453.

[30] See A. C. Graham, "Liberty and Equality," *Mind*, 74 (1965), 59-65.

to consider claims for departure from it.[31] It is true, as critics
of this line of reasoning point out, that the presumption of
equality is but one side of a coin, the other being the presumption that unequals should be treated unequally. In
some cases the inequality is so obvious that we jump immediately to the other side of the proposition. Thus if, while
walking in the woods with a friend, I find a ten dollar bill
and offer to share it with him, I have not acted unjustly because I did not offer to share it with other nearby users of
the path. It is also true that what should be treated equally

[31] For a sensitive treatment of the question of presumptive equality
—one that is critical of the concept as often used but yet not, I believe, inconsistent with the discussion above—see Joel Feinberg, *Social
Philosophy* (Englewood Cliffs, N.J.: Prentice-Hall, 1973), pp. 99-102.
J. R. Lucas, in his "Against Equality Again," has set forth a vigorous
argument against presumptive equality. Some of it appears to me to
be answered by what is said in the text above, while other parts are
not relevant to the use of the term made in this book. One point,
though, calls for special mention. He argues that a society in which
more than one hierarchy exists will be a happier one than a society
in which all are confined to a single hierarchy. (He assumes that some
hierarchical ordering is inescapable.) This argument for two or more
"pecking orders" has much to commend it. I would simply point out
that the democratic state, by using the "one person, one vote" principle assures this plurality.

Julius Stone has recently launched an attack on presumptive equality as central to the concept of justice. Even he concedes that "recognition of common humanness, of human equality in that sense" is *prerequisite* to raising questions of justice." The notion of equality, he
insists, however, cannot *answer* questions of justice because it does not
tell us what differences or similarities between persons or cases are relevant to justice. This is quite true. Equality is not the whole of justice
by any means; but to consider questions of justice without it as a starting point would be like conducting a race without a starting line.
Stone's argument is set forth in "Justice in the Slough of Equality,"
(mimeographed) paper presented to the World Congress on Philosophy
of Law and Social Philosophy, Sydney and Canberra, 14-21 Aug. 1977.
See pp. 4-5. On this question see also Carl Cohen, *Democracy* (Athens,
Ga.: University of Georgia Press, 1971), pp. 263-267, and Stanley I. Benn,
"Egalitarianism and Equal Consideration of Interests," in Pennock and
Chapman, eds., *Equality*, NOMOS IX (New York: Atherton, 1967),
pp. 61-78.

146

are, in the first instance, cases rather than persons. But "persons" are "cases" until shown to be otherwise, although the "showing" may be too obvious to require demonstration. The point is partly procedural, as was suggested above, but this protective procedure is further justified by our common humanity, a point to which I now turn.

By "common humanity" I refer to the principle I have elsewhere denominated "human dignity." In Chapter Three that principle was variously derived. In part it was derived from the valuations we place upon equality and our general opposition to exploitation and discrimination. To use those arguments here would be circular, since it is about equality that we wish to make certain conclusions. However, other arguments were set forth in support of the value of the individual, of human dignity. They need not be repeated here, but they did include the fact that man, uniquely, possesses certain abilities which enable him to be a moral being, to engage in what we may call the moral enterprise. It seems not unreasonable to hold that when we are dealing with moral questions, as we are when we consider how people should be treated, beings capable of morality should be considered as constituting a class. They have one highly relevant factor in common. They alone can raise and discuss moral issues, develop rules of right conduct, and regulate their own behavior to conform to them. Other considerations apart, this fact is persuasive that such creatures have a presumptive claim to equal treatment. There may of course be all kinds of differences relevant to the moral enterprise that justify differential treatment. But these differences must be pointed out and their relevance to the moral enterprise and to the demand for differential treatment made evident. That is the meaning of calling the claim to equal treatment "presumptive."

What is this "moral enterprise"? Whatever else it may be, it clearly involves two principles: those of impartiality —of finding rules that will be applied alike to me and to all others who are similarly situated—and of benevolence. The

147

latter may indeed be implied by the former, at least if those rules are to gain general acceptability.

Hume puts the matter with characteristic lucidity. When one uses ethical terms, he writes, he "speaks another language, and expresses sentiments, in which he expects all his audience are to concur with him. He must here, therefore, depart from his private and particular situation, and must choose a point of view, common to him with others; he must move some universal principle of the human frame, and touch a string to which all mankind have an accord and symphony."[32]

The "good will" as contrasted with the "impartiality" point is also well put by P. F. Strawson. He writes: "It is important to recognize the diversity of possible systems of moral demands, and the diversity of demands which may be made within any system. But it is also important to recognize that certain human interests are so fundamental and so general that they must be universally acknowledged in some form and to some degree in any conceivable moral community. Of some interests, one might say: a system could scarcely command *sufficient* interest in those subject to its demands for these demands to be acknowledged as obligations, unless it secured to them *this* interest. Thus some claim on human succour, some obligation to abstain from the infliction of physical injury, seem to be necessary features of almost any system of moral demands. Here at least we have types of moral behavior which are demanded *of* men as men because they are demanded *for* and *by* men as men."[33]

As a matter of fact, the line of reasoning just propounded is generally accepted. Rarely, if ever, do we meet the man who says that Jews should be exterminated "because I don't like them," or that blacks, *because of their*

[32] David Hume, *An Enquiry Concerning the Principles of Morals* (La Salle, Ill.: Open Court, 1947), p. 111.
[33] Strawson, "Social Morality and Individual Ideals," *Philosophy*, 36 (1961), 1-17, 11.

alized by some other form of government. A more likely line of attack would be to contend that other ideals, of equal or greater importance, would be secured less well, or even defeated, by democracy. Before turning to this line of attack, however, it will be well to say a little more about the implementation of the specifically democratic ideals of liberty and equality. (Fraternity pertains to social democracy, or the spirit that should infuse the citizens of a democratic government, rather than to anything that can be said to characterize the institutions of government themselves.)

Of liberty, most of what needs to be said has already been covered. A democracy that fails to protect the basic civil liberties is not likely to remain a democracy for long. Indeed, as was argued in Chapter One, unless it maintains those liberties essential to the free exercise of political power, it loses its claim to be called a democracy, for the essence of that institution has been destroyed. At the same time, some form of regime other than a democracy might provide significant freedoms. It might, for instance, provide for the rule of law and all the elements of fair trial and the like that normally go with that concept. It might, although the record suggests it is unlikely, even protect the freedoms of expression, assembly, and association. And when it comes to matters less central to the political process but nevertheless important parts of liberty—matters such as freedom to move about, to choose among potential employers and employments, to marry whom one likes, to be allowed important areas of privacy, and so on and so forth—a democratic regime could be quite antiliberal, while a nondemocratic regime could conceivably allow a great deal of freedom. It is here that the case for democracy must rely upon experience and common sense. It is probabilistic rather than definitive. In the past, nondemocratic regimes have not been notable for their protection of freedoms. This is as true of freedom as defined in Chapter Two as it is of a more strictly individualistic definition. Moreover, in today's modernized world, where the proportion of the popu-

150

lace that is articulate, uncowed by authority, released from
the "the cake of custom," and insistent upon having a say
about its fate, is almost certainly larger than it has ever
been before, the chances of the logical possibilities sketched
above coming to prevail for significant periods of time seem
extremely slight. Whether conditions favorable to the maintenance of a democratic regime will continue to prevail is
of course a different question.

Another, and more popular, line of attack is to contend
that the liberties just discussed are of little value without
economic equality. But this is not an argument against democracy; it is an argument for a particular economic policy. Its supporters may believe it is so important that if
necessary, democracy itself should be sacrificed (temporarily) in order to obtain such equality. In view of the record to date, critics may well wonder whether the sacrifice
would in fact turn out to be only temporary. And, if not,
would the gain in equality (and justice, if that it is) be
worth the losses of liberty and welfare? In such matters each
person must judge for himself.

Similar arguments also pertain to equality. If a particular kind of equality, economic equality, is selected as all-
important, it is possible to argue that if necessary, all other
forms of equality, including formal equality and political
equality, should go by the board. The whole line of argument in the discussion of equality above goes in the opposite direction. But there is one form of equality about which
little has yet been said directly. And that is the form most
centrally related to democracy, political equality, the principle of "one person, one vote." Does formal equality, or
even the minimum of substantive equality implied by the
principle of presumptive equality, entail the equality of the
franchise? Clearly no. Is it not true that some are better
fitted by intelligence and experience than others to exercise
political power? Just as clearly the answer is yes. Hence political liberty, as the equality of the vote is frequently
called, does not follow by logical necessity from the equal-

151

ity principle. To put the question in terms of the previous discussion, it is obviously true that men vary greatly in their ability to cast their ballot so as to maximize either their own welfare or that of society. They do not know their own interests, or how to further them, equally well. No one can dispute these statements; no one can deny their relevance to the issue of how political power should be distributed. How then defend the equality of the vote?

There is no easy answer. John Stuart Mill himself, great defender of representative government, was at best uncertain on this point. But telling points, I believe, can be made. In the first place, one must note the distinction just made between "political power" and "the vote." It is of great importance. Without the vote, a man's political power may be slight or nonexistent; with it, if he is stupid or ignorant, it may still be very slight. On the other hand, if he is reasonably intelligent and feels sufficiently interested to make the attempt, he can use his franchise with considerable effect. He may achieve a position of influence in a political party, or of authority in the government. In short, the vote is a bare minimum—not without great importance, as will be argued, yet little more than an entitlement, which may or may not be exercised. For the person with sufficient ability, energy, desire—and luck—it may become the key to the most powerful position in the land. Many others, with intelligence and energy among other qualifications, will parlay it into positions of considerable power. Thus "one person, one vote" by no means condemns the able to impotence, nor treats those with the ability to pursue their interest and the general interest wisely and effectively on a par with the most stupid and ignorant.

On the other hand, it hardly needs to be said that the ability to attain political office is no guarantee of either the ability to promote the general welfare or the single-minded will to do so. Here one must rely on the ability of the average man at least to know when things are not going well with him, and upon a competitive political system that will make it worth someone's while to organize the discontented. These are no mean reliances. It is true that the large body of literature on the effects of political competition is inconclusive. Whether a system in which inter-party competition is keen is more responsive to popular demand than a system in which the competition between political parties is moribund is far from clear. But these studies deal with noncompetitive systems (states or political subdivisions thereof) within a competitive system, and in a country where the whole milieu is democratic. They would seem to have little bearing on the differences between democratic and nondemocratic systems.

In the last analysis, democracy is our most powerful weapon against tyranny. Moreover, in a modern industrial or postindustrial society the only likely alternative to democracy seems to be an authoriarian regime that becomes tyrannical whenever its security is threatened. As Walter Lippmann wrote many years ago, speaking of the fun that is often poked at parliaments as "talk-shops," "deride the talk as much as you like; it is the civilized substitute for street brawls, gangs, conspiracies, assassinations, private armies. No other substitute has yet been discovered."[35] The fact that democracy provides a peaceful means for bringing about change, including the inevitable change of leaders, is one of its important accomplishments. Yet it would be a mistake to assume that other forms of government can never deal with the problem of succession in a peaceful manner. The Soviet Union has on several occasions proved the contrary.

Perhaps the most important single argument for the equality of the vote, at least as contrasted with some qualified form of representative government, is simply that it symbolizes the principle of presumptive equality, which is one of democracy's central values. To legally brand some

[35] *The Essential Lippmann*, ed. Clinton Rossiter and James Lare (New York: Random House, 1963), p. 229.

153

individuals as unequal, to deprive them of that badge of democratic citizenship, the franchise, an equal franchise, would not only be a denial of a core principle of democracy, it would at the same time be an affront to the human dignity, the self-respect of those who were thus discriminated against. And to do this would not only be in itself a great blow to the self-esteem of the people affected, it would also be an invitation to all to belittle them and to be disregardful of their welfare. As Bertrand Russell once remarked, "any class which is destitute of power will be despised, and accused of every kind of crime, and harried and ill-treated and subjected to cruelty."[36]

4. DEMOCRACY AND THE ENDS OF GOVERNMENT

It was suggested before that if the case for the democratic idea was to be effectively refuted it would have to be in terms of other ideals than those that specifically pertain to democracy. One thinks in this connection of other general objectives of political organization, particularly of justice, of welfare, of order and security. As for justice, little more need be said. If the democrat's arguments for equality are sound, then it can hardly be alleged that democracy as such is unjust; for that argument has been met above in the discussion of equality.

One of the major counterarguments to democracy, the

[36] Quoted in E. M. Sait, *Democracy* (New York: Appleton-Century-Crofts, 1929), p. 96. It is important to realize the nature of this reasoning. The case for democracy is not based upon an abstract and doctrinaire argument to the effect that all individual preferences should count equally, and that if I wish you to sleep on your back, my preference in this matter should weigh equally with yours. (The example and the argument is borrowed from Amartya K. Sen, *Collective Choice and Social Welfare* [San Francisco: Holden-Day, 1970], Chap. 5.) But most people are self-assertive enough about their own desires to fend off the nosiness of others. In short, giving all adults equal *minimal* political power will not result in their using the power equally in support of their basic needs and their whimsical preferences.

one just discussed, is based upon the contention that the general public is too unintelligent, ill-informed, and inattentive to public affairs for a form of government that gives even marginal control over its policies to the mass of the people. In short, the charge is that democracy is inimical to welfare. It should be noted at once that today particularly, the charge does not rest solely on the alleged stupidity, ignorance, and apathy of the average voter. These shortcomings might conceivably be overcome by better education. But will even informed, intelligent, and interested voters act in such a way as to promote their own interests and that of the general public? If one thinks only of "the public" versus some self-interested minority, the answer seems obvious. But "the public" is made up of many groups, ultimately of many individuals. If each pursues his own interest, or even that of a particular group, the result may be to defeat his interest. If the citizens of each town vote for a new post office, to be paid for from the national treasury, too much money will be spent on post offices. All will suffer. Yet if the citizens of a particular town (or their representative in the national legislature) vote against a post office for their town, they will suffer. No one wants *his* gasoline taxed to encourage the development of other resources, but the result of his opposition to such a tax may be disaster in the not far distant future.

How serious this general problem will prove to be in today's world remains to be seen. It is certainly not to be taken lightly; and, like many others, it becomes more serious as the proportion of social (and especially economic) activity that is regulated by government increases. It can be minimized (perhaps at some cost) by appropriate constitutional arrangements, as is discussed in Chapters Nine and Ten. Beyond this, certain more general points need to be made. Any alternative form of government will also be responsive to certain interests. If it seeks, in spite of its unaccountability to a general electorate, to be responsive to a very wide spectrum of interests, it will be likely to fall

155

into the same trap of yielding to pressures that are, in their consequences, mutually conflicting and self-defeating. If, on the other hand, it is narrowly based and responsive, the interests of most people, almost by definition, will be overlooked or at least underrated. Perhaps more fundamentally, but also more problematically, one should note that the problem would not arise if voters tended to vote on a Kantian-Christian principle of doing to others as they would be done by. Or even if they recognize the necessity of compromise, and of compromise on a basis other than one that will prove to be self-defeating to all in the long run, the worst results of the process we are discussing will be avoided. And the publicity attendant upon democracy— the widespread discussion of probable consequences of various possible courses of action, with the opinions of experts fed into this debate, the necessity for all interests to appeal to some general interest or principle in order to gain the support of others, and the commitments on the part of group and party leaders as to how they will act under varying circumstances—all tend to ameliorate the disease.[37]

Finally, it might seem that the best answer to the welfare argument would be to invite comparison, in terms of welfare, between the democratic and nondemocratic nations. The facts about material welfare are so notoriously favorable to the democracies that it is unnecessary to recite the evidence. However, this argument is less conclusive than might first appear, for in large measure the countries that are industrialized and possess the conditions of democracy are democracies, and vice versa.

It would be wrong to leave the impression that welfare is confined to material well-being, or even to all the outputs of government. What was said earlier about the effects of participation in politics, directly or indirectly, is rele-

[37] See Jack Lively, *Democracy* (Oxford: Basil Blackwell, 1975), pp. 122-126; and Brian Barry, *Political Argument* (London: Routledge & Kegan Paul, 1965), pp. 253-256.

vant here. If in fact the cititzen's role has an educational, a developmental, and a morally broadening influence, these results of the democratic process also come under the head of welfare. Even more direct in its influence on welfare is the enlistment of energies and the drawing upon the talents and skills of the largest possible number of people.

Among the traditional goals of the polity, the closely related values of order and personal security remain to be considered. Here, however, it seems to be less a question of what is the effect of democracy on these goals than a matter of what is the effect on democracy of the conditions that determine order and security. I do not mean, of course, to suggest that it is not a major function of the state to maintain order. Obviously it is. It is undoubtedly true, however, that a country may be so unruly, its people so bitterly divided, that democratic government can not operate or survive. Under such circumstances, it is less a question of whether democracy can maintain order than of whether it can survive. In short, we are dealing here with an end or objective of the state that at the same time is intimately related to a requisite for democracy, a subject discussed in a later chapter. Whether a people who cannot maintain order among themselves by means of a democratic government can be effectively ruled by *any* form of government in a modernized society is another question. And whether a democracy can hope to operate successfully in a society that has not been modernized is still another. All that needs to be said here is that given a society with a reasonable degree of unity, not necessarily of homogeneity, but of tolerance, feeling of community, and commitment to democratic methods of settling disputes, there is no reason the objectives of order and security should not be adequately attained. If that statement seems in part to be circular, it is so only because the question as posed related to the requisites of democracy rather than to its merits. It has been more than once noted, in the preceding pages, that democracy is not for all times and places; and that in the case of large aggregations like the nation-state it had not been tried or thought feasible until modern times.

5. CONCLUDING REMARKS

The essence of the justification of democracy can be simply categorized. Half of the case derives from democracy's relation to the value, worth, dignity, and moral uniqueness of man. On the positive side, this appears in terms of liberty and its various contributions to the life and growth of the individual. On the negative side, it is a matter of democracy's being the most effective means for avoiding tyranny—itself almost the very antithesis of the dignity of the individual.

The second justification of democracy relates to the distribution, rather than to the maximization, of good. I refer to the concept of distributive justice, or equality. But, while the idea of formal equality is basic to this whole line of argument, its connection with the equality of the franchise depends upon arguments founded in the first half of the case: human dignity and the avoidance of tyranny.

One important fact must not be obscured by the brevity of this summary. The democratic form of government is designed to achieve, as best can be done, the democratic ideals. But it may fail to do so. And if it does, the soundness of the argument for the ideals becomes irrelevant. The argument has relied at various points upon presumptions, upon "burdens of proof," and upon probabilities. The latter, moreover, have included assumptions about the probable nature of nondemocratic regimes. I think these various assumptions are well founded; but, like Hobbes's arguments for monarchy, they do not pretend to have the certainty of logical demonstration. They rely heavily, as a last-ditch defense, upon the belief that power not subject to an accounting corrupts, and that the ballot provides the most civilized method of ensuring popular accountability.

What I have referred to as the last-ditch defense of democracy—that it is the best defense against tyranny—could serve as the sufficient and only defense for anyone who is not prepared to defend tyranny. In brief, ideals far short of liberty and equality for all would serve as well to vindicate democracy. Why then make the more elaborate argument advanced in this chapter? The answer is that if we wished to defend only the procedural concept of democracy, it would have been unnecessary, indeed pointless, to spell out the case for liberty and equality in general. But, as we have seen, controversies are constantly arising as to whether this or that democratic procedure is better, or whether any particular democratic procedure is, under certain circumstances, operating democratically. In short, the democratic ideal is constantly being appealed to as a test for what is "really" democratic. This is why it has been necessary to discuss the nature and justification of that ideal.

Finally, I would add something about how my argument relates to various other justifications of democracy. For the most part, I have not spoken the language of the utilitarians, although, both in arguing that democracy is the best defense against tyranny and in some of the arguments supporting the value of liberty, I have borrowed from them. On the other hand, I have rarely used the term *rights* and have relied upon the argument that democracy tends to "maximize" the values of liberty and equality and, even more basically, that of respect for persons. It should be observed that in so doing I am not using the type of argument to which John Plamenatz took such vigorous exception.[38] In dealing with the ultimate value of the indi-

---

[38] See Plamenatz, *Democracy and Illusion* (London: Longmans, 1973), where he argues: "Neither [democracy's] champions nor its critics are concerned with maximizing the satisfaction of wants or the achievement of goals. They favor it because it gives men certain rights and opportunities; or they reject it because it does not. But these rights and opportunities are not valued because they make it easier for people to maximize the satisfaction of their wants" p. 168. See also p. 172.

CHAPTER V

Types of Operational Democratic Theory

DEMOCRATIC political theory is by no means confined to a single system of logically connected propositions. The discussion of the tensions in democratic theories in Chapters Two and Three underlines this fact. The subjects of those chapters might serve as a basis for the classification of democratic theories. Thus we would have theories emphasizing (or starting with) the individual and theories emphasizing (or starting with) the collectivity; and theories stressing liberty and theories stressing equality. But, as we have seen, these two pairs of theories would overlap considerably. Another objection might be made to the whole project of classifying democratic theories: namely, probably no two writers accept identical theories of democracy. Yet some order can be brought out of all this chaos.

Classifications inevitably and properly reflect the purpose or purposes of the classifier. For the remainder of this volume, which will deal with operational rather than justificatory democratic theory, it appears that two classifications are especially useful. One relates to the manner in which power is or ought to be exercised and distributed in a democratic government. Although this is not the classification to which major attention will be given, it is sufficiently important to merit considerable attention. More basic theories of democracy relate to the key values that the theorists believe do and/or should motivate the bulk of political actors.

1. POWER THEORIES

What are here called power theories are more accurately described as theories of power-exercise and -distribution.

161

They do not refer to whether power is exercised harshly or benignly, arbitrarily or reasonably, but rather to how the people are organized or organize themselves, formally or informally, for the purpose of exercising their sovereignty.

Power theories of democracy may be classified as follows: (1) elitist, (2) populist, (3) constitutionalist, and (4) social pluralist. Each of them, at least potentially, stands for three different kinds of theories: descriptive theories, prescriptive theories, and models.

A descriptive elitist theory, for example, would hold that in fact democracies operate through a relatively small, homogeneous, and permanent group exercising effective power. (Or, in a less general version, the theory might state simply that this is one type of democracy—that this is the way it works in certain countries.) It would tend to emphasize stratification and group dominance in the society, and also either apathy or deference by most of the electorate. A prescriptive elitist theory, on the other hand, is a theory of what ought to be. (It is normative rather than empirical, although it is operational.) It is the theory that in a democracy a small, relatively permanent and homogeneous group *ought* to exercise predominant power. It emphasizes the importance of energy in government, of prompt decisions, and of right answers.

Finally, if one were to use this same theory as a model, he would assume a "pure type" of democratic regime embodying effective rule by an elite and then proceed to make deductions how such a regime would operate. Thus one might assume, as many have done, that regardless of forms and appearances in a democracy (or perhaps in a certain democracy, or a certain kind of democracy, such as American local governments) an identifiable elite does in fact rule. Then one could deduce that this elite would be able to prevent political action contrary to its interests, and, conversely, to obtain legislation and administrative action favorable to its interests. Next comes a long process of attempting to identify various groups that might constitute

162

such an elite, investigating their interests (a nice theoretical as well as practical task in itself), and attempting to discover whether in fact those interests have been protected and promoted by the actions of the government. If they have, so much the better for the hypothesis and for the model of which it was a part; and conversely. It might be said with some justice that this is less a separate kind of theory than it is simply a method—or *the* method—of testing descriptive theory. The distinction is worth making, however, because in some cases the model makes no pretense at being accurate description. It is deliberate exaggeration or oversimplification, designed to illuminate just how wide of the mark predictions based upon this deliberate oversimplification are likely to be. Although this kind of theorizing is possible in any of the theories treated here, by all odds the chief example is provided by radical individualism, to be discussed below.

Populism is at the opposite pole from elitism. It assumes a maximum of popular participation, so that power tends to be distributed equally. In its normative version, equality is its primary value. It also tends to assume that all decision making will be by a simple majority. Nothing should, or, on the descriptive side, does obstruct the will of the majority.[1] Both types of theory tend to assume most decisions will be made centrally, at the level (local-central) that permits an overview of all the relevant facts.

The other two major types of power theory see the governmental process as involving a great deal of conflict, with public policy emerging as a byproduct or a resultant of struggle. In the case of constitutionalism, the struggle is structured by the forms and procedures of government. In fact, the organized branches of government, the legislature,

---

[1] In practice, populism tends to appear as a prescriptive theory only. For a justification of the use of this admittedly vague term, see Peter Worsley, "The Concept of Populism," in Ghita Ionescu and Ernest Gellner, *Populism* (London: Weidenfeld and Nicolson, 1969), Chap. 10.

the executive, and administrative agencies, acquiring interests of their own, tend to become important principals in the contest. The social-pluralist theory attributes less significance to governmental forms and constitutional provisions, and more to social groupings of all sorts. According to this theory, it is these groups, whether their basis be ethnic, class, occupational, religious, sectional, or whatever, that provide the motive forces for politics. From their competition and coalitions, policy decisions emerge. In the case of both of these theories, decisions are made less on the basis of overview than by the kind of process that Charles E. Lindblom once dubbed "disjointed incrementalism," a highly descriptive phrase he later, more euphoniously, called "partisan mutual adjustment."[2]

It will be noted that the classification of power theories presented here is based on two principles: that of the number exercising power and that of the means for distributing or otherwise limiting the exercise of power. In its theoretically complete form, it would be represented by the six-cell matrix in Chart 1.

In practice neither constitutionalists nor social pluralists tend to make the distinction as to whether the few or the many are in the dominant position; hence the four cate-

[2] David Braybrooke and Charles E. Lindblom, *A Strategy of Decision* (Glencoe, Ill.: Free Press, 1963), Chap. 5; and Lindblom, *The Intelligence of Democracy*, Part 2. An interesting variant on the classification set forth above is one. provided by Robert E. Putnam in his *Politicians and Politics*, (New Haven: Yale University Press, 1970). Putnam adopts essentially the same four types of theory suggested above, using different names and arranging them in a different order, but adds a fifth category. His types of theory, followed in parentheses by the name given them here, are as follows: guided democracy (elitism), polyarchal democracy (social pluralism), liberal democracy (constitutionalism), classical democracy (populism), and socioeconomic democracy. The last category stands for a system in which social and economic inequalities are minimized. Both the order and the addition of the fifth type befit the purpose of his classification, which is to array democratic theories in terms of their approximation to the democratic ideal of equality.

164

CHART 1: Power Theories of Democracy

Holders of Power	Limitations on the Exercise of Power		
	None Specified	Constitutional Arrangements	Social Arrangements
The few	Elitism	Constitutional elitism	Social elitism
The many	Populism	Constitutional populism	Social populism

gories originally introduced are the only ones normally encountered.[3] Thus in this simplified version of the chart, the boxes labeled "Constitutional elitism" and "Constitutional populism," respectively, would be combined in a single box, labeled simply "Constitutionalism," occupying the space previously covered by the two terms. Likewise, "Social elitism" and "Social populism" would be merged into "Social pluralism."

2. MOTIVATIONAL THEORIES IN GENERAL

The theories to which the classification discussed above applies assume that the important variables are the distribution of political power and the means for limiting its exercise. I turn now to a different kind of theory, calling for a different classificatory scheme. These theories are, or at least may be, more general in scope than power theories.

[3] While elitists and populists are by implication described above as providing no limitations upon the powers of government, in fact they traditionally assume some such limitations, usually without actually specifying what these limitations are or should be. A theorist of either category who believed that no such limitations should exist and that in fact governments should attempt to regulate the whole of social life would be a totalitarian democrat, whether elitist or populist, calling for subdivision of the "elitism" and "populism" cells in the chart.

They tend to deal with people considered generically, rather than with political organization, although they may also be applied in a more restricted fashion, as will appear. Being based upon theories of human nature, or at least upon theories of the nature of political motivation, and upon ethical theories, they constitute theory on a higher, more abstract level, more suitable for deductive purposes, than do explanatory theories tied more specifically to time and circumstance.

The variable elements that are the basis for the next classification relate to what I call "key values," a term applied both to the values actually operative in society and to those that the upholders of motivational-ethical theory believe either ought to prevail or do prevail to a considerable extent. A discussion of these kinds of theory (which, for simplicity's sake, I shall generally call "motivational" theories) should help to identify the roles played in various theories by assumptions both as to fact and as to value. A common factual assumption, for example, would be that voters pursue personal benefit as their dominant political goal.[4] A value assumption (using "value" in a broad sense) might be that they ought to behave in this fashion, or, alternatively, that they should place great weight upon the welfare of others. The whole discussion should throw light upon the relations between prescriptive and descriptive theories. It should also, as subsequent chapters will demonstrate, make it easier to see in what respects different the-

[4] I refer to this as a "factual" assumption, which of course it is, but it should be noted that the fact assumed has to do with what values people hold, what motivates them, hence the term *motivational theories*. Clearly, a personal-benefit theory could be at any of numerous levels of generality. It could claim applicability to all democratic voters, or to all voters in "mature" or "stable" democracies, to all voters in Western democracies, or in English-speaking democracies, or to voters in a particular country; or it could be thought to vary by socioeconomic status. The tendency is for such theories, however, to claim a high degree of generality.

166

ories lead to the same policy recommendations—e.g. as to the best decision-making rules.

Considering both the practice of democratic theorists and what appears to provide the most useful classification of democratic theories of this kind, I select four values, variously stressed by different theorists as being especially characteristic of man in his political behavior. They are (1) personal benefit or advantage (self-interest); (2) the public interest; (3) moral values—rights and duties, justice; (4) the collectivity (conceived as being valuable in itself as well as that which determines the nature and values of individuals) and collective action. These are convenient and useful categories, but are not rigorously defined and distinguished. They can be combined in various ways and can also be further refined. Benefit, for instance, is ambiguous: it can be defined in terms of "satisfaction," "self-development," or "giving effect to preference"; it can be material or nonmaterial, including under the latter heading "social acceptance" (leading to enhanced self-esteem) as well as "self-development," or "self-actualization."

Exposition and provisional classification of democratic theories can be shown in a simple chart that uses the key values understood as a descriptive concept (relating, that is to say, to actual behavior) for one classification, and the key values taken prescriptively (or normatively) for a second set of categories, subdividing the first set, or vice versa, however one prefers to look at it. In the resulting sixteen-cell matrix, only a few of the major theories out of the sixteen possibilities have been found plausible.

The key values are not all of the same order. They can be tentatively subclassified as to whether a value is to be maximized, using a process of rational calculation, or whether it is of a different kind. The values of the second type are not easily described except as "nonmaximizing" theories; but it may be said that they are nonutilitarian and tend to be based either upon a deontological ethic or

167

upon sentiment or a different concept of rationality from that which utilitarians use. (Although I have classified the collectivists as nonmaximizers, this is not completely accurate. Insofar as they wish to maximize collective action, they belong in the other subcategory, leaving the rights and duties theorists as the only pure example of the nonmaximizers. See Chart 2.)

This classification is provisional. From time to time, various explanations and qualifications will be introduced that show its limitations and inaccuracies. For the present, it seems best to operate with the system as it appears in the chart. As to the blanks, it would be possible, for example, to hold that people *should* try to maximize their personal benefit but that in fact they give primary weight to the interests of others (or to their rights and duties, or to the collectivity), and to build a democratic theory upon these assumptions. An individualist of the type described by Tocqueville, especially if he subscribed to a Physiocratic or Smithian theory of the "unseen hand," might indeed adhere to just such a theory, arguing that the public interest would be better served if individuals minded their own business rather than going against inclination in pursuit of a goal they could but dimly perceive and the means to which were at best uncertain. In fact, however, if any democratic theorists hold that people ought to act politically from self-interest, they are extremely reticent about the matter. Or again, a theorist could contend that people ought to be guided by their rights and duties (in accordance with "natural rights" theory) but that in fact they tended to pursue their personal benefit. Thus it is possible that the quasi-democrat John Locke belongs in the box two columns to the left of the box in which his name appears on the chart. Finally, it might be suggested that Karl Marx subscribed to a collectivist normative theory and a personal-benefit descriptive theory, as far as concerns bourgeois democracy; but it may be inaccurate to ascribe *any* normative views to him for bourgeois society. (For what

Chart 2: Types of Motivational Democratic Theory

Prescriptive ("Normative") Key Value		Descriptive Key Value			
		Maximizing theories		Nonmaximizing theories	
		Personal benefit	Benefit to others (as well as to self)	Rights and duties (moral values)	Attachment to the collectivity and to collective action
Maximizing theories	Personal benefit	Radical Individualism*: Anthony Downs, Buchanan, and Tullock ‑ ‑ ‑ ‑ ‑ ‑ Individualism: James Mill			
	Benefit to others (as well as to self)	Bentham (?)	Public-interest theory: J. S. Mill, Dewey		
Nonmaximizing theories	Rights and duties			Rights and duties theory: Locke (?), Plamenatz, Rawls	
	Attachment to the collectivity and to collective action	Marx (for bourgeois society) (?)			Collectivism: Marx (for Communist society)

* Radical individualism falls only under Descriptive Key Value in this category.

NOTE: Names of theorists are suggestive only. Seldom does an individual perfectly fit a "pure type." Furthermore, many theorists have written entirely about prescriptive theory or entirely about descriptive theory, leaving us in the dark as to where they should be classified on the other axis. Thus British idealists, such as Bernard Bosanquet and F. H. Bradley, clearly belong somewhere along the bottom line. But where?

Marx would consider "real" democracy, he would belong in the collectivist camp throughout.)

For the most part, however, democratic theorists, insofar as they deal with both descriptive and prescriptive considerations, assume that the value they believe ought to be generally preferred is in fact so preferred at least to a substantial degree.[5] Actually, therefore, the most widely held democratic theories tend to fit in the cells where a given normative key value corresponds to the same key value assumed as descriptively preponderant. The four resulting types of democratic theory then are: (1) individualism; (2) utilitarianism (or, as it will be called here, the theory of the public interest); (3) the rights and duties (deontological) theory; and (4) democratic collectivism.[6]

The reader must constantly remember that the categories enumerated are in the nature of "pure types." While it is true that the most widely held democratic theories fit in one cell or another, most theorists tend to mix the elements in some measure. They are likely to fall predominantly in one or another of these categories, but not completely. And some, like Rousseau, manage a very considerable mixture.

3. RADICAL INDIVIDUALISM

One feature of the chart remains to be explained: the theory of radical individualism, and its anomalous location, unrelated to any normative value. Radical individualism is a theory of rational behavior based on the assumption that people do, on the whole, seek to maximize their personal benefit or advantage. It is a positivistic

[5] As will be explained below, this statement does not apply to many collectivists, because they are not advancing descriptive theory.

[6] It will be clear at once that the first and fourth types of theory are substantially the same as the sources of the tensions discussed in Chapter Two. Present purposes, however, call for somewhat different treatment of these theories than was appropriate for the earlier discussion.

theory, making *no* assumptions about how people ought to behave. It is true that other democratic theorists take a positivistic stance, eschewing all value judgments, but a unique feature of radical individualism is that as a theory of rational self-regarding behavior, it is a *kind* of normative theory—the norms coming not from any assumed "right" or "best" key values, but simply from the application of the standard of rationality to the assumption that people are essentially self-regarding in their political behavior. It tells people how they ought to act if they wish to be rational. Furthermore, radical individualism is an extreme form of individualism. It is tempting to think of it as being one pole of an axis the other pole of which is radical collectivism; but as will presently appear, this would be an oversimplification. Which form of individualism is most extreme depends upon which of its aspects one is considering.

Radical individualism is also unique in that it denies the possibility of interpersonal comparisons. Further, along with individualism generally (see Chapter Three), it affirms the proposition that "human beings are the 'ultimate constituents' of the social world."[7] Thus, for instance, it makes no sense for radical individualists to talk about "the public interest" in most situations, for normally a judgment as to which of two states of affairs is more in the pub-

[7] These basic assumptions correspond closely to the traditional (but perhaps inaccurate) interpretation of Hobbes, with the important omission of the self-assertive, prideful nature of Hobbes's natural man. For contemporary statements and defenses of the doctrine, see James M. Buchanan, "An Individualistic Theory of Political Process" in *Varieties of Political Theory*, ed. David Easton (Englewood Cliffs, N.J.: Prentice-Hall, Chap. 2; and Ludwig von Mises, *Human Action*, pp. 11-35 and 41ff. Jerome Rothenberg's *The Measurement of Social Welfare* (Englewood Cliffs, N.J.: Prentice-Hall, 1961), Chap. 2, also argues for the radical-individualist position, in the absence of an empirically demonstrable alternative. The quoted passage in the text above is from the excellent article "Holism and Individualism," by W. H. Dray, in the *Encyclopedia of Philosophy*, 3:58, but is not stated as his own position.

lic interest involves comparing the interests of two or more individuals. If a given change makes even a single individual less well off than he was before, it cannot be said, without comparing his interests with the interests of those who have gained, that the public interest has been served.[8] However, if the change improves the position of at least one person and makes no one, in his own view, worse off (in other words, if it is a movement toward Pareto optimality), it would be considered "efficient" or "rational" by radical individualists, and might be thought of, even by him, as in the public interest. They adopt this element of their model not because they believe it is completely realistic but, as will appear, because it enables them to make rational calculations and develop testable hypotheses in a way that would otherwise be impossible, given the subjective nature of interpersonal comparisons.

In another way as well, the radical individualist transcends individual judgment sufficiently to compare social states. (Of course he does not actually transcend individual judgment; he obtains unanimous agreement, so that the distinction between individual judgments and social or aggregated judgments disappears.) The other way by which the radical individualist attains a basis for a generalized judgment, as will appear, is by forcing the individual to choose decision-making rules in ignorance of his future circumstances and therefore of how the rules will affect him. This device compels him to look at himself as a sort of generic person, taking a kind of "public" point of view. It is worthy of note that in taking this stance the radical individualist assumes the possibility of one's knowing what his future preferences will be. Although he avoids an interpersonal comparison, he compares the self at different periods of time.

As a further aspect of its individualism (and of its posi-

[8] See James M. Buchanan, "The Relevance of Pareto Optimality," *Jour. of Conflict Resolution*, 6 (1962), 341-354, 347ff.

tivism), the theory makes no assumption that one man is better or more worthy than another, that one man's prefences have precedence over those of another, or that we can specify certain people who know and can be trusted to serve the interests of others better than they themselves. When two adults disagree, neither has any moral claim to overrule the other. In spite of its positivism, then, by denying the possibility of comparing individuals, and thus of placing one man's claims above another's, the theory becomes *effectively equivalent* to one based on the principle of moral equality, even though the positivist says nothing about what is legitimate and denies concern with such questions. In practice, he tends to assume that anything the individual willingly and knowingly consents to is legitimate, at least in the sense that he has acted rationally.

Collective action thus calls for unanimous agreement. Assuming, as the radical individualist does, the existence of differing and sometimes conflicting individual values and preferences, for any sizable community the unanimity requirement would be a prescription for perpetual turmoil or anarchic deadlock. It being to the advantage of everyone under these circumstances to have some form of government, at least some machinery for collective security, some mechanism for securing rights of person and property, rational men, it is argued in contractualist fashion, would unanimously agree on some set of rules for settling disputes and taking joint action. Since, by the initial hypothesis, the only acceptable way to distribute either the costs or the benefits of government is by consent of the individuals concerned, the problem is to find a set of rules to which all rational men would consent because all would have a reasonable expectation of benefitting. They would in fact seek a Pareto optimal set of rules. To insure that no one is worse off than he was before, those rules must be subject to change only by unanimous consent, unless some other rule for amendment is unanimously agreed to. But once the

173

rules were established, particular decisions (which might involve the creation of subsidiary rules—laws) would require only the degree of consent provided for by the rules.[9]

Radical individualism is, in the strict sense of the word, a model, not simply a theory. In other words it is about rational political behavior. Adherents to it may or may not add certain assumptions as to the prevailing key values. Although they frequently use the language of "utility maximization," today's radical individualists do not assume that various goods, satisfactions, and the like, can all be reduced to a common factor, utility. It is assumed that rational man orders his preferences and makes his decisions (choices) accordingly; that he decides, for example, whether to spend his money for an auto or for an improvement on his house, or to save it against a rainy day.

An alternate, and arguably more realistic, concept of rationality could be substituted for the one just described. This theory is less exclusively one of maximization than is the standard utilitarian theory commonly used by economists. It is defined in terms of the following principles: (1) selection of the most effective means for the accomplishment of the desired end; (2) the "dominance principle" ("given several plans of action, one is to choose that plan which secures all the desired ends of other plans, and more, *ceteris paribus*"); (3) the lottery principle (a complicated statement the essence of which is that one should seek to maximize his *chances* of securing maximal satisfaction of desires); (4) the principle of postponement (one should postpone making a choice among plans of action, when it is not clear what ends will be desired or how they will be best secured, *ceteris paribus*); (5) and finally, "if principles 1-4 do not apply, and *ceteris paribus*, one is to choose that plan which, after a dispassionate, well-informed weighing of

[9] This theory is most fully elaborated in James M. Buchanan and Gordon Tullock, *The Calculus of Consent* (Ann Arbor: University of Michigan Press, 1962).

probabilities and preference intensities, will better secure one's desired ends."[10]

Still another version of the rationality concept that might be utilized, *in part*, by individualists is "satisficing," as proposed by Herbert Simon. According to this model, it is not assumed that men can discover the optimal path either for maximizing satisfaction or for behaving rationally as defined by Richards. Rather, men would be assumed to plan short, purposive behavioral sequences, enough to provide some satisfaction for salient desires; but it would not be assumed they could commensurate their desires in a way that would make it possible to calculate the path to maximum efficiency.[11]

Of the same type is the theory of Charles E. Lindblom, referred to earlier, the chief difference being that while Simon concentrates his attention on individual behavior, Lindblom is more concerned with the effect on public policy. Simon stresses the limitations of the human organism; Lindblom emphasizes the enormity of the task involved in planning human affairs. He would quite agree with Simon's conclusion that "we should be skeptical in postulating for humans, or other organisms, elaborate mechanisms for choosing among diverse needs."[12] Simon goes on to say, in the same passage, that "common denominators among needs may simply not exist, or may exist

[10] David A. J. Richards, *A Theory of Reasons for Action* (Oxford: Clarendon Press, 1971), pp. 28-30 and 43 (quotation at 43).

[11] Herbert Simon, *Models of Man*: (New York: Wiley, 1957), 204-205 and 270-273.

[12] Ibid., p. 272. In Lindblom's most recent book, his intellectual kinship with Simon is apparent: "One commonplace strategy for a policy maker is to proceed incrementally and sequentially, with close interplay between end and means. In such a strategy, he is less concerned with 'correctly' solving his problem than with making an advance. He is also less concerned with a predetermined set of goals than with remedying experienced dissatisfaction with past policy while goals and policies are both reconsidered." Lindblom, *Politics and Markets* (New York: Basic Books, 1977), p. 314.

only in very rudimentary form; and the nature of the organism's needs in relation to the environment may make their non-existence entirely tolerable." Lindblom has stressed the relative efficiency of a political system that minimized overall planning and allowed maximum opportunity for groups to form and to seek to influence the governmental machine in the direction of their perceived interests.

Returning to the main stream of radical individualism, contrary to what is usually the case in discussions of welfare economics, the radical individualist, as was remarked above, applies the concept of the Pareto optimum to rules, not simply to states of being or conditions. Moreover, according to him, a form of government, a constitution, or a specific decision-making rule does not guarantee a particular outcome for a particular individual. All that can be maximized under the uncertainty prevailing at the constitution-making stage is the *probability* of outcomes more reflective of preferences than could be obtained under any other set of decision-making rules.

Since the radical individualist is trying to calculate what sort of *constitution* the rational man, considering his own long-run interest and that of his immediate descendants, would adopt, he cannot at this stage confine himself to the short-run calculations entailed by the Simon-Lindblom theory. This is why that theory of rationality could be utilized by the radical individualist only "in part." For the post-constitution-making stage, it would suffice; but for the constitution-making stage, with which the radical individualist is primarily concerned, it is insufficient.

The assumption of rational self-interest is not quite enough to guarantee unanimous agreement on a set of rules for government (i.e. a constitution). Rational self-interested men would probably agree on the need for government and the corollary proposition that they would have to agree to certain limitations upon what they had previously been free (i.e. without obligation to the contrary) to do. But they would not necessarily come to agreement on what these limitations should be, that is to say on a particular set of rules or, more simply, on a particular ruler. Each of various contending groups might hold out for what they wanted, believing that they could eventually get their way, or that to give in would mean annihilation. Presumably the radical individualist must get around this difficulty in one of three ways. He may assume that some individual or group will in fact establish an effective government, obtaining obedience, though not willing consent, from some of the subjects by force. After this has been accomplished, it might indeed be rational for everyone to give willing consent to the continuance of the regime thus established. Or, he may assume that the members of the nascent polity already are characterized by a minimum of mutual sympathy and trust. Still a third possibility is to assume a nonrational commitment to the political system itself (assumed to have already been created), as Anthony Downs explicitly does. Radical individualists may of course differ among themselves as to how much of this nonrational element is required to make their assumption of self-interest realistic as the basis of political unity. But it would seem clear that any qualification introduced to account for the original agreement must likewise be assumed when considering subsequent political behavior.

More difficult problems arise when it comes to the key values assumed by the radical individualist. What is meant by "personal benefit or advantage"? Some supporters of this theory have attempted to make the concept broad enough to include any preference, or even more broadly still, any action that the individual decides to take or would take if given the opportunity. Thus, if the individual "prefers" to act out of sympathy, compassion, feeling of obligation, desire for unity, love of the collectivity, or pursuit of some other ideal—counter to what, *other things being equal,* he would like to do—he is still acting as a

177

rational individual.[13] A theory of this kind is individual-istic in the methodological sense. Further, it can be made to serve certain limited purposes by way of logical demonstra-tions. However, by abolishing any basis for distinguishing between altruism and action based upon personal benefit or advantage it seriously limits the usefulness of those terms. At best the theory provides but a bare framework for explanations. It supports no predictions; it yields no testa-ble propositions. It is a theory only in the weakest sense, its motivational assumption being in fact tautological.

What is here called radical individualism in fact goes further than this, as do the radical individualists whose work has already been referred to. While admitting the existence of political motivations that are neither selfish nor even self-regarding, they assume that in the political as in the economic realm these motivations generally give way where they conflict with perceived personal interest.[14] They assume that each individual seeks the greatest pos-sible satisfaction of his desires (or, more accurately, cor-respondence between preferences and outcomes) at the least cost; and that he alone may assign priorities to his various

[13] Buchanan and Tullock, *The Calculus of Consent*, p. 4, state that "the representative individual in our models may be egoist or altruist or any combination thereof." The radical individualist is using the word *rational* to refer to the calculation of, or the ability to calculate, means-ends relations. (The refinements of the Richardson theory or of the Simon-Lindblom theory remain within this framework.) The calculation of consequences is a rational act; the weighing of one set of consequences against another is a nonrational act. Feelings are nonrational. Unless it is otherwise indicated, this common, but not universal, usage will be followed below.

But a broader usage is also common. For instance, a person who reacts to the suffering of others by showing sympathy is said to behave rationally. On the other hand, a person who habitually laughs with fiendish glee at the sight of human suffering and with similar regu-larity reacts with inconsolable sorrow when others express happiness would be generally held to behave irrationally.

[14] Buchanan and Tullock, *The Calculus of Consent*, p. 306, and see James M. Buchanan, "An Individualistic Theory of Political Process," pp. 27-28.

178

wishes and evaluate the anticipated costs. Action in accordance with preference does not necessarily lead to satisfaction, much less "utility maximization," whatever that might mean; but the radical individualist holds that we have no basis for judging what will satisfy another individual and imposing it upon him. Accordingly his own preference must control.

For the same reason, radical individualism departs from other forms of individualism, at least verbally, in a slightly different respect: it deals with "desires" or, better, "preferences," rather than with "interests." It assumes, however, that rational individuals perceive their own interests and act in ways which serve them, or at least that no one else (since he cannot be privy to their preference schedules) can know what their interests are. (This is not to identify interests with preferences; but it is to assert the impossibility of knowing what a person's interests are without knowing his preferences.)

In its strictest form, radical individualism treats each individual as a unique unit; he must express and evaluate his own preferences through the franchise, a function no one else is psychologically in a position to perform for him; furthermore, in the strongest form of the theory it is assumed that his preferences will reflect his view of what will contribute most to his material advantage. In that strict form few would support it as realistic, but some would consider that models built on this set of assumptions would yield hypotheses worth testing. Moreover, insofar as a model based upon these assumptions gave rise to hypotheses that proved to be tenable, that corresponded to reality in significant degree, an important service would have been rendered in at least two respects. In the first place, it would be persuasive that the assumptions, on the average, were nearly correct (perhaps because individual variations tended to cancel out). Secondly, hypotheses deduced from the model but not yet supported by evidence would have a high degree of presumptive validity.

179

4. QUALIFIED FORMS OF INDIVIDUALISM

a. *Admission of Sympathy, Low-cost Impartiality, and Nonmaterial Interests*

In practice, theorists tend to relax one or more of the assumptions of the extreme forms of individualism, in greater or lesser degree, giving rise to several other varieties of individualism, as we saw in Chapter Three. Even Hobbes admitted that a person might be moved by "the pain of compassion." Many would accept Harsany's notion of "low-cost impartiality" or Hume's "selfishness and confin'd generosity" as a fair description of political man.[15] Likewise, individualists admit nonmaterial benefits. With George Homans, for example, they may hold that one of the greatest personal benefits, especially as it affects political action, is social acceptance.[16] These modified forms of individualism also do not appear to retain the assumption of the impossibility of interpersonal comparisons.

Within limits, various relaxations of the theory's assumptions may be subjected to empirical testing just as may the original model. The limits are relatively severe, however, inasmuch as each relaxation makes the theory less precise and therefore less testable. Thus if one postulates that individuals in their political activities seek both social acceptance and material benefits, it is not difficult to imagine many situations in which the individual is forced to choose between the two. In default of any basis for knowing how he would choose, the theory loses effectiveness.

[15] For the Harsanyi discussion, see John C. Harsanyi, "Rational-Choice Models vs. Functionalistic and Conformistic Models of Political Behavior," *World Politics*, 21 (1969), 513-538, at 521-522. Harsanyi himself adopts a somewhat more complicated motivational theory. For Hume, see *Treatise of Human Nature*, ed. Selby-Bigge (Oxford: Clarendon Press, 1896), p. 495.

[16] Homans, *Social Behavior* (London: Routledge & Kegan Paul, 1961); also Harsanyi, op.cit., pp. 523-524. Similarly, David L. Miller argues that the desire for significance, or self-esteem, is the most basic element of human nature. *Individualism*, p. 176.

180

The dilemma of rigor versus realism appears to be finally unavoidable; yet the degree of discrepancy is a subject that can be further explored by a combination of theoretical analysis and empirical research.

On the other hand, the postulate of low-cost impartiality—the assumption that men will voluntarily act justly at some cost to themselves, providing the cost is not very great, is susceptible to testing. A recent experimental study, while not purporting to be conclusive, finds that in general egoistic models are much more predictive of committee behavior than are nonegoistic models, but that models based on "fairness" find some support in situations where the cost is slight.[17]

b. Other Variants of Individualism

Among other variants of individualism, two types may be described as "romantic" individualism. First, the idealists think of the individual as seeking (and as rightly seeking) self-development, or self-realization. Some of the complications these terms introduce are self-evident. Curiously enough, the first and last of them at least may provide bases for a type of political theory that moves a long distance from individualism toward collectivism. In short, if the development or "realization" of the self leads toward the identification of the self with the collectivity, individualism and collectivism tend to merge. Insofar as this version is properly called individualistic at all, it might be dubbed romantic individualism. It is held by such idealists as T. H. Green, Bernard Bosanquet, and F. H. Bradley, the last two of whom were discussed in Chapter Two. (Of these three, probably only Green is properly called an individualist of any type.)

As with other kinds of individualism, the chart provides no separate box for romantic individualism, because its

[17] See Morris P. Fiorina and Charles R. Plott, "Committee Decisions Under Majority Rule: An Experimental Study." *Amer. Polit. Sci. Rev.*, 72 (1978), 575-595.

variation from other forms of individualism is entirely in terms of the interpretation of what constitutes "personal benefit," and especially of what is the "person." This points to one of the chart's over-simplifications.

If such a thing as a distinctively existentialist democratic theory exists, it too probably falls under the "romantic" heading. Its emphasis is on "authenticity" and on feeling and sentiment, with accordingly less stress on rationality. Like radical individualism it would appear to deny the possibility of interpersonal comparisons. Unlike idealism it does not assume that the "realization" (or, as existentialists would say, "actualization") of the self involves development toward overall societal unity. In this respect it is more like radical individualism. On the other hand, it departs from that model in being nonmaterialistic and nonhedonistic.[18] Lacking any theory as to what direction "self-actualization" is likely to take, it can yield little in the way of predictions about political behavior. Its contribution is rather to prescriptive than to descriptive theory. Thanks to the primacy given to the goal of "self-actualization," freedom generally, and political liberty in particular, becomes the primary social good.[19]

Still another type of theory is not so much a variation on individualism as a separate type of theory—one that would belong in the cell below individualism. That is to say, one who held such a theory would believe men *ought* to act po-

[18] The political theoretical implications of existentialism are notoriously ambiguous and ill-defined. Sartre, in particular, has striven valiantly, but with questionable success, to reconcile a kind of Marxist position with his basic individualism. See Frederick A. Olafson, *Principles and Persons* (Baltimore: Johns Hopkins University Press, 1967), Chap. 8, esp. pp. 224-234.

[19] Jean-Paul Sartre, although a declared Communist, has recently given expression to his extreme individualism by saying, "then, by way of philosophy, I discovered the anarchist being in me. But when I discovered it I did not call it that, because today's anarchy no longer has anything to do with the anarchy of 1890." "Sartre at Seventy: An Interview," *New York Review of Books*, Aug. 7, 1975, pp. 10-17, 14.

litically for the general welfare, though he believed they primarily seek their own self-interest in fact. If such a theorist also believed that interests are sufficiently harmonious that even under these circumstances actual and desirable behavior tended to coincide, he might be described as a Benthamite.[20]

5. THE THEORY OF THE PUBLIC INTEREST

The second major motivational variety of democratic theory is the theory of the public interest. According to it, a concern for the public interest should and does constitute a major supplement, if not a replacement, for rational self-interest as the basis for political behavior. This type of theory includes utilitarianism but is not confined to it. For instance, it would include the theory expressed by Cicero, who, repudiating Epicurean individualism, declared: "I shall content myself with this one assertion—Nature has implanted in man so strong a need of virtue and so strong a dedication to the defense and salvation of the community that its force has conquered all the allurements of pleasure and leisure."[21] More typical, however, would be the position of D. D. Raphael, who speaks of "the claim of the members of society in general not to be harmed," and of "the interests of society" as contrasted with "the interests of the individual" (which are the special concern of justice), using the former phrase to designate something that

[20] Bentham's philosophical position is notoriously ambiguous. In particular, he vacillates on the question of psychological hedonism as well as on the theory of the harmony of interests.

[21] *Republic*, 1, 1, quoted by Robert Denoon Cumming, *Human Nature and History* (Chicago: University of Chicago Press, 1969), 1: 188. It could be argued that this theory in upholding virtue rather than interest as the major and approved motivating force, would be rightfully classified under the heading of the third type used here, the rights and duties theory. However, if the one duty featured is the duty to defend the community, it would seem to be more properly classified as a public interest theory.

183

we know from experience "is likely to benefit or harm a number of members of our society, while not knowing which particular members will be affected on this occasion."[22]

The term *the public interest* has been the subject of a great deal of controversy, and some have contended it is so vague as to be useless or even meaningless.[23] For the skeptics, suffice it here to raise a single question: If the government (and the government only) could find a cure for cancer, who would deny that it would be in the public interest, *ceteris paribus*, for it to do so? To be sure, the "other things being equal" clause, covers a multitude of difficulties. But they are difficulties in the application of a concept whose central core of meaning is clear enough. If the cost, in the example above, were to be to give up one tenth of one percent of the national income for one year, it would be hard to conceive that anyone would think it not in the public interest.

Variations in the meaning of the term not inconsistent with what has just been said will appear in the discussion below. In some respects the differences between this theory and radical individualism (and collectivism as well) are matters of degree. In one respect, however, a sharp and clear distinction marks off this theory from radical individualism, although not from most of the less extreme forms of individualism. Unlike radical individualism, this theory, perforce, admits and relies upon interpersonal com-

[22] Raphael, *Moral Judgement* (London: Allen & Unwin, 1955), pp. 73-74.

[23] See discussions in the following works Wayne A. R. Leys and Charner Perry, *Philosophy and the Public Interest* (Chicago: Committee to Advance Original Work in Philosophy, 1959); Carl J. Friedrich, ed., *The Public Interest*, NOMOS V (New York: Atherton Press, 1962); Richard E. Flathman, *The Public Interest* (New York: Wiley, 1966); Virginia Held, *The Public Interest and Individual Interests* (New York, Basic Books, 1970); and Clarke E. Cochran, "Political Science and 'The Public Interest,'" *Jour. of Politics*, 36 (1974), 327-355.

parisons. It holds, for instance, that it is valid to make a judgment of the form "A's desire is more intense or his interest greater than that of B," and to take political action accordingly. In other words, it is empirically (psychologically) possible to make the comparison and ethically right to be influenced by it in determining one's conduct.[24]

Perhaps this theory and that to which it is opposed will be more sharply etched if a word is said about the arguments used in their support. On the psychological point, it is the radical individualist who is on the defensive, for it is readily apparent that by a kind of extended sympathy we do constantly make interpersonal comparisons. We make judgments of the form "This will benefit them more than it will hurt us." We even make a rough comparison of the amount by which A is happier than B with the amount by which B is happier than C. It is clear, as I.M.D. Little says, that "if one accepts behavior as evidence of other minds, then one must admit that one can compare other minds on the basis of such evidence. Therefore, those who 'deny' interpersonal comparisons must deny the evidence of other minds."[25] At the very least, it would seem, they

[24] Even Bentham conceded the necessity of assuming that the happiness of one individual could be compared with that of another; otherwise, he said, all reasoning in politics would be "at a stand." Bentham MSS, U.C. No. 4, quoted by Elie Halévy, *The Growth of Philosophical Radicalism* (New York: Macmillan, 1928), p. 495. He also laid down as a moral principle that each person should seek "the greatest happiness of the greatest number," a prescription which could not be followed without making interpersonal comparisons. Incidentally, it is this prescription that distinguishes utilitarianism from the egoistic position of radical individualism. While Bentham's ethical theory thus looked to the public interest, his motivational theory was egoistic, individualistic. Hence his location on the chart above, in the box below radical individualism. His individualism was further underscored by his vigorous insistence that "society" is only a fiction; but it should be noted that this form of individualism is shared by many, perhaps most, of those who subscribe to the theory of the public interest, thus distinguishing them from collectivists.

[25] Little, *A Critique of Welfare Economics*, 2nd ed. (Oxford: Claren-

185

must deny that we can know anything about those other minds, and deny too that we can accept behavior (including verbal expression) as evidence of experience comparable to our own. Yet these assumptions must be made by even the most rigorous of sciences. Moreover, and this is the crucial test, scientists, depending upon these assumptions, are able to make accurate predictions.

In fact, it appears that the difficulty about satisfying the radical individualist as to the validity of using interpersonal comparisons is not that he fails to recognize either the universality with which we make them or the confidence we feel in their validity. The problem, it would appear, is the difficulty, if not impossiblity, of formulating a general rule describing what we do when we make these comparisons. Kenneth Arrow himself, protagonist of the modern welfare economics, which eschews interpersonal comparisons, has this to say: "The principle of extended sympathy as a basis for interpersonal comparisons seems basic to many of the welfare judgments made in ordinary practice. But it is not easy to see how to construct a theory of social choice from the principle."[26] In short, the radical individualist sacrifices some degree of realism for a greater degree of rigor. This is substantially what was meant above by saying that radical individualism is, in the strictest sense of the term, a "model," not simply a theory.

One consequence of abandoning the assumptions that one can not make interpersonal comparisons is that one is no longer confined to taking account of preferences. We can look beyond the preferences and the desires, wants, wishes, or even ideals that dictate the preferences, to the real interests or welfare of the individuals concerned. This again is what we do all the time. Insofar as we govern our

---

don Press, 1957), p. 57. See also John C. Harsanyi, "Cardinal Welfare, Individualistic Ethics, and Interpersonal Comparisons of Utility," *Jour. of Polit. Econ.*, 63 (1965), 309-321.

[26] Arrow, *Social Choice and Individual Values*, 2nd ed. (New York: Wiley, 1964), p. 115.

behavior out of consideration for others, we take account not only of what they themselves say they want, although we may weigh that quite heavily, but we consider also their needs as *we* see them, what we take to be their interest. As David Braybrooke says, "Preferences do not imply satisfaction; satisfaction does not imply welfare."[27]

Yet supporters of democracy are committed to the proposition that *in the last analysis*, the individual must be the judge of his own welfare—in other words that his preferences must rule. Of course majorities, or whatever numbers may act for the whole under the decision rules agreed to, may, if they like, act for the welfare of minorities in ways that depart from the latter's expressed desires.[28] Yet it is interesting to note—and a token of our respect for the democratic postulate—how reluctant they are to do so. It is commonplace for people to remark how much better off many relatively poor people would be if they spent less on such luxuries as television or such profligacy as lotteries and more on such basics as housing. Nevertheless, we do not normally find majorities imposing such judgments on minorities. In other words, while recognizing that the individual is not always the best judge of his own interests, we tend to act as though he were, and to do so because we think it is the best policy. We believe we must put up with some loss of welfare from ignorance, stupidity, and shortsightedness as the price for allowing the individual the opportunity to make his own choices, both as a weapon with which to protect himself against exploitation by those who are smarter and better informed and also as a symbol of his dignity and as an instrument for his development as a responsible person.

It would be a mistake to push this argument too far. But

[27] Braybrooke, *The Three Tests for Democracy* (New York: Random House, 1968), p. 134.

[28] Public-interest theories may support the interests of minorities either on the basis of rule-utilitarian reasoning or by importing into their theory certain elements of rights and duties theory.

187

the fact that we sometimes override our respect for individual choice does not disprove its existence. When we (that is, the polity) provide the needy with specified goods or services (thus leaving them no choice as to what they get), we probably justify this method on the ground that when the collectivity gives something to individuals it has a better claim to determine the nature of the gift than it would have to impose its values in the case of prohibiting action or taking something away. It is also worth noting that a substantial body of opinion today favors providing the needy with cash instead of specific goods and services. This policy is embodied in the so-called negative income tax proposal favored by many economists.

Returning to the main thread of the discussion, those who believe that pursuit of the public interest is and ought to be a major political motivating factor may explain this proposition in any of various ways, most if not all of which take off from one of the modifications of individualism previously described. Thus for Bentham the interest of the public, or of the community, is "the sum of the interests of the several members who compose it."[29] Interest he defined in terms of maximizing pleasure and minimizing pain. To pursue the interest of the community is his definition of the good—one that he believes to be practically self-evident upon adequate reflection—but not necessarily the course men will pursue.[30] Others, as for instance John Stuart Mill, would explain this altruistic behavior in terms of conscience, itself a "mass of feeling," whether growing out of sympathy, love, fear, or other forces.[31] Other theorists would distinguish between altruism based on sympathy and a purer form where people want, or feel they

[29] Bentham, *A Fragment on Government and an Introduction to the Principles of Morals and Legislation*, ed. Wilfred Harrison (Oxford: Clarendon Press, 1970), p. 126.

[30] Ibid., Chap. 1. .

[31] "Utilitarianism," in *Utilitarianism, Liberty, and Representative Government*, p. 26.

should pursue, the interest of others for its own sake. Thus Thomas Nagel defends "rational altruism" (not to be confused with what might be called "sympathetic altruism"), which "can be intuitively represented by the familiar argument, 'How would you like it if someone did that to you?' "[32] The answer he points out, cannot be sympathy, because the course of action that would call for might as well be to take a tranquilizer. The rational altruist, he argues, thinks the interests of persons should be protected and advanced; for this purpose "my self" is interchangeable with "other selves."[33] Although Nagel is not discussing political theory, he has obviously provided the foundation for a rather pure type of public-interest theory. For idealists like T. H. Green, a similar result is obtained by combining the standard of self-realization with an enlarged concept of the self.

More generally, and most basically, nonegoistic moral philosophers who take the concept of the good, rather than that of the right, as fundamental, agree on some principle of universalization. That is to say, they hold that the very nature of morality is for its principles to be in some sense universal; they should not be personal to the person making a moral judgment; they should be impartial, and capable of being cast in universal form. Minor differences as to how this principle should be expressed, whether by Kant, or Sidgwick, or J. S. Mill, or Marcus Singer, need not concern us. They all concur in a normative theory that commits the individual to pursue the interest of others who are similarly situated. Thus citizens, as such, are committed to the welfare of the general public.

Those who adhere to the public-interest theory of democracy today often identify the public interest not with any summation of private interests nor even with personal interests that include the interests of others because of one's

[32] Nagel, *The Possibility of Altruism* (Oxford: Clarendon Press, 1970), pp. 79-83, 82.
[33] Ibid., pp. 83-89.

sympathy or identification with those others, but rather with objects of interest that each person shares with all other members of the state. These would include such conventional "ends of the state" as security of person and property, liberty, and justice. In the general "welfare" category, they would include especially, but not solely, those public goods—like pure air—that no one can enjoy unless they are available to all. To be sure, the public interest must either be defined so as to include private as well as public goods or else the public interest itself must be commensurated with aggregated private interests before it is possible to determine the right or best public policy. Thus, to take an oversimplified example, if a one percent decrease in the amount of a certain pollutant in the atmosphere will decrease eye irritation by ten percent (assuming eye irritation can be measured), and if this decrease can be brought about by increasing the cost of driving the family car by ten cents per mile and increasing the cost of public transportation by three cents per mile, the question of what is in the public interest may be debatable.

Still other elements may be thought to be part of the public interest. Cooperative activity may be valued; and so may the community. Here, it will be observed, the public-interest theory verges on collectivism. Nor should it seem strange that each can be qualified to the point where it merges with a qualified version of the other, just as, in similar fashion, individualism and the public-interest theory converge at the margins.

Clearly then, public-interest theories of democracy are not all alike, just as with other types of democratic theory. If they are descriptive theories they do hold, however, that persons in their political actions significantly take into account what they believe to be the interest of others—and not just of some others (like members of their families) but of others generally, of the polity as a whole. This will include both interests that are collective goods and those that are simply aggregated private interests, an interest in

190

clean air, and an interest in less poverty and a higher standard of living for most people. Prescriptive theories will hold that this is the way people ought to be motivated. Probably most theorists who hold the first position (the descriptive public theory) hold the second as well. The converse is of course not necessarily true, but I suspect that most of those who hold the second either hold the first or believe that under favorable circumstances the first will tend to become true.

6. Rights and Duties (Deontological) Theories

The theories described thus far are "maximizing" theories. Those who adhere to rights and duties theory argue that any maximizing model applies, descriptively, to only a small part of the realm of politics. For the most part, they assert, we are not such calculating beings as these theories imply. Rather, they contend, a major part of our political activities is and ought to be governed by a sense of justice and, more specifically, by respect for a whole panoply of rights and duties that have gained acceptance in any given society. For such a theory, moral obligation is the most important basis for unity; moral values are the most important values in determining political action, and rights and duties tend to overshadow interests and preferences, both as standards and as controllers of behavior. Theories of this type might equally well be called deontological. A theory that included natural rights would belong in this category, but the latter is by no means confined to theories of natural rights. It is sufficient that at a given time and place political conduct is and ought to be predominantly shaped by beliefs in rights and duties, in justice, and generally in moral values. Interpersonal comparisons are not only admitted, they are entailed.

Among classical theorists, this category is most systematically exemplified by John Locke. In relying upon natural law, natural rights, and consent, he stresses moral obliga-

191

tion, although he does not rule out rational self-interest nor would he have believed that a polity could long be sustained without it. Locke's more democratic predecessors, the Levellers, likewise relied on the theories of natural law and natural rights; and the same is true of the great popularizer of democratic principles, Tom Paine.

Among more modern and more fully democratic theorists, this type of theory is manifested primarily among justificatory theorists and those who deal mainly with theories of rights.[34] John Plamenatz, however, clearly places himself in this category with respect to operational as well as normative theory. He declares that "our ideas of justice, equality, and freedom, vague though they may be in certain respects, are a good deal less vague than our ideas about preferences, interests and goal achievement."[35] Moreover, our wants suffer from two weaknesses as bases for political theorizing: they are less stable and less definite than are rights and duties, and moreover, they are themselves affected by our beliefs about justice and freedom, and "about what is honourable or respectable or generally useful.[36]

A supporter of this view of democracy might point to American attitudes (and resultant political activities) toward the Vietnam war as an example of what he is talking about and as an argument for his position. Consider the number of people who demonstrated, marched, made trips to Washington, and contributed substantial sums of money for organizing and propagandizing against continuation of

[34] Elements of it may be found in A. C. Ewing, *The Individual, the State and World Government* (New York: Macmillan, 1947), and in Braybrooke, *Three Tests for Democracy*. See also Downie and Telfer, *Respect for Persons.*

[35] Plamenatz, "Some American Images of Democracy," in *The Great Ideas Today, 1968*, ed. R. M. Hutchins and M. J. Adler (Chicago: Encyclopedia Britannica, 1968), pp. 251-300, 286.

[36] John Plamenatz, *Democracy and Illusion* (London: Longmans, 1973), pp. 164 and also 182.

the war. For some, self-interest may have been involved; but the behavior of many, probably most, supporters of this cause can hardly be explained in those terms. Moreover, ideas of justice and morality appear to have played a larger role than those of national interest. Other examples of disinterested political behavior abound. Much of the drive among whites for black rights and welfare belongs in this category. So does the controversy over the death penalty. Support of school bond issues or higher school taxes by persons who have no children in those schools, presently or prospectively, strongly suggests either an element of altruism or a concept of justice in their motivation, although an explanation in terms of enlightened self-interest is possible. Old-style conservationists and new-style environmentalists provide further examples.

A rights and duties theory of a different order from that of John Plamenatz is presented by John Rawls in his monumental work on justice, a small part of which was discussed in Chapter Two.[37] Apart from the fact that unlike Plamenatz Rawls's treatise is an ambitious philosophical work dealing with the whole subject of justice, the two writers differ in three significant respects. Rawls focuses on ethical norms, while Plamenatz is emphasizing behavior as influenced by ideas of liberty, rights, and duties. That is to say, Rawls's theory is largely prescriptive, while Plamenatz's is mainly descriptive. Moreover, unlike Plamenatz, Rawls not only develops a complete system of justice, he also devotes a great deal of his attention to the derivation of this system. Finally, more explicitly than Plamenatz, he makes clear that he has a motivational apparatus separate from his theory of justice. To be sure, men do feel a commitment to the principles of justice. But they may also have an ideal of a well-ordered society—a good and rational society of shared ends; and this, too, may provide a basic political motivation.[38] To this extent he is a public-interest theorist.

[37] Rawls, *A Theory of Justice*.   [38] Ibid., pp. 520-523.

To explain Rawls's system in any detail would be to give it disproportionate attention for the purpose of this book. Certain points, however, are of interest and relevance here. Most interesting is its mode of derivation. Harking back to the contractualists in method, it is at once rationalistic and individualistic (in its theory of justice). Rawls assumes a group of families living together behind what he calls a "veil of ignorance." They would not know their own talents or capabilities, their likes or their ideals, or their social or economic condition. They would be interested in constructing a system of rules (rules of justice which would, in turn, govern the form of their polity) that would give themselves, their families, and their children a fair deal in life. They would be concerned especially about the primary social goods: rights and liberties, power and opportunities, and income and wealth, in that order. Liberty takes priority, because rational men would want the fullest opportunity to pursue their goals and interests and develop their powers, without interference from others. General agreement on a system of justice could not be obtained except on this foundation. The two principles of justice completely stated in Chapter Two then emerge. First, each person should have an equal right to the most basic liberty compatible with a like liberty for others. Second, social and economic inequalities should be arranged in the following fashion: (1) they must reasonably be to everyone's advantage, and (2) they must be attached to positions and offices open to all on the same terms.[39] Thus, if it is a question of whether action should be taken that would benefit a certain group, the answer is not to be determined by weighing their advantage against the disadvantage (cost) incurred by some other group, in utilitarian fashion. Rather no such step should be taken unless all would in some measure benefit (or at least none would suffer and the worst off would benefit). This priority of concern for the least advan-

[39] Ibid., pp. 60-65.

taged Rawls believes is required by the principle of fairness, which is at the heart of his theory.

It should be stressed that the principles of justice in the first instance apply to a constitution. In general, the theory lays stress on the development of procedures that will, as far as possible, insure that justice is done. Here the similarity between Rawls and Plamenatz is notable. Both are antiutilitarians. They stress rights and duties and procedures rather than preferences. Both argue that ideas of justice, once formed, affect wants.

Although Rawls begins from an individualistic base, his principles of justice lead him far from the egoism of the radical individualists. He himself contrasts the ideal market process (the model of the radical individualists), whose goal is efficiency, with his ideal legislative process, whose goal is justice. And, as he remarks, "The intensity of desire or the strength of conviction is irrelevant when questions of justice arise."[40]

It will perhaps be apparent from this account that Rawls's theory is stronger on the normative than on the operational side. The principles of justice he develops correspond with considerable accuracy to our intuitive ideas of what is just, especially after some explication and argumentation in case of the less obvious applications. On the other hand, our social behavior and social institutions can hardly be said to make a good fit with them. For instance, Rawls holds that legislators ought first to pursue justice (since this is the citizen's first interest in government) and only secondarily consider the interests of his constituents.[41] One may properly wonder whether this represents normal legislative behavior in all important areas of legislative activity. It is notable and relevant that candidates for elective office notoriously appeal to the special interests of each of many groups whose support they are seeking. And when a McGovern places unusual stress upon justice and other

[40] Ibid., p. 361.   [41] Ibid., p. 227.

traditional virtues, the results raise further doubts as to the accuracy of Rawls's theory as applied to political behavior in the United States.

Yet Rawls does not claim his principles of justice prevail today, not at least in the sense that they are generally adhered to. But he does claim that certain principles of moral psychology operate in such a way that if people were brought up in a just society which was perceived as just, they would tend to develop a corresponding sense of justice and to behave accordingly.[42] To the extent then that our society is not just, Rawls's theory is neither operational nor does it claim to be.

Summarizing with reference to rights and duties theories of democracy in general, they clearly suggest the maintenance of individual rights (and liberties) as one of the main tests for the acceptability of a democratic regime; and, by the same token, the maintenance of rights would, for these theories, be one of the most important criteria for the evaluation of decision-making rules and other institutions of government. From the same point of view, they may figure largely in justifications of democracy. As operational theory, they are somewhat less useful and less likely to be adopted as comprehensive theories of democracy than as qualifications of a maximizing theory.

This statement is especially applicable in Plamenatz's version of rights and duties theory, where the number and diversity of rights and duties that might affect political behavior is so great as to militate against the use of such a theory for either explanatory (except in the most general terms) or predictive purposes. For Rawls's theory, this difficulty is mitigated by the facts that his system is procedural and that it is all comprised by his two principles of justice.

Like the theory of the public interest, rights and duties theory may be considered as an important qualification of

42 Ibid., pp. 453-462, 490-496, and 138.

the egoistic assumption of individualism. It may set limits to this assumption. If I am a farmer I am likely to favor various forms of agricultural subsidies; and if I am a laborer I am likely to favor an increase in the minimum wage. However, in either case, limits to my demands may be set by ideas of fairness or the concept of the equal rights of other groups.

This way of putting the matter will appear to some as too weak. Rights and duties theorists would likely hold that if one assumed all political activity was motivated by a sense of duty rather than a calculation of maximum personal benefit, the result would be a more realistic account than would that of the radical individualist. In this respect the theory is parallel to that of the public interest. Moreover, the two are by no means mutually incompatible; the same theorist may stress both the idea of the public interest and concepts of right, duty, and justice as key motivating factors. The utilitarian will emphasize the former; the deontologist the latter. The deontologist will argue that the average voter does not engage in elaborate calculations of interest—particularly so if he is not being motivated by self-interest. Thus when white people are voting on the busing of black children to school, they are likely to be thinking, the deontologist would argue, in terms of justice, of what is fair. Similarly, when the merits and demerits of wage and price control measures are being discussed, the inequities of the way the system operates in practice are likely to be very important considerations. The distribution of tax burdens is another subject where, it is highly arguable, the calculation of the public interest— an extremely complicated affair—is likely to be a matter for less debate than is the apparently much simpler matter of fairness. On the other hand, it would appear that when it is a question of whether to spend public funds for highways or for subsidizing rail transportation, the public-interest theory is more useful (realistic) than that of rights and duties. Furthermore, the unwillingness of people to

197

give up private-car commuting even in the most smog-ridden areas strongly suggests that in this issue-area at least, radical individualism paints a more realistic picture of political behavior than does either of the other types of theory now under discussion.[43]

The examples above can prove no more than that each of the theories thus far discussed is valid for certain situations and none is valid for all. Clearly, theory could be helped by much more empirical research. A statistical study of one session of the Iowa legislature provides an example of what I have in mind. The greatest concern was found to be for questions of morality (liquor, crime, capital punishment), and contests over monetary matters were at a surprisingly low level. Generalizing beyond the specific study, the researcher remarks that "a clue to what is going on is suggested by the ease with which samples of mass publics answer questions about 'important issues' or 'matters requiring government action' not in terms of personal interests convertible into private demands on government but in terms of general 'problems' confronting 'the country' or 'the state.' " And again he remarks that "even if the task of the legislature is defined as dealing with clashing interests, the primary goal almost inexorably becomes reconciliation, reduction of conflict, not mere registry of preponderant demands."[44]

Finally, it should be noted that just as a "maximizer" may stress either individual or social welfare as the goal, so a deontologist may place his emphasis either on rights or on duties. In the former case, he leans toward individualism, while in the latter case he moves in the collectivist direction.

[43] See Ward Elliott, "The Los Angeles Affliction: Suggestions for a Cure," *The Public Interest*, Summer 1975, pp. 119-128.

[44] John Wahlke, "Policy Determinants and Legislative Decisions," in S. Sidney Ulmer, ed., *Political Decision-Making* (New York: Van Nostrand-Reinhold, 1970), pp. 76-120. The two quotations are at pages 108 and 109, respectively.

7. COLLECTIVIST DEMOCRATIC THEORY

The fourth and last type of democratic theory I have labeled collectivist, for reasons set forth in Chapter Three. Although some students of political theory regularly use some such term (e.g. *organicism, organismic theory, idealism* or *holism*), definitions tend to vary or to be avoided. Indeed, collectivism, like individualism, has a cluster of meanings. In the following pages types of collectivism will be distinguished, partly but not wholly in terms of shadings of degree.

For present purposes at least, the most important subclassification is the one made in Chapter Three between hierarchical, organic collectivism on the one hand, and egalitarian, communitarian collectivism on the other hand. Although the distinction is of great importance, most of what is said in the following paragraphs applies to both types. Most democratic collectivists today belong in the second category, and so it is of the greater contemporary interest and relevance to the subject of this book.

If radical individualism is the epitome of rationalism (in the narrowest sense of that word) in democratic political theory, collectivism occupies the other end of what might be called the rationalist-romanticist spectrum. For the differences between the two ends of this spectrum little needs to be added to what was said in Chapter Three. It was noted there that in saying the state (or the whole) must be valued in and for itself, the collectivist takes an ambiguous position. In part, and for some, it may be no more than stressing the point that one should consider the welfare of everyone, the beneficent effects of the whole on all of its members, and the claims of future generations. In part, and for others, the emphasis is upon a psychological point—that the individual self reaches out and includes the selves of others, that the more fully developed a person is the more he has incorporated in his psyche the selves of others (at the limit, all others) in his society. Or the point may be, in

199

Rawls's words, that "human beings have in fact shared final ends and [that] they value their common institutions and activities as good in themselves."[45] Different individuals develop different capacities; and none can fully enjoy these attainments except in participant activity. Logically distinct though these points are, they tend to go together. A person who holds either of the first two is likely to hold the third. How far the implications of these points are carried in an antiindividualist direction is another matter. Here variation is wide and ambiguity common.

Two points should be noted about this general position. First, though the common institutions and activities are viewed as good in themselves, they *may* be so viewed only because they are satisfying to individuals. A game of bridge may be a good in itself only in the same way that may be true of a game of solitaire. But what the collectivist seems to stress is that the *kind* of value the individual derives from conjoint activity is distinctive; it derives from its conjointness. Second, the reference may be to society but not to the state. To transfer to the state everything that is true of society runs the danger discussed in Chapter Three The individual may be so identified with the whole that all sense of separateness is lost, and with it the foundation-stone of democracy.

While collectivism emphasizes feeling and emotion, and is at the opposite end of the scale from rationalism, *narrowly defined*, to identify it with irrationalism would be a great error, although some irrationalists may be collectivists. Plato was no irrationalist; and the same is true of the idealist democratic collectivists, as exemplified by Bernard Bosanquet and F. H. Bradley. For such men, reason includes more than calculation, it includes the process by which our feelings, sentiments, and moral beliefs are brought into a rational harmony, both within the individual and as among individuals in society.

[45] *A Theory of Justice*, 522.

The modern democratic collectivist is likely to be less of a holist, less of a Platonist, than were his nineteenth-century predecessors. His concern is to oppose individualism. He detests a theory that portrays man as self-interested and self-sufficient, for whom the state is merely a means to reconcile conflicts and to maximize individual freedom. He admires rather "the politics which concerns itself with the good life, which is grounded on man's inadequacy as a solitary being, and which aims at virtue rather than at mechanistic freedom. . . ." He sees privacy as "an arena for greed, in individuality the specter of loneliness and alienation, and in negative freedom a rejection of the bonds of human commanlity."[46] For these reasons he places a high value upon cooperation both for its own sake and for the unity it promotes.

Although democratic collectivism's modern proponents tend to be highly critical of what they call pluralism, both normative and empirical, in fact collectivism can support placing a high value on group life and on providing a substantial degree of group autonomy. Moreover, it favors the hypothesis that the behavior of groups is of primary importance to the understanding and the dynamics of political life. Yet, as the case of Rousseau reminds us, a caveat must be entered here. A collectivist is primarily concerned about the whole and he may believe that groups within the state, including political parties, threaten the unity of the whole. For any sizable polity, he is likely to recognize their necessity, but he may consider them a *pis aller*. (But not so Hegel or the British idealists.)

Finally, it seems apparent that a natural affinity exists between collectivism and a systems approach to the study of politics. High valuation of the whole and determination of the individuals' values and behavior by the collectivity strongly suggest that the state will be found to respond to laws and tendencies of its own, which could not be derived

[46] The quotations are from Benjamin R. Barber, *Superman and Common Men*, pp. 96-97.

from the study either of individual nature or motivation. Moreover, insofar as one studies individual political behavior, it would be more fruitful, from the collectivist point of view, to study the process and results of political socialization than to concentrate on the individual considered as an autonomous unit.

8. Comparisons and Contrasts among Motivational Theories

It will be recalled that the classification of theories set forth in Chart 1 was provisional. It is now clear that the nonmaximizing theories are not just extensions of the spectrum of individualism and public interest theory, nor of the key values of personal benefit and benefits to others. The collectivist does of course have much in common with the public-interest theorist. Like him, he lays great stress on benefits to others both as an ideal and as an operative goal. But he is interested in how this goal develops and believes that powerful social psychological forces are at work to foster its growth; and he values the processes as well as the end state. He also tends to stress the interest in the future, to lengthen the time-span over which the public interest is calculated, and to stress the value of enduring institutions, especially of the state itself (except for Marx and his followers). He sees the public as a corporate entity, a unit rather than an aggregation, and emphasizes interests peculiar to that entity. He places great value on the social aspects of life and on the man who identifies with society, while he feels that men who are lost in their private interests are lost indeed. He not only values cooperation for its own sake as well as for its consequences, but he disvalues competition. This is what most definitively distinguishes the egalitarian collectivist from the public-interest theorist.

The rights and duties theorist, as he stresses either individual rights or duties to others, may lean in the individualistic or in the collectivistic direction. Moreover, he may

202

or may not see rights and duties as deriving from rationality in the second sense defined above.

Neither the rights and duties theorist nor the democratic collectivist denies that personal benefit is important both as motivation and as moral guide. Rather they tend to qualify, in effect though not always in their rhetoric, the tenets of the maximizing theories.

Furthermore, all of the theories discussed above may and generally do assume some tension between what men do strive for and what they ought (and think they ought) to strive for. While the major theories fall in boxes on the chart that equate a given normative value with its operational counterpart, this must not obscure the fact that the normative value tends to run ahead, so to speak, of the operational value, as our aspirations generally exceed our accomplishments. This is perhaps most true of collectivist theories.

The question might be raised, Why begin with individualism and treat other theories, in large measure, as variants or modifications of it, or as departures from it? Could this procedure not be as well reversed? An easy answer would be simply that one must start somewhere. But the choice was not arbitrary. Discussions of political theory generally begin with the individual, with his interests, desires, preferences, obligations, and so forth. Even Plato followed this course before turning to the "larger letters." Moreover, if indeed the individual can be fully understood only in relation to some collective entity, this fact is not obvious to the naive questioner. One needs to work up to such an explanation.

9. CONCLUDING REMARKS

It may be appropriate to say a few words about what is to be gained from these typologies of democratic theory as well as about their shortcomings. The key-value classification certainly will have failed in its purpose if it does not

203

show the close relations between normative (evaluative) and empirical theory, between the prescriptive and the descriptive theory. One sees here why it is so difficult, and so dangerous, to treat either in permanent abstraction from the other. Rationality, whether on the level of efficiency, of ends and means, or whether on the level of morality, that is of discovering rules, modes of behavior, that lead to enduring fulfillment, is the link between the normative and the behavioral (operational) approaches. Neither, it would appear, can be complete without the study of rationality; and rationality itself leads in both directions. What ought to be is conditioned by the actual and the possible; the existential, what is, is likewise conditioned, and directed in its development, by what ought to be.

In arraying operative theories of democracy on a spectrum running from the most radically individualistic to the most radically collectivistic, it may become clearer in what sense and to what degree democratic theory is incorrigibly individualistic and in what sense it is not only compatible with collectivistic theory but is made more psychologically sound and morally acceptable by modification in this direction. Further, this schema makes it possible to deal with the topics considered in the remainder of this volume in a way that shows how the problems in question relate to the various theories, and even how they can be dealt with in detail in terms of one theory, and then in terms of the others as variants on, or departures from, the first.

Not much needs to be added regarding the power theories of democracy. They are of definitely secondary interest in the present context. Yet it would give a distorted view of democratic theory to neglect them. They are in no sense rivals to the motivational theories. They concentrate on institutions and on the manner and extent of popular mobilization. No one of the motivational theories leads necessarily to any particular one of the power theories, although it will be apparent from what has been said above that a

collectivist will more likely be an elitist (if he is a hier-
archival collectivist) or a populist (if he is an egalitarian collectivist) than he will a constitutionalist or a social pluralist.
Constitutionalism, with its stress on the rule of law and
formal procedures to check arbitrary governmental action,
is much more congenial to the individualistically inclined
theorist (of whichever of the first three types of motivational theory) than it is to the collectivist, with his stress
on commitment to the whole. Social pluralism, because of
its stress on intergroup competition, is generally anathema
to contemporary collectivists. It must be recognized, however, that the hierarchical or organic collectivist (e.g.
Hegel) may be both a social pluralist and a constitutionalist, a point which brings out the fact that the latter two
types are not necessarily mutually exclusive.

The remaining chapters of this book, except for the Conclusion, discuss a series of problems common to the operation of democratic institutions. In addition to analyzing
these problems for their own sake, I also consider each of
them in relation to the various types of democratic theory.
Often the analysis of the problems throw light on the
theories, tending to support some and limit the validity or
usefulness of others. In one case, this process is reversed
and each of the theories is used to see what solution for the
problem in question (decision-making rules and machinery)
gains support, if any, from each of the theories.

CHAPTER VI

Conditions of Democracy

In considering the justification of democracy, in Chapter Four, no claim was made that it would in all circumstances be a desirable form of government. On the contrary, the discussion specifically related only to democracy "under favorable circumstances." I now turn to a consideration of what circumstances are favorable to the formation and survival of democratic regimes. In doing so, especially in conclusion, I shall relate what is said to the key-value (motivational) typology set forth in the preceding chapter, looking for either support or qualification or contradiction of each of the major types of theory included in that typology. To the limited extent that it lends itself to this treatment, the same will be done for the power theories of democracy.

1. Introductory Remarks

Although no theory of democracy can afford to neglect this subject, it is beset by difficulties. It was once common in the literature to speak of *pre*requisites for the establishment of democratic government or of requisites for its maintenance and successful operation; but it is questionable whether the distinction between prerequisites and requisites can be sustained, and it is now seldom made. Certain African leaders have maintained that no such thing as a "prerequisite" for democracy exists; that a democracy, once established, can create the conditions essential for its continuation. As a general proposition, the latter statement is extremely dubious; but the argument does point to an important truth. Many "conditions" (the term I shall generally use instead of "requisites" or "prerequisites") are

conducive to the establishment of a successfully functioning democracy. If all were lacking, a democracy could
probably not be established. But it is difficult to identify
any one of them as so essential that it could not be fore-
gone until later, assuming other favorable conditions were
present.

In other words, not only does the distinction between
requisites and prerequisites tend to break down, but it may
also even be impossible to say of any particular condition
that it is either "necessary" or "sufficient" for either the
establishment or the maintenance (stability) of a democratic regime. Certainly it seems impossible to specify a
group of conditions as being both necessary and sufficient.
A variety of reasons account for these difficulties. For one
thing, most of the conditions discussed here are matters of
degree, and are frequently not susceptible of precise measurement. They tend also, within limits, to be mutually interchangeable. A strong sense of national unity may com-
pensate for deep religious cleavages. A very low literacy
rate, one that would doom democratic regimes under most
conditions, may be compatible with democratic success
where a small, highly competent elite is deeply committed
to democratic ideals. And so on.

Many of the conditions favorable to democracy are matters of degree, and it is often extremely important how they
are distributed, either geographically or by categories of
the population. For instance, the presence of a large intransigent minority, if it is geographically concentrated in
a central part of the country, might make democracy unworkable, especially if the matters on which it was intransigent extended to subjects that called for nationally
uniform treatment. The same minority, if widely scattered,
might not cause a serious problem at all. For many purposes, the distribution among levels of the population is
even more important. (Reference is to levels in terms of
political involvement, competence, and resources.) The
most important determinants of success or failure in a

democratic or would-be democratic regime will be found in the quality and characteristics of the political elite, the higher levels of political activism.

Another point that must be borne in mind: the conditions of democracy operate at various levels of causation. The quality of the political elite is immediately important; it in turn is partly determined by the educational system; the latter will depend, in some measure, upon the output of the economy; and the economy, of course, is determined by all manner of factors, including the work habits of the masses and the supply and quality of managerial talent, for example. No one of these causal stages completely determines the next, but each is important enough to be included in a discussion of the conditions of democracy.

Yet the difficulty is even greater still. While the level of education will be influenced by the output of the economy, it is equally true that the level of education will influence the output of the economy. Here the circularity of influence is benign. But it need not be. If, for instance, the rate of education outruns the development of the economy so that many educated youth cannot find suitable employment, the resulting discontent may, at least in the short run, do democracy more harm than good. This is a not uncommon phenomenon in the early stages of political development, but the specter of a large number of unemployed Ph.D.s in the United States today suggests it has more general applicability.

The causal linkage between the social and the economic on the one hand, and the political on the other, also exerts its influence in both directions. Thus political factors in the form of governmental outputs (e.g. the construction and maintenance of an irrigation system) may be vital determinants of the level of economic output. Moreover, it will do no harm to spell out what has already been implied: the conditions for democracy are not necessarily the same at all times and places.

It is easy to confuse the conditions of democracy with two other sets of conditions, with which in fact they overlap to an important degree. One of these is the set of conditions essential for the existence of *any* form of polity. In some measure the two are the same, except that they differ in degree. Political talent, a sense of unity, and so on, are more essential for a democracy than for other forms of government. But there is a point below which no stable form of government can be maintained. In some instances, the difference may not be very great.

The second set of conditions closely connected with democratic requisites relates to political development. Some would even define political development as development of, or toward, democratic institutions. But it is not generally defined in precisely that way, and the conditions for the one are not necessarily identical with those for the other, although a large degree of overlap is practically inescapable. All students of the subject would agree that the development of a strong sense of national unity would constitute an aspect of political development. "Nation-building" is sometimes used almost as a synonym for development, yet in England, for instance, that process was well accomplished long before democracy was established. Today the two developments are not usually so widely separated in time; yet Brazil might be suggested as an example of a well-developed nation in which democracy has yet to flourish. A sense of national unity is by no means a sufficient condition for a lasting democracy, but it is clearly a necessary one.

With all these difficulties, it might seem that the subject defied any useful approach. Yet, as is generally the case in such situations, a look at the extremes reveals some order in the apparent chaos. Only the brave would contend that a successful democracy could be established in Saudi Arabia today. And it seems clear enough that the Swiss have something the Haitians lack. In general, we know a great deal

209

about the conditions favorable to democracy and also about those that are harmful to it; it is primarily when we are dealing with borderline cases, of which there are many, that we get into difficulty. Indeed it has been clear from the beginning that most of the new states in Africa faced at best a rocky and uncertain road in attempting to establish democratic institutions. One can more readily get a sense for the overall situation than define it with particulars in a way that admits of generalization. As long as it is understood that the complex of favorable conditions herein discussed cannot be precisely specified, whether we call them requisites, prerequisites, or conditions is of little moment. At best they provide raw material for very weak theory.

Political theorists, and other students of politics, have long known that the kind of constitution practicable in a given situation depends on various factors precedent. Thus Aristotle declared that where the numbers of the poor were more than enough to counterbalance the superior quality of the rich, the natural form of government would be a democracy. Likewise, he held that where the middle class outweighed the other two classes, or even one of them, a "polity" (which would more nearly correspond to a modern representative democracy than would his "democracy") could be "permanently established."[1] If Aristotle stressed the economic condition of the various classes—the distribution, not the quantity, of wealth—it was not because he overlooked the importance of attitudes but because he believed that for the most part, political attitudes were determined by economic interest. Nevertheless, by modern standards Aristotle's account appears woefully incomplete.

John Stuart Mill, in considering this topic, addressed himself to the qualities of the citizens rather than to economic or other conditions that he presumed would determine those qualities. He wrote:

[1] *Politics*, IV, xii, Secs. 3 and 4, 1296 b. By a democracy, of course, Aristotle meant a direct democracy.

210

The people for whom the form of government is intended must be willing to accept it; or at least not so unwilling as to oppose an insurmountable obstacle to its establishment. They must be willing and able to do what is necessary to keep it standing. And they must be willing and able to do what it requires of them to enable it to fulfil its purposes. The word 'do' is to be understood as including forbearances as well as acts.[2]

In fairness to Mill, it should be noted that he is here speaking of the conditions for *any* form of government. The chapter from which the quotation was taken, the only one in which he discusses the subject, is a consideration of the extent to which forms of government are a matter of choice. His argument was that, subject to the limitations outlined above, they *are* a matter of choice. He goes on to say, too, in a passage suggestive of remarks made above about the possibility of a government creating its own requisites, that even though a people is unprepared for good institutions, an essential part of their preparing for such institutions may be to kindle the desire for them in the people. He asks:

What means had Italian patriots, during the last and present generation, of preparing the Italian people for freedom in unity, but by inciting them to demand it? Those, however, who undertake such a task need to be duly impressed, not solely with the benefits of the institutions or polity which they recommend, but also with the capacities, moral, intellectual, and active, required for working it; that they may avoid, if possible, stirring up a desire too much in advance of the capacity.[3]

Alhough the latter remarks in particular are quite perceptive, Mill's treatment of the subject remains highly inade-

[2] Mill, "On Representative Government," in *Utilitarianism, Liberty, and Representative Government*, p. 177.
[3] Ibid., p. 181.

quate. It is quite right to say the people must be "willing and able" to support the government and do what it requires of them, but this tells nothing about the kinds of attitudes and abilities thus entailed. Even less does it move to the next level of causation and suggest what conditions favor the development of a citizenry possessing these attitudes and abilities.

Yet, perhaps because they were primarily concerned with democracies already in being, students of politics had little more than this to say on the subject until quite recent times. The failure of democracy in Italy and Germany after the First World War gave rise to some speculations about democratic prerequisites. Mainly, however, it was the formation of new states at a heretofore unheard of rate following the Second World War that turned the attention of many students of political science to this subject. It is to the findings of these researchers and the resultant theoretical constructs that we now turn.[4]

The various factors and propositions about democratic requisites to be discussed here will be grouped under three headings: (1) history, (2) the socioeconomic order, and (3) political culture. These are broad categories. If they were made more numerous they could be more precise; their contents would be less heterogeneous; but this simpler classification has compensating virtues.

The material just outlined will comprise the body of the chapter, while the bearing this material has on the validity of each of the types of democratic theory developed in Chapter Five will be reserved for the concluding section.

[4] For the most part I shall merely state the conclusions that empirical research has supported, with at most summary statements of the evidence and references to the researchers who have discovered and compiled it. Fortunately, Robert A. Dahl has done a magnificent job of systematizing most of the propositions that have been advanced on this subject and bringing together a great deal of evidence bearing upon them. See his *Polyarchy* (New Haven: Yale University Press, 1971).

2. HISTORICAL AND POLITICAL FACTORS

The heading "history" is perhaps the most discouraging from the point of view of anyone who would like to see democracy make substantial headway among the new states in the near future. Partly, this is simply a matter of the development of political institutions taking a long time. If a group of people are united in, let us say, a business enterprise, especially if it is a relatively small enterprise, the effect of what they and their fellows do is easily perceived. With skillful management, including selection and rejection of personnel—a means not generally open to the polity—both self-interest and affect can be readily mobilized in support of the organization. The case of a state is a very different matter. Nation-building is generally a slow process, partly because the new loyalty must in some measure displace some system of old loyalties, tribal or other, and partly because the state is large, vague, impersonal, and often associated in the subject's mind at least as much with taxes and onerous regulations as with benefits. Even if we assume that a democratic constitution has been adopted and an elected regime installed, the battle is only begun. To get the individual citizen to identify with the regime— to feel that its interest is his interest, that his little share of sovereignty (especially if he was in the minority!) amounts to anything and makes it either his duty or his interest to put himself out for the sake of helping the system function successfully—is a large order. Loyalties, by definition, tend to be longlasting. Once a substantial part of a nation has acquired not only a sense of identity but also loyalty to its system of government, it possesses a buffer that can absorb many blows. Moreover, these feelings are passed on from generation to generation, even without conscious attempt, by a process of socialization that begins in the home, as parents' attitudes are uncritically adopted by their children. But in a new democracy where no strong nation has been developed, the bulk of the nation, not just a single

213

generation, must be affected in a brief period. To repeat, it is not simply a matter, as with children, of developing a loyalty where previously none had existed; rather, for large numbers of people, old loyalties must be displaced. Furthermore, in the first instance it is likely that loyalties will attach to a particular leader or group of leaders; but only when these personal attachments have been transformed into impersonal ties to a system can that system be presumed to be stable.

To be a bit more specific on this matter of elapsed time, on the basis of a wide-ranging survey of political modernization, Dankwart Rustow found that the comparatively few new states which have attained relatively stable democratic institutions shared these features in common: (1) a history of from 40 to 130 years of administrative and educational modernization; (2) a stable geographical base for their political system for the same period of time; and (3) a tradition, dating back at least from one to three generations, of political parties that provided some organic link between rulers and ruled, and that became progressively more inclusive.[5] Approaching the problem from a slightly different point of view, Professor C. E. Black divided the process of political modernization into three stages: (1) consolidation of modernizing leadership, (2) economic and social transformation, and (3) integration of society.[6] Of 148 political entities studied, he found 68 that had completed the first stage. (None of those that had not completed that stage could be considered stable democracies, the closest approximations being Malaysia and Singapore.) For the United Kingdom, probably the most successfully functioning democracy, the first period occupied 183 years. For all but three of the others that have become stable democracies, it occupied over 50 years. The three exceptions,

[5] Rustow, *A World of Nations* (Washington, D.C.: Brookings, 1967), pp. 228-229.

[6] Black, *The Dynamics of Modernization* (New York: Harper & Row, 1966), pp. 90-94.

followed in each case by the number of years in stage one, were Iceland (46 years), the Philippines (47 years), and India (28 years). Today the democratic institutions of the last two, at the very least, have been substantially qualified.

The establishment of a democratic fundament then takes time. But the mere passage of time is not enough. A series of problems, even crises, successfully resolved seems to be almost a necessary condition for the formation of a democratic regime. If these problems take the form of conflict, perhaps armed, with other nations, they will contribute to national unity. But at least some of them should be internal and should involve severe contests between major social or political groups.[7] By successfully dealing with such problems, a political system establishes support for its procedures. Thus this kind of experience should characterize the early stages of a democratic regime.

The last observation points to another, closely related, point. How the democratic regime comes into being is of great importance: whether in some way that unites the people and infuses them with a sense of the new regime's legitimacy or in a fashion that leaves a powerful minority defeated, disgruntled, and with a strong sense of having been unjustly treated. Either revolution against a colonial power or gradual and peaceful development may provide the first condition; some form of internal war may leave it with the second. But obviously these conditions cannot be stated precisely. Would Nigeria be better off politically if it had had to fight for its independence? Internal wars, perhaps especially if spread over a considerable period of time, may serve the purposes of unification and of legitimation of a new and more democratic regime.[8] But it is far from clear that they always produce this effect.

[7] Cf. Rustow, op. cit. At the same time, conflicts may leave cleavages so deep as to be inimical to democracy. (See below, subsection b.)

[8] Perhaps the most striking example of this process is provided by the Mexican revolution, which appears to have advanced Mexico, relative to many other Latin American countries, in its evolution toward democracy.

215

The final item under the heading of history, and perhaps the most discouraging to the democrat, concerns the order in which various stages of development take place. Liberal democracy may be thought of as a compound of constitutionalism and simple democracy; democracy, as defined here, requires various constitutional devices if it is to operate as it should; democracy as Dahl defines it consists of two dimensions, "contestation" and participation, one measure of the latter being "inclusiveness." These are three different ways of saying much the same thing, although the last of the three is more restrictive.[9] Among the most stable democracies of the world, in virtually every case, constitutionalism or liberalism developed before universal suffrage; institutions of political competition were operating long before they were extended to anything like the whole of the adult population.[10]

It is easy to see why this order of development should encourage the stability of an ensuing democratic regime. Attitudes favorable to compromise, habits of political moderation, commitments to procedures designed to limit arbitrariness and to insure that decisions are not made without hearing all sides and without adequate information and deliberation, have an opportunity to develop and become well ingrained in the national character and especially in

[9] Dahl's emphasis is upon political competition; the way it is put here is intended to bring out other elements of liberalism as well, such as respect for individual rights of person and property. These other components are extremely important, especially because they extend to elements of the population not included in political competition at the stage of development under discussion.

[10] The charts in Black, *The Dynamics of Modernization*, substantiate this statement. See also Rustow, *A World of Nations*, Chaps. 3-4 and p. 276. He argues that the best sequence of development is (1) the achievement of unity; (2) the establishment of authority and development of public services; and (3) movement toward equality, including equality of political participation. In some cases, he says, the best order would be to reverse the sequence of the first two items. But to start with equality, he contends, will likely lead to breakdown and civil war.

the character of political activists before the political system is opened wide to the struggle among the full panoply of social interests. Mass man has sometimes been defined as the man who does not think of the morrow but governs his life by considerations of immediate advantage. Insofar as this characterizes the average person, a successful democracy will clearly depend upon institutions that check impulsive action and upon deeply entrenched respect for these institutions. It is difficult to develop this kind of respect in the mass of the people while they are in a position to exercise their power to obtain immediate advantages at the expense of orderly procedures.

Thus, while it does not follow automatically that the order of events which characterized the development of democracies in the nineteenth century must also occur in today's emerging nations, sound reasons favor establishing constitutionalism firmly before the suffrage is made universal. Yet that has not been the pattern in the second half of the twentieth century; nor does it seem likely to be in the foreseeable future. It might even be argued that the reasoning used above to explain why a substantial period of constitutionalism with limited democracy should precede full democracy also explains why it is no longer likely to happen that way. Today's masses, unlike those of the nineteenth century, are surrounded by democracies; at least they live in a world where they are made aware of the fact that peoples elsewhere are self-governing. Democracy has become the norm, the ideal to which all aspire. And the very unwillingness to postpone enjoyments until tomorrow that is peculiar to the undisciplined mind makes it practically very difficult, if not impossible, to postpone the advent of full democracy without imposing repressive controls that are incompatible with constitutionalism.

All of this is not to deny that new or newly democratic states can develop stable democratic governments; but one fears that if such development does take place it is likely, at best, to resemble that of France in the nineteenth cen-

217

tury rather than to follow the course of English or American history during the same period. Possibly Mexico displays a less discouraging pattern of political development. In that country, after sixteen or seventeen years of continual violence and upheaval, a stable regime has been maintained for nearly half a century. To be sure, Mexico is not newly independent, but though it is by no means fully democratic, a significant fact is that inclusiveness has outrun contestation, in Dahl's terms. One should add, however, that while political competition is minimal, it does exist. Moreover, the court system maintains a significant element of constitutionalism in the form of protection for private rights.[11] If Mexico does progress to a full measure of democracy and stabilize at that level, it will provide a significant counterexample to the line of argument advanced above.

For the most part, historical considerations relate to political rather than to economic matters. The latter are undoubtedly of great significance, but so much discussion of the subject assumes they are primary, and all else secondary (if not "epiphenomena"), that it is essential to point out the crucial and basic role of the political factors.[12]

3. Socioeconomic Factors

In turning next to the socioeconomic order, two broad principles provide a useful starting point: (1) a democratic society must be an "open" society; and (2) power must not

[11] See Robert E. Scott, *Mexican Government in Transition* (Urbana, Ill.: University of Illinois Press, 1959), pp. 267-273. See also Barry Ames, "Bases of Support for Mexico's Dominant Party," *Amer. Polit. Sci. Rev.*, 64 (1970), 153-167. Ames's study by districts shows that the higher the level of development, the less relatively powerful is the dominant party—in other words, the greater is the "contestation."

[12] Political factors are of basic importance not only for political development but for economic development as well. See J. J. Spengler, "Economic Development: Political Preconditions and Political Consequences," *Jour. of Politics*, 22 (1960), 387-416.

be concentrated to the extent that individual autonomy ceases to be a significant force.

To say that a democratic society must be an open society means it must be porous and flexible. It must be open to new ideas and new ways of doing things. It must be neither a caste society nor one where tradition, or some nominally nonpolitical organization such as a church, rules with a heavy hand. What was said in an earlier chapter about the ideal of individual autonomy is relevant here. The socioeconomic order, then, must encourage flexibility, or at least not destroy it.[13] It must not have a class system that makes it extremely difficult for members of a rising class, whether it be the middle class or labor, to rise to positions of power and prestige. In Pareto's terms, it must provide for "the circulation of the elites."[14]

Flexibility and mobility tend to go together and mobility is a feature of city life. Hence it is often thought that urbanization is a prerequisite for democracy, and indeed some correlation between urbanization and democratization can be found, as will appear. But most of today's older democracies were only slightly urbanized in their beginnings. (To be sure, democracy as an institution had its origin in city states.) Today both urbanization and de-

[13] The case of Britain is a useful reminder that we are dealing with matters of degree. Compared to the openness of American society, that of Britain is relatively closed. See the discussion in Seymour Martin Lipset's *The First New Nation* (New York: Basic Books, 1963), Chap. 6. But when the British aristocracy was pressed for the admission of new classes to the electorate in 1832 and at subsequent periods, it showed a willingness to "give" that distinguished it from the hard-shelled traditionalism of Germany, for instance, even as late as the Weimar period. It has been plausibly suggested that England's institution of primogeniture, which forces younger sons to leave the land and find their own livelihood, has had much to do with breaking the rigid class barrier between aristocracy and others. See Robert Ulich, *Education of Nations* (Cambridge, Mass.: Harvard University Press, 1961), p. 95, cited and quoted by Lipset, *First New Nation*, p. 244.

[14] See Vilfredo Pareto, *The Mind and Society*, 4 vols., ed. Arthur Livingston (New York: Harcourt, Brace, 1935), 4: §§2025-2046.

219

mocratization tend to be aspects of "modernization," so it is easy to see them as necessarily related. But even if urbanization sets up forces which tend to bring about democracy, it does not follow that urbanization is a necessary condition of democracy. When one thinks of the highly democratic cantons of rural Switzerland, of such countries as Canada, Australia, New Zealand, or Denmark, not to mention the earlier history of the older democracies to which reference has already been made, it seems clear that the relation between urbanization and democracy is far from necessary. Agrarian society is not incompatible with democracy; what is incompatible is such fixity, such rigidity, that all individual autonomy in matters political is balked either by tradition or by social structure. Thus a highly *traditional* peasant society is incompatible with democracy, but a society of free farmers is not.[15]

If individuals are to be free to exert their autonomy with political effectiveness, more is required than the absence of a rigidifying traditionalism. Power must not all be concentrated in one identifiable and intercommunicating group of men. Otherwise, all the devices of constitutional government cannot be expected to prevent individuals and minorities—or even majorities—from being abused and exploited. Not only this, but the competition for political power and office itself is unlikely to be free where political power provides the only route to wealth and fame. That is to say, powerholders will be willing to relinquish power to their rivals only if they have a reasonable chance of obtaining prizes elsewhere. Thus Robert Dahl concludes that "a competitive regime is unlikely to exist in a country with highly centralized direction of the economy, no matter what the form of ownership."[16] In fact, in no country where the government owns or monopolizes the major

[15] On this distinction see Dahl, *Polyarchy*, p. 56.
[16] Dahl, "Governments and Political Oppositions," in Fred A. Greenstein and Nelson W. Polsby, eds., *Handbook of Political Science* (Reading, Mass.: Addison-Wesley, 1975), 3:115-174, 141.

means of production, controls the church, and does not permit free trade unions and other voluntary organizations to function does democracy as it has been defined here exist. Taken together, this set comprises a requisite, a necessary condition, for democracy. When analyzed, these requirements embody the important principle stated above, that power must be dispersed. This much is clear. And it has important corollaries, including, for instance, the proposition that too great a concentration of wealth and income in the hands of a few is inimical to democracy. But how much is too much? How extensive must social and economic pluralism be? Or, to put it the other way, how far can a democratic government safely go in gathering power into its own hands? And further, to what extent must government, in this context, be treated as a unit, and to what extent, on the other hand, can federalism or other forms of political decentralization provide the defenses to liberty and equality of political power without which a democracy cannot survive? Unfortunately, many obstacles stand in the way of any satisfactory answers to these questions. All of the matters referred to are matters of degree; they are not susceptible to precise measurement; generally more of one will make up for less of another; and in some measure, this interchangeability extends beyond this group of factors to all the other conditions of democracy.

To go beyond the kind of analysis presented above, with respect to the socioeconomic order, is both easy and difficult. Here we move into the realm of measurement. The extent of urbanization, the gross national product, various indices of industrialization, such as per capita energy consumption, number of automobiles, and the like, and facilities for communication, such as telephones and radios and newspaper circulation, can be ascertained fairly accurately for most countries. Correlations between such data and degrees and rates of democratization can be readily worked out within wide but still useful latitudes of accuracy.

The latitudes are as wide as they are because of the diffi-

country in which democratic institutions are not firmly established.

Still another problem arises out of the reliance upon comparative studies using cross-national aggregates, the method upon which nearly all but the most recent studies have relied most heavily. Studies of this kind are likely to be seriously distorted by the idiosyncratic nature of the subject. That is to say, often factors that are unimportant in many, perhaps most, states are of great significance in one or more others. It is now widely believed that longitudinal studies, covering long periods of time in a single country, provide better bases for study, at least in the early stages of generalization, than do the studies using cross-national aggregates.

In spite of all these difficulties, some of the propositions thus far advanced, and especially some of the research findings, are well worth examining. Among so-called developing countries, James S. Coleman found a high degree of correlation between economic development, as measured by eleven separate indices, and type of political system ("competitive," "semicompetitive," or "authoritarian"). Among forty-six Asian and African countries, seven were classified as competitive political systems. These seven were among the nineteen countries with the most-developed economies, three of them among the first four (the exception being South Africa, rated semicompetitive); only one (India) was below twelfth place. Of the fifteen authoritarian countries, all but three (United Arab Republic, Iraq, and Libya) were in the bottom half of the economic-development scale, and even Libya was only barely above the median. The twenty-four semicompetitive polities were more evenly distributed. The twenty Latin American countries exhibited a similar pattern, with seven of the twelve authoritarian regimes occupying the last seven places in the economic rank ordering, while none of the five polities rated competitive appeared below ninth

223

place. If the study were to be brought up to date, some changes would be in order, but not enough to affect the general picture.[19] As Dahl says, granted thresholds and deviant cases, there is clearly a close relation between socio-economic development and democracy.[20]

This proposition is further confirmed by Bruce Russett's findings. Using the same political classification used by Almond and Coleman, he classifies eighty-nine countries (ranging from the United States to Burma) according to per capita GNP in five levels or stages. (He calls them, in order, "traditional primitive," "traditional civilizations," "transitional," "industrial revolution," and "high mass consumption.")[21] The results are presented in Chart 3. Russett concludes, "There is good evidence that a reasonably high level of economic development makes the success of democracy much more likely."[22]

A more recent study, based upon factor analysis of over twenty political and social indicators, finds that a group of factors we might generally associate with stable democracy correlate highly with per capita GNP.[23] The authors are

[19] Gabriel A. Almond and James S. Coleman, eds., *The Politics of the Developing Areas* (Princeton: Princeton University Press, 1960), pp. 536-544. Of the eleven indices of economic development, the classification of two is open to question. They are both measures of education: the literacy rate and the percentage of school-age children enrolled in primary schools. Of course they are highly dependent upon an economy that at least rises above the subsistence level.

[20] Robert A. Dahl, *Polyarchy*, p. 74.

[21] Bruce M. Russett, *Trends in World Politics* (New York: Macmillan, 1965), p. 140.

[22] Ibid., p. 138. See this and the following pages for an excellent discussion of ten ways in which this assumed causal relation probably operates.

[23] Irma Adelman and Cynthia Taft Morris, "A Factor Analysis of the Interrelationship between Social and Political Variables and Per Capita Gross National Product," *Quar. Jour. of Econ.*, 79 (1965), 555-578. The indicators comprising this factor were as follows: strength of democratic institutions, freedom of political opposition and press, degree of factionalization of political parties, basis of the political party system, strength of the labor movement, political

CHART 3: Classification of Political Systems in Five
Stages of Economic Development (by percentage)

Political System	Stage of Economic Development				
	I	II	III	IV	V
Competitive	13	33	12	57	100
Semicompetitive	25	17	20	13	0
Authoritarian	63	50	68	30	0

SOURCE: Adapted from Russett, *Trends in World Politics*, p. 140.

quick to point out that they are not inferring a causal
sequence from their data. In fact, they believe both the
political and the economic developments might best be
explained by certain underlying forces that bring about
"a transformation of basic attitudes affecting the habits,
beliefs and emotions of the individual members of society."[24] This change in attitudes, they suggest, breaks
down traditionalism and ascriptive norms, thus opening
the way for both economic and political development.
However, another of their findings seems to cast doubt
upon, or at least to qualify, this argument: for the early
stages of development they find the political indicators are
relatively insignificant, becoming much more important as
social institutions become adaptable to the needs of economic growth.

Daniel Lerner, in a study of fifty-four countries, performed a multiple correlation with their indices of urbanization, literacy, media participation, and political participation. These items were found to be highly correlated,
the highest correlation coefficient (.91) going to literacy and
the lowest (.61) to urbanization, with media participation

strength of the military (negative-correlation), degree of administrative efficiency, and degree of centralization of political power (negative-correlation). Ibid., p. 562.

[24] Ibid., pp. 566-567.

and political participation registering .84 and .82, respectively.[25] He further found that literacy and urbanization begin to correlate quite directly after urbanization reaches about the 10 percent level and up to about the 25 percent level. After that, literacy continues to increase, regardless of urbanization. He hypothesizes that this minimum of urbanization provides the conditions for widespread participation.[26] Incidentally, it also makes the development of mass communication media economically feasible. This theory would account for the fact that urbanization scored lowest on his multiple-correlation test. What emerges is a theory that urbanization increases education, that education increases communication, and that communication increases political participation. That theory, with political participation defined as representative democracy, has been largely confirmed by another study using data drawn from American experience from the period 1781-1960.[27] Further confirmation is offered by McCrone and Cnudde.[28] On the basis of a statistical analysis of seven logically possible causal models relating the four variables, these authors conclude that the urbanization $\to$ education $\to$ mass communications $\to$ democracy model best fits the data.[29]

[25] Lerner, *The Passing of Traditional Society* (Glencoe, Ill.: Free Press, 1958), p. 63.

[26] Ibid., p. 60.

[27] Gilbert R. Winham, "Political Development and Lerner's Theory: Further Test of a Causal Model," *Amer. Polit. Sci. Rev.*, 64 (1970), 810-818. This study is particularly impressive because of the long time-span involved and its reliance upon data from only one country.

[28] Donald J. McCrone and Charles F. Cnudde, "Toward a Communications Theory of Democratic Political Development: A Causal Model," *Amer. Polit. Sci. Rev.*, 61 (1967), 72-80. And see Phillips Cutright, "National Political Development," pp. 253-264. For evidence tending to confirm the proposition that democracy ("democratic performance") depends on economic factors rather than the reverse, see Jackman, *Politics and Social Equality*, Chap. 4.

[29] Again, the results are obtained by the use of cross-national aggregate data. As a further qualification, it should be noted, the au-

226

It must be added, however, that another recent study suggests a contrary conclusion. Precisely what is argued, together with the author's qualifications, can best be put in his own words:

> . . . sufficient evidence has been presented to support the hypothesis that there is a general tendency for political stability, democratic performance, and modernization to vary positively, at least for the noncommunist nations during essentially normal conditions of political life. Finally, evidence has been advanced to call into question the assumption by some analysts that modernization tends to precede democracy in the course of political evolution. On the basis of the research reported in this paper, a contrary assumption would appear to be tenable.[30]

Two points about this study should be noted; the evidence for his first hypothesis, as the author recognizes, is stronger than for the second; moreover, while data cover a long time-span (nearly a century), they are of the cross-national aggregate variety.

If participation is to be representative rather than manipulated, if in other words it is to be democratic, it is of prime importance that the information sources and communications systems should be widely accessible and of various kinds, not all subject to control by the same interests.[31]

Clearly, both education and communication systems depend on a certain degree of prosperity, so it should be no surprise that very poor countries tend not to be demo-

---

thors point out they are compelled to assume that democracy is the dependent variable and that causation operates only in one direction.

[30] Arthur S. Banks, "Modernization and Political Change: The Latin American and American-European Nations," *Comp. Polit. Studies*, 2 (1970), 405-418, 417.

[31] Cf. David E. Apter, *The Politics of Modernization* (Chicago: University of Chicago Press, 1965) , p. 456.

cratic, as has been shown to be the case. It does not follow that once a stable democratic regime has been established its politics will be made more democratic by further affluence. But that of course is not the question. We are considering the conditions for establishing and maintaining democratic regimes.

Supporting and demanding education and mass communications are not the only ways an industrialized society provides a tremendously important, even if not essential, base for democracy. An industrial society, as contrasted with a primarily agrarian one, is more mobile, more flexible in its beliefs and attitudes, and more complex and varied in its associational and organizational patterns and structures. The mobility and flexibility, which it both requires and accentuates, spells death to traditionalism, at least in its extreme form. The varied competences, statuses, interests (both vocational and avocational), and life experiences of the members of an industrial society lead inevitably to a plurality of interest groups, both organized and unorganized, that is bound to weaken any monolithic power structure. By the same token, it will give rise to demands for broadly based participation in the political system, as many interests seek to make themselves felt, to bargain with each other for mutually satisfactory public policies.

Also a mobile, industrialized society tends to be a competitive society, one in which achievement rather than birth determines ranks and rewards. Moreover, rights and opportunities tend to become universalized—equal for persons of equal competence. That at least is the ideal. All of this is in accordance with the principle of an open society and is destructive of the ascriptive principle, which is completely counter to the democratic ethos.[32]

[32] For an interesting discussion of the ways in which the principle of openness may operate, see Lipset, *The First New Nation*, Chap. 6. He argues that the principle may be operative in the economy but not in the polity or vice versa, and that either situation makes for at

Reference was just made to "a mobile, industrialized society," with the implication that such a society provided a condition for democracy. Perhaps the stress in the preceding discussion should be more on mobility and less on industrialization, although the two tend to go together. "Social mobilization," that is to say the process by which individuals and groups are freed from old commitments and thus made available for new social arrangements, may be the most important single socioeconomic condition for democracy. Such is the impressively supported argument of a recent study.[33] It is doubtful, however, whether our measures of such processes as "social mobilization," "industrialization," and "liberal democracy" itself, are precise enough to establish priorities of influence among the several important socioeconomic factors.

Despite the whole general trend of analysis put forth in this section, it must be admitted that deviant cases do exist, which should not be surprising. Yet the obvious examples, Nazi Germany and the USSR, are less serious exceptions than might at first appear. Hitler's regime lasted for less than seven peacetime years. And the war that brought its end may well have been the price the regime paid for even that degree of success. The Communist regime in the Soviet Union established its powerful hold on the country long before industrialization had made great progress. Today the evidences of internal stress are numerous and experiments in various forms of decentralization

best an uncertain foundation for democracy. He finds that prewar France exemplified an open polity with a closed economy, while in prewar Germany just the opposite condition prevailed.

[33] Philip Coulter, *Social Mobilization and Liberal Democracy*, Chaps. 1-2. In this connection too, see Ronald Rogowski, *Rational Legitimacy* (Princeton: Princeton University Press, 1974). Rogowski argues that the ideal type of society most favorable to democracy is one in which the citizens are completely "interchangeable." Stable parliamentary regimes will, he contends, also characterize certain "mixed" types of society, where both factionalism (vertical) and segmentation (horizontal) are considerably eroded (thus allowing for substantial mobility).

or relaxation are common. Although at present the trend seems to be in a reversionary direction, few competent observers foresee a return to anything like the monolithic centralization of power that characterized the Stalin era.

The United States, where democracy preceded industrialization, might also be mentioned as an exception. But the United States had no feudal background, no entrenched landed aristocracy; and, with its Westward movement, it was a decidedly mobile society, and mobility, as was mentioned above, is one of the most significant effects of industrialization with respect to the development of democracy. The erstwhile British dominions of Australia, Canada, and New Zealand fall in the same general category.

Finally under the heading of the socioeconomic order, a few words about the distribution of wealth and income. It is important in this connection once more to distinguish between agrarian and industrial societies. While gross inequality always creates problems for democracy, it is much more serious in an agrarian than in an industrial society. Another of Russett's studies found that among the twenty-three countries in which the inequality of land distribution (measured by the Gini index) was below the median, thirteen were democracies and one (Finland) a near-democracy. Among the twenty-four countries above the median (greater inequality) on the other hand, only four could today claim to be "democratic."[34] The direct relation between equality of land distribution and democracy was strong.

Unfortunately, the same kind of calculation cannot be made for industrialized countries because nearly all of them are democratic; and in the case of exceptions, such as the USSR, information on income distribution is not available. Data of some interest and relevance are available, however. Among twenty countries for which Gini

[34] Bruce M. Russett, "Inequality and Instability: The Relation of Land Tenure to Politics," *World Politics*, 16 (1964), 442-454; see chart at 454.

indices for inequality of income distribution before taxes are available, seven that rank among the lowest ten in terms of inequality (least unequal) are among the top 10 percent among twenty-two nations in terms of per capita GNP. Only one nation that ranks low (ninth decile) in terms of GNP is high in terms of equality—the perennial deviant, India. The nine countries that score above the median for inequality include five that are below the median GNP ranking. (The twenty countries for which these data are available include 29 percent of the world's population.)[35] Higher per capita income seems to be accompanied by less inequality.

In short, great inequality of land distribution is a counterindication for democracy; considerable inequality in the distribution of income, such as prevails among the highly industrialized nations, is obviously not incompatible with the existence of stable democracy. The reasons for this difference appear to be as follows. In a landed economy where ownership is highly concentrated, wealth carries with it knowledge, status, and political power. In an industrial society, political resources, such as education, organizational skills, access to leaders, and the like, tend to be much more widely distributed.[36] In addition, it is perhaps of equal importance that in a landed society those at the top of the pyramid have interests in common and little to divide them. In a complex industrial society, on the contrary, interests are highly diversified. The extractors, processors, and fabricators of aluminum may have much more in common with their employees than they do with their competitors in the steel industry. Importers tend to be at odds with manufacturers, cotton farmers and processors with the makers of synthetic fibers and fabrics, and so on and so forth. An important political consequence, then, of the

[35] Bruce M. Russett and others, *World Handbook of Political and Social Indicators* (New Haven: Yale University Press, 1964), pp. 153-157 and 245.

[36] Dahl, *Polyarchy*, pp. 82-88.

231

situation just described is that a given degree of economic inequality does not produce the same sharp political alignment of haves and have-nots in an industrialized society that it does in a society where land is the chief form of wealth. To this should be added the fact that industrialized societies tend to have less inequality than agrarian societies, and also greater class mobility.

Further, industrialized societies are middle-class societies. Ever since Aristotle, theorists have been saying that regime stability, and especially the stability of a democratic regime, depends upon the existence of a large middle class, preferably large enough to counterbalance both rich and poor together, certainly large enough to maintain the balance of forces by throwing its weight with one side or the other. In part, Aristotle's theory was one of balance of power, as just suggested; in part, it was to the effect that a moderately well off class would be neither so envious and generally dissatisfied as the poor nor yet so ambitious and undisciplined, and hence unwilling to obey constituted authorities, as the rich.[37] Today this theory tends to be comprised within the larger theory just discussed. Industrialized societies develop a large middle class, however that rather vague term be defined. And both the reasoning set forth above and Aristotle's may be valid.

That both industrialization and economic growth tend to favor the development and the stability of democracy seems fairly clear, at least up to a point. But, as usual, the "other things being equal" qualification must be assumed. Otherwise, for instance, the Soviet Union might be advanced as an embarrassing deviant case, as was mentioned above. Where a new (not traditional) authoritarian regime has preceded and fostered the process of industrialization, it will thereby have gained a degree of legitimacy that may protect it against democratizing forces indefinitely. Another qualification: it also seems true that

[37] Aristotle, *Politics*, IV, xi.

very rapid economic growth, especially in a country still relatively low on the economic scale, causes dissatisfaction and discontinuities in the social structure that tend to be politically disruptive.[38]

The last comment suggests the following speculation. What is the effect on a democratic system if economic growth is drastically decelerated or even comes to a halt? Is continuing economic growth a requisite for democratic stability? We have little information bearing on this question. To be sure, all advanced industrial nations have suffered periods when growth slowed temporarily or ceased. Such a period was a very important factor in bringing the Weimar Republic to an untimely end. Other democratic regimes, including our own, have weathered such experiences. But I am thinking of a permanent change rather than one most people assume will be temporary and that in fact turns out to be so. Today we are becoming painfully aware of the fact that continued economic development may exhaust essential resources and destroy the environmental conditions for a good life. Or suppose the increasing problems of pollution and exhaustion of resources compel us to take steps that slow or stop economic growth. Then what? Clearly democracy would suffer severe strain. Change always involves strains. Vested interests are interfered with, or at least threatened. What we perhaps have hardly been aware of is the fact that while an economy is expanding, this very expansion greatly alleviates the pains which would otherwise attend change. While an economy is growing rapidly, it is always possible to accommodate new interests, to give increased power and material rewards to elements of society that have previously been excluded from these benefits without depriving anyone of what they are presently enjoying. In short, it has been a positive-sum

[38] H. H. Gerth and C. W. Mills, eds., *From Max Weber* (New York: Oxford University Press, 1946), pp. 193-194. See also Bert F. Hoselitz and Myron Weiner, "Economic Development and Political Stability in India," *Dissent*, 8 (1961), 172-179.

233

game; but as economic growth declines we approach a zero-sum game. The people who have been looking forward to the day when a rising standard of living would enable them to enjoy material comforts and luxuries they had heretofore been denied would find they could gain them only by taking them away from someone else. Or, more to the point, this fact would become evident to those who already enjoyed these benefits; if anything is worse than having dreams frustrated, it is to have present enjoyments taken away. Whether the have-nots were forced to remain have-nots or whether the haves were compelled to give up something of what they had would hardly influence the political effect. Either way, the strain upon the machinery of democracy and even more upon the democratic temper would be terrific.

This is not the place to indulge in wild speculations about the outcome of the potential struggle just outlined. It is pertinent, however, to indicate that the economic conditions of democracy carry with them pessimistic as well as optimistic overtones for democracy's future. We are accustomed to thinking of this subject in terms of states in the early stages of emergence from traditionalism or at least in the early stages of industrialism. But if we cast our eyes rather at the postindustrial society, the outlook is less favorable. It is easy for those who are now among the haves, or who at least have enjoyed lasting benefits from our material civilization, to say and doubtless believe we are about to experience a tidal shift in our value schemes, that future generations will bring us an abundance of men and women whose values can be satisfied without an ever-increasing output of material goods. Perhaps. But what about the great mass of people who have never been able to wallow in crass materialism? Will it seem so crass to them? Such speculations apart, the theorist has performed his role when he points out that economic growth has provided an important condition of democracy and has greatly eased our political growing pains, and that this fact raises important questions about the consequences for democracy if this condition were to be removed or substantially qualified.[39]

The discussion to this point, so far as it goes beyond mere correlations to causal relations, suggests that higher income is important for democracy because it is essential to improved education and communication, and because increasing absolute incomes relieve the strain caused by the relative losses inevitably incurred by many in any dynamic society. Two other nexuses exist. In countries where the struggle to secure a living is intense, mutual trust tends to be low. Except for the closest bonds of kinship, at least, trust is a luxury that can be indulged in only by those who can afford to lose some of their material goods. This reason-

[39] On socioeconomic conditions, I should refer also to the work of Deane Neubauer. On the basis of a study of twenty-three democratic nations, using a measure of "democraticness" that he devised, Neubauer found almost no correlation between this measure and the socioeconomic variables used by Lipset and others. His conclusion is that these variables constitute a "threshold effect," and that once the threshold has been reached and democracy has been established, a further improvement in those conditions has little effect in increasing the "democraticness." Although Neubauer's methodology (for example, the basis for selecting the twenty-three countries) and conclusions have been questioned, it is unnecessary to appraise his work here. As was remarked above, we are here concerned with conditions for the attainment and maintenance of democracy rather than with what favors its further development once it has been established. The latter question is certainly of considerable interest; but it is inherently difficult owing to the problem of obtaining agreement upon what constitutes an increase in "democraticness." See Deane E. Neubauer, "Some Conditions of Democracy," *Amer. Polit. Sci. Rev.*, 61 (1967), 1002-1009, and the interchange between Neubauer and Phillips Cutright, "National Political Development," *Amer. Polit. Sci. Rev.*, 62, (1968), 578-581. The threshold theory is further confirmed by Robert Jackman, *Politics and Social Equality*, pp. 66-73. Measuring democratic performance in sixty countries in terms of (1) the proportion of voting age adults who vote, (2) the competitiveness of the party-voting system, (3) a measure of electoral irregularity, and (4) a measure of freedom of the press, he concludes that the threshold hypothesis fits the data much more closely than does the idea of linear correlation.

ing appears to hold true even above the poverty line, at least for businessmen risking their capital.[40] As the struggle for survival relaxes, trust develops, and without mutual confidence a democratic system has little opportunity to develop.

The second nexus relates to the valuation of liberty. This key democratic ideal seems also to depend on a measure of economic development. Thus John Rawls argues that "as the conditions of civilization improve, the marginal significance for our good of further economic and social advantages diminishes relative to the interests of liberty. . . ."[41] An argument based upon findings of psychology reaches a similar conclusion.[42] Thus in these two additional ways economic development is causally related to more direct conditions of democracy.

4. THE POLITICAL CULTURE

a. General

From "historical" and "socioeconomic" conditions of democracy, we turn to a final rather vague and elastic category, "political culture." This concept includes a congeries of individual characteristics, values, attitudes, beliefs, myths, sentiments, and ideologies. It also, as will appear, includes features of the whole that relate to its form rather than to separate aspects of it. The present treatment must be highly abbreviated. The items that could properly be discussed are extremely numerous. They shade off gradually from those of most central importance as nearly necessary conditions (or absolute contraindications) for stable democracy, to those mildly favorable or unfavorable conditions at the periphery of the subject.

[40] On businessmen, see Sayre P. Schwartz and S. I. Edokpayi, "Economic Attitudes of Nigerian Businessmen," *Nigerian Jour. of Econ. and Soc. Studies*, 4 (1962), 257-268.

[41] John Rawls, *A Theory of Justice*, p. 542.

[42] I refer to the Maslow-Davis theory. See Chap. 4. n. 17.

It has already been remarked that the subject of conditions of democracy unavoidably includes more than one level of causation. Some conditions are properly thought of as such not because of their direct effects but because of their indirect effects. In other words, they may cause other conditions that are in turn requisite to or supportive of democracy. If we could always identify the causal paths and precisely evaluate their operation, we might treat the subject of conditions of democracy entirely in terms of immediate conditions, in which case political culture would bulk very large indeed; or we might deal with it in terms of the factors found to be (directly or indirectly) the causes of the democratically favorable and unfavorable aspects of political culture. In the latter case, we would have reduced political culture entirely to other factors. This kind of reductionism would be attractive if it turned out that in this way a large number of conditions could be reduced to a significantly smaller number—ideally to one. It should be apparent from the discussion up to this point that reductionism in this case does not hold out the promise of great simplification. In this connection, too, Robert Dahl has performed a great service. In the study already referred to, he faces this question directly. After studying numerous aspects of political culture that appear to be important requisites for stable democracy ("polyarchy," in his terminology), and after examining a number of concrete cases and the literature relating to them and to the subject generally, Dahl concludes that "at present and for an indefinite future no explanatory theory can account satisfactorily for the beliefs of political activists and leaders."[43] They must accordingly be treated as "major independent variables" by any theory that attempts to account for variations in regimes in different countries.

[43] Dahl, *Polyarchy*, p. 188. One of the cases which resists reductionism is that of Argentina, where he finds polyarchy has not succeeded in spite of the fact that the socioeconomic factors were as favorable as in other countries where it has succeeded. Ibid., pp. 132-140. Perhaps today the case of Chile would provide another example.

Thus far nothing has been said to relate theories of the conditions for democracy to the more general theories of democracy. What was said above about the ways in which industrialization provides support for democratic institutions does lend support for one of the power theories of democracy: namely, the social-pluralism theory. The motivational theories, however, have found little if any application or support in the discussion up to this point, simply because the historical and socioeconomic requisites do not embody values. It is among the cultural conditions of democracy, which comprise its *immediate* conditions, that we would expect to find values. And that indeed proves to be the case.

The term *political culture* might suggest a degree of homogeneity that would be neither realistic nor, from the political point of view, desirable. It is well known that in all democracies the levels of political attentiveness and activity vary tremendously. They range from the work of those whose full-time employment relates to the very highest levels of political activity (in the United States the president), constituting the apex of this pyramid, to the involvement of those at the other extreme who are completely apathetic, not participating in the political process, knowing little about it, and perhaps caring even less. Any attempt to draw lines between these extremes must be largely arbitrary. Nonetheless, it may be helpful to think in terms of various levels, such as "professionals," "activists," the "attentive public," the "vaguely interested," and the "apathetics."[44] Even this number of groupings is more elaborate than will be made use of in the following analysis.

Two points, however, should be made about levels of political awareness and activity. The first is that we must give our primary attention, for most purposes at least, to the upper levels. It is their beliefs, their attitudes, their

[44] Regarding the important role of attentive publics, see V. O. Key, Jr., *Public Opinion and American Democracy* (New York: Knopf, 1961), p. 546.

energy, that will be of fundamental importance. Edward Shils is typical of students of this subject in listing first among the preconditions of political democracy the stability, coherence, and effectiveness of the ruling elite.[45] I am speaking now not about a desirable state of affairs, a subject about which differences of opinion exist, but about facts. The fact is that most people have no clear and consistent set of political beliefs and do not care enough about politics in normal times to become actively involved (beyond voting, at least) and thereby have an important effect on its fate, whether the politics is democratic or not.

The second point, closely related to the first, is that different characteristics are important for different levels of the political culture. While the political beliefs of a large proportion of the population may not be very important, it may be exceedingly important whether or not the people speak the same language and whether they are sharply riven by ethnic divisions.

b. Dignity, Autonomy, and Respect for Persons

Let us begin by discussing certain characteristics of the individual and his beliefs. In view of what was said in Chapter Five about the close relation between democracy and the belief in human dignity and autonomy and the respect for persons, it should come as no surprise that a widespread commitment to these values is exceedingly important—perhaps essential—for a stable democracy. In fact this is saying, and little more, that if a democracy is to succeed, the people, especially the active and attentive

[45] Shils, *Political Development in the New States* (s'Gravenage: Mouton, 1962), pp. 52-60. The other preconditions he lists are (1) the practice and acceptance of opposition; (2) adequate machinery of authority; (3) institutions of public opinion (among which he includes trade unions and other voluntary organizations, and local governments); and (4) "the civil order"—a mixed bag, including a sense of nationality, interest in public affairs, the acceptance of the regime as legitimate, and a sense of personal dignity and rights, among other things.

239

members of the public, should believe in its principles.[46] If indeed "eternal vigilance is the price of liberty," one cannot expect that price to be paid by persons who care nothing about it. And if democracy's key value of liberty is not maintained, democracy will have ceased to exist. Edward Shils is worth quoting at some length on this point, even though in the following passage he is discussing political development generally rather than the conditions of democracy more specifically.

> At the very bottom of all the factors which are likely to determine prospective development in the political systems of the new states is the rudimentary state of individuality and of the consequently feeble feelings of individual dignity and worth within the polity. From this comes the insensitivity toward the rights of individuals, among both rulers and ruled. It is this deep-lying factor which makes for the frailty of public opinion, its reluctance to criticize authority, its unbridled abuse of authority, and the un-empirical, unfactual nature of its political criticism.[47]

c. Belief in Individual Rights

A strong sense of self, of personal autonomy, carries with it, as Alex Inkeles points out, a belief in individual, perhaps inalienable, rights. A sense of privacy too, a demand for areas of life that are sacrosanct, not to be touched by government, is an important component of the individ-

---

[46] What is important of course is that they should vote and otherwise act in accordance with these principles. I am assuming that people tend to act in accordance with their beliefs—their real beliefs, not necessarily their professed beliefs. To be sure, sometimes people may alter their beliefs to accord with their behavior, where the latter is controlled by some other force. See Leon Festinger, *A Theory of Cognitive Dissonance* (Evanston, Ill.: Row, Peterson, 1957).

[47] Shils, *Political Development in the New States*, p. 37. See also Alex Inkeles, "National Character and Modern Political Systems," in Francis L. K. Hsu, ed., *Psychology and Anthropology* (Homewood, Ill.: Dorsey Press, 1961), p. 195.

ualistic complex. An attitude of healthy skepticism toward authority is an outward-looking aspect of individualism that is also important. This is not to be confused with resistance to authority, with unwillingness to pay taxes, cooperate with the authorities, or otherwise obey the law and indeed to lend a hand in its support. Such attitudes as these are all-too-common characteristics of developing countries that seriously handicap their efforts at modernization, political and otherwise. I have in mind not an attitude that favors evasion or defiance of the law but rather one that encourages the individual to stand up for his rights when they are threatened by over-zealous bureaucrats, and that resists, by legal means, attempts to extend the authority of the state in ways which threaten privacy and individual autonomy. I cannot attempt here to define that line, much less to justify a particular definition of it. The main points, however, are these. Democracy needs citizens who respect the law and resist its abuse, whosoever rights are being abused. It also needs citizens with clear ideas of the proper limits of state authority (though these ideas may vary with time and circumstance) and readiness to do battle, at least by legal means, in support of these limits.

d. Trust, Tolerance, and Willingness to Compromise

Closely related to the beliefs, values, and attitudes just discussed is a group comprising trust, tolerance, and willingness to compromise. Any form of government, assuming it is to be legitimate, entails trust. That is part of what legitimacy means. In a democracy this trust must extend generally to the political activists. At the very least it must prevail *among* the political activists. The man in the street, the apathetic, may profess complete cynicism about government and all politicians. Democracy can tolerate a fair number of such people as long as theirs is a passive cynicism that does not lead them to take action or even to resist performing such civic duties as tax paying. But activists are another matter. Party leaders, and indeed the

241

whole party structure, must trust the other side. A competitive political system will not survive if either side believes the other is seeking to destroy it and will resort to any means to do so. Either the side in power will use the law to crush the opposition or the opposition will resort to illegal means, or both. Attitudes of this kind are likely to be widespread. That is to say, politicians are not likely to trust each other unless attitudes of trust prevail widely throughout the society. I mean simple trust between people, which seems to be a prerequisite of a successful democratic government, rather than their trust of government or politicians, which might be more the product of such a government. The former, however, seems less likely to originate in this way. What both common experience and knowledge of developing nations does suggest, however, is that poverty breeds thievery and distrust, while economic security makes for mutual trust.[48]

A willingness to compromise needs no definition. Its opposite is intransigence. Insofar as tolerance goes beyond the willingness to compromise, it refers to a willingness to accept beliefs and practices with which one is in sharp dis-

[48] The findings of Almond and Verba are interesting in this connection. The following question was put to respondents in five countries: "Some people say that most people can be trusted. Others say you can't be too careful in your dealings with people. How do you feel about it?" The percentages of respondents who said they believed most people could be trusted were as follows: United States, 55 percent; United Kingdom, 49 percent; Germany, 19 percent; Italy, 7 percent; Mexico, 30 percent. The most striking fact about these figures is probably that the two countries with the longest democratic history showed by all odds the highest "trust" scores. The differences among the other figures, especially the relatively high ranking of Mexico and Germany's low score are less easily explained. Even the argument about economic security and general trust is called into question by the Germany-Mexico contrast. However, the German anomaly, if that it be, almost disappears when only persons with some university education are considered. The figures for the respective countries then are: 19 percent, 29 percent, 58 percent, 48 percent, and 59 percent. Almond and Verba, *The Civic Culture*, pp. 267, 269.

agreement. It does not mean that a tolerant person must necessarily accept with equanimity the existence of beliefs and practices with which he is in sharp disagreement. He may indeed vigorously oppose them. But he must be willing to "live and let live," not seek to impose his way of life upon them. Recent events in Northern Ireland provide a striking, though extreme, example of the point. Further elaboration hardly seems necessary; nor is space available to speculate on the causes—religious, historical, economic, ideological, and otherwise—of widespread intransigent and intolerant attitudes.

That nations vary in this regard was brought home to me many years ago by an amusing incident in a graduate seminar of which I was then a member. The professor was discussing this very subject. He suggested that political differences in certain countries were much sharper and more antagonistic than they commonly are in Anglo-Saxon countries. Using a particular country as an example, he said it was common there, following an election, to change the names of streets that had been named after prominent leaders of the now-defeated party. A national of the country in question, who was a student in the group, took sharp and heated issue with the professor, who did his best to undo the damage he had done. The professor's efforts at pacification were to no avail, and his argument received striking reinforcement from the fact that this student never again attended the seminar.

e. Literacy and Education

Literacy, and education more generally, are of primary importance for democracy. Because they are so closely related to the socioeconomic structure, they were discussed above, where it was pointed out that literacy seemed to be more important as a foundation for democracy than were other aspects of modernization. It is not simply that education enables men to read and to comprehend the news, campaign literature, and the like. To an important extent

243

the radio and, where it is available, television diminish the importance of literacy. But education does much more than provide literacy and train people to comprehend the issues of politics and to be effective political leaders and members of the bureaucracy, although these things are of immeasurable importance. Fully as important in the case of developing nations is the fact that it helps to break down traditionalism, and to develop new attitudes and values, such as openness to new experience and willingness to participate in civic affairs.[49]

f. Commitment to Democratic Procedures and Values

Certain commitments on the part especially of the political elite (including important administrative and judicial officers) are of obvious importance. It seems safe to say that a commitment of the elite to democratic principles and procedures and a willingness to do all in their power to support the democratic regime is virtually a necessary condition for a stable democracy. It cannot be said to be a sufficient condition, but the case of India suggests it goes a considerable distance in that direction. As has been stated at various points in this chapter, India is frequently a deviant case. Relatively, it stands very low both in literacy and in GNP; yet its democratic record is far better than that of other countries with comparable GNP or comparable scores in terms of literacy or in terms of percentage of the population attending primary schools. (This statement stands even though democracy in that country was

[49] This statement is well documented by Alex Inkeles in reporting on a study based upon interviews with 6,000 people in six developing countries. He found education to be the most powerful factor in making men "modern," in which term he included the factors mentioned above. It is worthy of note that second only to education in this regard was occupational experience in large-scale organizations, especially factory work. "Making Modern Men: On the Causes and Consequences of Industrial Change in Six Developing Countries," *Amer. Jour. of Sociology*, 75 (1969), 208-225, esp. 208.

for a while eclipsed and is even now in a somewhat parlous state.) No other country with a functioning competitive political system even approaches it for low scores in these particulars. It is not a nation. It has serious linguistic barriers and religious differences. It did, it is true, enjoy a measure of constitutionalism before it became a democracy —but while it was under foreign rule. Observers seem to agree its record for a quarter of a century is primarily attributable to the education, the training, and the commitment to liberal democratic values that its leaders received at the hands of the British, in British universities, in schools and universities in India largely manned by Englishmen and governed by British traditions, a commitment also inculcated in the Indian Civil Service under English leadership.

Almost equally important is the case of Argentina. Dahl points out that one of the great weaknesses of the Argentinian efforts to maintain a democratic regime has been that the political elite has never been committed to democracy, as is demonstrated by their regular and massive use of force and fraud to prevent electoral results unfavorable to them.[50] In fact, the Argentine case provides a beautiful complement to that of India; for in the case of Argentina such conditions as urbanization, education, size of the middle class, and per capita income were as favorable as in many countries where democracy succeeded. The controlling difference seems to have been the lack of commitment to democracy by the political elite.

g. Public Spirit

Closely related to commitment to democratic procedures and, especially, values, is a commitment to the public welfare generally—what is often referred to as "public spirit." A priori, the value of this attribute for democracy seems clear, but hard evidence is difficult to find, partly because

[50] Dahl, *Polyarchy*, pp. 132-140.

of the difficulty in measuring it. Some interesting and relevant information was secured by Almond and Verba, however. When people were asked what leisure activities they preferred, charitable and welfare activities were named by 8 percent of the respondents in the United States, 5 percent in the United Kingdom, 2 percent each in Germany and Italy, and 1 percent in the least politically competitive country of the list, Mexico.[51] A rather similar pattern emerged when people were asked what quality they admired most. Generosity ranked highest in the democracies that have been the most stable in their adherence to democratic regimes.[52]

h. Nationalism

Any viable, legitimate polity, but especially a democratic one, needs to be held together in part by a basic loyalty, a commitment to something more evocative of emotion, more warming to the cockles of the heart than a set of procedures, and probably even more powerful than the democratic values of liberty and equality. In the modern world that glue, that political cement, is the sentiment of nationalism. As a leading student of the subject has remarked:

> The rise of democracy as a political phenomenon has coincided too closely with the emergence of nations as conscious entities to be explained in terms of random chance. The lines of interconnection between the two are many. The most evident is . . . the fact that nationalism is one of the major manifestations of the modern social ferment which overturns traditional social relationships and gives

[51] Almond and Verba, *The Civic Culture*, p. 263. The percentages naming civic-political activities, by country in the same order, were as follows: 2, 2, 3, 1, and 0.

[52] Using the same order, the percentages were as follows: 59, 65, 42, 25, and 36. When respondents with some university education are segregated from the rest, the percentages are: 80, 83, 85, 39, and 34. Ibid., p. 265.

new consequence to formerly submerged elements of society.[53]

Nationalism performs two functions in this connection: it unites people to the state[54] and it unites them to each other. In each case it supports the public interest as against private interest and tends to sustain loyalty in those instances and for those periods where public policy seems to go seriously contrary to individual interest. Needless to say this is an invaluable service.

But this should not diminish the importance of a plurality of associations. While nationalism is almost wholly a sentiment, and the national group is normally not organized as such, although it may be coterminous with the state, smaller groups not only have their own loyalties, which move men part of the way from particularistic self-interest toward concern for the whole, but also are organized and may conduct activities that foster thought about the basis in interest for supporting the whole.[55]

i. Consensus and Cleavage

A sentiment of nationalism, or something closely akin to it, may come close to being a necessary condition for both statehood and democracy, but it is not a sufficient condition, even within the complex of political culture, to constitute a requisite for democracy. In search of sufficient conditions, we must move on to concepts with more intellectual content, such as "consensus" and "agreement on fundamentals." Such terms as these are constantly recurring in

[53] Rupert Emerson, "Nationalism and Political Development," *Jour. of Politics*, 22 (1960), 3-28.

[54] I am assuming we are dealing with a nation-state or, if it is a multinational state, that a state-wide nationalism overrides that of the constituent nations.

[55] For a sensitive and enlightening discussion of the relations between national identity and self-respect (itself of key importance to democracy), each contributing to the other, see Lucian Pye, *Personality and Nation Building* (New Haven: Yale University Press, 1962).

the literature. In discussing commitment to democratic ideals and precedures, I have already given some attention to this subject, especially as it relates to the political elite. A few further remarks are in order. The relation between consensus and stable democracy has been the subject of study by numerous investigators in recent years. While their findings are not always completely in accord, the agreements are much greater than the disagreements. These studies have been well summarized and compared with each other in a book by Ian Budge, the bulk of which is devoted to his own very substantial monograph on this subject and based upon field research in Great Britain.[56] After summarizing evidence indicating that democratic beliefs and opinions are capable of influencing behavior, he notes that "all empirical research points to the conclusion that agreements on democratic procedures do differ in their extent and content (and by implication, in their intensity) between the members of strata distinguished on the basis of education, income and political activity."[57] In summarizing his own research findings, he concludes that both politicians and politically oriented citizens in Britain are highly agreed on both abstract and procedural democratic norms, and that the politically uninterested citizens agree highly on the more abstrast norms of democratic behavior and somewhat less than the politically oriented citizens on the application of these norms. On substantive issues agreement is much less, and the lineups between the activists and the apathetics vary widely. It is significant to note, however, that disagreements on such matters, among both groups, are seldom of the zero-sum variety. Finally, Budge concludes, "the system works in normal times because politicians are strongly attached to both specific and abstract ideas, see established institutions and procedures as putting

---

[56] *Agreement and the Stability of Democracy* (Chicago: Markham Publishing Co., 1970).

[57] Ibid., pp. 18ff. The quotation is at page 22.

these ideals into practice, and have few political goals which are completely blocked under present procedures. . . ."[58]

All this of course falls short of proof that any specific amount of agreement on these matters is either a necessary or a sufficient condition of stable democracy. It does, however, give strong support to the proposition that the attitudes and beliefs of the politicians and secondarily of the attentive public are by all odds the most important.

Vagueness in this area arises not only from the fact that it is impossible to specify the amount, kind, and distribution of consensus necessary for stable democracy, but also from the fact that too much consensus, it is widely argued, becomes an *un*favorable factor. Thus it is widely held that a stable democracy requires a proper balance between consensus and cleavage.[59] This proposition has been criticized from at least two points of view. In the first place, it is argued that the formulation is so vague as to be virtually meaningless. It is indeed ill-defined. All it does is alert us to the fact (or the alleged fact) that consensus beyond a certain point is harmful to democracy and cleavage beyond a certain point is likewise injurious. If these propositions are sound, however, they are of some interest, although certainly their value is limited owing to the fact that the proper balance between consensus and cleavage cannot be accurately specified, and probably could not be even if con-

[58] Ibid., p. 176. A similar point is made, with supporting data and argument, in a study by G. Lowell Field and John Higley, "Elites and Non-Elites: The Possibilities and Their Side Effects," Module 13, Warner Modular Publications (Andover, Mass., 1973), 1-38. Stressing the importance for democracy of an elite unified not by ideology but by a tradition of political contest, an "agreement to disagree," they further argue that such an elite, once established, is "reliably self-perpetuating" for at least a generation. Ibid., p. 15.

[59] See, for example, Bernard Berelson, Paul F. Lazarsfeld, and William N. McPhee, *Voting* (Chicago: University of Chicago Press, 1954), Chap. 14. For an attempt to prepare the way for the measurement of political cleavages, see Douglas W. Rae and Michael Taylor, *The Analysis of Political Cleavages*.

sensus and cleavage could be precisely measured. A theory is not to be condemned for being only a little bit helpful unless the critic has a more helpful theory to substitute for it.

The second criticism goes more to the heart of the matter. It questions the need for cleavage. If agreement prevails, why arouse sleeping dogs? Just because it is the government's job to reconcile conflicts, it does not follow that the absence of conflicts is a bad thing. The difficulties with this argument are two: it assumes that the absence of conflicts means the absence of problems; and it overlooks the whole developmental argument, the benefits to the voter of being alerted to problems, being sensitive to their implications, and being forced to think about them. Dankwart Rustow, stating this point and somewhat more, puts it this way: "Only by means of dissension can democracy become a learning and a problem-solving process, a way of finding proximate solutions to insoluble questions. Only through continual expression of disagreement by sharply rivalling groups can political participation be maximized and political equality thus approximated. Agreement and consensus can only be the end-product, not the prerequisite, of the democratic political process. . . ."[60]

Yet about both cleavage and consensus something more must be said. First, while they may be good, especially where they are cross-cutting,[61] dominant and deep cultural cleav-

[60] Rustow, *A World of Nations*, p. 234.

[61] A cross-cutting cleavage is one which divides a society along a line that is different from another cleavage in the society. Instead of reinforcing one another, such cleavages tend to ameliorate divisiveness. For instance, if all White Anglo-Saxon Protestants (WASPS) in a given society are well-to-do, and all non-WASPS are poor, divisiveness may reach the danger point. If half the WASPS are poor and half the non-WASPS are well-to-do, so that the rich-poor cleavage cuts across the WASP/non-WASP cleavage, most people will be sufficiently cross-pressured that the intensity of political conflict will not threaten the society. For a formal proof of both points, see Robert E. Goodin, "Cross-Cutting Cleavages and Social Conflict," *Brit. Jour. of Polit. Sci.*, 5 (1975), 516-519.

ages may make democracy unworkable. The difficulties posed for democracy by divisions along ethnic, religious, and racial lines are amply illustrated today by the experiences of Canada and Belgium, Nigeria and Northern Ireland, not to mention Great Britain itself. It is interesting that in each of these cases ethnic and religious differences tend to coincide with economic differences. With the drive for greater equality in most of the world today, this situation aggravates latent conflict between culturally disparate groups. What Dahl calls "subcultural pluralism," then, must be put down as a decidedly negative factor in our listing of the conditions for a stable democracy.[62]

Nor can ethnic diversity be lightly dismissed as bound to give way to "nation-building," yielding to the impact of improved communications. The fact of the matter is, as we see on all sides, even in the most "developed" countries, ethnicity is on the rise. Improved communications serve to encourage ethnic political consciousness rather than the reverse. A perceptive observer has put it in the following words:

> Quite aside from the question of who rules, there is the matter of cultural self-preservation. An unintegrated state poses no serious threat to the life-ways of the various ethnic groups. But improvements in the quality and quantity of communication and transportation media

[62] See Dahl, *Polyarchy*, Chap. 7. He argues that certain democratic political institutions cope more effectively with subcultural pluralism than others. In particular, he finds the evidence favors a strong executive and a two-party system or some variant thereof, such as the Swiss system, where all political parties are represented in the executive. Two other scholars believe that "the resolution of intense but conflicting preferences [are not] manageable in a democratic framework." They consider the case of Switzerland as a "persistent counter-example" and conclude that its success depends upon its tradition of cantonal independence long preceding the federation and upon the great need for unity for self-defence in its situation. Alvin Rabushka and Kenneth A. Shepsle, *Politics in Plural Societies* (Columbus, O.: Merrill, 1972), p. 217 (for the first quotation) and pp. 208-211.

251

progressively curtail the cultural isolation in which an ethnic group could formerly cloak its cultural chasteness from the perverting influences of other cultures within the same state. The reaction to such curtailment is very apt to be one of xenophobic hostility.[63]

It is not only ethnic or cultural pluralism, as the examples just mentioned might suggest, that lead to unworkable cleavages. In a longitudinal study of twenty-six countries, Richard A. Pride has found that most democracies are short-lived, that they are so because of deep and irreconcilable social cleavages, generally dating from the mobilization phase of development.[64]

In stating the importance of some (but not too much) cleavage, the finger has already been pointed at a second kind of cleavage also a counter-indication for democracy. Paradoxically, it is "communalism." By communalism is meant the existence throughout a society of tightly knit territorial groups sharing a common culture and including members of all ages and classes. In African new states in particular the extent and toughness of these groups presents a formidable barrier to social mobilization, to nation-building, and hence to democracy. To a certain extent a similar phenomenon may be observed among several Asiatic countries.[65]

The existence in numerous countries of these counter-indications for the successful establishment of democratic regimes serves as a dual warning: a warning that the conditions for democracy are complex indeed and that simple statements of them are surely wrong, and also a warning that not only may democracy be very slow in coming in

[63] Walker Connor, "Nation-Building or Nation-Destroying?", *World Politics*, 24 (1972), 319-355, 329. The whole article is of interest for the subject here under discussion.

[64] Pride, *Origins of Democracy* (Beverly Hills, Cal.: Sage Publications, 1970), p. 744.

[65] On all of this see Coulter, *Social Mobilization and Liberal Democracy*, Chaps. 7-8.

Still another approach to the subject under discussion, like Huntington's focusing on the stability of democratic governments, is that of Harry Eckstein. It is different from any of the analyses discussed up to this point, including Huntington's, in that it takes the whole culture, or at least a major portion of it, as its unit of analysis rather than a more specific aspect of the culture. Moreover, it relates to form rather than substance and, most ambitiously stated, it would not be considered as an added item to those already discussed; rather it would aspire to replace them. Although it is an exceedingly complex and subtle theory, I shall attempt to capsulize it, recognizing that such an attempt can at best achieve only partial success. Broadly and crudely stated, Eckstein contends that a stable and effective democracy depends upon the congruence of authority patterns throughout all or most of the society. By "authority patterns" he means the institutionalized relations between elites and masses, which may be democratic, authoritarian, or constitutionalist. Such patterns appear not only in government but also in political parties, pressure groups, business organizations, voluntary organizations, clubs, the family, schools, and so forth. "Congruence" may mean identity or near-identity, or it may mean some "fitting" or dovetailing, such that an institution gives support to a democratic political regime even though it is not precisely democratic itself. Moreover, the closer to government an institution is (e.g. political parties) the closer should be the resemblance, while an institution such as the school or the family, dealing with relations between adults and children, would not need or be expected to correspond so closely.[67]

[67] The original statement of Eckstein's theory, published in 1961 as a research monograph, is reprinted as Appendix B of his *Division and Cohesion in Democracy* (Princeton: Princeton University Press, 1966). This book is designed as a test for the theory, which, in large measure, he finds confirmed. He summarizes his theory in the following words: "Government will be stable (1) if social authority patterns are identical with the governmental pattern, or (2) if they constitute a graduated pattern in a proper segmentation of society, or (3) if a high degree

The theory recognizes the point made earlier in this chapter about various conditions of democracy being to a considerable degree mutually substitutable. Thus a diffuse social deference in England may play the role of greater reliance on legalistic norms in the more egalitarian society of Norway.[68]

Eckstein, and especially his study of the Norwegian system, gives support to the importance of a balance between consensus and cleavage (or "cohesion and division," as he puts it). Going beyond this theory, he makes it somewhat more specific, while maintaining his position that it is form rather than substance which counts, by distinguishing three types of balance. "Consensus" systems are those, like the system of Great Britain, where the degree of division is low. The American system, which depends upon a high degree of overlapping of memberships and cross-cutting cleavages, he calls "mechanically integrated." Finally, a system may be characterized by numerous and quite deep divisions and yet also manifest an overarching attitude of solidarity, a feeling of community, such as he found to be the case in Norway. Thus, in his words, "the forms as such seem to be far more important than the specific attitudes, actions, and structures that constitute them."[69]

5. CONCLUSION

For the most part, the chapter has dealt with conditions, without regard for the question of whether they must precede the establishment of democracy if it is to be stable and without the specification that they were necessary conditions. Nonetheless, much of the discussion, like most of

---

of resemblance exists in patterns adjacent to government and one finds throughout the more distant segments a marked departure from functionally appropriate patterns for the sake of imitating the governmental pattern or extensive imitation of the governmental pattern in ritual practices." Ibid., pp. 239-240.

[68] Ibid., p. 190.   [69] Ibid., p. 197.

the relevant literature, has largely proceeded as though once the conditions for democracy had been secured, all would be well. It is not necessarily so, as was pointed out immediately above. A key condition may be lost—as was already suggested in the discussion of the implications of a contracting economy, as well as in that of ethnicity. This or other developments may call the legitimacy of democratic institutions into question and ultimately lead to their decay. The combination of subcultural pluralism with a rising demand for equality may have the same effect. Even without subcultural pluralism a radical egalitarianism that downgraded liberty might undermine support for democracy, and likewise with liberty unchecked by any regard for quality.

It is worth asking whether any of the items discussed in this chapter constitute necessary or sufficient conditions for democracy. I believe it is clear none is a necessary *and* sufficient condition. Nor do I believe any one or two could be said to be sufficient conditions. "Necessary" is another matter. Several conditions seem to come close to deserving that designation, if they do not in fact do so. One reason it is difficult to speak with more assurance about this point is that the items under discussion are necessarily vague. It is impossible to specify, for example, just *how much* individual dignity and autonomy is possessed by any particular person, much less by the average person in a state. Still more, it is impossible to specify how much is requisite, and likewise with most of the other items that have been discussed, especially those under the heading of "political culture." Yet it is precisely under this heading that the most likely candidates for "necessary" conditions are to be found. I would go further and hazard the opinion that none of the items discussed under the headings of "history" or "socioeconomic condition" qualifies as necessary, while asserting that most of those discussed under "political culture" at least come close to meriting that designation. Clearly subcultural pluralism (absence of) cannot so qualify. But one would be hard put to find any of the others about which one could say that a stable democracy might reasonably be expected even in its complete absence.

In short, nearly all the elements of political culture, in significant degree and especially for the political activists in a polity, may be said to be necessary conditions for democracy. Furthermore, this group may well comprise a sufficient condition for democracy. Whether these conditions can obtain without the presence of a goodly number of the historical and socioeconomic conditions is at least sufficiently doubtful to justify our discussion of those conditions.

What light does this consideration of the conditions of democracy cast upon the general theories of democracy discussed in the preceding chapter? It has already been noted that the importance of social mobilization and its usual concomitants (industrialization, urbanization, communication, and education) as conditions for democracy supports the theory of social pluralism.[70] The special importance of the beliefs and values of the elite hardly supports populism, but rather the contrary. In fact, it might appear at first glance to give support to elitist theories. It should be noted, however, that the elites important for political development need not be homogeneous. In fact, a social-pluralistic society with each organized or unorganized special group characterized by elites is likely to provide more opportunity for effective political leadership by those with special qualifications in this direction than is a less heterogeneous society. Finally, it would appear that the importance of individuals who are conscious of their rights and willing to stand up and struggle for them against actual or threatened tyranny gives support to the theory of constitutionalism, which is entirely compatible with social pluralism. This conclusion is reinforced by the fact that the most stable democracies are those in which constitutionalism was firmly established before democracy was highly developed. Yet, as Eckstein's

[70] Not just any pluralism will do. The theory calls for groups that are at once permeable and nonexclusive.

257

argument in particular makes clear, the importance of a highly institutionalized polity will depend upon the nature of the social structure. Examination of the conditions of democracy, then, appears to give its major support to the power theories that value the dispersion, by one means or another, of political power rather than its concentration.

Turning to the motivational theories, it appears that some propositions to which the findings in this chapter give support call for qualification of the theories in this classification. Thus the need for some unifying force above and beyond rational self-interest calls for a qualification of the assumptions underlying radical individualism.[71] The importance of individual autonomy is incompatible with an extreme version of collectivism, although probably not with what democratic collectivists would affirm. The need for some cleavage of interests and opinions and for the social pluralism that is perhaps the same thing looked at from a different perspective would also require qualification of collectivist theory. The collectivity and its values must not dominate at the expense of all else. At the same time, under this heading, both the need for trust and willingness to compromise and the need for public spirit constitute at least additions to the assumptions relied upon by the more extreme forms of individualism.

Finally, further clarification may be secured by approaching the question from the other end, beginning with the types of democratic theory and asking what assumptions about conditions of democracy each of them would tend to make. The individualist clearly would assume the importance of individual autonomy, of intelligence, and of education. He would probably also stress the importance of industrialization, because of its encouragement of a secular,

[71] It is true that some radical individualists recognize this need, but in doing so they qualify their theory. It is true also that insofar as their theory is predictive, it is possible this qualification would not greatly alter their predictions—or that their predictions would prove reasonably accurate even without qualifying their assumptions. That is probably what Buchanan and Tullock would contend.

258

rationalistic approach to life. The public-interest theorist would also see education and rationality as essential for calculating the public interest. He would be distinguished from the individualist, however, by the emphasis he would place upon consensus and "public-spiritedness." When we come to the rights and duties theorist, we have to make a distinction between elite and masses, between the political activists and those who assume a more passive role. The political activist would stress the commitment to democratic values and, especially, procedures. By the same token, he would be quick to see the virtue of attaining liberalism or constitutionalism before full-fledged democracy. With respect to the more politically passive part of the population, he would emphasize commitment to an ethical code.[72] Finally, the collectivist would stress the need for a powerful unifying sentiment, such as nationalism, and also, perhaps more than the others, see the great importance of communications, as a vital means for developing community. Trust, tolerance, willingness to compromise, and public spirit would also be high on his list.

Putting the two approaches together, clearly no one of the motivational theories, except for the most extreme versions of individualism and collectivism, is rendered unsupportable or implausible by the facts adduced in this chapter. On the contrary, each of them receives considerable support, suggesting that the theories are more complementary than mutually antagonistic.

[72] The significance of the distinction between elite and mass might be recognized by theorists of all four motivational types, but the points that distinguish the rights and duties theories especially call for this distinction.

259

CHAPTER VII

Responsiveness and Responsibility

DEMOCRACY, it has been argued, is roughly "the multitude's rule," organized in accordance with the principles of liberty and equality. In this and the succeeding chapters we turn to the practical linkage between rule by "the multitude," i.e. the electorate, and the democratic ideals of liberty and equality together with the generally recognized purposes of government—order, security, justice, and welfare. Obviously, the details of such a vast subject cannot be discussed here, nor the myriad problems they involve. What will be attempted is to define and analyze the crucial concepts; to relate the most general problems their analysis reveals to relevant empirical materials; and to make use of motivational and power types of democratic theory both to systematize and to illuminate the issues discussed. In some cases, too, the analysis of problems and review of empirical materials will bear upon the validity or plausibility of some of the various theories.

The present chapter will be devoted to the concepts of "responsiveness" and "responsibility," and to the closely related institution of political parties. These two concepts are perhaps the most crucial for democratic theory, bringing together as they do the problems of securing expression of desire and rational action. In fact, once more we note a tension in democratic theory, one suggested by the power theories and especially the first two of them: elitism and populism. Like other tensions in democratic theory, this one reflects a tension inherent in man himself: that between desire and interest; between having one's way and having what is good for one; or sometimes simply between short-run and long-run interest.

260

1. RESPONSIVENESS

The term *responsiveness* is widely used in contemporary discussions of democracy, especially in criticisms of democracy's operation. Democracies are frequently criticized, indeed attacked, for not being sufficiently responsive. Just what the term means, however, is often left for the reader to decide. Here again where we should have clear concepts to conduct scientific and theoretical analysis, we often confront terms whose unexplored ambiguities constitute standing solicitations to fallacy—solicitations, one may add, that receive a bountiful response. At least in part, disagreements among those who theorize about democracy may be attributable to this fact.

The word *responsive* has to do with responding or answering. One dictionary defines it as "reacting easily or readily to suggestion or appeal." Responsiveness might be said to be the counterpart of influence. The person or group that exerts influence is influential; the person or group on whom it is exerted is responsive. In government, this is largely what democracy is all about. A democratic government should respond to, reflect and give expression to, the will of the people. How else can democracy, in the terms of our original definition (see Chapter One) be "rule by the people"? Yet phrases like "the people" and "the will of the people" are slippery at best.[1] Saying instead "public opinion" does not avoid the basic difficulty that often there are many wills, many opinions (and many "no opinions"), but neither a consensus nor even a majority.[2] Under such cir-

[1] At least until recently, this fact was sufficiently recognized that these terms had been largely eliminated from the vocabulary of serious political scientists. Today, however, they are rife in the rhetoric of controversialists and even seem to be creeping back into the language of scholars.

[2] For instance, reports on ten opinion polls on capital punishment in the United States taken between 1950 and 1973 showed that in six of them "no opinions" or "not sures" held the balance of power between the pros and the cons. Data from *The Public Opinion Quarterly*, 34 (1970), 290ff; *The Gallup Poll—Public Opinion, 1935-1971* (New

cumstances (which are probably more prevalent than their contrary on important issues requiring governmental decision), the primary meaning of responsiveness has no applicability.

The problem is more complicated than has yet been indicated. It is not only that wills or demands, even when they exist and are known, are often splintered, so that no majority supports any one proposal; but also, popular demands may conflict with each other. The same people may demand lower taxes and increased benefits or services entailing increased expenditures. Or, two pressures (demands), while being in the strictest sense compatible with each other, may lead to mutually self-defeating results. (Perhaps the government that yields to both rather than neither of these pressures would be generally considered the more responsive; but would it be more desirable? This question raises an important issue to which attention will be given in a moment.)

Moreover, another problem should be noted. Demands, desires, may vary greatly in their intensity. Is the responsive government simply to *count* demands, or should it somehow measure their strength? And how should it respond to a situation in which 35 percent of the electorate strongly favor a certain proposal, 55 percent mildly oppose it, and the remaining 10 percent are indifferent? The definition of responsiveness provides no answer.

Meanwhile other difficulties present themselves when one begins to think in detail of applying the test of responsiveness. To whom should government be responsive? To the majority of "the people"? Apart from the fact that on most issues no such majority exists, if we are speaking of representative government, as for practical purposes we must be, this question raises issues regarding the role of the repre-

York: Random House, 1972); *The Gallup Opinion Index*, March 1973, Report No. 93, p. 15; and *Current Opinion* (Roper Public Opinion Research Center, Williams College, Williamstown, Mass.) 1, Issue 8, August 1973.

sentative. These issues will be discussed more fully in the following chapter, but it may be pointed out here that for reasons already mentioned regarding the "will of the people," any representative system will be imperfectly representative at best. Whether or not it is desirable that a majority of the electorate have its "way," as the populist theory of democracy holds, no good reason appears for insisting that a bare majority (which is what maximum "responsiveness" suggests) of elected *representatives* should always be able to enact *their* wishes, even though no popular or majority will may exist. This conclusion is further reinforced when one considers that on any particular question the representatives may not even reflect the views of a plurality of those who have an opinion on the matter.

Two other complications arise for anyone who would hold that democracy's task is simply to be responsive to popular wants and demands. Government itself in no small measure creates and shapes our wants. Not only does the president, in ways made famous by FDR's fireside chats, use the media to persuade the public as to what they *should* want, but all kinds of governmental agencies, at all levels of government, consider it part of their function to alert citizens to what they believe the citizens' interests to be, whether it is a matter of new legislation to protect the environment or a question of appropriations for agricultural research. Moreover, it appears that even apart from any conscious governmental policy to influence opinion, in fact public opinion often changes to accord with existing public policy.[3] It would be highly unrealistic to think that government acts simply in response to wants and demands. And it would be circular to contend it *should* be responsive to demands that it may itself have engendered (although of course it might be that for other reasons it should pursue the policies represented by those demands).

[3] See William R. Shaffer and Ronald E. Weber, "Political Responsiveness in the American States," paper delivered at the Annual Meeting of the American Political Science Association, Washington, D.C., 5-9 Sept. 1972.

263

Not only are wants often shaped or even created by government, but also they may call for the impossible. Moreover, they may be satisfied by something other than what is "wanted." In part they may be satisfied by their very expression. Thus we hear much today of "expressive" demands. Further, government may take action that is more symbolic than effective and that is yet satisfying by giving expression to demands and by providing reassurance. Thus, as one writer puts it, "responsiveness to the will of the people means rather less than meets the eye."[4] In a sense, to be sure, this kind of action is responsive to demand, but in a subtle and sophisticated way.

Perhaps partly because of the difficulties just described, but probably even more because of the one alluded to above —that in certain situations responsiveness may not be desirable, or may not be the *most* desirable thing—people often find themselves talking about "responsiveness to need." Now responsiveness to need is a perfectly good concept, the meaning of which needs no explication. In a general way, it is obvious; yet as with demands, the questions of intensity and of *whose* need immediately rise to plague us. The point here, however, is to insist that it must be sharply distinguished—as it frequently is not—from responsiveness to demands, wants, or preferences. Should democracy give the people what they want, or should it give them what, in the judgment of their elected representatives and other officials, is good for them? Wherever what the people want can be ascertained and is found to vary from what the government thinks should be done, we are faced with a serious dilemma. No attempt will be made to resolve that dilemma in this chapter; but it is important to recognize the existence of tension between demand and need. In fact,

---

[4] Murray Edelman, "The State as Provider of Symbolic Outputs," International Political Science Association, IXth World Cong., 19-25 Aug. 1973, nr. I, 3, 11, p. 1 (mimeographed). Further on this subject, see the same author's *The Symbolic Uses of Politics* (Urbana, Ill.: University of Illinois Press, 1964).

264

the phrase "responsive to need" is so likely to mislead that it is often better to use another term, such as "responsible," to avoid confusion. The latter term, however, does include more than the idea of responsiveness to need, so that the latter phrase will sometimes be used; but "responsive" will never be used alone to mean "responsive to need." Its association with the democratic ideal of responsiveness to public opinion, will, or demand is so strong that this connotation will be assumed unless other phraseology makes it obvious that a different meaning is intended.

Enough has been said to show that "responsiveness" is vague and ambiguous and that tensions exist among its alternate meanings and applications. Now what are the implications of this finding for democratic theory? With respect to power theories, the only relevant observation is the obvious one, that populist theory, and it alone among these theories, places primary, indeed almost sole, emphasis on responsiveness as the test for democraticness. The populist, that is to say, has complete faith in the ability and proclivity of the individual to protect and advance his own and society's interest with the minimum of reliance upon deference, political institutions, or social structure to "refine" the popular will. This points to the conclusion that the populist theory is subject to inherent difficulties and also, insofar as the theory is capable of application, that the desirability of its use as the sole principle of democracy is open to serious question.

As to the motivational types of democratic theory, no one of the four is committed to the idea of responsiveness as the sole test of how a democratic government should operate. With regard to collectivist democratic theories, this proposition hardly needs demonstration. However collectivists may define the good of the collectivity, it is certainly not some sort of summation of individual desires, for that is precisely what they are seeking to avoid. As for the deontological, or rights and duties, theory almost the same thing may be said. "Duty" implies potential opposition to "de-

265

sire." Likewise the theory of the public interest distinguishes "interest" from "desire" (although of course they may, and perhaps more often than not do, coincide). Individualism, especially radical individualism, comes closest to embracing the ideal of responsiveness as the sole test of good government, for it insists that the role of a democratic government should be to respond to individual preferences. In fact, if the radical individualist is held strictly to the assumption of individual rationality, including perfect information and accurate calculation, he would appear to be committed to this test. In the interest of saving the time required to obtain all the relevant information and make the necessary calculations, he might wish to delegate considerable responsibility, thus leading him to create institutions that might not be perfectly responsive to his desires. But their responsiveness would remain the test by which he judged their performance. If, however, the radical individualist, as rational constitution maker, recognized human fallibility and the consequent desirability of distinguishing between long-run and short-run judgments, he might then arrange institutions (and constitutions) in such a way that responsiveness to desires is postponed. So it might be also if he recognized that a person's desires may change over time, or that they may even change as the result of the actions of government itself.

In other words, if responsiveness is used as the chief test of democraticness, whichever one of the sets of motivational assumptions we make, we may arrive at substantially the same result, although least clearly so in the case of radical individualism.

2. RESPONSIBILITY—MEANINGS

"Responsibility" has long been a favorite of political scientists, both for describing certain phenomena and for appraising the operation of political institutions. It is, moreover, closely related to "responsiveness." It has at least two quite separate and distinct meanings. In the first place, responsibility means accountability, in the sense of answerability. Clearly here the relation to responsiveness is close. A person is responsible to another for his actions when that other person can hold him to account for them. A government is responsible when its tenure of office is subject to control, within limits, by the electorate. Similarly a ministry that holds power at the pleasure of the legislature is said to be responsible to the legislature. By way of extending this meaning, where a government comprises many elective officers, and especially where its functions are divided among several elective organs, responsibility is frequently said to involve the identifiability of particular individuals or groups who are the effective causes of the government's actions. In other words, it is maintained that under such circumstances it does not suffice for the government as a whole to be accountable to the electorate; but rather the voters should be able to identify the responsible authorities and hold them accountable as a group for their deeds and misdeeds.

Responsibility also has a second meaning. Indeed, one can easily distinguish at least two or three meanings besides accountability. However, these meanings are so closely associated with each other in common usage that they will be treated here as a single complex of ideas. Rationality and morality are the keys to this second meaning of responsibility. A person's conduct is responsible if it is conditioned upon deliberation and sound reasoning based upon the relevant facts and upon consideration of, and due regard for, the consequences. A person, or a legislative body, that acts impulsively and without consideration of the bearing of his or its acts is said to be irresponsible. Likewise the attitude of *"après moi le déluge."* Responsibility implies rationality, honesty, attention to duty, concern for the rights and welfare of others, and for the public interest.

Responsibility in this second sense is closely related to

267

rationality, and no one would be likely to deny its desirability, in government as elsewhere, other things being equal. To be sure, other things may not be equal; many might prefer a less responsible democracy to a more responsible benevolent despotism, if that were the choice. The question then would be how far to go in that direction, how much responsibility to sacrifice for the sake of greater responsiveness. Responsibility, in this sense of rationality and morality, involved some limitations upon absolute majority rule and upon responsiveness. A government that responds immediately, with positive action, to majority wishes cannot take time for full ascertainment of facts, for adequate analysis, for calculation of consequences, and for the weighing of values. It may be assumed that only a few would, in principle, push the demand for responsiveness so far as to sacrifice completely the opportunity for such research and deliberation, although the procedures they support might have this practical effect. The important point to note here, however, is simply the existence of tension between the ideals of responsiveness and responsibility, and to observe that this tension adds support to the positions taken above in the discussion of responsiveness.

3. Accountability, Motivational Theories, and Political Parties

Turning to a consideration of responsibility as answerability, we find the issues complicated. To be sure, it is of the essence of democracy that the government should be accountable to the people. How is this objective to be accomplished?

Let us look at this question from the standpoints of each of our four motivational types of democratic theory. Do they serve as adequate descriptive theories? Beginning with radical individualism, what would rational, self-interested men do when confronted with such a problem?[5] We have

[5] At the outset it should be made clear that the rational-man model

268

assumed we are dealing with the representative form of democracy. (The rational man in a modern state would, in any case, soon be driven to this arrangement.) The question arises, How are representatives to be selected and held accountable (and thus, presumably, made responsive)? By elections, yes. This much, again, is provided by definition and appears obviously to be a rational device for the purpose. But how are candidates to be selected? This task requires some form of organization. It could be ad hoc, but the practical advantages of specialization and division of labor tend to lead to the adoption of permanent organizations of professionals and quasi-professionals. For local representatives, to be sure, these organizations might be purely local. But if any issues are of nationwide importance it is likely that certain individuals throughout the country will find it in their interest (or in accordance with their ideals) to support a particular policy or program for dealing with a given issue. Moreover, since a particular representative will have to deal with many issues, a nationwide organization for selecting and supporting candidates suggests itself even to the rational egoist as the logical solution.

It may be useful to spell out the argument in slightly greater detail, using a highly simplified set of assumptions. Let us suppose that at a particular juncture the country confronts three issues (I, II, and III), and that in general proposed solutions or policies can be grouped in one of two categories (A and B) for each issue. Thus a candidate (or representative) might stand for IA, IIA, and IIIA, or he might stand for IA, IIA, and IIIB, and so on. One can easily fill out the matrix of twenty-seven possible positions, each with its own candidate. The result would be confusion for the voter, or at the very least the necessity for possessing a great deal of information. To be sure, for any given voter, one issue might have such saliency that he

set forth in Chapter Five and used here should not be confused with the model of the "rational activist," sometimes used as a model for democratic political theory.

would find it rational to disregard the others. His problem would be quite manageable. Even so, the resulting elected body would in all probability be made up of representatives standing for each of the twenty-seven possible positions. Their problem of building majorities would be quite complicated. Compromises would be negotiated, and at the next election the rational voter would have to be familiar with the ultimate positions taken by his representative in order to hold him accountable according to the voter's preferences. A lot is being demanded of the voter. To obtain all the information he needs both about the merits of the issues and about the actions of his representative and to give this body of information the requisite thought might well consume all his waking hours—or a great deal more, if that were possible.

What to do? Some time-saving device is obviously called for, and the national political party, whether organized on the basis of commitment to certain leaders or on the basis of specified issue stands or more general ideological orientations, seems a natural device to serve this purpose.[6] Other forces tend in the same direction. Under the presidential system of government, the power of the executive office, plus the fact that it is held by a single individual and is therefore indivisible, exerts a strong force toward the nationalization of politics. In the United States, it appears to be responsible for the fact that we have two national parties (that is to say, a two-party system), weak though they are, in spite of the regional heterogeneity of the country and its interests, and in spite of the decentralizing influence

---

[6] There are functions to be performed at the local level, at the national level, and specifically within the legislature; and a party system that embraces all three is most functional. Historically, some party systems have developed first at the legislative level and then spread to the constituencies, while in other cases the reverse order has been followed. Sometimes, too, as in France, they have started at both levels and the linkage between the two has never been completely developed, with unfortunate effects and with consequent inefficiency in the performance of their representative function.

of our federal structure. Even under a parliamentary system, forces tend in the same direction. As governments become involved in more activities the need for a centralizing force has increased, with the result that the prime minister in most modern democracies has long since ceased, in the old phrase, to be simply *primus inter pares*; his powers tend rather to approximate those of the American president. To the extent that this happens, the same logic that applies in the United States makes for national parties and a two-party system.

Although the rational voter may find a party that is more to his liking under a multiparty system than another under a two-party system might be, he is likely to be thwarted at the next stage. Since at the legislative level with a multiparty system normally no single party will command a majority, coalitions must be formed, and compromises must be worked out after the election. This is one problem with enforcing accountability without political parties. In other words, the apparent gain at the electoral level tends to be lost before policies can be effectuated. As is well known, many factors (ethnic and religious commitments, for instance) have entered in to prevent the logic of rational individualism from being carried to what is here suggested as its logical conclusion, a two-party system; but it is interesting that in two major democracies, France and West Germany, postwar developments, especially in West Germany, point in this direction.

Were attitudes toward a number of issues facing a modern democracy both stongly held and randomly distributed, in the way suggested by the twenty-seven-box matrix hypothesized above, it is unlikely that the development suggested here as logical would take place. Too many people would feel too strongly about a variety of matters to be able to find common ground on which they could compromise. In that situation it might well be that a democracy could not survive, for lack of sufficient consensus. On many economic issues facing a modern democracy, however, the

271

attitudes of rational individuals are likely to cluster. If the people are strongly egalitarian, this fact will tend to dictate their position toward welfare measures, taxing policy, and many noneconomic issues as well, such as those having to do with race or the distribution of educational opportunities. On the other hand, if they place their stress on individual liberty and if they believe that increased productivity is both important and endangered by egalitarian measures, they will tend, insofar as they are rational and informed, to line up on the opposite side from their more egalitarian countrymen. To be sure, not all issues cluster in this simple fashion. Often attitudes toward racial questions, or matters of religion or nationality, not to mention foreign policy, tend to complicate the pattern. The only suggestion made here is that for the rational individualist strong forces make it desirable to have a party system and as simple a one as possible (preferably a two-party system, combining the maximum of simplicity with competition between parties to enforce accountability).

Now democracies do in fact develop systems of political parties. Moreover, a case can easily be made for the proposition that in the absence of strong religious, ethnic, or ideological divisions, these systems tend to be of the two-party variety. This does not prove that people's political behavior is rationally motivated, as the individualist assumes it is, but the proposition is at least compatible with such an assumption and may be thought to give it some support.

Yet a qualification is in order. We are confronted here with the problem of public goods, that is to say of goods that benefit everyone, or nearly everyone, whether or not everyone contributes to the support of these goods.[7] Assuming then that it is in the interest of all to have a democratic government and, to this end, to have political parties and an active electorate, it does not follow that it is in the in-

[7] See Mancur Olson, Jr., *The Logic of Collective Action* (Cambridge, Mass.: Harvard University Press, 1965).

terest of a given individual to participate in political activities to the extent necessary for the maintenance of democracy. It is perfectly rational for an egoist not to bother informing himself about the issues and personalities at stake, or even to take the trouble to vote. It is rational for him to behave in this fashion, that is to say, if he thinks the chances of his vote's affecting the result are very slight. To put it very crudely, if he thinks it might be worth $1,000 to him for Candidate A (or Party A) to win, and if he places a value of $10 on the time it would take him to make that estimate and then to vote, it is not *evidently* rational for him to vote unless he thinks the chance of his vote's determining the outcome of the election is better than one in a hundred—a very unlikely circumstance indeed. "Rational" is qualified by "evidently," because the voter may get pleasure from doing whatever is required to make up his mind, from making up his mind, and from actually casting his ballot. He may find this mode of expressing himself enjoyable in itself, as an exercise of his rights of citizenship, as a means of expressing his support for A (or his contempt for B!) or for some other reason. Such reasons as these may explain why so many people do vote. Of course it may be simply because party leaders have urged them to vote and have led them to believe they could have an appreciable influence, and that they have not been sufficiently thoughtful to realize what the actual odds are.[8]

In short, the individualist theory suffers from a serious weakness at an early stage in the political process—not in explaining why people vote as they do but in explaining why they vote at all. What about the theory of the public interest? At the point of weakness in individualism just noted, the public-interest theory lends some support, although less than might at first appear. Even though the voter thinks he should, and in fact does, relate his behavior

[8] On all this, see William H. Riker and Peter C. Ordeshook, "A Theory of the Calculus of Voting," *Amer. Polit. Sci. Rev.*, 62 (1968), 25-42.

to his perception of the public interest, that would not rationally move him to invest a significant amount of time and effort in voting if he thought the chances of its being effective were *insignificant*. But the calculus of the public-interest voter is different from that of the individualist. Assume now that, as before, the voter thinks it would be worth $1,000 to him for Candidate A (or Party A) to win. But also assume he thinks it would be worth a like amount to each of 999 other voters. The net gain for the public would now be a million dollars. Even if he thinks the chances of his vote's determining the outcome are only one in ten thousand, the discounted value to society of his vote would now be $100. Surely this ought to be worth a $10 effort on his part if he is motivated to support the public interest, assuming he identifies the welfare of these one thousand people with that of society.

Moreover, if the voter thinks, perhaps quite reasonably, that the public interest will be promoted by the mere fact of his voting (preventing the development of the cynicism which may be as much effect as cause of low local electoral turnouts), that is likewise a rational reason for voting. To the extent that voters react in this fashion, the public-interest theory is again supported. It should be noted, however, that this reasoning applies also—but much less strongly —to the rational individualist.

Going beyond the act of voting, the reasoning of the public-interest theorist would parallel that of the rational egoist (the radical individualist). Once he had accepted the commitment to vote and otherwise engage in political activities, the reasoning advanced above to explain the formation of political parties applies as well for him as for the egoist. For both it is desirable to minimize the cost of participating in the political process and to maximize the ability of the voter to give practical effect in public policy to both his wants and his ideals. As was argued above, these are the objectives a competitive party system seems fitted to foster.

274

Turning to the rights and duties theory and testing it first by the problem of why people vote, it is possible—even plausible—that they do so because they believe it is their duty. They know that if everyone behaved like our putative rational egoist, democracy would probably break down. One of the most elementary principles of ethics, which most of us are taught and accept from an early age, is the proposition that we ought to behave the way we would like others to behave in like circumstances. We may or may not do it, but few would deny the validity of the proposition. So at least until it is further explained, the fact that large numbers of people do vote would support this theory as much as that of the public interest. On the other hand, the rights and duties theory by itself could hardly explain the fact that democracies universally are characterized by the institution of political parties. It appears that, concerning political parties, this theory must be confined to a supplementary, though possibly important, role.

One further comment about the rights and duties theory as compared with individualist and public interest theories. It is possible—indeed it seems reasonable to suppose—that the political elite and the active public, by definition giving more thought to the subject of politics than do the more apathetic masses, tend to operate in accordance with one of the interest-maximizing theories. Also, since their focus is on the public, they may well tend to adopt a public-interest stance. On the other hand, it is plausible that those whose interest in and attention to politics is more limited tend to react to public questions more in terms of conventional ideas of right and wrong, of justice and injustice, insofar, that is to say, as they were not governed by habit or the personal charm of leaders, or other emotional factors.

As for the application of the problem of accountability to the theory of democratic collectivism, we are met, as always, with the difficulty that no authoritative elaboration of such a theory for the modern state is available. Rousseau

275

was opposed to both representation and political parties. But then he was discussing a city-state, the only kind of state in which he thought democracy was feasible. Nevertheless, his opposition to all parties within the state is based upon reasoning that would seem to be equally applicable to a larger polity. Wishing to stress the value of the whole and of a deep appreciation for the unity of the whole by all its members, and to give all support to the creation of a General Will, he was fearful of parties and factions. In his ideal polity they would not be tolerated. Yet, he was realist enough to recognize that that was a counsel of perfection, and that in practice, at least in a large state, they would be unavoidable.[9] From the standpoint of political parties as instruments for enforcing accountability, indeed, collectivist democratic theory finds little support either in rational analysis or in practical experience, as an operational (descriptive) theory. What it does is to set up an ideal—doubtless an unattainable ideal but nonetheless one that serves a useful purpose. It stresses the importance of a moral and emotional commitment to the whole, a loyalty that overrides group loyalties and prevents or at least moderates the ills of factionalism. In this respect it is similar to the rights and duties theory in playing a supplementary role to that of radical individualism (or to that of the theory of the public interest, which is itself a highly modified form of individualism). Finally, here as elsewhere, if the collectivist aspect of democratic collectivism got the better of its democratic side, if it sought to supplant rather than to supplement the other theories, political parties might be ruthlessly suppressed, as endangering the General Will or community consensus.

In short, with respect to responsibility as accountability, two facts are especially important: democratic citizens, in

9 See Maure L. Goldschmidt, "Rousseau on Intermediate Associations," in J. Roland Pennock and John W. Chapman, eds., *Voluntary Associations*, NOMOS XI, (New York: Lieber-Atherton, 1969) 119-137. What is said above is in agreement with Goldschmidt's interpretation of Rousseau, but his emphasis is upon the fact that Rousseau did not oppose all voluntary associations but indeed saw their great value.

large numbers, do vote; and democratic politics is conducted in important measure through the instrumentality of political parties. The first of these facts lends support to both the public-interest theory and the rights and duties theory. To a lesser extent, the same can be said for radical individualism. It would seem to have no bearing on the theory of democratic collectivism. The second fact more or less equally supports each, or any, of the first three theories. Collectivism, on the other hand, does not seem to comport well with the existence of political parties. Moreover, it at least sometimes leads to a negative evaluation of this democratic institution.

4. LIMITATIONS OF POLITICAL PARTIES AS AGENCIES OF ACCOUNTABILITY

Now, against this general theoretical background, it will be useful to pursue the matter of the role of political parties a bit further. The theory of political parties as discussed above implicitly assumes the party is able to enforce its collective will upon all concerned, president, senator, and congressman, alike. This is known as the theory of party government. The voter need only look to see which party is in power. If he approves of what has been done and of what that party promises to do in the future, he should vote for the candidates of that party. If he prefers the program of the opposition party, he votes for its candidates. Walter Lippmann long ago gave a clear and simple statement of this theory. He wrote: "To support the Ins when things are going well; to support the Outs when they seem to be going badly, this, in spite of all that has been said about tweedledum and tweedledee, is the essence of popular government."[10]

Although in fact, as Lippmann recognized, parties must generally be judged on the basis of quite general and vague

[10] Lippmann, *The Phantom Public* (New York: Harcourt, Brace, 1925), p. 126.

standards, accountability would be sharpened, the electorate's control over policy strengthened, in proportion as they would take clear stands on specific issues. For the system to work it is also necessary for the party members in the legislative and executive branches to adhere to the party positions. Those who would stress the role of political parties as instrumentalities of government and as means for enforcing accountability to the electorate, as opposed to mere nominating devices, in other words, must emphasize the elements of party program and party discipline.[11]

Together with the elements of program and discipline goes a third element of the party-government complex, that of the so-called electoral mandate. The idea embodied in this concept is that the party winning an election receives a mandate, conceived of as authorization and sometimes also as direction, to carry out the party's program.

Now it is clear that party government, in the sense just described, is today at a low ebb in the United States. The theory speaks in terms of the party that is "in control of the government." This party should be held accountable for what the government does and does not do. But for roughly half of the time since the conclusion of the Second World War no party has been in this position. The party that controlled the presidency did not control one or the other or sometimes either of the houses of Congress.[12] Add the facts, as found by Stokes and Miller, that most voters know very little of what goes on in the national legislature, that few

[11] The literature on this subject is almost without limit. A number of years ago, a committee of the American Political Science Association submitted an extensive report on the subject. In normative terms, it was strongly in favor of programmatic and disciplined political parties for this country, and proposed various measures designed to aid in moving in that direction. "Toward a More Responsible Two-Party System," Supplement to *Amer. Polit. Sci. Rev.*, 44 (1950).

[12] The weakness of party government in earlier years is clearly demonstrated in Julius Turner, *Party and Constituency* (Baltimore: Johns Hopkins University Press, 1951), pp. 28-34, especially Table 3, at p. 28. (Turner did find, however, that the party was the strongest *single* factor in influencing congressional voting.)

judgments of legislative performance are associated in the minds of the electorate with the parties, and that a large part of the electorate is not even aware of which party controls Congress, and it becomes even clearer that party government is weak, at least at the Congressional level.[13]

Indeed, it seems the theory that the party, at least as considered apart from the system as a whole, is the primary agency for the enforcement of accountability with respect to particular issues—the mandate concept—is largely outmoded in contemporary America. When issues were relatively few and simple, as they could be when the role of the national government was far more restricted than it is today, the theory made considerable sense. Half or three quarters of a century ago a few great but relatively simple questions, such as the attitudes to be taken toward tariffs and trusts, were predominant. Today the situation is obviously very different in this respect. When each of the major parties must give some indication of its position on such issues as the form and amount of foreign aid, foreign policy toward each of the world's great areas, the form and amount of aid to our decaying cities, health insurance, income redistribution, racial problems, pollution control, tax reform, inflation control, and so on ad infinitum, it is unlikely an election can give a clear indication of what a majority or even a plurality of the public wants. A mandate, in most instances, is undiscoverable. This must be so for several reasons. In the first place, on many issues the general public does not know what it wants; or its wants are mutually incompatible (lower taxes, higher expenditures, and no inflation) and it has not brought itself to make the hard choices. It lacks the information, the education, the time to study, and the interest required to form clear and mutually consistent opinions on most of the issues facing the government. Secondly,

13 These findings have been well documented by Donald E. Stokes and Warren E. Miller, "Party Government and the Saliency of Congress," *Pub. Opinion Quar.*, 26 (1962), 531-546. See also William Buchanan, "An Inquiry into Purposive Voting," *Jour. of Politics*, 18 (1956), 281-296.

even if the public had opinions on these questions, party voting would not reveal them. This would partly be the case because however the party positions were formulated, many voters would find themselves favoring the stand of one party on certain issues and that of the other on other issues. In this situation, no clear conclusions could be drawn from the outcome. Partly, uncertainty and lack of clarity would result from the fact that the very competitiveness of a two-party system compels the parties to seek a vague happy medium on many if not most issues.

This proposition finds both empirical and theoretical support. The facts about the narrow differences between American political parties are too well known to require substantiation here. Moreover, that competition among rational actors would tend to produce this result has been rigorously demonstrated under certain reasonable assumptions.[14]

Let us pursue the matter of specific mandates a little further. Franklin Roosevelt, in 1933, devalued the dollar and launched large spending programs, although he had no mandate to do either and the second ran exactly counter to his campaign promises. Operationally, the "mandate" had no effect. He was reelected in 1936 by a landslide vote. He had apparently convinced the people (or enough people) that what he had done was in their interest. Lyndon Johnson, on the other hand, was elected president in 1964 on a platform of minimizing or eliminating our involvement in Vietnam. The issue was sharpened by his opponent's outright stand for escalating the war. Yet LBJ in office acted contrary to his "mandate." The result, from his point of view, was less fortunate than FDR's experience. Probably because of his war policy, the polls turned sharply against him and he decided not to run in 1968. Yet few would doubt that, if his policy of escalation had worked, had brought

[14] See Peter C. Ordeshook, "Extensions to a Model of the Electoral Process and Implications for the Theory of Responsible Parties," *Midwest Jour. of Polit. Sci.*, 14 (1970), 43-70.

280

peace, the story would have been different. On the other hand, had he run and won on a policy of escalation, it seems likely the political outcome would have been the same. Electoral reaction appears to be more in terms of the consequences of the policies actually pursued than in terms of adherence to promises. One may also hazard the guess that the reaction of a representative (whether a president or a legislator) is more likely to be by way of anticipating future electoral behavior than by way of keeping promises *per se*. Of course, even on this line of reasoning it may often appear prudent to a representative to keep his promises, especially in cases where the issue was sharp and the pre-election posture of the representative clear and where a plea of changed conditions or of new information would be implausible. In such situations an elected official, if the issue is a salient one, will generally do well to stick to his promises or, at the very least, to qualify or pass the buck (e.g. by not pushing very hard on the matter in question).

Leon Epstein has conducted an interesting empirical study bearing directly on the mandate question. He analyzed a particular gubernatorial election in which a single issue—a tax question—was salient. It appeared to be an ideal situation for applying the mandate theory. In this case, there is a sense in which the tax issue appears to have determined the result. Yet the necessary qualifications are so great as to deprive the finding of much positive significance for the mandate theory. Only a small proportion of voters were motivated by the tax issue. About a third of them could not identify the stands of the parties on the issue. Moreover, a third of the Democratic voters preferred the Republican side of the tax issue. Finally, most of those who voted for the winning (Democratic) candidate would have done so regardless of the tax issue. In short, even in this favorable case, to call the result a mandate would deprive that term of most of its presumed significance.[15]

[15] Epstein, "Electoral Decision and Policy Mandate: An Empirical Example," *Pub. Opinion Quar.*, 28 (1964), 564-572.

In England, the birthplace of party government, it is generally supposed that the system operates much more closely in accordance with the model. Yet recent studies cast doubt upon this assumption. One student of the subject finds grounds in surveys for concluding that "it is clearly fallacious to believe that success in a general election indicates that the voters have endorsed the policies advocated by the winning party."[16] Thus voters who supported Labour in the 1970 General Election presumably assumed, if they gave the matter any thought, that a Labour government would support England's entry into the European Economic Community.[17] Yet in the final analysis the party leadership opposed entry and tried to enforce its policy upon the whole of the parliamentary party. The fact that on this issue eighty-nine members defied the leadership is a further, though quite unusual, example of action contrary to the model. Incidentally, the Conservative party leadership, while allowing a "free" vote, contrary to the model, supported entry, in spite of the fact that the polls showed decisive opposition to this policy from the general public. Accountability in this instance did not produce responsiveness to current public opinion. Yet of course the Government remained accountable for what it had done. Interestingly enough, while it lost the next General Election (in

[16] A. H. Birch, *Representative and Responsible Government* (Toronto: University of Toronto Press, 1964), p. 121. Birch goes on to demonstrate that the channels of communication between people and government are numerous, complex, two-way in operation, and continually shifting. Chap. 16.

[17] Although hedged, the statements of Harold Wilson clearly pointed in that direction. The 1966 Labour Party Manifesto declared, "Labour believes that Britain, in consultation with her European Free Trade Association partners, should be ready to enter the European Economic Community, provided essential British and Commonwealth interests are safeguarded." *Times Guide to the House of Commons, 1966* (London: Times Office, n.d.), p. 283. Harold Wilson relied upon the concluding proviso of that sentence to explain Labour's opposition to joining the EEC in 1971. (No party manifestoes were issued in 1970.)

282

1974), this issue does not appear to have been a significant factor in the result.[18]

5. THE PARTY-GOVERNMENT MODEL FURTHER CONSIDERED

Thus it appears that in the United States, and to a lesser extent in England, the operation of party government with respect to accountability does not accord with the theory. These discrepancies prompt further reflection upon the party-government model in the light of our discussion of responsiveness above. In the first place, it is worth noting that the system of government through the agency of disciplined political parties may run counter to the democratic principle of majority rule, at least in the sense of responsiveness to the majority of the electorate. (Thus responsibility and responsiveness are here at odds.) If a party that controls the legislature and the executive submits to group discipline and supports whatever is agreed upon, either by its membership or by its policy-making body, this majority of a majority may itself represent only a minority of the electorate. Nor is such a hypothetical case improbable. In Great Britain, the most striking examples arise out of the nationalization issue. The militant left wing of the Labour party has successfully insisted upon a policy of extended nationalization of industry with the result that when it is in power, policies to this effect are implemented, in spite of the fact that a majority of the electorate clearly opposes it. In 1950, for instance, a majority of the voters cast their ballots

[18] Further interesting data on the British case may be found in Richard Rose, *Politics in England*, 2nd ed. (Boston: Little, Brown, 1974). See the chart at p. 381. Out of eight clear pledges made by the Labour party in its 1964 manifesto, only five were carried out during the ensuing six years of office, while the Government acted contrary to the other three. The Conservatives in 1970 took clear stands on thirteen issues. During the next three years, they carried out their pledges in nine cases and took the opposite action in four.

for candidates who were opposed to the program; yet Labour won the election and steel was nationalized.[19] In 1967, steel having meanwhile been denationalized by a Conservative Government, and with opinion polls showing no more than 25 percent of the voters favoring renationalization, steel was once more substantially nationalized. Nor can it be argued that the pronationalizers made up with intensity of feeling what they lacked in numbers. The evidence is quite to the contrary. The opponents of nationalization appear to have felt more strongly about the matter, at least if constancy of opinion is any indication.[20]

With respect to a single issue, then, party government and majority rule may come into conflict with each other. But in such a situation, it might be argued, the voters presumably cast their ballots with their eyes open and must be assumed to have preferred other parts of the Labour program *with* nationalization of steel to the programs of the other parties without it. This is perfectly true. It is also true, however, that to force such a harsh alternative upon the voters is a disadvantage which might be avoided under a looser party system. It is a disadvantage, that is to say, in terms of maximizing responsiveness to public opinion on separate

[19] It may even be questioned whether most of the nationalization program carried out between 1945 and 1950 had the support of the majority of the voters. See the excellent analysis by R. B. McCallum and Alison Readman, *The British General Election of 1945* (London: Oxford University Press, 1947), pp. 250-253.

[20] Interviews of a random sample of voters in the summer of 1963, the autumn of 1964, and the spring of 1966 (the same persons being interviewed each time as far as possible), showed great shifts on this question, especially among those inclined to favor nationalization. The aggregate proportions pro and con were remarkably stable, but individuals shifted, apparently indicating weakness of conviction. Only 10 percent remained constantly in favor of more nationalization throughout the three times, out of about 20 percent on this side of the issue on each occasion. On the other hand, out of over 50 percent who each time opposed further nationalization, 40 percent adhered to the same position on each of the three occasions. David Butler and Donald Stokes, *Political Change in Britain* (London: Macmillan, 1969), pp. 177-180.

issues. In some cases, of course, popular demands may be such that they tend to defeat each other. In such cases forcing a "harsh alternative" would be all to the good. Voters would find themselves forced to act responsibly (rationally).

As a footnote, it may be observed that the system of direct primaries, as practiced in the United States, not only makes it more difficult to enforce party regularity in the legislature, but would also make the result of such enforcement more unrepresentative, more contrary to rule by the majority of the voters. And yet—and in this case the significant point— the institution of the direct primary is aimed directly at the objective of securing responsiveness to the majority will. The potential conflict between party government and majority rule, in other words, is once more brought to the fore.

A second consequence of the party-government system is that it encourages sharp reversals of policy. Curiously enough, here the bare majority rule aspect of the model has this effect, while in the analysis presented above it was the party-discipline aspect that was under discussion. In brief, where the majority, on a particular issue, extends across party lines, party government is likely to be at odds with the objective of responsiveness; where, on the other hand, the majority and one party tend to be coterminous, sharp policy reversals are likely if the parties are highly competitive (that is, if the party in power frequently changes). Again the case of British nationalization of steel is in point. The industry was nationalized in 1950, denationalized in 1951, and substantially renationalized in 1967.

While the example of steel is by no means unique,[21] it is exceptional. The reason it is exceptional, however, is that even in England political parties, although disciplined, are not highly programmatic. More often than not, an election does not contribute greatly to clarifying the majority opinion about issues, because the parties hedge, or agree, on

[21] See the account of the effects of changes of Government on housing programs in Britain during the twenties in Barbara Wootton, *Freedom under Planning* (Chapel Hill: University of North Carolina Press, 1945), pp. 131-133.

many of the issues. In other words, party responsibility does not necessarily mean greater clarity as to issues. Parties cannot clarify what is inherently unclear. When a large proportion of the electorate is unfamiliar with an issue, or is undecided, or in any case takes no clear stand—a common state of affairs—party discipline will not change the situation.[22] More to the point of this discussion, to the extent that this situation prevails, party government does not further accountability on specific issues.

The last statement requires amplification. Most of what has been said relates to accountability by issue or group of issues. If we consider answerability to the highly generalized satisfaction or dissatisfaction with "the way things have been going" that Lippmann spoke about, the picture is quite different. Clearly party government facilitates accountability of the government as a whole on its record as a whole. Insofar as parties anticipate that voters will react in this fashion, party government should maximize responsiveness to this kind of voter sentiment.[23]

[22] In Great Britain, as in the United States, neither positions on individual issues nor broad ideological orientations are sufficiently clarified in the minds of the rank-and-file voter that they can be used to account for the content of political change. Butler and Stokes, *Political Change in Britain*, Chaps. 8 and 9.

[23] The theory here attributed to Walter Lippmann, which he set forth in 1925, is similar, as concerns the point under discussion, to that advanced by Joseph A. Schumpeter in his *Capitalism, Socialism, and Democracy* (New York: Harper & Row, 1942). Schumpeter attacked the notion of a common will, which might through the device of representation be converted into public policy, and contended instead that "the democratic method is that institutional arrangement for arriving at political decisions in which individuals acquire the power to decide by means of a competitive struggle for the people's vote." Ibid., p. 269. Although Schumpeter's attack on the theory that public opinion is either unified or rational is similar to Lippmann's and has similar consequences for a more rationalistic and simplistic (sometimes called classical) type of democratic theory, Schumpeter was more cautious than Lippmann about denying that public opinion can be effectively directed, through the ballot, at specific governmental policies. Although the "revisionist" type of democratic theory repre-

6. RATIONALITY AND ACCOUNTABILITY

A serious question has been haunting our discussion for the last several pages. It can be ignored no longer. Speculation about the putative behavior of the rational individual led to our discussion of political parties, party government, and electoral mandates. Now, ironically, in demonstrating that the party-government model and the concept of an electoral mandate depart widely from the realities of political life, we have said a good deal that tends to cast doubt upon the rationality (including possession of relevant information) of electoral behavior. And much more could be said to the same effect. Have we undermined the very foundation of our argument and of democratic theory more generally?

For a number of reasons, I do not believe so, but the question cannot be lightly dismissed, for the early studies of voting behavior did point in this direction. The authors of *Voting*, for example, showed that the voters in their study who contributed most to changes in party control were those who possessed least of the characteristics desirable for a rational democratic system.[24] On the basis of another study, the author concluded that "it appears that the orthodox view of the electorate as deliberately controlling policy through the choice of candidates seems to apply to only a minority of the citizenry and to be to them a rather peripheral concern. . . ."[25] According to Warren Mil-

---

sented by Lippmann and Schumpeter and many others was dominant at least among American political scientists for many years—perhaps still is—today it is widely under attack. A current "reader" on democratic theory devotes over half its pages to "challenges to democratic revisionism." Henry S. Kariel, ed., *Frontiers of Democratic Theory* (New York: Random House, 1970). Interestingly enough, not one of the twelve selections that comprise this section of the book says anything to contradict the view of the facts upon which the Lippmann-Schumpeter theory is based.

24 Berelson, Lazarsfeld, and McPhee, *Voting*, p. 316.

25 William Buchanan, "An Inquiry into Purposive Voting," pp. 281-296, 295.

ler, reporting on a portion of the work of the University of Michigan's Survey Research Center, in 1958 scarcely 3 percent of the voters "could identify, in even the most gross terms, a single policy stand taken by their Congressman in any given major policy area." From the same study it appeared that in this off-year election, few voters deviated from their normal party alignment, and these deviations appeared to be related to factors irrelevant to the issues. At the same time, there were wide departures from the party-government model, produced not so much by constituency demand as by constituency ignorance.[26]

Although much more evidence could be adduced to the same general effect, most of it dates back several years. More recent studies and reevaluations of the earlier data paint a more favorable picture of the democratic process. As early as 1955, Janowitz and Marvick, in a study of the first Eisenhower-Stevenson campaign, found a fairly high correlation between the preferences of voters for these candidates and their respective programs.[27] Perhaps the turning point in the analysis of voting behavior from the point of view of democratic theory was marked by the appearance in 1966 of V. O. Key's, *The Responsible Electorate: Rationality in*

[26] Warren Miller, "Majority Rule and the Representative System of Government," in E. Allardt and Y. Littunen, eds., *Cleavages, Ideologies and Party Systems* (Helsinki: Transactions of the Westermarck Society, 1964), pp. 345-376. However, it did show a quite good correlation between congressmen's roll-call behavior and policies supported by the constituencies on civil rights questions and a significant correlation on social-welfare legislation. Ibid., pp. 345 (for the quotation) and 350-351. See also Stokes and Miller, "Party Government and the Saliency of Congress," pp. 531-546.

[27] Morris Janowitz and Dwaine Marvick, "Competitive Pressure and Democratic Consent: An Interpretation of the 1952 Election," *Pub. Opinion Quar.*, 19 (1955-1956), 381-401, 391-393. Well over half the supporters of each candidate supported his program, while roughly half the others were ambivalent or neutral on the issues. This kind of study does not tell us why voters vote as they do, but it at least shows that less than a quarter of them voted so as to defeat their policy preferences.

288

Presidential Voting, 1936-60.[28] He summed up his message: "The perverse and unorthodox argument of this little book is that voters are not fools." Writing before the Goldwater campaign, which would have provided more ammunition for his guns, and accepting the assumption that partisans tend to stick with their party even when they disagree with its policies, Key concentrated upon the "shifters." Here he found unmistakable evidence that defecting was related to opinion on issues.

Key dealt with presidential elections, where perhaps policy preferences play the largest role. But other students have reexamined and reinterpreted the Survey Research Center data on midterm elections of congressmen, bringing out more emphatically than Miller and Stokes had done the very high correlation between the Representative's perception of his constituents' attitudes and his roll-call behavior, and the quite high correlation between roll-call behavior and the actual attitudes of constituents.[29] A similar review of earlier studies of congressional elections concludes that "election outcomes are in substantial part responsive to objective changes occurring under the incumbent party; they are not 'irrational,' or random, or solely the product of past loyalties and habits, or of campaign rhetoric and merchandising."[30]

[28] Cambridge, Mass.: Harvard University Press, 1966.

[29] Charles F. Cnudde and Donald J. McCrone, "The Linkage between Constituency Attitudes and Congressional Voting Behavior," *Amer. Polit. Sci. Rev.*, 60 (1966), 66-72.

[30] Gerald E. Kramer, "Short-Term Fluctuations in U. S. Voting Behavior, 1896-1964," *Amer. Polit. Sci. Rev.*, 65 (1971), 131-143, 140. For further evidence in support of voter rationality, see James L. Sundquist, *Politics and Policy* (Washington, D.C.: Brookings, 1968), Chaps. 9-11. In a careful path analysis of a sample of voters from the 1968 presidential election, Theodore F. Macaluso not only finds support for the thesis that vote switchers vote "rationally," using the conventional definition of that term, but also that the influence of issues is markedly lower among those with low education, those who read about the election infrequently, late deciders, and those whose financial condition is unchanged since the year before than it is for a cross section of all

Recent studies argue even more strongly that issues are more important determinants of electoral results than has been generally argued on the basis of survey studies.[31] In fact, it may be argued that the American electorate, *when it feels that political issues are important to it*, behaves as rational-man theory would lead one to expect; that is to say, it finds it worth its while to pay attention to politics,

switchers. "Parameters of 'Rational' Voting: Vote Switching in the 1968 Election," *Jour. of Politics*, 37 (1975), 202-234. Rational consideration of issues as a significant factor in determining voting decisions is also supported by the research findings of David M. Kovenock, Philip L. Beardsley, and James W. Prothro. See their working paper "Status, Ideology, Issues, and Candidate Choice: A Preliminary Theory-Relevant Analysis of the 1968 American Presidential Election," (Specialist Meeting B:XI, Eighth World Congress of the International Political Science Association, Munich, 31 August-5 September, 1970). See also John E. Jackson, "Issues, Party Choices and Presidential Votes," *Amer. Jour. of Polit. Sci.*, 19 (1975), 161-185. Finally, still further evidence of voter rationality is supplied by a recent study of voting at midterm congressional elections. Shifts in voting patterns at midterm elections as compared with the preceding congressional elections are shown (for the period 1938-1970, omitting the wartime election of 1942) to correlate very strongly with changes in the popularity of the president (as measured by the Gallup poll) and in real disposable personal income per capita. Regardless of how many individuals may vote irrationally, the net effect of all voting shifts is in line with what a consideration of these two factors would dictate. Edward R. Tufte, "Determinants of the Outcomes of Midterm Congressional Elections," *Amer. Polit. Sci. Rev.*, 69 (1975), 812-826.

[31] P. B. Natchez and J. C. Bupp, "Candidates, Issues and Voters," *Public Policy*, 17 (1968), 409-437; David E. RePass, "Issue Salience and Party Choice," *Amer. Polit. Sci. Rev.*, 65 (1971), 389-400; Gerald M. Pomper, "From Confusion to Clarity: Issues and American Voters, 1956-1968," *Amer. Polit. Sci. Rev.*, 66 (1972), 415-428, now appearing in revised form as Chap. 8 of Pomper, *Voters' Choice* (New York: Harper & Row, 1975); Richard W. Boyd, "Popular Control of Public Policy: a Normal Vote Analysis of the 1968 Election," ibid., 429-449; Richard A. Brody and Benjamin I. Page, "Comment: The Assessment of Policy Voting," *Amer. Polit. Sci. Rev.*, 66 (1972), 450-465; and Kendall L. Baker and Oliver Walter, "Voter Rationality: A Comparison of Presidential and Congressional Voting in Wyoming," *Western Polit. Quar.*, 28 (1975), 316-329.

290

and attitude consistency increases as does consistency between attitudes and voting behavior.[32] Going a step further
in support of the rationality of the whole political process
in American democracy (when the results are combined
with the study just referred to), Gerald Pomper finds a
limited and often indirect but still significant linkage between the demands of the electorate and electoral results,
including the actions of the parties on their platforms after
the election. He notes a fact too often overlooked, that
actual electoral control is often greater than appears because representatives often anticipate electoral behavior.[33]

On a slightly different tack, a study of all candidates for
the House of Representatives in the 1966 election is also
relevant. The authors found that on the whole a substantially significant choice of policy was offered the voters and
that the winning candidates generally voted their preelection promises.[34]

A recent study of ticket-splitters in American politics is
also of particular interest. In the first place, contrary to
earlier findings about "independents," it appears that the
person who splits his ticket is just as well informed about
American politics and is just as concerned about public

[32] Norman H. Nie and Kristi Anderson, "Mass Belief Systems Revisited: Political Change and Attitude Structure," *Jour. of Politics*, 36
(1974), 540-591. See further, Stephen Earl Bennett, "Consistency
among the Public's Social Welfare Attitudes in the 1960's," *Amer.
Jour. of Polit. Sci.*, 73 (1973), 544-570; and Roger Douglas, "Economy
and Polity in Australia: A Quantification of Common Sense," *Brit.
Jour. of Polit. Sci.*, 5 (1975), 341-361. Still another study is impressive in
testing the rationality of voting behavior both on the inductive side
(focusing upon perceptual mechanisms with the aid of social-psychological theory) and on the deductive side (using economic type analysis). The author concluded that for the sample studied, voters' choices
were rational in both aspects. Michael J. Shapiro, "Rational Political
Man: A Synthesis of Economic and Social-Psychological Perspectives,"
Amer. Polit. Sci. Rev., 63 (1969), 1106-1119.

[33] Gerald M. Pomper, *Elections in America* (New York: Dodd,
Mead, 1968), pp. 244ff.

[34] John L. Sullivan and Robert E. O'Connor, "Electoral Choice and
Popular Control," *Comp. Polit. Studies*, 2 (1969), 7-67.

problems as the more conventional voter who selects a straight party ticket. Moreover, "in rating the candidates and officeholders on the basis of the issues and how they handle them, the ticket-splitters make rational decisions."[35]

The data relied upon in the preceding paragraphs is entirely from American sources simply because that is where most of the relevant research has been conducted. One recent British study, however, is directly in point. On the basis of survey data, the authors conclude that, contrary to the conventional wisdom, voters do tend to support the parties whose stands on issues they agree with. They also find that, especially in the case of weak party identifiers, the choice of party is based upon the voters' preferences regarding issues, rather than their support of certain issues being mere rationalizations of their party commitments.[36]

In concluding this section, three general points are pertinent. First, it must be remembered that voters who vote along their customary party alignment, unthinkingly, and those who vote blindly, in complete ignorance or misunderstanding of the issues, are likely to be randomly distributed among the different parties. Their votes tend to cancel each other out, leaving the final determination to those who are better informed. Especially over the long run, this becomes an important consideration.

Second, much of the evidence recounted earlier dealt with congressional elections. Stokes and Miller, who were quoted in that context, also state that accountability operates more effectively through the presidency; and that in certain issue areas, especially social and economic welfare matters, accountability is more effective than in others.[37]

[35] Walter DeVries and Lance Tarrance, Jr., *The Ticket-Splitter* (Grand Rapids, Mich.: Eerdmans Pub. Co., 1972), p. 122.

[36] James A. Alt, Bo Särlvik, and Ivor Crewe, "Partisanship and Policy Choice: Issue Preferences in the British Electorate, February 1974," *Brit. Jour. of Polit. Sci.*, 6 (1976), 273-290. For further evidence drawn from the British electorate supporting voter rationality, see Marion R. Just, "Causal Models of Voter Rationality, Great Britain, 1959 and 1962," *Comp. Polit. Studies*, 21 (1973), 45-46.

[37] "Party Government and the Saliency of Congress," p. 546.

Third, even if all that the voters do, through the mechanisms of parties and elections, is to give a general nudge to the ship of state, indicating approval or disapproval of the course it is taking, that is no mean contribution. It may be presumed that citizens know more about what their desires are than about how to attain them; and more about their satisfaction or dissatisfaction with public policy than about how to improve it. If their indication is an unfavorable one, those they elect will be under pressure to find out how to change the situation if they wish to avoid a fate similar to their predecessors'.

7. WEAK-PARTY SYSTEMS

Having dealt with the problem of voter rationality, which was raised in the course of considering the party-government model, it is time to return to the main thread of the argument and consider an alternative to that model. If the system of disciplined programmed parties tends to conflict with the objective of responsiveness to the majority will on specific issues, and if it encourages instability of policy or avoids this evil only on pain of losing its claimed advantage of greater accountability, what of a system of weak parties? Is it unresponsive?[38] Irresponsible?[39] These questions are too large to be given anything like a complete answer in this chapter. They will be returned to at appropriate points in succeeding chapters. Some light can be shed upon them, however, from the point of view of the preceding analysis.

[38] By now it should be clear that this question is not susceptible of a simple yes or no answer. One must ask, Responsive to what? And, of course, How responsive? Nor is it to be assumed that responsiveness is always desirable.

[39] The question of responsibility as it applies to acting in the light of full information and deliberation was not discussed in the preceding analysis of responsiveness, accountability, and strong political parties, for reasons of convenience and clarity in exposition. That omission will be corrected below. In the case of weak parties, however, it has seemed best to combine the discussions of responsiveness and of responsibility in the rationality sense.

293

The American system of loose and undisciplined parties, which must vie with pressure groups and other devices for giving expression to public opinion, is frequently referred to as government by consensus, or by "concurrent majorities." By permitting representatives to regroup themselves from issue to issue, influenced but not bound by party affiliation, it fosters the maximum response to majority or plurality will. On the other hand, the system of checks and balances, with its attendant multiple constituencies, tends to make the enactment of legislation more difficult, unless it either has strong general support or is not vigorously opposed by any of the great pressure groups. It will be apparent that this second feature of American government considerably modifies the first (the party system). Weak parties make for more responsiveness, checks and balances for less.

Let us look briefly at the legislative process under the American party and governmental systems. A bill is drafted, perhaps by a legislator, more likely by the staff of an administrative agency, a pressure group, or a policy-leading group such as the Committee for Economic Development or Common Cause. If it is an important bill with substantial backing, it will be the subject of extensive hearings and subsequent deliberations by committees in both houses of Congress (or of a state legislature). The testimony of experts from within and without the government, arguments and persuasive efforts of all kinds, the views of concerned administrative agencies and of the president, will all be presented. The staff experts of the congressional committees are likely to play an influential role. Abundant opportunities will present themselves at various stages along the legislative path to adjust conflicting interests by means of amendments to the original bill. If the measure is highly controversial, it is unlikely to emerge from the legislative mill in its original form. The result is typically the product of many minds and many interests, acting with the aid of extensive research facilities bringing to bear the relevant facts and pointing out distortions and omissions in each other's arguments and factual presentations. The process is designed to maximize the opportunities for criticism, for fresh ideas and insights, and for achieving the result that will receive the widest possible acceptance. By the same token, however, the product is likely to be quite different from what would have been desired by any of the interested groups in the first instance—perhaps quite different from what any of them would still consider ideal. It may, for better or worse, be a patchwork of compromises.

How should such a process be appraised for responsiveness and responsibility? Clearly it does not accord with the party-government model. Key votes may not divide sharply along party lines. No "recognizable group, interest, or individual" can be held responsible for the outcome, a fact sometimes considered a serious defect of the system.[40] Yet it is clear the process described above involves considerable pains to achieve action that is responsible in the sense of being explicable, rationally supportable. Decisions are reached only after extensive investigation, opportunity for interested parties to be heard, and deliberation.

What about responsibility as answerability or accountability? First, it seems that the lack of an identifiable group, interest, or individual as responsible for a given piece of legislation is not *ipso facto* contrary to any democratic canon, for such a lack may indicate virtually unanimous support. In other words, the kind of lack of responsibility that can be attributed to the legislative process as described above, or as it operated in the enactment of the Employment Act of 1946 as described by Bailey in great detail, is a function of facts which add to its general acceptability. Responsibility for steel nationalization in England in 1949 was clear; but it was purchased at the price of such low acceptability that the decision did not stick. Nationalization of the mines, not to mention "cradle-to-the-grave" security,

[40] Stephen Kemp Bailey, *Congress Makes a Law* (New York: Columbia University Press, 1950), pp. 236, 237.

295

on the other hand, had bipartisan support from the outset. It is hard to view with dissatisfaction the consequent diffusion of responsibility.

If we look again at the example of the Employment Act of 1946 (and the same could be said of countless laws passed more recently), it appears that the only way in which responsibility could have been made clearer would have been to pass a different Act—something closely resembling the original bill—or else to have had the whole idea defeated. That is to say, if the result had been more to the liking of one or the other of the (relatively) extreme groups, responsibility would no doubt have been clearer. But such a result would have been not only more displeasing to the defeated group but also less responsive to modal opinion, probably not supported by any majority, and therefore more likely to prove unstable.

We must look further, however, at this matter of accountability. Its purpose is to enable the electorate to control policy. If something is done of which the electorate disapproves, a workable way should be provided for the voters to express their disapproval and bring about a change. Of course, legislation that has received general approval, which represents a substantial consensus, is much less likely than legislation enacted by a slim majority to become the subject of popular disapproval. The very process that beclouds accountability makes it less essential. Nevertheless, the proof of the pudding is in the eating; that which was approved as a bill may be condemned in operation. Yet, in practice, neither in England nor in the United States does it generally work out this way.

Moreover, opinions on specific issues or issue areas have some tendency to cluster, easing the problem of making government accountable through the political parties. In Great Britain, it is true, issue polarization between parties on a national scale is more common than in the United States. In some measure this contrast reflects the difference in party systems; but here, as always, one must be careful

296

about assuming what is cause and what is effect. The very size and variety of conditions in the United States, as compared with Britain, create a strong presumption that in large measure the differences in party systems are more reflections than causes of the differences in the structure of public opinion.[41] It would, moreover, be easy to exaggerate the difference between the British and American systems. As Butler and Stokes remarked, speaking of the British general election of 1966, "Only on the issue of nationalizing the steel industry did the Labour Party stake out a position that was strongly discrepant from that of the Conservatives —and the calculation that actuated the Labour cabinet certainly had more to do with placating left wing M.P.'s at Westminster rather than with winning votes in the country."[42]

In the United States, the behavior of Southern Democrats exaggerates but nonetheless typifies the conditions underlying our party structure. Southern Democrats have in the past been willing to choose to vote for a prolabor presidential candidate only because they can elect congressmen who will join with Republicans to defeat many of his policies. Nor is this situation confined to the Democratic party. The basic condition it reflects lies in the number and complexity of issues facing the country and the almost equal number and variety of group interests comprising the electorate. Such a plurality of views cannot be forced into the confines of dichotomous statement. Opinions cluster, but not in a simple, two-camp style.

The facts suggest that increasingly American voters are sufficiently rational and well informed to meet this situation by discriminating voting, going beyond the manoeuvre of the Southern Democrat. This conclusion is supported by the

[41] For substantiation of the statements in the text above, see the careful study by Donald E. Stokes, "Area and Party in Representation: Britain and the United States," mimeographed, paper presented at the 1967 meetings of the American Political Science Association, Chicago, 5-9 Sept. 1967.

[42] Butler and Stokes, *Political Change in Britain*, p. 447.

rapid growth of ticket-splitting in the United States since 1945.[43]

What has just been pointed to as evidence of the system's rationality may also present a problem. Independent voting indicates a weaker commitment to political parties. A rapidly increasing number of voters—especially among the younger voters—declare themselves "independent," refusing to identify themselves with any political party.[44] Can the party system survive with only a relatively small core of party professionals and activists, while the bulk of the electorate is "independent"? This question, at the moment unanswerable, may pose a problem for democracy in the United States. But it is hard to see that it is a serious problem so long as party organizations perform the nominating functions and if "independent" voters exercise their independence in a way rationally calculated to advance their interests (as evidence recited earlier gives some reason for thinking they do).[45] At least this should lead to responsiveness; whether it is likely to lead to responsible action in the sense of socially rational action is another question, to which some remarks will be addressed later on. It may be noted here, however, that an important contributing factor to the current decline of political parties is the great increase in the scope of governmental responsibilities and

[43] See DeVries and Tarrance, *The Ticket-Splitter*, pp. 29, 32n, and 121-122.

[44] Mr. Gallup finds this trend continuing. He reports an increase in the number of persons under thirty who classify themselves as "independents" from 36 percent in 1972 to 39 percent in 1975. *The Gallup Opinion Index*, June, 1975, p. 21.

[45] A similar argument is made by James Coleman, "Collective Decisions and Collective Actions," in Peter Laslett, W. C. Runciman, and Quentin Skinner, eds., *Philosophy, Politics and Society*, 4th series (New York: Barnes and Noble, 1972), pp. 208-219, 218. See also James F. Ward, "Toward a Sixth Party System? Partisanship and Political Development," *Western Polit. Quar.*, 26 (1973), 385-413. Ward takes issue with Walter Dean Burnham's defense of the decline-of-party thesis, as set forth in his *Critical Elections and the Mainsprings of American Politics* (New York: Norton, 1970).

action, with resultant variety of issues to which the parties address themselves. The wider the spread of issues the less likely is it that opinions will cluster—the less likely that a mass of voters will be able to agree on any *program*. Clearly this is a more serious problem for the party-government model than it is for a weak-party system. As for the latter, whose main function is to attend to nominating candidates, one can only hope that the same reasons which led to their development in the first place, as recited above, will assure their continued existence. Yet it is not at all clear that they will. Both the increase of independent voting and the weakening of party organizations brought about (especially in the case of the Democratic party) by recent changes in the rules governing the selection of delegates to the national conventions have contributed to party disintegration even for the nominating process. An ominous sign is provided by the increasing reliance of presidential candidates on special committees for their election, unrelated to the regular party organizations and appealing to voters from both parties as well as to independents. Within limits this development has its positive aspect—it facilitates the kind of pluralistic representation that permits voters to express themselves in more complicated issue-patterns than would otherwise be possible. But if it were to go too far it might result in a very complicated situation that more voters would find confusing than liberating.[46]

To assume that either political parties or the elections to which they are adjuncts provide the only, or even the chief, link between the voters and the government would, however, be a great mistake. Much that is relevant happens both before and after this dramatic, but not necessarily climactic, event. In the choice of candidates and in the formulation and pronouncement of party policy in party

[46] Gerald Pomper suggests one way to combat party disintegration would be to channel federal contributions to campaign expenditures through the regular party organizations instead of directly to candidates. For this suggestion and more general discussion on the subject, see his *Voters' Choice*, Chap. 10.

platforms and campaign speeches, the law of anticipated reactions is at work. The very statement that party competition forces parties to seek a fuzzy "happy medium" suggests they are responsive to what they believe modal effective opinion is.[47] As their beliefs about what will be popular with new voters and potential switchers shift, so does their position change. In a perfect market, sellers offer similar products for similar prices; and if demand increases they all raise their prices. The similarity of party platforms has led many observers to false conclusions: in particular, to the conclusion that the party system is not responsive to public opinion. These observers commit a methodological error. They should compare this year's platforms to those of the preceding general election. If they discover, as is frequently the case, that both major parties have changed in the same direction, if both opposed a Women's Rights Amendment on one occasion and both came out in favor of it four years later, the evidence in favor of responsiveness is strong; and so, too, with antipollution legislation. The gradual edging toward a comprehensive system of health insurance in the United States during the 1970s provides another example of this process.

In addition to preelection influences of the kind just discussed, two other factors must be taken into account: postelection influence and the effect of leaders. It is true that most of the people on most issues are ignorant or indifferent or both. But the same statement cannot be made of political activists and influentials. Leaders, elites, activists, in thousands of both special-interest and general-interest groups, are informed, active, and influential. Among them, they express almost every conceivable point of view and support almost every substantial interest (whether or not in just proportion). It is especially because of these individuals that responsiveness does not end with elections,

[47] Use of the word *effective* here is intended to reflect the fact that party leaders will seek to weigh as well as to count opinions, in the effort to determine which ones are firm enough to affect voting.

that the avenues through which public opinions can be brought to bear upon policy formation and implementation are manifold, operating at all levels, from precinct to administrators, and using all manner of techniques and forms of organization. The difficulties of achieving democratic and responsible policy making at the legislative level through the sole—or even the dominant—agency of the political party are magnified when it comes to the administrative level, where so much of the policy-making process takes place.

While to distinguish conceptually between preelection, election, and postelection influences and also between leader and rank-and-file influences is important, it would be unrealistic to insist that these influences can always be distinguished in practice. Two further examples will illustrate this point and also emphasize the fact that the American system can be highly responsive. The growing opposition to the Vietnam War in the late sixties led to numerous responses. Lyndon Johnson decided not to run for a second term of office.[48] Both of the major parties came out in 1968 for bringing the war, or our participation in it, to an end. While that process proved to be slower than most would have hoped, in fact the participation of American ground troops was brought to a virtual end by the close of 1971, and American casualties were reduced dramatically; and in March 1973, all remaining military forces were withdrawn. Growing economic recession in 1971 led the Nixon administration, doubtless partly in response to increasing popular demands and partly in anticipation of the 1972 elections, to scrap his preelection opposition to Keynesian economics and to plunge headlong, if temporarily, into price and wage controls, despite his earlier stand against them. Neither action would accord with the theory of electoral mandates, but both represent responsiveness to popular demand.

[48] Observers generally believe that this decision was prompted by the unpopularity he acquired as a result of his escalation of that war. Johnson himself denied this was his motivation.

301

The preceding discussion, it must be stressed, relates to responsiveness achieved through accountability *on specific issues.* It does not negate the crucial fact that governments remain accountable on the basis of the generalized public reactions to their policies and that political parties play a significant role in this operation, even if only by providing a mechanism by which the dissatisfied can be organized in support of a particular alternative.[49]

8. RESPONSIBILITY AS RATIONALITY

This discussion of political parties, strong and weak, disciplined and undisciplined, has had much more to say about responsiveness and accountability than about responsibility in the sense of rationality, taking action on the basis of full information and careful deliberation after hearing arguments from all sides. Quick responsiveness to simple majorities would threaten responsible action. Beyond this statement, generalizations are hard to make. The two models of party systems that have been discussed cannot be neatly classified according to their effects upon the degree to which governments act responsibly. Party government, as it has been described in these pages, is sometimes upheld as a model for responsible democratic government in the rationality sense as well as in terms of accountability. The theory is that the party in power is able to put together a coherent and well-thought-out program and then, by party discipline, to see that it is carried out by appropriate legislative and administrative action. Unfortunately, this model

[49] For simplicity's sake, the discussion here has been confined to two-party systems. Under multiparty systems, party positions are often more clearly enunciated. Also the voter has a wider choice with a consequently greater possibility of finding a party that approximates his particular position on each of several issues. But under such a system, normally no single party will be able to effectuate its program. As was pointed out, coalitions must be formed and compromises worked out after the election has taken place: the apparent gain at the electoral level tends to be lost before policies can be effectuated.

contains serious flaws. In the first place, political parties in such a system, just as much as under the weak-party system, must build a majority in a competitive struggle for votes. The inevitable result is to seek the support of many groups by making promises that appeal to their particular and intense interests, even though making good on each of these promises is likely to prove impossible, because they will often be mutually incompatible. As Professor Lindblom has acutely remarked, "A party can easily win a majority of electors to it by appealing to each subsection of the electorate on an issue on which it is an intense minority, thereby winning the election with a majority of the electorate opposed to the party's policy on each point."[50] The same process of yielding to pressures that lead to mutually conflicting policies may take place as well after the election as before. This process is in some measure self-limiting, to be sure. Insofar as the mutually conflicting policies are expected to produce bad consequences that will be perceived as such by the electorate and entered as a black mark in the record of the party in power, it may be that the party leadership will seek to check the process of combining inconsistent programs; and it may be that the leadership under a strong-party-government model is in a better position to accomplish this objective than is the case under a weak-party system. Unfortunately, the matters we are dealing with here—inconsistent policies—are not sufficiently specifiable and measurable (by the degrees of inconsistency and the likely consequences) to render any more rigorous judgment possible.

The combination of disciplined parties and the parliamentary form of government does at least make for the implementation of policy that is *planned*, whether or not it is planned with a view to consistency. The American system, on the other hand, is much less controlled. It is more responsive, both positively and negatively, to minority groups with intense interests. The resulting policy outputs

[50] Lindblom, *The Intelligence of Democracy*, p. 141.

are less planned and less orderly. They are not necessarily less the result of informed deliberation. It has been argued that this "pluralistic" method brings together a greater wealth of information, more different points of view and types of experience, and a greater sensitivity to varying intensities of need than does the more orderly, planned procedure of the party discipline/parliamentary government model.[51]

9. CONCLUDING REMARKS

This chapter has been devoted to some of the most basic concepts of democracy, and some aspects of the operation of certain democratic institutions, especially political parties, have been discussed. It has been argued that such terms as responsiveness and responsibility, and for that matter, majority rule, are not so simple and straightforward as they sometimes seem. They have different meanings and, moreover, meanings that tend to conflict with each other. Responsiveness to wants may be quite different from responsiveness to needs. Responsiveness to the majority may not be compatible with responsiveness to certain intense minorities. Responsibility as accountability, and responsibility as rational action may also be at odds with each other.

Discussion of these distinctions and of the resulting relations led necessarily to some discussion of public opinion. No more than a most superficial consideration of this immense topic was necessary to make clear its complete inadequacy for the tasks set for it by some naive theories of democracy. (Whether any serious thinkers have ever held the theory in this naive form is not a question that need trouble us.) "Activists," "influentials," "leaders," "elites"— people in these categories must clearly play key roles in any

[51] For a powerful statement of this case, see Lindblom, ibid. The case for party government is ably put by Samuel H. Beer, "New Structures of Democracy: Britain and America," in William N. Chambers and Robert H. Salisbury, eds., *Democracy in Mid-Twentieth Century*, pp. 30-59.

democratic state. The ordinary voters are greatly influenced by them. Without them they would be much more confused than they are. But, with their assistance, as V. O. Key remarked with considerable supporting evidence, "voters are not fools."[52]

The introduction of these terms led to some discussion, under the heading of weak political parties, of the institutions and processes often designated by the overworked term *pluralism*. If democracy cannot get along without at least one elite, one body, group, or class of people with more than average political skill and, accordingly, more than average political influence, should this aggregation of influentials be organized into a single body, should they be divided into two fairly closely knit competing groups, or should they be scattered more widely? The question of pluralism comes up in other contexts in succeeding chapters. Nonetheless, in the present context I have given reasons for favoring the pluralist solution to this problem, insofar as it is a matter of choice. Pluralism is today under wide attack. For the most part the critics are directing their attacks at different issues from those discussed in this chapter. They tend to identify pluralism with the belief that if narrowly defined interest groups—that is, groups of people organized on the basis of some common selfish interest—are allowed to dominate the political scene, somehow the public interest will take care of itself. As will appear later, I do not defend that position; but I also question whether the system of strong-party government gives any more assurance that the public interest will be protected and advanced than does a system of weak parties with checks and balances and separated powers. Many critics of pluralism would also contend that greater use of participatory democracy would both minimize the necessity of relying upon elites and make it possible to achieve consensus and not to have to rely upon partisan competition. This argument is discussed in Chapter Eleven.

Both sets of theories or models of democracy set forth in

[52] Key, *The Responsible Electorate*, p. 7.

Chapter Five have some applicability to the subject of this chapter, especially in connection with political parties as instruments for enforcing accountability to the electorate. In the discussion of the most general aspects of voting and the organization of voters, the set of motivational theories was the most applicable. Although the discussion of party systems has had little either to gain from or to contribute to these theories, it will be recalled that the discussions in the early part of the chapter both of responsiveness and of accountability considered the implications of those subjects for the motivational theories. Our discussion of responsiveness seemed to bear only on radical individualism, and here it was ambiguous. The most obvious form of that theory seemed to be controverted by our analysis of responsiveness. On the other hand, in a more sophisticated form, radical individualism was quite compatible with responsiveness. And when attention was turned to accountability, the theory of radical individualism seemed a good start for explaining both what actually happens and what the needs of a democratic system demand. At the same time it was found wanting in certain respects, both in explaining why people do vote and also in providing any argument as to why they should vote.[53] Here both the theory of the public interest and the theory of rights and duties come to the rescue. As supplements to individualism, both on the descriptive and the prescriptive side, they (either or both of them) supply what would otherwise be lacking. The individualistic theories place a heavy, perhaps unsustainable, burden upon rational far-sightedness, which becomes more realistic to the extent that commitment to the public interest, or to public-interest-supporting rights and duties, can be relied upon. In fact, either the public-interest or

[53] Strictly, radical individualism, being a positive and not a normative theory, could not be expected to explain why people ought to vote. The last remark in the text above, then, must be taken as applying to individualism generally, although least to the self-realizationist variety.

306

the rights and duties theory could stand alone, though such a construction would appear to do much less than justice to the realities of political behavior, which exhibit a great deal more self-interestedness than either of these theories calls for. Finally, democratic collectivism is compatible with the facts of political behavior only if assigned a purely ancillary role. In no case did the facts compel us to assert the validity of one of the theories to the complete exclusion of the others.

As for the second set of democratic theories, it must be concluded that neither elitist nor populist theory seems adequate to describe or account for responsiveness and the enforcement of responsibility. The populist model would give public opinion a role. it is incapable of playing. It is therefore an inadequate model, either descriptively or prescriptively. If by elitist it is simply meant that a few are politically more able than the many and also that it is right and proper that institutions recognize this fact and permit the elite to exercise their inevitable influence legitimately, one need not quarrel. But if elitist means more than that, in general something like the party-government model, reasons have been given for questioning elitist theory's desirability, as well as suggesting that even in England, its home, the reality departs considerably from the norm. This theory, in short, must be confined to a subsidiary role. Populism, it may be added, is not only an inaccurate description of reality in the mature democracies of the world, but also it is theoretically deficient in demanding too much of the average voter and in failing to allow for the need for organization and for leadership. (The latter subject is discussed more fully in Chapter Twelve.)

Finally, then, the analysis above has provided support for both constitutionalism and social pluralism as prescriptive as well as (especially in the United States) descriptive theories. Their relations to each other have not been discussed, except perhaps by implication. In other chapters it will become increasingly evident how constitutionalism

CHAPTER VIII

Representation[1]

To achieve responsiveness and responsibility, all modern governments rely heavily upon representation. Political representation in the broadest sense is not necessarily democratic. In a proper sense of the word, all legitimate governments are "representative." Thus medieval kings were thought to be made legitimate not only by hereditary right and divine ordination but also by the acclaim of the nobles. They owed their authority as well, at least in some dim past, to the people more generally, or so it was widely held. Part of their office was to see that justice was done, "to protect the poor as well as the rich in the enjoyment of their rights."[2] The most absolute rulers, whether James I or Adolf Hitler, have sought legitimacy by claiming to represent the people.

It will be noted that the two main claims of monarchs and dictators from which their legitimacy appears to have derived were (1) that they stood for, gave expression to, and supported the interests (and ideals and aspirations) of their people; and (2) that they were in some fashion authorized to act (generally within variously stated or implied limits) in the people's behalf. All this is not of mere historical interest, nor applicable only to nondemocratic states. *All* regimes gain legitimacy by being in some degree representative (in one or, generally, both of the senses

[1] Parts of this chapter, in identical or similar form, appeared as the first chapter of *Representation*: NOMOS X, ed. J. Roland Pennock and John W. Chapman. Reprinted by permission of the Publishers, Lieber-Atherton, Inc. Copyright © 1968.

[2] R. W. and A. J. Carlyle, *Medieval Political Theory* (Edinburgh and London: William Blackwood & Sons, 1915), 3: 33.

mentioned) or at least by convincing an effective majority (sufficient number) of their subjects that they are.

As certain elements of the realm in traditional monarchies became dissatisfied, they demanded a more accurate and responsive form of representation, one over which they had control.[3] Thus today the man in the street tends to think of elected officers as the primary representatives, and he especially thinks of the elected legislature as *the* representative body and its members as *the* representatives. Elections are thought to constitute the great sanction for assuring representative behavior, by showing what the voters consider to be their interests by giving them the incentive to pursue those objectives. But the role of representatives is not entirely a one-way affair. They are intermediaries, which is to say they have also a role to play in "representing" to their constituents the organ of which they are a part. They tell voters about the interests of the country as seen from the center. Moreover, in analyzing and interpreting that information and seeking to persuade their constituents of its significance, they exert leadership. They help to "socialize" the public.

The chief concern of this chapter is elected representatives, especially the members of legislatures. Yet elections are certainly not the only means whereby persons in positions of authority are encouraged to act representatively, even today, nor are elected officers the only ones whose behavior is in some measure representative. Members of the bureaucracy, even though they may be practically immune from even indirect elective pressure, are expected to subject their discretionary authority to at least some norms of representation.[4]

[3] Of course, this is schematized history at best. In England, for instance, elected representatives were first created at the king's instance (although it is doubtful that they had legislative power): but the statement is valid for a later period.

[4] It is at least arguable that as the policy role of bureaucracies in both England and the United States has increased and become more widely recognized, the ideal of administrative "neutrality" has weak-

In arguing that administrators act in a representative role, especially those having broad discretionary powers or exercising great influence on policy making, it is not contended that this is the only role they play or even that the role in this context calls for the same behavior as it would in a legislative context. The circumstances attending the grant of administrative authority, especially the basic legislation, committee reports, and legislative debates, may indicate that the wishes of a particular segment of the polity, perhaps a particular industry, are to be given exceptional weight. Or they may suggest that the representative role of the administering agency should veer sharply away from the responsiveness-to-desire pole toward that of estimation of the public interest.[5] In the United States, the poverty program, whose statute calls for "maximum feasible participation" by the beneficiaries, illustrates departure from the norm in the opposite direction, toward responsiveness.

1. Elective Representation—Preliminaries

First, it is only fair to note that some writers believe the whole concept of representation might well be dispensed with. H. B. Mayo, for instance, has written: "Democratic theory has little to gain from talking the language of representation, since everything necessary to the theory may be put in terms of (a) legislators (or decision-makers) who are (b) legitimated or authorized to enact public policies, and who are (c) subject or responsible to popular control at free elections. The difficulties of policy-makers are practical, and there is no need to confuse democratic politics by a

---

ened and the demand to strengthen popular control over those administrators who in fact make policy in important matters has grown. One thinks, for example, of Britain's recently created specialized select committees for the supervision of administration and of the notorious efforts of Congress and its committees to control administration.

[5] The distinction between these two aspects of representation will be discussed below.

theory that makes the difficulties appear to be metaphysical or logical within the concept of representation."[6]

I believe, however, that something important would be lost by failing to deal with the concept of representation. Parts of the government other than legislative bodies serve representative functions, so the concept of representation links or mutually relates these various instruments of representative roles. Furthermore, even the people more specifically thought of as representatives, i.e. members of an elective legislature, have various roles from which conflicting directives frequently emerge that can be reconciled only by reference to some superior set of norms. It is suggested here that in some measure the concept of representation, *considered in the specific contexts in which it is applied,* provides this superior set of norms. Much that would be hopelessly vague, considered in the abstract, becomes more precise in actual application. In making this point below, some indication will be given of the relation between the theory of representation and empirical studies of legislative roles.[7]

Second, I assume that "representation" may not always have had the same meaning, and that it may not always mean the same thing today in different countries. Where the context does not indicate otherwise, the reference is to Anglo-American usage in the twentieth century. In fact, much of the discussion relates primarily to the American situation, being rendered not wrong but largely irrelevant to the British system by the strength of party discipline there.

Third, while the "concept" of representation will be treated at some length, reference will also be made to various "theories" of representation. The two may be kept

---

[6] Mayo, *An Introduction to Democratic Theory* (New York: Oxford University Press, 1960), p. 103.

[7] I have in mind especially the extensive and valuable study by John C. Wahlke, Heinz Eulau, William Buchanan, and LeRoy C. Ferguson, *The Legislative System* (New York: Wiley, 1962).

312

mutually distinct, but they tend to merge; and where the line is to be drawn between them is in a measure arbitrary. For instance, if "representation" meant—as it does not—that a "representative" was a person who should do what and only what his constituents demanded of him, one would not need a theory about his proper role. The substance of such a theory would have been incorporated into the definition. If, on the other hand, the word meant that a person was empowered to do whatever he chose on behalf of those whom he represented, and this was all it meant, then only a theory about how representatives should acquit themselves could supply such a normative element. In other words, in default of agreement upon a single theory, no theory would become part of the concept itself, but the concept would tend to be supplemented by two or more alternative theories.

Fourth, as has already been implied, it will not be argued that all vagueness can be eliminated from the term. Nor is vagueness always a shortcoming; indeed, in moderation it may be an asset! Ponder the popular (and useful) term in modern political science *consensus*; or consider *power, liberty, cleavage*, or *the public interest*. Imprecise terms, in this case terms that lay down standards (as contrasted with rules) of conduct, often have the virtue of holding together, before the mind's eye, related though distinct ideas. They show linkages and continuities that might otherwise be overlooked. Synthesis as well as analysis has its uses in contributing to the understanding of systems of all kinds, including political systems. As the use of the word *standards* may suggest, terms with some elements of vagueness are especially likely to be required where norms are involved, but the examples of *power, consensus*, and *cleavage* show that not only normative terms are difficult to make at once precise and useful.

Fifth, it must be understood that the elected representatives here discussed (whether members of a legislature or chief executives) are not simply advisory or expressive.

313

They have powers to make policy and enact laws, and in doing so they are frequently resolving conflicts among various sections of the public. But whatever they do, whatever roles they play, they are representatives and therefore should act representatively, subject to the norms of representation, whatver they may be.

A. Phillips Griffiths has argued that political representation is a variety of ascriptive representation.[8] An ascriptive representative is one who has authority to act for and commit those whom he represents. At best, this theory seems to place the emphasis in the wrong place—on the powers of the representative rather than on his responsibilities. Further, it is not clear in what sense political representatives *can* always commit those whom they represent. If my congressional representative makes a speech condemning the president, or libeling someone, it would hardly be said that I am "committed" by his action. Moreover, it would appear to be not the representative who has the power to commit me, but the body of which he is a member. Even then I am "committed" only in the sense that I am legally bound to obey duly enacted legislation, as I might be—perhaps less strongly—even in the absence of "representative" government.

Two other concepts of representation discussed by Griffiths should also be mentioned. He disposes effectively of "descriptive" representation—representation by persons who as nearly as possible reflect the complexion of the constituency. As he says, no one would argue that morons should be represented by morons. It is desirable to have a given group represented by members of that group (as is recommended for women and minorities by the revised rules governing Democratic conventions), insofar as it is as a means to having that group's point of view effectively expressed and its interests advanced. In any given case, de-

[8] Griffiths, "How Can One Person Represent Another?" *Aristotelian Society*, Suppl. Vol. 34 (1960), 182-208.

scriptive representation may or may not be the best way to accomplish those purposes.

Griffiths's final category is representation of interests, meaning thereby that various interest groups, rather than geographical constituencies, should elect representatives. This is not a theory of what constitutes representation but of what should be represented. It will be discussed later in the chapter.

Not only do representatives do more than represent in the narrowest sense of that term; also legislators do more than legislate, and much of what they do falls under the concept of "representing": "errand-running," acting as lines of communication between constituents and administrators, and arguing the interests of their constituents before administrative agencies.

Sixth (returning now to the main line of the argument), just as the concepts of authorization (power to formulate and effectuate policies) and representation are intertwined —because roles of legislation and of representation are to a large extent performed by the same persons—so are the concepts of leadership and representation. Clearly leadership either is an aspect of representation, or is entailed by it, or is a necessary means to performing the representative function. However that may be, leadership is clearly a subject that must command our attention. It will be dealt with separately, in Chapter Twelve.

2. "Linkage" between Representative and Represented

In the preceding chapter, eventually it seemed necessary to consider a crucial point: whether people voted so arbitrarily that any analysis based on voter rationality was worthless. Only after finding evidence that this was probably not so did we proceed with our discussion. Now, in considering the subject of representation, we have reached a similar pass. Our denial of the validity of the mandate theory in connection with responsiveness and responsibility raises the question of what linkage, if any, exists between representative and represented. (Insofar as this is a question of voter rationality, that subject has already been treated; but more than this is involved.)

First, it may be helpful to say a few more words about the mandate theory here as it more specifically applies to representation. (The theory is largely in disrepute among American political scientists, but it still has its adherents even in the United States, and especially abroad.) More clearly than other theories of representation, the mandate theory relates specifically to elections and the supposed—and here enters ambiguity—authorization *or* direction to a representative that an election creates. Thus by being elected, a representative may be said to have been authorized to use his own judgment in pursuing justice, or the interest of the nation, or the interest of his constituency. Or, it may be said, that he has been authorized to act in one or more of these ways especially (or only) on a certain key issue that was featured during the campaign. But others may construe a mandate to mean not only authorization but also instruction, making the representative more of a delegate. And again the instruction may apply to all his campaign promises or only to a specific issue. The concept of a mandate is generally applied to the legislative members of the majority party as a whole, or to the government they have established.

As to "authorization," this generalized idea of a mandate is so broad as to be unfalsifiable; and, in any case, it amounts to no more than a denial of the delegate theory, to be discussed below.

If one fixes upon the "instruction" definition, as being more precise, difficulties remain. It tends to go with the theory of "party government"; and the weaknesses of that theory, especially as applied to American government, were pointed out in the preceding chapter. Even in the case of

This last finding suggests a further line of thought. If indeed representatives do defer to constituency opinions, may it still be that this phenomenon demonstrates accountability enforced by elections, in spite of the fact that it seems to make its appearance more in "noncompetitive than in "competitive" electoral districts? I believe so. Consider the case of a representative who has been elected by a narrow margin (that is, in a "competitive" district). He must decide how to vote, let us say, on a measure to limit eligibility for food stamps. Let us assume further that he desires to be reelected, that he has no information about his constituents' opinions on this matter other than what he can derive from the results of the election, which he won by a 1 percent margin, after having voiced sentiments that might have led his constituents to expect his negative vote on the measure. Since being elected, however, he has become convinced that, in the public interest, he should support the measure. Now consider the case of another representative whose situation is the same, except that he comes from a "safe" district, having won the last election by a margin of 15 percent. Which representative, other things being equal, is more likely to vote responsively to the presumed views of a majority of his constituents? Surely it is the representative of the "safe" district. He can be relatively much more sure of the majority opinion in his district. To vote his own (changed) views *might* offend 65 percent of the electorate. On the other hand, his colleague from a competitive district, by the same type of crude measurement, would offend only 51 percent. He could much more safely bet that either (1) the issue was not sufficiently salient with enough voters to affect the result of the next election; or (2) that he (or the course of events) would persuade 1 percent (actually, one-half of 1 percent, plus one) of the voters to change their minds; or (3) some combination of these two.[11]

[11] For further speculations on the significance of Miller's findings, see Bryan D. Jones, "Competitiveness, Role Orientations, and Legislative Responsiveness," *Jour. of Politics*, 35 (1974), 924-947, at 934ff.

Of course the second of our hypothetical representatives would not mind offending 65 percent of his constituents (assuming pure self-interest) if he was sure his seat was "safe." But no seat is safe from a turnover in the primary election, and over a reasonably long haul virtually none is safe even in the general election. Hence, responsiveness by occupants of so-called "safe" seats in no way disproves that elections are effective instruments of accountability.

At the same time, I am not suggesting that the linkage *on specific issues* between constituency and representative is a strong one. To do so would be contrary to what has been argued above about the mandate theory. It would also be negated by numerous special studies. For instance, a study of the Iowa state legislature serves as a warning against assuming too close a relation between constituency and legislator's behavior.[12] In this study it appeared that on four issues for which a relatively high degree of constituent knowledge and interest was to be presumed, and which were submitted to a referendum vote, representatives were unable to predict correctly how the majority of their constituents would vote in a large proportion of cases. The percentage of representatives' accurate predictions on constituent voting for the respective issues were: (1) home rule, 91.5%; (2) reapportionment, 81.7%; (3) annual sessions of the legislature, 58.9%; and (4) item veto, 64.3%.

To be sure, representatives are subject to numerous influences other than their own attitudes and those of their constituents as they perceive them. For instance, they are influenced by their party leadership in their constituencies, in their states, in their own legislative body, and of course

---

[12] Ronald D. Hedlund and H. Paul Friesema, "Representatives' Perceptions of Constituency Opinion," *Jour. of Politics*, 34 (1972), 730-752, 741. Interestingly, those representatives who said they viewed their role as that of delegates (reflecting constituency opinion) were least well informed about the opinions of their constituents, while those who asserted they considered themselves as "trustees" (that is, following their own beliefs) were best informed about their constituents' views. Ibid., p. 743.

by the president (or governor), if he is of their political party. What is the significance of this fact? Insofar as the party is interested in keeping its men in office, the basic reference point is the same—the voter—except that party leaders, especially those at the national level, are likely to take more of a national than a local point of view. They tend to relate, that is to say, to a broader constituency and possibly to a longer time span.

Also, the individual representative and the party leaders must take account of the views of past and potential financial contributors. That this is an important factor in many cases is beyond doubt; but measurement is difficult if not impossible. How much it varies from constituency or national preference is equally problematical; but there is certainly no reason to assume coincidence. Organized groups, whether of business, labor, or agriculture, all have access to this means of influence. Specific interests, through their pressure groups, constitute an important though certainly distorting factor in the process of linking electorate and public. They may give financial support to particular candidates within the limits of campaign financing legislation. Perhaps, however, they are best perceived as carriers of information (bearing both upon the nature and intensity of constituency opinion and upon the merits of issues) and as persuaders and analyzers and attention-directors. Doubtless they both accentuate the influence of constituency opinion and distort it. Often they also bring to bear a national (though partial) point of view to supplement a local one.

The most massive empirical study of representation made to date not only stresses the point just made—that other forces than elections influence representative bodies—but also concludes that elections perform important linkage functions that substantially increase responsiveness.[13] To the

[13] Heinz Eulau and Kenneth Prewitt, *Labyrinths of Democracy* (New York: Bobbs, Merrill, 1973), pp. 443, and *passim*. See also the same authors' "Political Matrix and Political Representation: Prolegomenon to a New Departure from an Old Problem," *Amer. Polit. Sci.*

same effect is the cautious conclusion of V. O. Key, Jr., with which this section may appropriately be concluded. He found that although constituency pressures often leave representatives considerable latitude, they tend to exercise their discretion in a way that suggests a relation between the votes they cast and the characteristics of the constituency (as revealed by demographic data).[14]

3. THEORIES OF REPRESENTATION

In what has been said above, reference has been made, at least by implication, to four distinct theories of how representatives ought to act.[15]

They may be stated in the form of the following propositions:

1. The representative acts (should act) in support of what he believes an effective majority of his constituents desires. (Local delegate theory.)[16]

2. The representative acts (should act) in support of what

Rev., 63 (1969), 427-441, where it is pointed out that even where a constituency has been generally satisfied to allow a legislative body to pursue its own views of the public interest, if the members of the public become dissatisfied they can intrude into the deliberations of the legislative body and force responsiveness.

[14] Key, *Public Opinion and American Democracy*, pp. 486-487.

[15] Note the distinction between "theories of how representatives ought to act" and "theories of representation" (the abbreviated heading of this section). Theories of representation are not confined to political representation. They relate to all meanings of the word. Even with respect to political representation, they are not confined to how representatives ought to act but encompass theories of the meaning of the word, such as "authorization" theories and "accountability" theories, touched on above, and theories stressing the ideal of representation and others stressing the meaning of the concept as reflected in practice. For an exhaustive and enlightening discussion of this subject, see Hanna Fenichel Pitkin, *The Concept of Representation* (Berkeley and Los Angeles: University of California Press, 1967).

[16] Desires need not be self-regarding; they may relate to the realization of ideals.

he believes is in the constituency's interest. (Local trustee theory.)

3. The representative acts (should act) in support of what he believes an effective majority of the nation desires. (National delegate theory.)

4. The representative acts (should act) in support of what he believes is in the nation's interest. (National trustee theory.)[17]

We shall first examine each of these theories in the light of an analysis of what "representation" is generally understood to mean, especially in particular contexts. (The relations between these theories and the various types of democratic theory will be discussed in the following sections.) It will be observed that the theories rely heavily upon the distinction between "interest" and "desire." Because "interest" is notoriously ambiguous or vague, a digression to discuss the meaning intended here is called for. For present purposes the word's ambiguities can be confined within reasonable limits. The "interest" of a person or a constituency or a nation, means its advantage. An action, policy, law, or institution is in the interest of a person if it increases his opportunity to get what he desires, including the realization of his ideals.[18] To spell this out a little further, the distinc-

17 These are pure type theories. Their number could be increased by developing mixed or compromise theories. See for instance Wahlke, et al., *The Legislative System*. Their analysis of the roles of a representative is more detailed. They speak of representational "styles" in a way that closely corresponds to the analysis above, except that they add the intermediate category of "politicos." But further, under the heading of "focuses," they consider such "clientele roles" as the "party role," the "areal role," "the pressure group role," and the "administrative role." (Ibid., p. 14, and Chap. 12.) It seems clear that these various roles impose conflicting demands upon the legislator and that they all relate to his role as representative. It is one contention of this chapter that the concept of representation considered in the context of particular situations can help clarify the forces at work, both normative and otherwise.

18 See Brian M. Barry, "The Use and Abuse of 'The Public Inter-

tion between "desire" and "interest" is the distinction between what is immediately demanded and what in the long run, with the benefit of hindsight, would have been preferred or would have contributed to the development of the individual into a person capable of making responsible decisions.

If, after he has done his best to form an enlightened opinion, the representative believes that a given measure would in fact improve, for example, the economic or educational level of his constituency, other things being equal he would be entitled to conclude that it is in their interest. Of course, most of the time he will be making the kind of judgments that involve weighing an advantage against a disadvantage (both being incurred by the same course of action), just as when an individual tries to decide whether something is in his interest. All that can be demanded is that the representative make this kind of judgment as wisely and impartially as he can. In most cases the standard will not be more vague than the one we all must use for our private choices. The same will be true when a decision must be made between what is judged to be a great advantage for a sizable minority and a lesser advantage for a bare majority. All must be within the framework of what the society in question has established (whether or not in the form of a written constitution) as proper for the state to do—i.e. it must respect recognized rights.

a. Delegate versus Trustee

Among these theories, it is probably safe to say that the dichotomy between acting as a delegate and acting as a trustee is most fundamental. It also seems clear that neither

---

est,'" in Carl J. Friedrich, ed., *The Public Interest*, NOMOS V, pp. 191-204; also Brian Barry, *Political Argument* (London: Routledge & Kegan Paul, 1965), p. 176. See also, especially for what follows in the text, S. I. Benn, "'Interests' in Politics," *Proceedings of the Aristotelian Society*, n.s. 1959/60 (London: Harrison & Sons, 1960), pp. 122-140, 139. On the terms *interest* and *public interest*, see as well Richard R. Flathman, *The Public Interest*, Chap. 2.

pole of this dichotomy is adequate to explain democratic representation in the modern Anglo-American tradition. For a representative to act purely and simply as a delegate would be to make him functionless most, if not all, of the time, for it is seldom clear precisely what a constituency, or even its majority, wishes. Most of the individuals who compose it either do not know enough or do not care enough (or both) about the issues on which their representatives must vote to have clear opinions of their own; and even when opinions are formed, a majority is likely to be lacking. Representing a constituency is not like representing a client, whose wishes, on a single issue at least, are presumably unitary. A constituency, on the contrary, is rarely unified, even on a single question. Of course, in some cases a clear majority has a definite view on an issue. It might be argued that in such cases the representative should act as a delegate, supporting the majority's desires even though he believes these desires are contrary to their own interests. Thinking for himself and deliberating on the basis of discussion with others, in other words, should be reserved for cases where no clear majority opinion unopposed by an intense minority exists. This is, to be sure, a logically possible position. My own view is that it would not be held by many thoughtful people who consider the implication of the legislative situation, with its opportunities for discussion, deliberation, and obtaining information. In any case, the burden of proof under these circumstances would certainly be on the legislator to justify voting contrary to the majority will.

Similarly, in other ways, what "representation" entails is affected by the context of the office of elected legislator. For instance, if the general attitude of the people in a given constituency were, let us say, anti-French, one would properly say a person who held that attitude was, other things being equal, "representative" of the constituency. It would not follow, however, that a representative elected by this constituency should vote for anti-French policies, regardless of other considerations. Interests would also need to be taken into account.

But the interest pole of the desire-interest axis is also untenable. Even Burke did not contend that it was the proper function of a representative to act without any consideration of the desires of those whom he represented.[19] In fact, it appears to be generally agreed that representation in a democratic context makes the satisfaction of popular desire itself a legitimate interest, thus blunting the sharpness of the contrast between representation of desires and representation of interests. It seems clear, then, that the proper role of a political representative today is generally believed to fall somewhere between these poles. Thus, it is argued here, the prevailing concept of political representation itself gives some guidance for the reconciliation of these conflicts.

Let us consider the delegate-trustee issue in the light of a series of examples illustrating various combinations of strong or weak (and positive or negative) majority desires, and strong or weak (and positive or negative) convictions on the part of the representative as to the constituency's real interest.[20] Suppose it is a question of whether funds should be spent on a fish hatchery and a research institute to study certain diseases that have been limiting the local fish supply, or whether the money should be spent on improving the roads. Assuming that motorists outnumber anglers by a staggering ratio, it is likely that a majority, while not feeling very strongly about the matter, might oppose the hatchery, whereas only the minority would have very strong feelings about it and support it. Suppose also the legislator's own study convinced him that the hatchery and research institute were, on balance, more in the public

---

[19] In his Bristol address, referring to his constituents, he said, "their wishes ought to have great weight with [their representative]; their opinion high respect; their business unremitted attention." *The Works of the Right Honorable Edmund Burke*, 6 vols., The World's Classics, Vol. LXXXI (London: Oxford University Press, 1906), 2:164.

[20] This "intensity" problem was very briefly discussed in the preceding chapter, in connection with "responsiveness."

interest than the additional funds for roads (perhaps partly because of a putative lift to the tourist industry and, through it, to the economy as a whole). Under these circumstances a vote for the fishermen would seem to be in order. If, however, his informed judgment was clearly to the contrary, he should vote for the roads. But what if it seemed to him a toss-up? Should he follow the rather passive majority or the relatively small but demanding minority? To this question no pat answer is available. If electoral considerations point in one direction or the other, that fact in itself would be significant and it would be right to allow them to govern.

Now take a proposal to fluoridate the water supply. Polls reveal that 45 percent of the electorate are mildly in favor of the plan, 40 percent are indifferent, and 15 percent are violently opposed and strongly organized. (The medical association, comprising about 0.5 percent of the population, is on record as strongly favoring the proposal.) The representative in question, having read the literature submitted to him by the medical association and by the antifluoridation society, as well as that supplied by the public health authorities (cf. Wahlke's "administration" role), is firmly convinced that the fears expressed by the "antis" are groundless and that in the long run fluoridation would be of great advantage to all members of the society. Here again the duty of the representative seems clear enough: to vote for fluoridation. Suppose, however, that the campaign of the "antis" has been highly successful. Opinion polls show the following distribution:

Strongly pro	10%
Weakly pro	20%
Indifferent	10%
Weakly anti	30%
Strongly anti	30%

How should the legislator "represent" his constituents in this situation, still assuming that he is convinced no harm to health or the security of the country, and a great deal of good, will come of the move? It would appear we are now in a gray zone where the norms of representation are at best ambiguous. A strong majority will opposes a strong general interest. He might argue (to himself) that while the satisfaction of desire is always a good in itself and exerts a claim upon the representative, the claim is weakened when the desire is clearly based upon a misconception of the facts. Such a weakened claim might be overridden by the strong claim based upon the enlightened view of interest. This would be my conclusion on the facts as stated.

As another example, let us consider proposed anti-closed-shop ("right-to-work") legislation. We shall assume a widespread popular prejudice against the closed shop, while the pressure groups of business and organized labor (the latter being considerably the larger but a minority of the electorate) line up, respectively, pro and con. This case is in some ways similar to the preceding one; but the question of "interest" here is much less susceptible to objective determination, and opinion among the experts is more sharply divided. Assuming the vote must be yes or no, the presumption would appear to be for following the legislator's own instructed judgment of what was in the constituency's interest.

But now suppose a substantial segment of business sided with labor on the issue (finding that the closed shop made for greater stability of labor relations). In this situation, even though the two made up only a sizable minority of the electorate, there would be a strong argument that representation of the people (a weighted amalgam of their desires and their interests) called for siding with the minority, unless the legislator's own instructed judgment of constituency interest pointed strongly in the opposite direction.[21]

[21] Note that in these examples the Wahlke categories of pressure groups and administration have been included and dealt with as aspects of the context within which the representational norms are applied. Both are suppliers of certain kinds of relevant information.

The very way in which these hypothetical cases have been discussed indicates that the concept of representation, while giving a fairly clear answer to some of the dilemmas created by the multiple roles a democratic legislator must play, is bound to leave large gray areas. Two devices for narrowing these areas are open to him. First, he may (and should) exert leadership in his constituency to narrow the gap between effective desire and constituency interest as he perceives it. The second means, likely to be effective in more cases than the first, is to find some accommodation between the opposing groups, some modification of the original proposal that at best might accomplish what each was really after and at the least might minimize the frustration of one side without seriously alienating the other. In the case of the anti-closed-shop proposal, a law that permitted the union shop might fill this requirement.

We need not cite further examples, although other combinations of weak and strong, and minority and majority desires and interests are possible and undoubtedly are found in practice. However, a few words about what Wahlke et al. refer to as the "consensual role" of legislators are relevant. Members of a legislative body must cooperate with each other in a multitude of ways, of which accepting the leadership of recognized party leaders in the legislative chamber is one, but not the only one. This role may call for behavior in certain cases that is not apparently compatible with what the representative norms would seem to demand. Yet even the requirements imposed by the existence of a group of friends in the legislature who frequently support each other's interest in informal return for like conduct on the part of other members of the group may be indirectly in the interests of the constituents of each of these members. Thus, whether or not the "consensual role" is thought of as distinct from "representation," it in fact may, and, I would argue, should, serve the same ends and be subject ultimately to the same tests of correctness. It is useful to point it out as a separate item;

but it would be a mistake not to recognize it as a part of a larger whole whose norms help to define its legitimate claims.

Now a word about electoral considerations, a factor that was deliberately put aside in the preceding discussion. Suppose our model representative, having made the kind of analysis we have been discussing, decides that he ought to vote for X. At this point he considers the probable effect of this course of action on his chances for reelection and decides they will be considerably diminished.[22] What effect, if any, should this have on his decision, if he is to stick to the norms of "representing"? In the first place, it might properly serve as a warning to recheck his previous calculations and judgments. Perhaps he had misjudged the intensity of certain desires. Assuming, however, that he found no reason to alter his appraisal, he might have decided to support what he felt to be the true interest of his constituency against its own misguided judgment (for example, in the fluoridation case). Now if indeed he were convinced, after careful study, that this would cost him his seat, should that fact, within the norms of representation, affect his decision? (We must assume that his vote in the legislative body might determine the outcome.) It would appear the only rational way for him to answer this question would be to estimate the alternative to his occupying the seat and the balance of representativeness for the constituency, on all issues, if his opponent held it. By this judgment, barring party and national interest considerations, to be discussed below, he must be bound. In considering the practical operation of this formula, it must be re-

[22] Of course, this is quite different from saying that he had decided to vote in a way the majority would oppose. Voters will not necessarily switch their position just because they disagree with the stand of their representative on a particular issue—or, for that matter, on a great many issues. Conversely, even though he had decided to vote in a way that a majority of the voters would approve, his action might still cost him his seat (if most of the majority were made up of members of the opposition party).

329

membered that if, for example, voting for fluoridation would cost him his seat, his opponent would probably also vote for fluoridation.[23]

But one must consider the question of whether in certain instances a representative may have (at least according to certain theories of democracy) a higher duty than to represent his constituency (still putting aside considerations of party and national interest). The clearest, if not the only, case would be a matter of conscience, a case where justice or moral right might be thought to conflict with constituency desire and possibly even with constituency interest. The case of segregation naturally comes to mind. Of course, if a segregationist constituency has elected an integrationist, knowing him to be such and in the absence of any pledge on his part to support the constituency views in this matter, no problem arises. They have waived any right to object; they have made the judgment that, all things considered, he will represent them better than any alternative open to them.[24] But suppose he has kept silent (or equivocated) on the subject and is certain that casting an integrationist vote would cost him his seat at the next election. If he acts as a representative, he must go contrary to his conscience (i.e. to another ethical norm).[25] He faces a di-

[23] It is because electoral considerations do play this role, which it is argued here they should, that the matter of apportionment is important. It must be recognized, however, that evidence may be found to support the proposition that well-apportioned and malapportioned legislatures arrive at very similar policy results. Thomas R. Dye, "Malapportionment and Public Policy in the United States," *Jour. of Politics*, 27 (1965), 586-601. Insofar as this finding is generally true, it is at least consistent with the proposition that ethical norms of representation are not without effect.

[24] This reasoning makes the not improbable assumption that on such a salient issue as one involving a sharp conflict between the conscience of the representative and the majority will of the constituency an alternative would have been presented (through the primary election or otherwise) had the majority not been prepared to make the judgment imputed to them in the text.

[25] For the sake of sharpening the issue, it is assumed that con-

330

lemma in which he must choose between ethical norms, a not unusual circumstance in life, and he must work out his solution by calculating and weighing consequences or by whatever other means his ethical principles may demand.

What about the relation of a representative to the minority in his constituency? Do people who did not vote for him and do not expect to vote for him have any claim upon him? Should he take their desires or their interests into account? If we speak now of their desires insofar as they are opposed to those of the majority (and no more intense) and of their interests insofar as they are in irreconcilable conflict with those of the majority—and this is a substantial narrowing of the issue, justified by what has already been taken into account by the preceding analysis—the answer would seem to be that the minority is entitled to consideration within the bounds set by the underlying consensus in the society in question.[26] In addition to recognized rights, this consensus would normally include commonly accepted notions of justice.

Thus a geographically isolated minority would have a claim on all representatives to supply them with police protection—or bomb shelters—in the same proportion to need as in other parts of the country. At least as far as desire

stituency desire, and possibly even constituency interest, might reasonably be judged so strong in this case as to override any consideration of an opposing national interest. In fact, it will be only in the rarest of cases that the issue between the dictates of conscience and those of representational norms will be in such direct conflict.

[26] It is, of course, the feebleness, if not utter lack, of such a consensus in many new states that makes the operation of representative government in them so precarious at best. It may well be, as Lucian Pye contends, that representation of particularistic groupings is essential for the viability of such polities. The fact is, however, in many instances leaders' fears that lack of consensus would either lead to civil war or at least prevent all positive accomplishment have led them to seek to impose a national consensus from above at the expense of the effective operation of the elected representatives. Pye, *Aspects of Political Developments*.

331

rather than interest is taken into account, this may seldom be a real issue, for one would not normally expect to find situations in which common notions of justice were accepted and yet the majority desired to neglect a minority in this way. Still, consideration of the treatment of Negroes in many places suggests that a wide gap between the implications of generally accepted standards and expressed desires is quite possible.

b. District versus Nation

The second big problem for representational theory, after that of desire versus interest, is that of part versus whole, constituency versus nation.[27] The tension appears only as one moves toward the interest pole of the representational standard; for no one would think that a representative should be influenced, per se, by the demands (as distinct from the interests) of any constituents but his own, even though they included every citizen of the country save his own constituents. But let us suppose it is a question of a direct conflict between what he is convinced is the national interest on the one hand, and, on the other hand, what both he and his constituents are convinced is their interest. What then?

The situation posed is not likely to occur very often. On most questions the constituency will not be looking.[28] That is to say, very few of its members will have any opinion; nor would an impartial observer believe that the public-policy issue involved raised any question of conflict between the constituency and the nation. So we are dealing with the exceptional situation. We are not here considering the question of whether the representative should act solely as a delegate. As at least a partial "trustee," he must

[27] Curiously, Wahlke does not list the nation among the various "clientele-roles" he enumerates. Wahlke et al., *The Legislative System*, p. 14.

[28] See Stokes and Miller, "Party Government and the Saliency of Congress," pp. 531-546.

inform himself so that he can determine the constituency interest. As a member of a deliberative assembly he should also discuss the matter with his colleagues in further search of sound judgment. But beyond all this, does his membership in an assembly with responsibility for national policy imply pursuit of what Burke called the "general reason of the whole"? Perhaps it would be better to ask, as we did when discussing obligations toward the minority: What is the underlying consensus on the subject in this society? Some obligation on the part of all to support the welfare of the whole is implied by citizenship in any body politic. Without it a body politic would not exist. Surely, then, persons who are selected to represent others in the government of that body politic must, *inter alia*, be expected to represent their interest in and obligation to the whole (even when the constituents themselves might be inclined to overlook it).

This much would appear to be clear. The strength of the representative's obligation to support the national as opposed to the local interest, where the two clearly conflict, is a function of several factors. First of all, it must be judged in terms of some inevitably crude estimate of the strength in the particular case of each of the interests involved, local and national. Second, the system of government itself is relevant. In Britain, Parliament (including its "Government") is the only vehicle for representation in the legislative process. In the United States, on the other hand, the division of labor and responsibility among president, Senate, and House of Representatives somewhat alters the situation, the implication being that the representatives of lesser areas than the whole have some special obligation to espouse local interests. Finally, it is partly a matter of the strength of the particular national consensus. It would appear at least a priori probable that the national consensus in Great Britain is stronger than it is in the United States. (To get a clearer picture of the extent to which this is true would be an interesting aim for an empirical study.)

Conceivably, the generally accepted theory in a given country might be that the general interest would be best secured by each locality (through its elected representatives) pursuing its own particular interest exclusively. I personally doubt whether many people in the United States, barring a few sophisticated political scientists, accept this view.[29]

Furthermore, it is perhaps fair to say that where a strong and highly visible local interest seems to be opposed to the national interest, the representative may have to face the possibility of defeat at the next election and thus be forced to make the kind of calculation of alternatives that has been described here.[30] Frequently, too, it may be fruitless or detrimental for the representative to vote for the national interest against that of his constituency. Take the case of pork-barrel legislation. It may be assumed that the net effect of the legislation will be detrimental to the national welfare but beneficial to the constituency of the representative in question. It is likely that if, during the bill's formulation, he refused to commit himself to support it, he would lose his district's "pork" while not defeating the bill. Under such circumstances, the only effective line for the representative to take is to try to combine with other representatives to create institutionalized procedures to inhibit this sort of legislation. It is a measure of the "national" consensus in Britain that in the form of the procedure for private bill legislation, just such action has been taken.[31]

[29] One of the writer's experiences during a British by-election illustrates the national differences in question. The constituency was heavily agricultural and highly marginal. On being asked about the attitude of the (traditionally Conservative) farmers toward the election, a Conservative party official showed great moral indignation over the fact that some farmers were actually considering voting for the Labour candidate just because of certain promised agricultural benefits—and contrary, it was implied, to what they must know was the national interest! It seems unlikely that any American politician could make such an argument with a straight face.

[30] See pp. 325-328.

[31] It may be observed that the United States, in limited degree,

334

c. Representatives and Political Parties

At first glance, at least, the effect of a party system upon the role of representatives appears to create serious difficulties; and it most certainly does add complications. In principle, however, the problem seems fairly simple. Why do parties come into being? If their members were completely like-minded, no problem would arise. But political parties are typically composed of people with some interest in common but also with important differences of interest (or, at the very least, of desire), who find it worthwhile to "trade out" their differences, each giving up something for the sake of gaining support for what he does not give up. What then do the norms of representation say to a representative from a farming constituency whose party leaders tell him he must vote to cut farm subsidies? Let us approach the question obliquely by considering it as if it arose in Britain. In that case there could be little question, assuming the representative had done his best to press the views and interests of his constituents upon his party leaders, without success. Under the British political system today it is normally part of the understood rules of the game that he should bow to the party (although he might occasionally abstain, if doing so would not endanger the government's majority). His supporters were aware of that possibility when they voted for him. Even if they did not know what stand the party would take on this issue, they desired his party to be in power and were presumably willing to pay the price. Moreover, if the price turned out to be more than they had anticipated and more than they were prepared to tolerate, they could shift their allegiance at the next election.[32]

---

has such an institution in the form of the president's veto power, and also in certain procedures relating to the authorization and appropriation of funds for public works.

[32] It must be recognized, here and throughout, that we are talking in terms of the informed voter. To bring in the uninformed and apathetic members of the electorate would complicate the discussion but

If, on the other hand, we are dealing with the American loose-jointed party system, the same answer does not apply with anything like equal force. But the principles are the same. The conscientious representative must ask himself: To what extent was I elected as a party man? What would my own preelection statements and actions lead a rational constituent to expect my position on this issue to be? What might my constituency have to gain in other matters from my support for the party on this issue? In other words, with respect to party loyalty, under whatever system, the *ultimate* test remains the desires and interests of the constituency, including the extent to which it shares in a party consensus and a national consensus. But, especially where parties are powerful and can therefore obtain good things for the constituency (which may be things of national as well as of local interest, like effective national defense), this may take the representative a long way from direct response to constituency demand on a particular issue.

Let us press this analysis one step further. Can the tension created for the representative by highly disciplined parties withstand the ever increasing span of governmental functions? As the number and variety of issues increases, any theory of imperative mandate becomes completely unrealistic. Even the kind of theoretical support for a more limited mandate to the party that was outlined above becomes increasingly tenuous. The more functions the government performs, the more difficult it will likely be for a party to adopt a program on which all or most of its members agree. Consequently, disciplined parties find it increasingly difficult to be programmatic. They may also be forced to accept some relaxation of discipline, as exemplified by the revised code of the British Parliamentary Labour party, adopted in August 1966. Perhaps equally as important as either of these developments is the tentative

---

would not, I believe, lead to different conclusions. In fact, it simplifies the representatives' problem by minimizing the element of desire.

transfer of important representative functions to pressure groups (or "representative organizations") operating directly on government at the administrative level. The great extent of this process in modern Britain, both at the stage of legislative formulation and at the administrative stage, is well known.[33]

As was argued in the preceding chapter, in the United States at least the party government model corresponds only slightly to reality. We also know that electoral accountability (at least as it operates in competitive districts) does not produce the close correlation between voter attitude and roll-call votes that common sense might lead us to anticipate. At the same time it appears that in the absence of effective electoral competition representatives seem to represent their constituents to a remarkable degree—or at least that there is a remarkable coincidence of views and votes between representatives and constituency. How does this come about? At least a *prima facie* case can be made for the proposition that a concept of ethical norms, imposed by the acceptance of the role of representative, vaguely defined though those norms may be, has something to do with this phenomenon. How strong that case may be is a problem for further research.

4. APPLICATION OF MOTIVATIONAL THEORIES TO THEORIES OF REPRESENTATION

How do the motivational theories apply to these theories of representation? To begin with radical individualism, at first sight it appears to call for the delegate theory (and, by the same token, for a strong mandate theory). Voters seek their own advantage and presumably will reward (by reelection) those representatives who most accurately mir-

[33] See, for instance, S. E. Finer, *Anonymous Empire*, rev. ed. (London: Pall Mall Press, 1966). Professor Finer also expresses (p. 111) the judgment, relevant to the argument in the text, that the national consensus in Britain "appears to be on the wane."

ror, defend, and carry out their wishes. Moreover, it would appear that the *national* delegate theory would be applicable only in the case of an official (e.g. the president) who is elected by a national constituency. For others, the local-delegate theory would appear to be indicated. And this is the tendency of much individualist thinking.

However, a truly rational individual, after the fashion of Downs or Buchanan and Tullock, is aware of the problem of information costs. He would recognize that he could not possibly acquire the information or devote the time to study and deliberation required to arrive at a sound conclusion on most of the questions that come before his representatives. He would be forced, therefore, to take a longer-run view of his interests. Toward the close of a representative's term of office, the voter would decide whether on balance the policies that had been pursued were well conceived for the satisfaction of his preferences (or for the advancement of his interests as he conceived them) as compared with the alternatives that had been available. Perforce, then, the voter would grant discretion to his representatives, subject to ultimate judgment in terms of his own preferences.

The radical individualist voter might resort also to other time- and labor-saving devices, such as deciding that a particular political party or ideological position or individual best represented his preferences (or long-run interests), and casting his votes accordingly. Again he would be moving in the direction of the (local) trustee theory, driven to it not by lack of self-interest or rationality but by lack of time and expertise with which to acquire, analyze, and evaluate the necessary information. He would be forced, that is to say, to entrust his representative with power to act, not on behalf of the public, of course, but on his own (the constituent's) behalf. Another qualification: our typical voter would undoubtedly also be driven to recognize that since he could not have his own, private representative, he would have to combine with others with similar preferences; and,

338

in order to get his man elected, he would probably have to include many voters whose interests were by no means identical with his, and hence he would be forced to compromise.

The radical individualist, then, begins with a bias toward the local-delegate theory of representation but would probably be forced to move in some degree toward the local-trustee theory. The representative, on the other hand, would be motivated to act in ways that he judged would win the self-interested support of a majority of his constituents, or the support of the political party he judged most likely to assure his reelection. (Assuming rational voters, these last two statements should be equivalent.) Furthermore, according to the norms of rational individualism, this is the way he *should* act.

Finally, if individuals found they could pursue their interests more effectively by organizing themselves into political parties, and if they could save themselves time and energy by finding some ideological kinship on a nationwide scale (in other words by forming national parties), the radical individualist would find himself moving in the direction of the *national* trustee theory. With a strong presidency elected on a nationwide basis (or even on an approximation thereof, as in the United States), this tendency would be enhanced.

It will appear from what has been said that the radical individualist emphasizes the function of aggregating interests and resolving conflicts among them. Persons who accept radical individualism as a normative as well as a descriptive motivational theory would wish to do everything they could to see that representatives did in fact behave as that theory directs. To secure this kind of responsiveness they might be led to support such institutional devices as the recall. They might also favor the initiative and referendum as means for insuring that their own views of their interests rather than those of their representatives would prevail. But whether they did so or not would depend upon the extent to which they accepted the line of reasoning based upon information costs and the like that was suggested above.

The radical individualist might also be expected to favor short terms of office as a further means of seeing to it that his representatives responded to his preferences.[34] Again, the record does not suggest any strong pressure in this direction, but, if anything, the contrary. In the United States, the original compromise of two-year terms for members of the House of Representatives, six-year terms for senators, and four-year terms for the president appears to be quite firmly established. The only changes that have been seriously discussed would be to lengthen the term of representatives from two to four years and (with less support, one would judge) to lengthen the term of the president from four to seven years (adding a bar to reelection). Neither of these proposals has ever received anything like the requisite support for adoption. In England, the earlier maximum of seven years for the life of a Parliament gave way in 1911 to a five-year rule; and that too, although it could be changed by a simple Act of Parliament, has remained stable. The Chartists' demand, a century and a quarter ago, for annual elections failed to gain wide support, nor has it been repeated by any substantial group. It would appear, then, that in both countries a stable compromise between proponents of delegate and trustee theories has been achieved, with little support for either extreme (which one might interpret as meaning little support for either theory to the exclusion of the other). It would also appear that the practices of democratic representation are at least compatible with the rational man assumption of individualistic theory.

What of other forms of individualism? They can be dealt with briefly. The Tocquevillean individualist, being

---

[34] This statement to some extent is subject to the same reservation noted above about the possibility of a sophisticated, far-sighted individualist permitting his representatives to operate on a longer leash.

family-centered and finding the larger society distasteful, would presumably favor the local-delegate theory of representation. Insofar as his reason forced him, as it would the radical individualist, to qualify this position, to that extent he would be qualifying the very quality that is his distinguishing characteristic. What I have termed the romantic individualist, stressing self-development or self-realization through political activity, would likewise tend to favor holding as much political power in his own hands as possible. The existentialist is, almost by definition, hard to predict. It would appear, though, that insofar as he opted for being a political man he would be committed to the maximal retention of political power in his own hands. But perhaps this would only mean that he would be an activist, seeking himself to hold office, and if attaining it, exercising it according to his own lights. Finally, as for what I have called the "qualified" individualist, since the qualification was in the direction of the public-interest theory, he can as well be thought of as a qualified public interest theorist; and it is to the theorists of the public interest that I now turn.

The logical application of the public-interest theory would appear to favor the national-trustee theory of representation. The voter would be pursuing the public interest. Considering the wealth of facts and complicated analyses necessary for a sound judgment of the public interest, he would probably think it proper to accept his representative's judgment as to what the public interest entailed—assuming of course that he found a candidate in whose judgment and integrity he had confidence. His own evaluation of his representative's judgment and integrity might of course be reconsidered over a period of time and in the light of a cumulative record. The Whig or Burkean view (the national-trustee theory) is almost certainly not so widely held in this country as in England and probably not so widely held there today as it once was. In England even today we are told on good authority that substantial groups

341

believe it would be a serious breach of privilege for a newspaper to advise its readers to speak to their M.P. about a particular issue.[35]

It is possible, to be sure, that the public-interest-minded voter would insist upon making his own evaluation of the public interest. In that event, we would again get a local-delegate theory of representation. The difference would be that the policies he would insist upon (and that the representative would endeavor to pursue) would be the voters' views of the *public* interest (assuming that the rational and informed representative would correctly perceive these views) rather than some sort of compromise among the private interests of a majority.[36] Since, however, the public interest voter is by definition less self-centered than the radical individualist, it seems more likely he would adhere to the trustee theory.

Similar reasoning applies to the national-local issue. Voters concerned for the public interest presumably would not stop at the interest of their constituency but rather would seek to advance the national interest. So it would also be the national interest that the representative would seek to advance; or rather, pursuing the line of reasoning above, it would be his perception of their perception of the national interest.

Just as the radical individualist's eye is first and foremost on the constituency and then on the representative body as a means of aggregating the interest of the various constituencies and then reconciling their conflicts, so the pub-

[35] Birch, *Representation and Responsible Government*, pp. 227ff.

[36] This statement, insofar as it refers to the representative, is subject to the following qualification: if the representative himself was so strongly committed to the public-interest theory that he was willing to sacrifice his own interest in remaining in office for it, he would pursue his own view of the public interest, regardless of whether it coincided with what he perceived to be that of a majority of his constituents. But, since such conduct would be generally self-defeating (as Burke found it to be), it is probably not properly attributable to the public-interest theory.

lic-interest representative seeks to determine the true interest, as contrasted with the expressed desire, "real needs" as contrasted with "false consciousness." Interests, rather than demands, are what he seeks to reconcile; and if this requires persuading the electorate, that is what he will try to do.

As to institutional arrangements, what was said above about the radical individualist points to the line of reasoning applicable here. The populistic devices of initiative, referendum and recall would not find favor with the public-interest theorist; and the same considerations that would lead the latter to favor the trustee theory would presumably lead him to place less emphasis on frequent elections and indeed to favor longer tenure of office for representatives, on the theory that this would enable them to act for the public interest as they saw it, knowing they would have a reasonable period of time for their actions to prove their value to the electorate. All methods of legislative organization—for instance, the use of specialized committees that gave greater opportunity for informed deliberation—and all procedures that would increase the opportunity for discussion both within the legislature and between legislators and their constituents—would meet with his approval.

It would appear that the adherents of rights and duties theory would wish to move away from the local-delegate theory in the direction of the national-trustee theory, as was found to be the case with those who held to the public-interest theory. To be sure it would be possible under this theory for voters to be as insistent as anyone on their own interpretation of their rights and duties, not being willing to trust their representatives' discretion in this matter. However, one who assumes that people are moved, politically, by their conceptions of right and wrong is not likely to assume that each person's ideas of his rights and duties is idiosyncratic. Such assumptions would hardly be compatible with any form of operational democratic theory. Indeed, the very concept of a right usually implies its general recogni-

343

tion; otherwise, agreement could not even be secured by bargaining, as might be the case with selfishly motivated persons even if their individual preferences were quite at odds with each other. Rights and duties, unlike interests, are not matters about which one compromises easily, if at all. Accordingly, the rights and duties theorists must be assumed to believe in a high degree of correspondence among individual ethical systems. That is to say, their theory must be assumed to be descriptive as well as prescriptive. Under this assumption, voters would be less concerned with matters presumed to be peculiar to them and more willing to support representatives who were believed to share their own sense of right and wrong.[37]

The Rawlsian theory of justice leads to much the same conclusion. Self-interest is qualified—increasingly as one approaches the ideal polity—by commitment to principles of justice, alike for all. What the voter does, under this assumption, is to vote for a representative who is most committed to the fundamental principles of equal liberty and equal distribution of primary social goods, subject to the rule of permitting departures from the latter standard only insofar as all may be expected to benefit. Of course, in an imperfect world, the voter would wish to maintain some considerable tie with his representative. He would also not wish to give up the local tie entirely, recognizing that a representative who felt compelled to give special attention to a particular district would be less likely to overlook facts relevant to doing justice to its citizens. But again, as with the public-interest theory and the miscellaneous rights and duties theory, the Rawlsian man would subscribe to a

[37] It is not to be supposed that any of the theories yet discussed assume that voters will have *no* particularistic concerns which conflict with more generalized norms or that they will not be politically activated by such concerns. Rather, it is assumed that in the public-interest theory and the rights and duties theory, voters' concern for their particularistic interests will be substantially qualified by their concern for the public interest or, as the case may be, their sense of right.

theory of representation that gave wider scope[38] to the representative than would be the tendency under radical individualism.

For his part, the representative would behave accordingly. As Rawls puts it, "Each rational legislator is to vote his opinion as to which laws and policies best conform to principles of justice."[39] While Rawls is speaking here of a well-ordered society, he suggests that in fact evidence gives some support to the proposition that representatives are so motivated in today's highly imperfect society. "No political party," he declares, "publicly admits to pressing for legislation to the disadvantage of any recognized social group."[40] That statement cannot stand without qualification. Party platforms calling for elimination of depletion allowances, higher inheritance taxes, and the like, are common and appear to be to the disadvantage of certain recognized groups. What Rawls should say, and what would be sufficient for his theory, would be that no party publicly admits pressing for legislation that would be *unjust* to any recognized group. A party may publicly admit pressing for a group's disadvantage where that comprises only the removal of an allegedly unjust advantage. The real point is that the argument must be based upon the justice, or at least the absence of injustice, of the proposal. Stated this way, the argument rings true. That representatives should act justly all affirm. And, while standards of justice vary, it is probably safe to say that the area of agreement is far greater than the variance. No one professing to be a democrat would contend for any special tax advantage except on the professed belief that it would in some way benefit society.[41]

[38] I use this phrase here to cover two dimensions: (1) release from a close tie to the voter—trusteeship; and (2) release from a close tie to the locality.

[39] Rawls, *A Theory of Justice*, p. 361.

[40] Ibid., p. 319.

[41] Rawls of course would insist that it must be beneficial to *each representative man* in society. Here is a real difference in theories of justice. The utilitarian would contend that a law might be just even

The dispute over depletion allowances, tax exemption of municipal bonds, and the like, has far less to do with varying conceptions of justice (still less unwillingness to accept "justice" as a constraint) than it does with varying theories as to the effects of such arrangements on society.

As far as concerns institutional arrangements and the proper role of the representative, what was said about the public-interest theory appears to apply equally to the rights and duties theory in either of its versions.

Finally, concerning the collectivist it would seem that with his commitment to the whole and his insistence that people do, and should come to, value their political community and its institutions for their own sake (or at least for the quality of life that accompanies a true community), he would also tend to avoid the delegate theory. It would appear the only question is where the collectivist would stand on the national-local issue. While persons of the public-interest and rights and duties persuasions would be inclined, it appears, toward favoring representatives with a national point of view, it is not so clear that this would be the case with the collectivist. He sets great store by community. He is motivated less by an abstract commitment either to justice or to the public interest than by a strong emotional tie to his own (political) community. The question then is what he would consider that community to be. The stress on the bond of sentiment, feeling, raises a question as to whether it could be expected to characterize the whole of a large, multinational state. On the other hand, modern democracies (for

though it harmed some, providing that it added to net (or average) utility. I know of no direct evidence that would show which of these theories is more widely accepted in our, or any, society. It seems clear, however, that it is common to take public action which harms certain groups for the benefit of others, presumably on the theory that the benefit to some exceeds the harm to the others. For example, consider the effect of "no fault" insurance on certain groups of lawyers. Thus one might infer that society generally does not accept this part of Rawls's theory.

the most part) are not divided into electoral districts that comprise natural political communities. Usually their social composition does not lend itself to such districting. Perhaps all one can say is that, were a collectivist representative democracy to come into being, its theory of representation, on the national-local axis, would depend upon the nature of the political entity—whether it formed a single community or several communities. In the latter case, presumably electoral districts would correspond to those communities and the orientation would be "local." In any case, and most importantly, the collectivist representative would seek to be an active creator of unity rather than an instrument for aggregating interests and working out compromises. The whole concept of representation, in his hands, tends to be transformed.[42]

5. Review

Reviewing the discussion of democratic theories of representation to this point, we see it is true that the whole concept of representation, and especially the mandate theory, has been subject to considerable skepticism in certain quarters. The mandate theory is, indeed, of little if any use; but at the same time the evidence shows considerable causal linkage between constituent desires and legislative behavior, as appeared in the preceding chapter. Pursuing

[42] While the reasoning above is logical enough, other things being equal, other things may not be equal, as the example of Rousseau illustrates. Of course, ideally Rousseau did not believe in representation at all; but he recognized that in a large state it was inescapable if any semblance of democracy was to obtain. Under such circumstances, as he explained in his *Considerations on the Government of Poland*, it is the corruptibility of representatives that should be the governing consideration. Because of this, representatives should be bound to follow their instructions exactly, and should be required to make frequent reports to their constituents to show that they had acted accordingly. *The Political Writings of Jean-Jacques Rousseau*, ed. C. E. Vaughan (Oxford: Blackwell, 1962), 2: 459-461.

this line of investigation, four distinct theories as to how representatives behave were identified, together with four parallel theories as to how they ought to behave. With respect to the former, the weight of the available evidence seems to indicate that they do not in practice follow any one of these theories to the exclusion of the others. Rather, they compromise in the light of varying circumstances and beliefs about what their role should be.[43] Many influences play upon the representative; but most of them are, directly or indirectly, reducible to the perceived desires of constituents or to considerations of justice or of what is in the best interest of the nation or the constituency.

With respect to the normative theory of representation, it was argued that usage and commonly accepted ideas seem roughly in accord with the general picture of practice as just outlined, although many individuals doubtless depart from the "commonly accepted ideas." In both cases, some sort of amalgam of the four theories seems to be called for, with the relative weights varying with the context.

As to the four motivational theories of democracy, the theory of representation that has been propounded and defended here does not run contrary to the implications of any of them. Accordingly none of them is invalidated or seriously disqualified by this discussion of theories of representation. Moreover, in the case of the first three motivational theories, what they would lead one to predict and

---

[43] This conclusion is supported by Miller and Stokes, among others. They write: "The findings of this analysis heavily underscore the fact that no single tradition of representation fully accords with the realities of American legislative politics. The American system *is* a mixture, to which the Burkean, instructed-delegate, and responsible-party models all can be said to have contributed elements. Moreover, variations in the representative relation are most likely to occur as we move from one policy domain to another." (Evidence was noted of a strong delegate relationship in the field of civil rights and a considerable reliance on the trustee relationship in the foreign-policy area.) "Constituency Influence in Congress," *Amer. Polit. Sci. Rev.*, 57 (1963), 45-56, 56.

what they would lead one to uphold as norms are not widely dissimilar from each other or from the practice and normative theory sketched above. To this extent, then, they lend support to the empirical and normative theories of representation that were independently derived in this chapter. Institutional arrangements in Britain and the United States further confirm the theoretical structure.

It should be noted, however, that radical individualism would lean more toward the local-delegate theory if the rational man which that theory hypothesizes did not place considerable weight on information costs. With that important fact placed in the balance, however, it tends, in its application to the problem of political representation, to approximate the position of the public-interest theory. It must be remembered that the latter by no means loses sight of the factor of local and individual preference, where that exists, is known, and is strongly indicated. On the practical side, the representative must have an eye on his own re-election, for the sake of his constituents' interest as well as his own; and on the normative side, some weight must be given to the proposition that what people feel strongly has a claim in its own right, and to the parallel proposition that the representative of a particular district must place its welfare high among his priorities, if only because he, of all representatives, must be expected to know, appreciate, and support it best.

The rights and duties theorist might be expected to lean toward the national-trustee side, but similar considerations to those just mentioned would force him to qualify his position in a practical situation.

Democratic collectivism differs most from the other theories. It tends more to be exclusively a theory of the ideal, of how things ought to be. It is designed to change both beliefs and practice; and it does not pretend to explain reality. Accordingly the democratic collectivist in practice does not qualify his theory by practical considerations. Also, on the normative side, the collectivist tends to stress

349

participation, thus minimizing the role of representation in general.

6. POWER THEORIES AND THEORIES OF REPRESENTATION

Nothing has been said in this chapter about our second set of democratic theories; nor is there much to be said that is not obvious. An elitist theory is a Burkean theory, stressing the national-trustee concept of representation. A populist theory tends to the elimination of intermediaries between people and government. In terms of the theories of representation, that means a delegate theory—presumably a local-delegate theory. It follows from what has been said that neither of these is very realistic. Clearly the theories of constitutionalism and social pluralism are more compatible with the compromise theory defended here. For reasons that emerge below, constitutionalist theory is particularly important in this connection; but one need not hold one of these two theories to the exclusion of the other.

Reference was made at the outset of this chapter to the way in which a regime as a whole is representative. It now appears that the representativeness of modern democratic government is not achieved through any single channel nor in accordance with any pure theory of representation. In the United States, three sets of constituencies elect representatives at the federal level alone. Moreover, the bureaucracy and an informal but effective additional form of representation, that of organized groups, provide other avenues of representation. This variety is not without good reason. For a person to be represented with respect to all of his interests with which government concerns itself is immensely difficult and inevitably partial and inaccurate, as Rousseau recognized with typical hyperbole. Accountability enforced by elections is one device, a crude one, for making government representative. It has been suggested here that an idea of what representation means in the context of government, a set of ethical norms, also plays a role. Finally, the existence of numerous and varied avenues of representation, each by virtue of its own peculiar nature seeing, reflecting, attempting to effectuate a slightly different facet of that great conglomerate of desires and interests which make up the electorate, probably produces a more tolerable result than could be accomplished by any one of them alone.

It may be remarked that the existence of district, state, and national levels of representation for the federal government in the United States not only permits the expression of opinion of varying levels of generality but allows—indeed forces—the voter to consider larger issues in casting his ballot for the president and, to a certain extent, for senator, while not denying him the opportunity to speak to more parochial issues at the district level. Moreover, on more specialized issues, the pressure-group system provides for refinements of expression that would not be otherwise available. Undoubtedly this system gives disproportionate representation to the politically informed and active. What democratic system would not? It is notable, however, that ever new groups are achieving effective organization; *vide* the "welfare mothers." Britain, with its smaller and more homogeneous population, lacks this variety of opportunities for representation. Whether its more unified system will continue to be satisfactory in a world in which various interests continue to proliferate remains to be seen.

7. INTEREST REPRESENTATION

What has just been said suggests that the nature of constituencies is important as well as their relation to their representatives. It is not only a question of "trustee" versus "delegate" or of "national" versus "local"; it is also a matter of trustee or delegate for what kind of a "public." The nature of constitutencies is important and may be affected by the mode of their organization. Constituencies may be large or small; they may be relatively homogeneous or

351

heterogeneous, and so forth. Other things being equal, large constituencies, of course, tend to be relatively heterogeneous. But other factors may be more important than size. Two types of representation—neither of them in use at the national level in the United Kingdom or the United States —illustrate the importance of the nature of the constituency and the method of selecting its representatives. They are "interest" representation and proportional representation.

By interest representation, I refer to any system of representation in which a citizen votes not for a representative to speak for all his interests as they are affected by a given level of government, but rather for different representatives for each (or several) of the various interests he may have. The simplest form would be a system wherein each person is assumed to have only one dominant interest, that which pertained to his or her occupation. This idea reflects an extreme form of economic determinism. It was briefly tried in the early days of the Soviet Union and soon abandoned. To the best of my knowledge it is nowhere practiced now, nor does it seem to be widely advocated. Many writers have vaguely urged the adoption of representation according to "interests" rather than geographical location, without specifying what interests would be represented or how citizens would be organized into "interest" constituencies. The most specific plan that has been advanced to my knowledge was put forward by G.D.H. Cole.[44] According to Cole's plan, citizens would be represented in numerous capacities: by vocation; as consumers, broken down into subcategories, such as consumers of "utilities" and consumers of more variegated commodities; as being interested in cultural activities; and so on. Each resulting group of representatives would meet with other members of the same group, at local, regional, and national levels, for the settlement of matters

[44] Cole, *Guild Socialism Re-Stated* (London: Parsons, 1920). For an account of the Guild Socialist movement, see S. T. Glass, *The Responsible Society* (London: Longmans, 1966).

pertaining only, or chiefly, to the interest they represented. Matters of more general concern would be dealt with by councils ("communes") made up of representatives from each of the various interest councils.

More recent theorizing along this line appears to have made no advances and to be less detailed. Yugoslavia, with its workers' councils, is often cited as an example of a kind of organization by interests. These councils have no power, either directly or indirectly, over the policies of the central government, as would be necessary in a democratic polity organized on functional lines. A recent essay by C. George Benello exemplifies both a contemporary argument for interest representation by means of the democratization of industry and also reliance upon the Yugoslavian example. "If our major institutions (among which business corporations are specifically included) were internally democratic," he writes, "it would be functional and natural simply to have assemblies constituted of delegates from them."[45]

The underlying theory of interest representation in one sense goes back to Rousseau, although the conclusion is very different. Like Rousseau, the proponent of interest representation believes that no man can represent another. The un-Rousseau-like conclusion he draws, however, is that a man can represent another man, indeed many other men, not as a whole but with respect to a particular interest. While no one else may have the same constellation of interests I have, I share an interest in, say, the teaching profession, and in higher education, with many others. These interests, while not identical, are sufficiently alike to admit of representation by a single representative or group of representatives. No longer need I be frustrated when I go to the polls by having to choose between Candidate A, whose views on higher education I strongly support but whose position on concentration of industry I abhor, and Candi-

[45] "Group Organization and Socio-Political Structure," in C. George Benello and Dimitrios Roussopoulos, eds., *The Case for Participatory Democracy* (New York: Grossman, 1971), pp. 38-54, 54.

353

date B, of whom exactly the reverse is true. With "interest representation," I can vote for a man who represents my views on higher education and for another with whom I am in accord regarding the concentration of industry.

This theory is subject to many criticisms of which I shall detail only two, one theoretical and one practical. First, on theoretical grounds, interest representation's "solution" of the problem with which the voter under a geographical system of representation is confronted is all too simple. The problem of determining each voter's priorities remains. To take an example, let us make the not unlikely assumption that consumers instruct their representatives to support lower prices, while the representatives of producers are similarly instructed to hold out for higher incomes. Or suppose I vote in one constituency for higher teachers' salaries and in another for lower student-teacher ratios. It is likely that something will have to give. While, with great difficulty and a substantial amount of arbitrariness, mathematical weighting devices could be arranged, the system would provide no information about my own weighting of the two stated objectives. Under the single representative (geographical) system, in many cases I, the voter, will be forced to give some indication (by my vote) of my priorities, of the relative saliency of various issues in my scheme of values and interests. Under the system of interest representation I enjoy the luxury of avoiding such hard choices, at the price of losing all control over them whatsoever. I abdicate —or must abdicate—responsibility and hand it over to deadlock or mindless compromising, or at least compromising to which *my* mind has made no contribution.

Second, the practical problem has already been alluded to. It is the matter of reconciling many different, and often sharply opposed, groups of representatives. Interests—or at least desires—would be aggregated, and solidified, in such a way that their reconciliation would be difficult, if not impossible.[46] Moreover, if a single body is created from repre-

[46] In fairness, it should be pointed out that proponents of interest

sentatives of these groups, how will they be weighted? Further related problems can easily be imagined. How are the unemployed to be classified? Are workers to be classified by industry or by trade? Are all housewives not "gainfully employed" to be lumped together? To be considered as having identical interests with their spouses? Or could such persons classify themselves as "happily liberated," "unhappily liberated," "happily enslaved," and "unhappily enslaved"? And so on and on.

Finally, what would be the position of each of the four types of motivational democratic theory with respect to interest representation? It appears that three of them, and probably all four, would oppose it. Certainly the modern theory of democratic collectivism, with its stress on community and on egalitarianism, could not possibly support a system that would stress people's differences rather than what they had in common. Interest representation is based upon the denial of the collectivist's ideal of community. This statement is made in full recognition of the fact that one of the most carefully developed schemes for representation by interests was by a Socialist, G.D.H. Cole,[47] whose democratic theory would have to be denominated as collectivist. The incoherence of his theory was perhaps obscured from his own gaze by his faith that all serious divergence of interests would be eliminated by abolishing private ownership of the instruments of production.

The older, hierarchical or organic form of collectivism differs in this regard. Hegel, for example, placed associations ("corporations") at the center of his representative system. For him the monarch and the idea of the state generally

---

representation have a reply—if not an answer—to this objection. Each interest organization would be given power to settle for itself all matters affecting it alone. They would not go to a central body in which all interests were represented. The catch is that many important matters, as the examples given above illustrate, do not affect a single interest alone.

[47] See his *Social Theory* (London: Methuen, 1920).

would provide the necessary unifying factor. Subsequently, collectivism appears to have gone off in one of three directions. The British Idealists, descendants of Hegel, have dropped the idea of interest representation altogether. Syndicalists, like the Guild Socialists whom they greatly influenced, were not much concerned with how to integrate the various syndical organizations, because they were chiefly concerned with the unity that they believed would prevail within them, and because, in a noncapitalistic society, they saw no reason for the syndicates to quarrel with each other. Finally, fascists have found this form of organization, at least as a façade, congenial; but with their antidemocratic theory we are not concerned.

The rights and duties theory, in either of its versions, and the public-interest theory are also based upon the ideal and the assumption of common interests and common standards of and commitment to justice.

Accordingly it would appear that, if the believer in interest representation is to find support from any of the four motivational types of theory, it will have to be individualism in one of its forms (unless possibly from the syndicalist-collectivist). It is true that the individualist might be sympathetic to the idea that the individual cannot be represented, as a whole, since he is such a discrete and unique entity. We have seen that the radical individualist would have at least an initial leaning toward the delegate theory of representation, and in fact that theory appears to be favored by proponents of interest representation. The latter do not trust representatives to work out the individual's priorities for him, but try (unsuccessfully) to find a system by which he can give direct expression and effect to them. But we have seen that the radical individualist, once he takes information costs into account, is likely to move away from the strict delegate theory. Furthermore, even though the radical individualists would have an initial leaning toward the delegate theory, his reasoning and ultimate conclusions would differ from those of the interest representationist. Unlike the latter, the individualist (of whichever subtype) is a strong believer in the integrity of the individual, whom he would expect and wish to make his own choices of priorities once it became clear that these choices were inescapable. This would lead the individualist to support the geographical system of representation, which places exactly this responsibility upon the voter. The conclusion to which we are driven is that none of the motivational theories of democracy, properly construed, would support interest representation, unless one accepts the dubious reasoning of the guild socialists or the syndicalist.

8. PROPORTIONAL REPRESENTATION

Proportional representation (PR), in all its numerous variations, seeks a uniform objective: a mathematically accurate representation of opinions. It has much in common with interest representation; in fact, in one respect at least it might be said to represent a logical extension of that system. It permits voters to group themselves according to whatever interest seems to them most important, and to do so automatically, without the formation of special constituencies. All that is needed is to secure the nomination of a candidate who stands, say, for nationalization of the petroleum industry and all voters who share that point of view can flock to his standard. Moreover, if three candidates take this general position in varying degrees, or the extreme position combined with various other planks, voters may safely vote for all three, in rank order of preference, with no fear that their votes will defeat each other.[48] Nor will any votes be wasted, votes beyond the number required to elect being transferred to the candidates ranked next on the ballots in question. To be sure, PR does not permit voters to give separate expression to as many different interests as do

[48] This statement does not apply to all systems of PR, but does apply to its purest version, that of the single transferable ballot (the Hare system).

357

some forms of interest representation, nor does it compel them to think in these terms (which might be regarded by some as an advantage and by others as a disadvantage).

Although PR has this kinship with interest representation, the impetus for it generally comes from another direction. It is to prevent "wasted" votes and unrepresented minorities; it is, in short, the logical extension of the "one person, one vote" ideal. Under it, the likelihood that any person's vote will be ineffective or less effective than that of another is reduced to its absolute minimum.

Yet it has never been adopted at the national level in Britain or the United States (or in any of the Anglo-Saxon countries). In general it is used at the national level only in countries where religious or ethnic minorities are an important factor and fear they will suffer injustice under a "winner take all" system. The reason for the general acceptance in Anglo-Saxon countries of what is admittedly a compromise of the democratic principle of equality is the belief that PR encourages minority groups and ultimately minority parties, thus endangering the two-party system and making a substantial degree of consensus more difficult to achieve. While this is a controversial issue, the merits of which cannot be argued here, the weight of opinion seems to agree that the threat is real, leaving room for argument over its extent. Under the cabinet system of government, the difficulty with multiparty systems is that no one party is likely to be able to form a Government. Coalition governments tend to be weak and unstable. Under the presidential system, the very power of the presidency and the consequent importance of capturing that office has tended to hold parties together in the effort to win it.[49]

Again, it will be enlightening to look at PR through the eyes of supporters of each of the motivational types of democratic theory. Not surprisingly the results are similar

[49] The fact that PR is sometimes used in the United States at the local level, and only there, appears to result from the minor role that political parties play at that level.

but not identical to the case of interest representation. Clearly PR is at the opposite extreme from the philosophy underlying democratic collectivism. It seeks to find and reflect divisions rather than unity. Nothing more need be said.

Both rights and duties theory and the theory of the public interest are fundamentally consensual theories; they depend upon finding agreement upon a standard of justice, whether it be utilitarian, deontological, or contractual. To this extent, then, like the theory of democratic collectivism, they run counter to any theory (such as that of PR) which assumes and seeks to give maximum effect to differences in interests and standards of right. In this instance, however, both types of theory, and especially the Rawlsian form of contractualism, would be somewhat ambivalent in their reaction. This is because the equalitarian strain in their philosophy—especially strong in Rawls's theory—would be greatly attracted to PR. How they would ultimately come out on the question would tend to be determined by their calculations of probable effects on the practical operation of government.

Here again, individualism would appear, at least in the first instance, to have the greatest affinity for PR. Both seek voter equality; and the individualist is inclined neither to assume nor to set store by consensus to the extent that the other theories do. Yet, once more, qualifying factors appear. As the individualist places great stress upon the preferences of the voter and wishes representatives to be well aware of them, the PR system, under which the representative is elected by a self-selected and to some degree unknown (to the representative) constituency, might for this reason have less appeal to him than it otherwise would. To be sure, even in a single-member district system, the elected representative cannot identify his supporters completely. But the districts are smaller (assuming the same-sized representative body) and it seems reasonable to assume that the sense of some mutual understanding between voter and representa-

tive is, on the average, stronger. Also, the practical considerations that militate against PR might be considered by
the individualist at the constitution-making stage and might
lead him to reject it. All of this, however, is obviously
speculative.

On balance, one can conclude only that neither interest
representation nor PR receive unqualified support from any
of the four motivational democratic theories. Interest representation would probably be opposed by all four. PR is
in a somewhat more ambiguous position, partly because
of uncertainties as to how it would operate in practice in
any particular setting. At best, it would seem that it might
receive some hesitant support from the three noncollectiv-
ist forms of democratic theory. The fact that it is not widely
practiced in Anglo-Saxon countries (in spite of their relatively individualistic orientation) suggests that the practical
arguments against it are deemed to outweigh any theoretical
advantages it might otherwise have. Finally, once more the
fact of conflicting theories leading to not dissimilar results
strengthens the case for those results.

9. CONCLUDING REMARKS

As for our second set of democratic theories, it does not
appear they have much either to contribute or to gain from
the representational theories just discussed. An elitist theorist could hardly favor either of them, both being attempts
to make democracy more egalitarian, while the elitist leans
toward qualifying this element of democracy. And the populist, although strongly equalitarian, tends to think in terms
of "the" people, assuming a degree of homogeneity and
unity of interest that runs exactly counter to both of these
theories. As for the constitutionalist, it is not apparent that
he would take any particular position on these forms of
constitutional arrangement. The social pluralist, believing
that the heterogeneous nature of society is far more important than constitutional arrangements, might also adopt

an attitude of indifference toward both proposals. If anything, his attitude would probably be negative, especially about interest representation, on the entirely plausible assumption that to give institutional status to arrangements reflecting social differences would tend to increase the chances of stultifying deadlock and of effective protectionism on the part of selfish interests.

We were led into this discussion of interest representation and PR by a discussion of the effects of different types of constituencies. It was pointed out that homogeneous districts tended to make the task of conflict resolution in the representative body more difficult. Interest representation and, perhaps to a lesser degree, PR exemplify this difficulty in extreme form. The heterogeneous single-member district tends to minimize the problem, because normally the representatives elected do not stand for a single interest or at least they are much less likely to than under either of the other systems. To win election, candidates in such districts must gain the support of a variety of interests; in other words, they must accomplish considerable resolution of conflicts before they enter the representative body. Hanson puts it well. He writes: "It is not necessary to have a community of interest in order to manage the conflicts of a plural society. It is, however, necessary to organize political power, largely through the official system of representation, in such a way that a vested interest is created in resolving conflict rather than in maintaining it."[50]

A suggestion that runs directly counter to interest representation has, in fact, much to commend it. In metropolitan areas, election districts might be wedge-shaped, so that each would encompass "elements from the business and residential core to the fringe areas."[51] A democratic collectivist could hardly be expected to support this suggestion, but no reason is apparent why it should not meet

[50] Royce Hanson, *The Political Thicket* (Englewood Cliffs, N.J.: Prentice-Hall, 1966), p. 130.
[51] Ibid., p. 131.

361

CHAPTER IX

Decision-Making Rules and Machinery: Individualistic Theories

1. PRELIMINARY REMARKS

The last two chapters have referred to the electorate and to voting as a major device for linking the people with their government. How else is the "will of the people" to be discovered? How else are the people to select representatives, rulers, and hold them accountable? And yet the more the theory of voting is studied, the more complicated it seems. Possibly further analysis will resolve the difficulties, but at present it appears to lead to a morass. One writer declares that the problems in strict individualistic theory are "insoluble."[1] Yet it is on the assumption of individualism that most of the research has been done.

Because the theorizing in this area has thus far been so inconclusive, I intend largely to bypass it. In Chapter One it has already been partly indicated how this will be done. I stipulate a procedural definition of democracy that includes nonminority rule but does not exclude requirements for more than a simple majority. I further indicate that majority rule, by any definition, may, under certain circumstances, work out in such a way that the result would be judged "undemocratic" by reference to the ideal definition of democracy.

The next few paragraphs treat briefly and in only slightly more detail some of the difficulties that led me to adopt this procedure. First, what is the principle underlying any formulation of "majority rule"? More specifically, how does

[1] Barry Holden, *The Nature of Democracy* (New York: Barnes & Noble, 1974), p. 118.

one decide (democratically) what policy a sizable group should adopt when several options are before it and no one of them commands the support of a majority? The procedure that now seems to have most to commend it is one which uses the test long ago advocated by Condorcet.[2] Essentially this involves a series of votes testing each of the possible choices against each of the competing possibilities. Modern parliamentary procedure is designed to accomplish this objective. Yet not all problems can be resolved this way, because of the phenomenon of "cyclical majorities." If a society of three members must choose among three possible courses of action and preferences are distributed in a certain way, no solution will satisfy the Condorcet criterion, as is indicated by the following instance. Assume three voters, A, B, and C, whose preferences among the available candidates (or policies), x, y, and z, are ranked as follows:

Ranking	A	B	C
1	x	y	z
2	y	z	x
3	z	x	y

In paired comparisons, candidate (or policy) x defeats y two to one, by the votes of A and C; y defeats z, by the votes of A and B; yet z defeats x, by the votes of B and C. If an individual preferred x to y, y to z, and z to x, we would say that his preference ordering was intransitive. And transitivity is part of the commonly accepted (and individualistic) concept of "rationality."[3] In other words, an individual

[2] See Duncan Black, *The Theory of Committees and Elections* (Cambridge: Cambridge University Press, 1958), pp. 159-180.

[3] Many philosophers use the term in a more inclusive sense and at least one has attacked the individualistic usage as applied in precisely this kind of analysis, contending it is necessary to develop a concept of rationality that is in some way more "social" and, one might say, "socialized" than the standard individualistic concept. See David Gauthier, "Justice and Natural Endowment: Toward a Critique of Rawls' Ideological Framework," *Social Theory and Practice*, 3 (1974), 3-26. Yet, as

who expressed such preferences would be judged "irrational." The essence of Condorcet's finding is that in certain cases it is impossible to sum or aggregate individual preference rankings in such a way as to produce a rational, i.e. "transitive," social ordering.[4]

In the case of a choice among policies in a legislative assembly, if preferences are intransitive, standard parliamentary procedure would normally result in retention of the status quo. Alternatively, victory might go to the side that was most clever at manipulating the rules of order.[5] Yet, in the long run, it is not unlikely that some compromise or trade (involving another issue or set of issues) will emerge which partially satisfies two or perhaps all three parties. How likely this eventuality is will depend upon the relative

far as I am aware, no one has worked out such a concept in the detail necessary to use it for the kind of analysis here under discussion. For other hints at definitions of "rationality" that are less restrictive than the individualistic one, see Edward I. Friedland, "Introduction to the Concept of Rationality in Political Science," University Programs Modular Series (Morristown, N.J.: General Learning Press, 1974), esp. pp. 22-24.

[4] A modern writer puts the matter more strongly. He exposes what he calls the "paradox of social decision"—an extension of the paradox of voting—and concludes that, with only trivial exceptions, no rational method for constructing sets of individual orderings is to be found. Holding this to be a symptom of human imperfection, he concludes that "our human activities are always piecemeal, and piecemeal rationality never ensures overall rationality." Y. Murakami, *Logic and Social Choice*, pp. 130, 134.

[5] For a full and careful discussion of the procedural problems involved in attempting to give effect to the majority principle, see Gerald H. Kramer, "Some Procedural Aspects of Majority Rule," pp. 264-295. Much rather inconclusive research has been done on the probability of a cyclical majority's occurring. In the British General Election of 1966 this phenomenon apparently did occur; a majority of the electorate (on a nationwide basis, not necessarily constituency by constituency) appears to have been opposed to the actual result and likewise a majority would have been opposed to a victory by either of the other parties. See Andrew M. Coleman and Ian Pountney, "Voting Paradoxes: A Socratic Dialogue," *Political Quarterly*, 46 (1975), 304-309.

intensities with which each of the parties hold their positions.[6]

Another fundamental problem in voting theory is revealed by Kenneth Arrow's "general possibility theorem."[7] What Arrow proves is that no voting system can in all possible cases comply with all of a set of requirements each one of which seems to be a reasonable, and indeed a necessary, constraint imposed by our intuitive ideas of the logic of democracy.[8] Many lines of attack have been pursued in the effort to solve this problem. None has succeeded, not even in giving a clear idea of the dimensions of the problem —that is, how frequently the conditions which make a majority-rule decision impossible are likely to occur in practice. Only two of these lines of attack will be given brief attention here.

First, it has been established that if preferences are "single-peaked," if, that is to say, persons who prefer Candidate A to all other candidates on one issue also place him

[6] For an actual example of vote trading in Congress showing how it was made possible by skillful use of the rules, see Randall B. Ripley, *Party Leaders in the House of Representatives* (Washington, D.C.: Brookings, 1967), pp. 132-136.

[7] Kenneth J. Arrow, *Social Choice and Individual Values*, Chap. 5.

[8] In nontechnical terms, the requirements are substantially as follows: (a) the system must provide for all possible orderings of preferences by each of the individual voters; (b) the system must provide the most positive possible correlation between individual and social orderings; (c) the decision to be reached must depend solely on the orderings of the voters of the possibilities under consideration; and (d) one person, one vote (and, even more generally, no one shall be a dictator).

Among the vast amounts of literature on this subject, attention may be called especially to three items: William H. Riker, "Voting and the Summation of Preferences: An Interpretative Bibliographical Review of Selected Developments During the Last Decade," *Amer. Polit. Sci. Rev.*, 55 (1961), 900-911; William H. Riker and Peter C. Ordeshook, *An Introduction to Positive Political Theory* (Englewood Cliffs, N.J.: Prentice-Hall, 1973); and Kenneth A. Shepsle, "Theories of Collective Choice," in *Political Science Annual*, 5 (1974), ed. Cornelius P. Cotter (Indianapolis and New York: Bobbs-Merrill, 1974), pp. 22-44.

first on their list on all other issues, then the problem does not arise.[9] This amounts to little more than saying that the greater the consensus in a society, the less will be the problem of aggregating divergent interests. It is not quite that bad. If all the issue-positions could be divided into two or more clusters, and if a majority of the voters preferred each of the issue-positions in one cluster to any of the other issue-positions, then the problem would disappear. But again we find no reason to make this assumption.[10]

The other line of attack is perhaps but a variant of the one just discussed. It is to drop the assumption of the pursuit of individual self-interest (broadly interpreted) as the basis for preference and to assume rather that such a thing as the common interest exists, that voters tend to pursue

[9] For a fuller account of the meaning of "single-peakedness" and discussion of its significance, see Riker and Ordeshook, *Introduction to Positive Political Theory*, pp. 101-106.

[10] Undoubtedly some tendency in this direction does exist. People who are opposed to socialized medicine are likely to oppose many other forms of socialization; but will they agree with respect to détente or capital punishment? A recent study "strongly supports the assertion that, with three alternatives and two salient attributes, the probability of geting a single-majoriy cycle becomes vanishingly small as the number of voters becomes large." Peter C. Fishburn, "Single-Peaked Preferences and Probabilities of Cyclical Majorities," *Behavioral Science*, 19 (1974), 21-27. In this connection, the findings of a New York Times/CBS News poll of Massachusetts voters taken after they had cast their ballots in the 1976 primary election are of interest. (*New York Times*, March 4, 1976.) The majority of Democrats agreed on government guarantees of jobs, opposition to cutting social services to balance the budget, and the reduction of the power of big business. But there was a great deal of disagreement on whether the government pays too much attention to the problems of blacks (49 percent of those who had an opinion thought it did), on détente with the Soviet Union (56 percent disapproved), and on relaxing pollution laws to help the energy crisis (59 percent opposed). Moreover, on each of these last three questions, Udall voters were in sharp disagreement with Jackson and Wallace voters. Thus, unless they changed their minds, many voters for the winning candidate in the general election were bound to be dissatisfied with important policies of the winning party.

367

what they believe is the common interest, and that they tend to agree among themselves on what the common interest is. Again, these assumptions, especially the second and third, are hardly supportable as general propositions. No doubt they are true of some of the people some of the time, perhaps of some of the people most of the time, and most of the people some of the time—but enough to rescue voting theory from the morass? Especially when one considers other problems not yet alluded to, one tends to agree with Shepsle, who writes:

> What will emerge, I suspect, from an examination of the impact of rules and institutions on the definition of the collective agenda, on the specification of strategic alternatives and constraints, on the expression of preferences, and on the weighting and aggregating of expressed preferences, is a theoretical maze. The machinery of deductive logic . . . may not serve well to uncover theoretical relationships.[11]

Where does this leave us? First, it should be noted that this discussion does nothing to invalidate the justification of democracy developed in Chapter Four, which rests on the proposition that under certain requisite conditions, democratic institutions appear to have a greater probability, at the very least, of avoiding tyranny and, beyond this of maximizing the ends of liberty (including personal development) and equality than do nondemocratic institutions.

What remains unclear is which of the various methods of aggregating preferences or otherwise implementing the broad principle of majority rule would be fairest or most just, or most in accordance with "the majority principle," if such a thing exists.[12] Certain useful things can be said,

[11] Shepsle, "Theories of Collective Choice," p. 68.

[12] Starting from Kramer's demonstration of the difficulty, if not impossibility, of discovering a single fair method of determining the majority will, Arthur Kuflik has come to the conclusion that no such thing as *the* majority principle is to be found, there being many dif-

however. They mainly deal with the question of simple majority rule versus requirements of special majorities and equivalent devices.[13]

The attempt will be made, in particular, to find out what rules for decision making are best in accordance with the principles of each of the four motivational types of democratic theory. As the titles of the chapters suggest, however, the discussion will not be strictly confined to the decision-making rules themselves, but will touch also on the machinery through which those rules operate. Such power-dispersing devices as bicameralism, the executive veto, judicial review, independent regulatory commissions, federalism, and so on, are, in part, functional equivalents of rules requiring more than a simple majority for decision making. Like such rules, they tend to maximize information, to encourage and facilitate deliberation, and to provide plural channels of representation; all, in the terminology to be developed below, tend to cut external costs and to increase decision-making costs. It should be noted, too, that constitutional limitations on the scope of governmental power, as they operate in the American system, amount to requirements of special majorities, for they may be overridden by the majorities required to amend the Constitution. These limitations may affect either the subject matter of the policy (e.g. the First Amendment) or the procedures and means by which the policy is converted into law (e.g. the executive veto) and the manner in which it is carried out (e.g. procedural due process). The considerations to be adduced here thus have an important bearing on the merits of these institutions; but they are not the only factors relevant to the evaluation of such institutions. No attempt will be

---

ferent ways of construing and supporting "rule by majority," no one way being appropriate in all contexts. "Majority Rule Procedure," in Pennock and Chapman, eds., *Due Process*, NOMOS XVIII, p. 326.

[13] The vast majority of the extensive literature analyzing the problems of vote-aggregation deals with simple majority rule.

made here to evaluate them as a whole, but only to indicate the implications for such an evaluation of the analysis pertaining to decision-making rules. To explicate these implications is important, however, because often an objective that could be furthered by a specific decision-making rule could be promoted as well, or better, by a particular arrangement of the machinery for making decisions.

2. Democracy, Majority Rule, and Radical Individualism

In a discussion of decision-making rules for democracy, inevitably majority rule will be the center of attention much of the time. We must note at once that rule by the majority is often alleged to be the very essence of democracy.[14] In particular, the Bentham-James Mill tradition, especially strong in England, forges a strong link between democracy and majority rule. Its moral basis rested upon the conviction that in the calculation of utilities and more particularly in the determination of the greatest happiness of the greatest number, each must count for one and none for more than one (cf. today's "one person, one vote"); and its political foundation embraced the additional assumption that each person best knew his own interest (and therefore the path to his own happiness). In America, the populist tradition gave strong support to the same conclusion.

Yet other parts of our democratic heritage qualify strict majoritarianism—the proposition that on all questions the vote of 50 percent plus one should be determinative.[15] A

---

[14] See, for example, *A Dictionary of the Social Sciences*, ed. Julius Gould and William L. Kolb (London: Tavistock Publications, 1964). As a theory of government, democracy is here reduced to two main concepts, one of which stresses obedience to the people's will, while the other emphasizes the free participation of the individual in the formation of that will; both concepts make majority rule supreme, with the important exception that the second conditions it upon the maintenance of the conventionally accepted liberal rights.

[15] "Majority rule," the broader term with which this discussion was

strong emphasis on liberty of conscience and on other individual rights formed an important element of the democratic tradition that grew out of the English Civil War. A. D. Lindsay, who drew heavily upon the debates in Cromwell's army between Levellers and the officers, stressed the idea that each person must be taken account of and permitted to have his say and to have his views considered, as contrasted with the idea of the consent of the majority as central to the democratic ideal.[16] Whether John Locke, whose work gave systematic expression to the liberal and democratic ideas of the seventeenth century and cast it in a form destined to have great and lasting influence in England, Europe, and most of all the United States, was a majoritarian or not has been the subject of great controversy.[17] Clearly individual rights were of great importance to his way of thinking, but he advanced no institutional device for their protection. He did suggest the possibility that when the original social compact was agreed upon, the people might arrange to require more than a majority for decisions. Thus, unlike many modern majoritarians, he apparently did not consider such an arrangement contrary to the right of equality. With respect to the majoritarian interpretation of Locke, this fact assumes considerable importance. Yet he did not pursue this suggestion and appears rather to have assumed that for reasons of convenience, majority rule would be generally accepted.[18] Rousseau, for once, was

---

begun, is sometimes used to cover all nonminority rule, any government in which no specified minority has the right to rule over the majority. It is used here, however, as equivalent to "majoritarianism," as defined above.

[16] A. D. Lindsay, *The Essentials of Democracy*, especially Lectures 1 and 3.

[17] See Willmoore Kendall, *John Locke and the Doctrine of Majority-Rule*, Chap. 7; J. W. Gough, *John Locke's Political Philosophy* (Oxford: Clarendon Press, 1950), Chaps. 2 and 3; and M. Seliger, *The Liberal Politics of John Locke* (London: Allen & Unwin, 1968), pp. 302-311.

[18] John Locke, *Second Treatise of Civil Government*, Pars. 95-99 and 140.

371

much more clear, specific, and judicious. He recognized that the more nearly a vote approached unanimity the greater the chance that it was a wise (he said "right") decision, and that therefore in important matters it would be desirable to require more than a simple majority for a decision, except in cases where the urgency of the matter was of overriding importance.[19] It might be appropriate to add at this point that whatever theorists may have said, strict majoritarianism has seldom been applied in policy decisions at the national level. Most frequently it has been limited by provision for executive vetoes and "upper" houses. It is chiefly where ethical and traditional restraints in behalf of individual rights and group interests tend to be especially strong, as in Britain, that majorities are subject to minimal instiutional limitations.

It is well known that the United States has perhaps the most elaborate effectively operating system of checks on decisions by simple majority that exists in any democratic government. At the same time, a good case could be made for the proposition that no country is more democratic in its whole ethos.

This chapter examines decision-making rules from the point of view of radical individualism and its variants. (For reasons that will become clear in the following chapter the other motivational theories, as they relate to decision-making rules, can best be discussed against this background.) It is applicable to both direct democracy and to representative government. It will not, however, take account of the complications introduced by the institution of political parties. This matter will be addressed in the succeeding chapter.

What bearing the power theories of democratic operation have upon rules for decision making does not call for extended treatment, because it is largely self-evident from the very nature of those theories. Most obviously, constitution-

[19] Jean-Jacques Rousseau, *The Social Contract*, Bk. IV, Chap. 11.

alist theory, by definition, calls for checks on the exercise of power such as the requirement of more than a simple-majority vote. By contrast, the cry of populism is "all power to the majority." The other two cases are perhaps less clear. Social pluralists, however, hold that the checking effect of special decision-making rules is accomplished by the structure of society, so they would at the very least set less store by mechanical requirements than would the constitutionalists. Elitists are perhaps in a slightly ambiguous position. They believe that *an* elite, although not of course a designated one, should exercise predominant influence. They might well feel that checks on simple majorities would help assure this predominance; but also they might believe that the superior skills, intelligence, and political activism of the elite would assure this result without constitutional aids.

3. RADICAL INDIVIDUALISM AND DECISION-MAKING RULES

a. Preliminaries

The rational man hypothesized by the radical individualistic model would seek to discover rules to which all rational men would agree. They would be founded upon approximate unanimity; but, once established, they need not require unanimity for subsequent decisions. Rational men would seek a set of rules that would ensure the best chance of satisfying their preferences. What rules would meet this test?

It was demonstrated in Chapter One that the core notion of "one person, one vote" does not in itself require bare-majority rule. In fact, in the case of small groups at least, an extreme departure from majority rule, the unanimity principle, with which the radical individualist begins, is often considered the very acme of democracy. For larger groups, it would appear, it is still thought that a unanimous *decision* is considered most democratic of all; but for such groups a rule *requiring* unanimity is likely to mean that little or no action will be taken by the group, thus largely defeating the purposes for which government is maintained.

Even in the case of large associations, if individuals are bound together in large clusters by ties of sentiment or common interest, members of certain groups may find themselves in a permanent minority, unable to win over members of the majority or to have any significant influence upon them. In this case, their formal equality of political power is specious. The majority can tyrannize them just as truly as could a despot. Their votes are as ineffective as if they were never cast. (As a matter of fact, under such circumstances they are likely not to be cast.)

b. Method of Calculation

To discover what decision-making rules the radical individualist would establish, we must place ourselves in the position of a generic, rational individual, at the stage of devising a constitution to regulate his life with others, aimed at maximizing his own satisfactions, and unable to measure his preferences against those of others. His task is to lay down rules for his society for the indefinite future. He is unable to predict, except in the most general way, what issues may arise or how their resolution may affect him or his family.[20] What decision-making rules (constitu-

[20] In what follows, I shall borrow considerably from Buchanan and Tullock, *The Calculus of Consent*. It should be recalled, however, that I am dealing with normative theory in a sense in which they claim they are not. I am speaking about what rational individuals *ought* to do if they wish to maximize their preferences. Of course, it may be said that by definition rational individuals do seek to maximize their preferences; hence what I say they ought to do is in fact what they will do. If theirs is a positive theory, it becomes normative as well if it is assumed that men ought to be rational.

Note, too, the parallelism with John Rawls's method and results in establishing the principles of justice. Men in Rawls's "original position," like rational constitution-makers, seek rules that would be in the best interest of themselves and their descendants. One such rule would be that goods, values, should be distributed equally unless all

tion) would receive unanimous consent under such circumstances?

In performing the calculations necessary for establishing the best (for him) rules for collective decision making, the rational individual must take into account two kinds of factors: (1) the costs of participating in collective decision making, and (2) the net costs or benefits anticipated from whatever actions are taken under the decision-making rule in question.[21] In general, the costs of decision making vary directly with the percentage of the electorate required for taking governmental action. They would be greatest under a rule requiring unanimous consent; least under the rule stating the lowest feasible requirement—a plurality of votes cast.[22] The effects (costs/benefits) of decision making is another, and more complicated, matter. Would the rational individual at the constitution-making stage want it to be relatively easy to get a law enacted or relatively hard? At least at first, it seems the answer would vary with the type of question involved. For instance, take rules of the road; more specifically, the rule as to whether one drives on the right or on the left. A rule must be established, and it matters little what the rule is to be. Under these circumstances, rule by a bare majority of those voting would appear to be preferable.

---

rational men in the constitution-making stage (for Rawls, read "original position") would agree upon rules for exceptions. (For Rawls the fact [if it were a fact] that an unequal distribution would be everyone's advantage—including especially the least favored—would constitute such an exception.) John Rawls, *A Theory of Justice* (Cambridge, Mass.: Harvard University Press, 1971-, Secs. 4, 11, and 46.

[21] Of course some persons may derive a net benefit from the decision-making process because of the sheer joy of "politicking"; but the relatively small numbers of people who enlist as party workers suggest that the average man does not value politicking very highly.

[22] This statement applies either to a direct democracy or to the rules applied for decision by a legislative body. It also broadly applies, other things being equal, to the rule for electing representatives and other policy-making officials under representative government. See Buchanan and Tullock, *Calculus of Consent*, Chap. 15.

375

Even a more restrictive rule, however, say one requiring the concurrence of two thirds of the voters, would not do much harm (i.e. not entail great internal costs); for the matter being of so little consequence as to *how* it is determined and yet of such great consequence that it *be* determined, it seems unlikely that a minority, even one large enough to constitute a blocking minority, would hold out for its own preference. On the contrary, once the majority preference was determined, the minority would probably acquiesce, since for them to do so would appear to be rational—rational because it would maximize their preference-satisfaction.

c. The Case of a Law Abolishing Democracy

Now let us take a case at the opposite extreme. What about a law abolishing the democratic form of government and substituting, without time limit, the dictatorship of one man? Surely, rational men, deliberately framing a democratic constitution, and therefore preferring such a constitution, would wish to do all they could to preserve it. They might imagine circumstances under which it would be desirable to hand over all power to one man, but it is unlikely they would believe it necessary to provide for this in perpetuity. That would defeat their own premises; accordingly, it would be irrational. Therefore, they would do all they could to guard against it, including provision that more than a bare majority should be required to take such action; in other words, that something less than a majority, perhaps far less, would be sufficient to block this kind of action.

It is true, to be sure, that in the hypothesized case (of a majority desiring to abolish democracy), aggregated preferences (each counted equally) would not be maximized. That is to say, the action taken (or not taken) would thwart the preferences of more individuals than it would satisfy, *at that moment*. However, the hypothesis is that rational constitution-makers, believing in a system which

376

would be most responsive to individual preferences, and calling such a system democratic, would consider the long run. Most certainly, they would try to prevent action that would subordinate all future individual preferences to the will of one man.[23] Moreover, it would seem strange to dub as undemocratic a provision designed to prevent democracy from committing suicide.

Nonetheless, it is sometimes argued that any provision which permits a number of voters (or representatives) fewer than a majority to block governmental action violates the principle of "one person, one vote" because it permits a minority to have its way when a majority cannot do so. (Although it was argued in Chapter One that "one person, one vote" does not imply majoritarianism, in the present context further demonstration may be useful.) Thus, it is contended, the minority has greater power than the majority; therefore, *a fortiori*, each member of the minority has greater power than each member of the majority, thus violating the principle of equality. The example provided above should show the fallacy of this line of reasoning. The most the blockers can do is to prevent the destruction of democracy, thereby preserving their power, and that of everyone else, in the future. That is the limit of their power. On the other hand, the majority retains complete power, with this single exception. It is prevented from exercising only one wish, one preference: namely, that which would prevent it from exercising its preferences in the future. If such an arrangement is undemocratic, then the whole rea-

---

[23] It is true of course, as Douglas Rae has pointed out, that majority-rule democracy does not guarantee the maximum satisfaction of individual preference. Conceivably, dictatorship might do a better job of it, as Hobbes argued. Douglas Rae, "Political Democracy as a Property of Political Institutions," *Amer. Polit. Sci. Rev.*, 65 (1971), 111-119, 118, n. 22. It must be remembered, however, that the radical individualist assumes people are, in the long run, the best guardians of their own interests. He is forced to this assumption, if for no other reason, by his denial of the possibility of interpersonal comparisons. But democratic theorists of other types rely upon the same assumption.

377

soning underlying the acceptance of democracy in the first place is false, and we are engaging in a fruitless adventure.

d. The Case of Rights Fundamental to Democracy

Now it remains to be inquired whether the case just discussed is unique, or whether the same reasoning applies to other cases. Perhaps the most obvious candidates would be proposed actions that threaten the very existence of democracy, the requisites, that is to say, for the maintenance of a democratic system. Clearly the rational individual at the constitution-making stage would wish to preserve all of the essential elements of his scheme, even against the wishes (which, by definition, must be irrational) of a majority. (The reasoning of the previous section is equally applicable here.) The limits of what this proposition entails may not be clear, but certain implications are hardly debatable. The ability of the individual to exercise his franchise freely, to be free to persuade others, and to organize for these purposes—in other words the First Amendment freedoms of expression and association—fall in this category.

Basic though they are, it is generally agreed that the guarantee of First Amendment freedoms is not necessarily sufficient to prevent majorities from interfering with the equal political power of members of minorities—that is from taking action that in effect denies their political equality. Officials, even elected officials, may use their powers to preserve their positions against democratic processes. Specifically, they may harass the members of opposition groups. To prevent this sort of occurrence we generally rely upon such devices as the writ of *habeas corpus*, the assurance of speedy trials, and the procedural guarantees of "due process of law." Rights of this kind, then, would rationally be protected at the constitution-making stage against contravening action by majorities. The power that these rights entail is by no means equivalent to the general power to "rule." Moreover, no power is given to anyone that is not enjoyed by all.[24]

---

[24] Whether the limitations imposed by these rights should be abso-

A further consideration will underline this conclusion. Quite apart from *hypothetical* reasoning about what rational individuals would do, it is a well-substantiated fact that average citizens are much more prone to defend such rights in the abstract (as at the constitution-making stage) than they are in individual applications, where particular interests, prejudices, or passions have been called into play.[25]

e. The Problem of Consensus

Proceeding, then, with the general analysis, not all the requisites for democracy can be embodied in individual rights. One much-discussed condition for a successfully functioning democracy is that of consensus. It is notoriously vague.[26] How much agreement, on what subjects, and even

---

lute or should be cast in terms of a requirement for a special majority is a matter of expediency. In the case of the issues discussed thus far, the reasoning would call for an absolute limitation; but if more than, say, two thirds or three fourths of the electorate favored a change in the democratic fundamentals, it is doubtful in any case whether a stricter prohibition could retain legitimacy and effectiveness. For this reason, and also because it might prove desirable because of technological developments and the like to change the wording of prohibitions while retaining their objective, it is the general practice to forego absolute prohibitions, relying instead upon the requirement of an extraordinary majority, perhaps reinforced with procedural devices such as attend the amending clause in the United States Constitution.

25 See the review of polls on freedom of speech in *The Pub. Opinion Quar.*, 34 (1970), 483ff. The editor concludes that Americans believe in free speech in theory, but not always in practice. Many would like to see controversy limited and the Bill of Rights tailored to the times and to the occasion. Very few people have ever been willing to accord complete freedom of expression to political extremists, at least since formal opinion polls began their inquiries. P. 483. See also James Prothro and Charles M. Grigg, "Fundamental Principles of Democracy: Bases of Agreement and Disagreement," *Jour. of Politics*, 22 (1960), 276-294.

26 It is true, though, that analysis of the use of voting rules as social-welfare functions has sharpened our understanding of the role played by consensus. In commenting on the significance of Duncan Black's study for Arrow's "impossibility theorem," William Riker de-

by what people (whether or not primarily the political activists), are all subjects for debate. Clearly the contribution that can be made to this problem by limitations upon majority rule is uncertain and at best incomplete. Yet the subject deserves attention. It is true of small groups, at least, that action by a bare majority against what the minority considers its vital interests tends to embitter and consolidate the minority so that future satisfactory collective action is more difficult. Indeed, in small groups the majority commonly is sensitive enough to this problem to forbear behaving in this manner—if only to preserve the group from disintegration. In larger groups the importance of observing this constraint is more easily lost sight of; the more so since it is often impossible to know in advance just what will be the minority's reaction to a particular infringement of its interests. Experience demonstrates that some societies can achieve a working agreement—a constitution—only at the price of a system of government embodying generalized checks on majority action. In fact, it would appear that the United States was such a society at its inception—and may still be. The fact that such was (and may now be) the case does not *prove* that insistence on generalized checks on majority action was or is rational; but it perhaps creates a certain presumption to that effect. The rational individual should recognize, however, that minorities as well as majorities may abuse their power in such a way as to endanger or even destroy consensus. Their power is negative only and therefore less than that of a majority under simple-majority rule; but nonetheless it may be great and capable of serious abuse.

---

clares that "Black's notable discovery may be epitomized by saying that social welfare functions exist without inconsistency among their conditions [the problem that Arrow found] *if some sort of inner harmony exists among the persons in the society. . . .*" (Italics added.) Riker, "Voting and the Summation of Preferences," p. 906. Without this consensus, or "inner harmony," as was pointed out in the preceding chapter, preferences may be intransitive and there may be no solution to the problem of aggregating individual preferences in a socially rational way.

As far as consensus is concerned, at least part of the rational answer may be to exclude the most divisive issues from politics altogether. This is what the framers of the American Constitution sought to do by erecting the famous "wall" between Church and State.[27]

f. Ban on Arbitrary Action by Government

What else would it be rational for constitution makers, completely uncertain about what special or vested interests they might acquire in the future, to agree upon? They would agree, it would appear, not only on protections for the democratic process itself but also on restrictions upon arbitrary actions. Whatever else rationality entails, it is certainly in opposition to arbitrariness; and vice versa. Like cases should be treated alike. Despite all the difficulties inherent in applying this formal rule—the problem of what is and is not relevant in considering "likeness"—the history of the "equal protection" clause of the American Constitution shows that the task can be accomplished. It involves a large area of agreement, although with a peripheral area of disagreement, especially among interested parties. In any case, it is not our present concern to decide whether a court or other institution can be devised that will fairly apply this rule. The point here is that rational men, seeking to construct decision-making rules which maximize the satisfaction of preferences, counting each person's preferences equally, and knowing that by definition rational men prefer not to be treated arbitrarily, would do whatever was feasible to prevent arbitrary treatment.

It might be said that what the rational individual wishes to avoid is arbitrary action that *injures* him. He has no objection, assuming pure self-interest, to arbitrary action by which he benefits. In other words, he wishes to avoid being in the minority when arbitrary action is taken. If he were in the majority, he might actually benefit by it. So, it might be argued, under majority rule, all else being equal—or,

[27] On limiting politics to noninflammatory issues, see David Braybrooke, *Three Tests for Democracy*, pp. 170-171.

what amounts to the same thing, unknown and unpredictable—his chances of being in the majority would be slightly better than of his being in the minority. Hence he would favor majority rule. But this conclusion follows only if the benefit of being in the majority is as great as the detriment of being in the minority. Such an assumption, I believe, would be mistaken, as the following example demonstrates. Suppose the minority would be forced to attend certain schools not of their own choosing, while the majority may go to the school of their choice. The minority clearly has been stigmatized as in some sense inferior or undesirable. (It is assumed that no rational basis for the distinction existed, or at least not one that outweighed the stigmatization, otherwise it would not be arbitrary.) It seems obvious that a rational individual, contemplating these two possible outcomes for himself—being in the majority in such a case or being in the minority—would not be satisfied with a substantially fifty-fifty chance of being in either group. He would prefer an arrangement that would make it *much* more likely that he would *not* suffer the invidious discrimination than that he *would* suffer it. The requirement of an extraordinary majority to pass such legislation would accomplish precisely this result.

It might be objected that in certain situations individuals in a majority might gain more by discriminating against a minority than they would lose if they belonged to that minority. Assuming that such situations might exist, one must distinguish between the gain or loss from the substantive result and the gain or loss from inflicting or suffering arbitrary action. It is the latter about which we are here concerned, and it seems self-evident that while one always is pained by (and resentful of) arbitrary action of which he is the victim, he does not normally take pleasure in inflicting arbitrary action upon another. The voting requirement under consideration is directed at arbitrariness per se; as such, the requirement seems bound to benefit the rational individual. Gains or losses from the substantive results, not inherently related to the arbitrariness, could be counted on to balance out in the long run. They would be equally likely to be on either side of the gain/loss ledger.

g. *Local Interests*

Generalizing from the kinds of situations discussed above, one may say that the rational individualist would support limitations on majority rule wherever the potential costs to him of state action appear greater than the potential gains. Such situations may arise not only where majority rule is likely to lead to arbitrary action or to the exploitation of a minority by the majority, but also where it leads to actions that are uneconomic from everyone's point of view (prisoner's-dilemma situations). All cases involving the appropriation of funds from general revenues for projects that are largely for the benefit of particular interests, for instance the residents of the localities in which they are spent, fall in this classification. In this kind of situation, majorities are subject to the constant temptation to vote themselves benefits at the expense of the whole.[28] The reasoning behind this statement is fairly obvious, but it will do no harm to spell it out with a practical example. Suppose the country is divided into 100 districts of equal population, and that the government has proposed to build an indefinite number of buildings and other public improvements. Assume further that each of these units will cost $100 million and is worth $60 million to the district in which it is to be located, and is of no value to persons located outside the district. Under simple majority rule, with side payments barred (making the usual assumptions of rationality and perfect information), some entrepreneurial

[28] The general argument, but not the particular example, is based upon Buchanan and Tullock, *Calculus of Consent*, Chap. 10. Much of the argument, and indeed of the identical wording, of the next several paragraphs is lifted (with the kind permission of the editor) from my "The 'Pork Barrel' and Majority Rule: A Note," *Jour. of Politics*, 32 (1970), 709-716.

legislator would mobilize fifty of his colleagues and they would vote projects for their respective districts. Assuming the cost would be spread evenly throughout the country, each district that got a project would benefit by \$60 million, at a cost of \$51 million, for a net gain of \$9 million, while the losers would suffer a loss of over \$104 million each $\frac{(51 \times 100m)}{49}$. (Note that the case involves both exploitation of the minority by the majority and also uneconomic expenditure, for the society as a whole would suffer a loss of \$20.4 million.) If, however, a two-thirds majority were required for such projects, it would take the representatives from sixty-seven districts to enact the necessary legislation, the price of which would presumably be sixty-seven bases. Each of these districts would have to shoulder a cost of \$67 million and receive a benefit of only \$60 million for a \$7 million loss on balance. Consequently, no projects would be approved.[29]

Let us now return to the situation requiring only a simple majority. It should be noted that the action of the first majority might not be the last. The minority, or part of it, might repeat the process by combining with some members of the majority who still desired projects. If these alignments continued to form, no district would ultimately be left out in the cold, paying taxes for other people's benefits while receiving no benefits of its own. Injustice would be avoided, or minimized, but at the price of gross overexpenditure. Many projects would be built that, by hypothesis, would not be worth their cost. Always assuming the

[29] For a formal, generalized demonstration of the proposition that the requirement of more than a simple majority makes such logrolling more difficult, see Peter Bernholz, "Logrolling, Arrow Paradox and Decision Rules: A Generalization," *Kyklos*, 27 (1974), 49-61. More specifically, he argues that there are decision rules (between simple majority and unanimity) "that can prevent occurrence of strong logrolling situations either if the number of simple issues is small or if not all the group members are voting on each occasion." Ibid., p. 59.

absence of side payments, simple-majority rule works badly in either case.[30]

Anthony Downs disputes this argument. He believes it has more force as applied to the legislator than it has with

[30] If full side payments were permitted, with perfect information and ample opportunity for negotiation, the whole problem would disappear. No projects would be built that were not "economic," and costs and benefits would be distributed in such a way that each district would enjoy an identical gain. This would be the result of a free market in votes, as districts bid to get projects, or to avoid taxation without projects or taxation exceeding the value of a project to them. This would be the case under *any* voting rule. What is to be stressed, however, is that both practical and rational considerations operate in real-life situations to limit both side payments and extensive vote trading. As Uslaner and Davis remark, "It is not terribly difficult for a rational legislator to realize when to stop trading and when the Pareto optimal position has been reached (particularly if he has been 'stung' once by the occurrence of the paradox of vote trading)." Eric M. Uslaner and J. Ronnie Davis, "The Paradox of Vote Trading: Effects of Decision Rules and Voting Strategies on Externalities," *Amer. Polit. Sci. Rev.*, 69 (1975), 929-942, 937.

It is true that vote trading may have bad as well as good effects. The most recent study of which I am aware, however, shows that the "worst anomalies" that mathematical modeling purports to attribute to vote trading appear only under certain strong and perhaps unrealistic assumptions (e.g. the absence of nonseparable collective preferences and of nonseparable voter preferences). The author goes on to suggest that since the worst effects of vote trading come from the high costs of cooperation, it might be best to *facilitate* cooperation by lowering these costs. Thomas Schwartz, "Collective Choice, Separation of Issues and Vote Trading," *Amer. Polit. Sci. Rev.*, 71 (1977), 999-1010.

On the basis of the logic of prisoners' dilemma situations involving free communication among *n* participants, John M. Orbell and L. A. Wilson II have found grounds for concluding that majoritarian democracy will support socially optimal programs when the costs to individuals of doing so are modest; but that when these costs are increased the same is not true—rather no equilibrium solution is possible (anything can happen). This unfortunate result can be avoided only by the adoption of supplementary rules. Although they do not explore this possibility, their calculations suggest to me that the requirement of an extraordinary majority would improve the situation. "Institutional Solutions to the *N*-Prisoners' Dilemma," *Amer. Polit. Sci. Rev.*, 72 (1978), 411-421.

respect to the individual voter; but even in the case of the legislator he argues that a great difference arises from the fact that the legislator is not accountable to his constituents for each of his votes, *seriatim*, but rather that he comes up for election at stated intervals on the basis of his complete record. "Any legislator who returns to his constituents with a record featuring more costs than benefits," he argues, "is sure to be defeated by an opponent promising the reverse."[31] Under some circumstances, this reasoning appears plausible, but if the local benefits are paid for by remote and (as to its incidence) indeterminate general taxation (the case posited above), its validity is doubtful.[32] It is doubtful for the following reason. The assumption of rationality and perfect information, which underlies the whole model used both by Downs and by Buchanan and Tullock, is in this kind of case *systematically* unrealistic. Voters are more likely to know about and give attention to specific benefits for them or their group than to be aware of the costs to be levied by taxation that is more or less general and, insofar as it is not completely general, indeterminate in its incidence. Under these circumstances, the rational constitution maker would not assume that the voter would be as keenly aware of the costs entailed to him by his legislator's behavior as he would of the benefits that would accrue to him. Moreover, it would be likely that the representatives of some district or group would be especially anxious to gain a special benefit. But if they then seized their opportunity, others would see they must do likewise

[31] Downs, "In Defense of Majority Voting," *Quar. Jour. of Economics*, 69 (1961), 192-199, 196.

[32] Buchanan and Tullock make the valid point that, for many situations in which their reasoning indicates the desirability of requiring qualified majorities, it would be more feasible and perhaps even more effective to pursue the same objective by resort to user prices and benefit taxes. The resultant obvious one-to-one relation between cost and benefit would eliminate the situation out of which pork-barreling arises. Unfortunately, the types of situation in which this solution is feasible are strictly limited.

386

if they were not to be exploited for the benefit of these opportunists. And thus the "Kantian-Christian" rule of not doing unto others what you would not have them do unto you would break down. The fact that the phenomenon of the pork barrel does exist gives empirical support for the line of reasoning just set forth.

Another attack upon the Buchanan and Tullock line of argument has been launched by Brian Barry.[33] He begins by questioning the assumption that any of the forty-nine legislators who were omitted from the first coalition will be able to effect recombinations with some of the fifty-one. He questions this assumption on the theory that the fifty-one would make an enforceable contract to prevent defections. Of course such a contract could not be legally enforced, and it seems doubtful that it would be made. If, however, it were made and enforced, it would insure a situation in which the majority exploited the minority to the utmost. For the districts in the majority, it would be the ideal pork barrel, at least in the short run. Thus this attack fails.

Alternatively, Barry argues, no stable solution might be found. Bargaining and recombinations might continue indefinitely, or until some irrelevant factor, such as constitutional or legal provisions, brought an end to the session.[34] In the case posited, this seems unlikely. It will be recalled that new combinations must include representatives who have already obtained the assurance of one project. It does not require a great relaxation of the assumptions of pure rationality and unlimited energy and bargaining time (i.e. no "internal" costs) to support the conclusion that the process would soon wear itself out.

[33] Barry, *Political Argument* (London: Routledge & Kegan Paul, 1965), pp. 250-256 and Appendix T, pp. 317-318.

[34] Ibid., pp. 252-253. It should be noted that Buchanan and Tullock use a different illustration—the case of upkeep of local roads—from the one presented in the text above. Barry's arguments, in particular the one about the difficulty of achieving a stable solution, have, I believe, greater validity as applied to the case of the roads than they do to the one under discussion here.

387

Proceeding on the assumption of endless haggling or, alternatively, of overspending that becomes obvious to all, Barry argues that intelligent men would search for a way out of this dilemma. They would seek an "obvious" solution upon which implicit agreement might be found. In the road-upkeep case, used by Buchanan and Tullock, he suggests that such a solution might be to keep all roads up to a customary standard of repair.

Bypassing the problem of how the "customary standard" was established in the first place, and whether *it* was efficient or involved exploitation, this process might work in the case of the roads, where presumably such a customary standard exists; but in the case of benefits like those discussed here, it is difficult to imagine what solution would be sufficiently obvious to command general support. Possibly a procedural device might do the trick, such as the British system of handling Private Bills. Unfortunately, this device has not yet seemed sufficiently "obvious" to American legislators. I can see nothing about the principle of majority rule that explains why the British have adopted this mechanism and the Americans have not. One could even speculate that it was precisely the tendency of a simple-majority system to lead to pork-barreling that encouraged the British to engage in this bit of institutional inventiveness. In other words, the Private Bills procedure may have been the "obvious solution" under conditions of parliamentary government before party discipline reached its modern pitch. But it is equally plausible to suppose that differences in the political cultures of the two countries may provide the explanation. In any case, its applicability is limited to local benefits and does not apply to the much wider category of special-interest benefits.

Another difficulty with Barry's obvious-solution approach to the standard pork-barrel situation is that not only is there no obvious solution to the dilemma, but the dilemma itself may not be self-evident. Benefits of the kind in question are more obvious than costs. Again, any relaxation of the assumption of complete rationality and information tends to lead to inefficient (i.e. non-Pareto-optimal) results. Barry himself writes that "it is perhaps easy to guess that logrolling under conditions of imperfect information will tend to produce over-investment in projects which yield specific benefits to determinate groups, because such benefits are highly visible to the beneficiaries whereas costs are not so visible to the general taxpayer."[35]

Barry makes a final argument that is not applicable here but that must be discussed to show why it does not apply to the majority-rule question, as well as to show its true significance. He contends that legislators who, by their "strategic position along the legislative pipeline," are in a position to hold up all appropriations, or to threaten to do so, can use this power to secure "pork" for their own constituencies.[36] That this is true seems clear enough. It is a sound argument against the seniority system for selecting committee chairmen and perhaps against other features of the committee system; but it is at least not obviously an argument against bicameralism or the presidential veto, features that may be considered as functional equivalents of qualified majorities. Whether one can have these features of the American system while avoiding a committee system that gives toll-charging opportunities to specific individuals, like committee chairmen, is a question meriting serious study. The special virtue of bicameralism, rather than the requirement of qualified majorities for the purpose here in view, are discussed below, in the next section.

Insofar then as voters are motivated by rational self-interest, it would appear that decision-making rules calling for qualified majorities, or other institutional arrangements having similar effects, tend (as contrasted with simple-ma-

<hr>

[35] Ibid., p. 318. He is using the argument to support a different point from the one I am urging, but it serves equally well to support my argument that the dilemma itself would not be obvious, while the solution to it would be even less obvious.

[36] Ibid.

jority institutions) to minimize pork-barreling. Yet it is widely believed that the experience of the United Kingdom (corresponding closely to the simple-majority-rule model) and the United States (approximating more closely a qualified-majority model) runs exactly contrary to what abstract reasoning, as set forth above, would lead one to anticipate. How can we account for this discrepancy? It may be that Parliament's procedure for Private Bills together with the standing orders affecting money matters generally provide a sufficient explanation. The special powers possessed by committee chairmen in the American Congress must surely also bear an important measure of responsibility for the situation in this country. Still further considerations relevant to this point are brought out in the following subsection.

h. *Other Types of Special Interest*

The present discussion could be concluded with the observations just made, except for the fact that the reasoning which applies to the limited phenomenon of pork-barreling, as that term is usually defined, has much wider application. And again the comparison of Britain and America is instructive. Although Britain has no "pork barrel," if we look more broadly at the use of public funds in Britain for the benefit of identifiable groups, farmers, old-age pensioners, recipients of general public assistance, manufacturers, and the like, something bearing a distinct family resemblance to the pork-barrel phenomenon quickly appears. British farmers seem to have been more highly subsidized than their American counterparts, by any reasonable standard of comparison.[37] Certainly no single explana-

[37] In the late fifties, for instance, subsidies comprised about three times as high a percentage of gross farm income in the United Kingdom as in the United States. As a percentage of net agricultural income, British subsidies were over four times as high as those in the United States. J. Roland Pennock, " 'Responsible Government,' Separated Powers and Special Interests: Agricultural Subsidies in Britain and America," *Amer. Polit. Sci. Rev.*, 56 (1962), 632. See also S. E.

tion accounts for this phenomenon, which runs counter to traditional wisdom, but arguments used in parliamentary and other discussions of the matter strongly suggest that legally established wages for agricultural labor, and tariffs and other benefits to manufacturers, constitute in a large sense a "package deal" that resembles the American pork barrel. It is implicit logrolling, or vote trading, and it apportions benefits to special groups, the cost of which is spread throughout the taxpaying or, as the case may be, consuming public. This is the essence of the pork-barrel phenomenon. It tends to result in overspending and it is discriminatory.

In the United States, the same phenomenon occurs. Whether it occurs to a greater or lesser extent than in Britain would be hard to assess. I am familiar with only one attempt to make such a calculation—the study referred to above dealing with agricultural subsidies—and the comparison there is not unfavorable to the United States.

It must be recognized too that in the United States attempts have been made to bring the "pork-process" under control. In the case of tariffs, considerable success has been achieved under the Reciprocal Trade Agreements Act, which took the determination of tariff schedules out of the hands of Congress and gave it to the executive (in collaboration with other nations). Doubtless the American chief executive is less effectively insulated from local and other sectional pressures than is a British Private Bill Committee, but the necessity for securing agreement with other countries adds a powerful safeguard. On balance, this particular variety of pork barrel has been cut to a shadow of its former size. An attempt was made a number of years ago to regulate river-and-harbor improvements on the basis of experts' findings. Unfortunately, the anti-pork-barrel aspect of this legislation has been defeated by the fact that far more

Finer, *Anonymous Empire*; and Peter Self and Herbert J. Storing, *The State and the Farmer* (London: Allen & Unwin, 1962), esp. Chaps. 9 and 10.

projects have been approved than can be carried out with the funds appropriated, and probably far more also than could be economically justified. The result is simply to move the logrolling and pork-barreling processes forward to the appropriation point, where the available funds are allocated among the backlog of approved projects. The upshot of all this would seem to be that we have no definitive evidence that the pork-barrel phenomenon, *in the broadest sense,* is more characteristic of American than of British government.

Even if it were, however, we would have no reason to attribute the difference to the fact that the British system approximates simple-majority rule, while the American system is similar to the qualified-majority system; the reasoning set forth above indicates that this difference should have the opposite effect. Other explanations are available. As was mentioned above, one explanation relates to the prevailing political cultures of the two countries. In Britain, commitment to the "public interest" is believed to be relatively strong. In the United States, on the contrary, politics tends to be particularistic and pluralistic. These differences are reflected, among other ways, in the party systems; British parties are highly disciplined in comparison with the loose federations that constitute American political parties. One result is that in Britain logrolling operations (which, as we have seen, constitute an integral part of the pork-barrel process) must be built into party programs rather than being worked out, more or less openly, within the legislature and reflected in voting across party lines.

Another difference, not unrelated to the difference in political culture, is to be found in the American committee system, to which reference has already been made. It is notorious that given committees tend not to be cross-sections of Congress, but cross-sections of those members of Congress who have, or whose constituents have, special interests in the affairs with which the committees deal. Thus the agricultural committees are composed largely of members from heavily agricultural areas, while the public-works committee is heavily populated with representatives from areas where dams, flood-control projects, and harbor improvements are important elements of public policy. This system tends to favor expenditures that benefit special interests or areas at the expense of the general taxpayer. It should be noted, however, that the use of such a committee system is unrelated to the requirement of qualified majorities, or of unanimity, or, for that matter, to bicameralism.[38]

To recapitulate, the reasoning and illustration to this point tends to indicate that where particular identifiable groups can benefit by legislation whose cost is levied upon the general taxpayer, majority rule tends to lead to greater transfers from majorities to minorities than the balance of preferences would dictate, or, to the extent that logrolling occurs, to devote more public revenues to satisfying group interests than the efficient use of resources would justify. To the extent that the decision-making rule was shifted toward unanimity these externalities would be eliminated. (The question of the price in terms of an increase in internal costs will be discussed later.)

Another type of situation illustrates the same general point about majority rule, although here the result is entirely a matter of exploitation rather than overexpenditure. Posit a country that produces very poor cigars and cigarettes and where the amount that can feasibly be imported is limited by balance-of-payments difficulties. Sixty percent of the smoking population prefer cigarettes. The possibilities are (1) to import cigarettes only, (2) to import cigars only, or (3) some compromise. If one brings normal ethical standards to play, a compromise would appear to be best. But majority rule, under the assumptions of radical

---

[38] Whether such a committee system is essential in a government of separated powers, and more particularly in one where a strong president is elected independently of the legislature, is a more difficult question and one that will not be examined here.

393

individualism, would presumably result in the importation of cigarettes only. If, on the other hand, a two-thirds rule were in effect, those who preferred cigarettes could not have their way without making some sort of compromise with the cigar smokers.

The precise terms of the compromise cannot be predicted. Moreover, it is not out of the question that the result would be deadlock. But rational men would probably find some way out of such a universally self-defeating outcome. Indeed, it would seem that a solution which gave both cigars and cigarettes the same percentage of imports that each had enjoyed for, say, the last five years preceding the balance-of-payments difficulties, would have sufficient *a priori* plausibility to insure at least that this proposal would serve as a starting point for bargaining.[39]

i. The Problem of "Intensity"

Up to this point, we have been dealing with areas or types of potential governmental action where the (generic) rational individual at the constitution-making stage would feel that the chances for relatively high external costs from such action were great.[40] Accordingly, he would favor a re-

[39] The example is adapted from Harvey Leibenstein, "Notes on Welfare Economics and the Theory of Democracy," *Economic Journal*, 72 (1962), 299-319. See especially pp. 310-315. The author is comparing Pareto choices (and the market principle, with which it is in accord, both being universal-consent principles) with democratic choice, which he identifies with majority rule. But a qualified majority at least moves away from majority rule (winner-take-all) in the direction of equitable compromise, even though less precisely than the market principle would do.

[40] This assumes that the external costs were anticipated to be high enough to justify the increased internal (bargaining) costs of a qualified majority requirement. It must be remembered in this connection that with representative government, the internal costs would not be at all of the same order that would characterize direct democracy. Even more important, the internal costs, for a given piece of legislation, would be incurred once and for all, while the external costs must be presumed to continue for the life of the law.

strictive voting rule (qualified majority) for that subject. In other words, on these issues, rational men would see that they had more to lose by having unfavorable rules imposed upon them than they could gain by imposing rules on others; hence they would prefer a system that weighted negative votes. In substance, this is what a qualified majority requirement does.

The much-mooted intensity problem need not concern us here in its most common applications, for it deals with a particular set of people dealing with a particular problem or issue. Here we are concerned with the formulation of decision-making rules, as we must be continually reminding ourselves, and intensity becomes relevant only insofar as the rational individual might conclude that he would feel more intensely about some given issue that might arise if he found himself defending the status quo than if he were demanding action. Now, with respect to certain kinds of policy questions, this is precisely what underlies the argument in recent pages, as in the example of "equal protections" for minorities, although I have avoided casting the issue in terms of "intensity."

I have avoided the word *intensity* because a great deal of confusion attends this concept. The fact that the term can be avoided in the argument pursued here indicates that the confusions and difficulties often attendant upon that concept are not entailed by this line of reasoning.[41] To clarify the argument further it may be pointed out that the intensity problem as it is generally discussed involves interpersonal comparisons—comparing the intensity of feeling or interest of one group with that of another. The radical individualist, not believing in the possibility of such com-

[41] See Willmoore Kendall and George W. Carey, "The 'Intensity' Problem and Democratic Theory," *Amer. Polit. Sci. Rev.*, 62 (1968), 5-24; and Douglas Rae and Michael Taylor, "Some Ambiguities in the Concept of Intensity," *Polity*, 1 (1969), 297-308. Buchanan and Tullock also deal with it in some paragraphs that I find obscure and believe to be confused. *Calculus of Consent*, pp. 125-130.

parisons, is not at liberty to indulge in this kind of reasoning, a fact that Buchanan and Tullock seem occasionally to overlook.[42] But of course an individual can compare the intensities of his own feelings; and it is precisely this kind of comparison that leads to logrolling, where an individual trades his vote on an issue of relative low intensity (or "salience") for him in return for support on an issue about which he feels more strongly. Frequently this process leads toward optimal results and so should be encouraged; but where it tends to lead to inefficient allocations of resources, as explained above, the rational constitution maker would seek means to check it.

j. General Legislation

The question that remains to be considered is whether the rational individual would wish some protection against majority action *in general*. We deal here, that is to say, with issues not included in any of the special categories discussed above. This residual category may not be very large. When one thinks about the category of legislation involving special benefits and generalized costs (one of the special classes that has already been discussed), it soon becomes apparent that that class is very large indeed. Subsidies, whether to business, agriculture, the elderly, or those below the poverty line, all come under this heading. Thus the argument sometimes made[43] that the "minority veto" entailed by the requirement of special majorities gives advantage to the upholders of the status quo (with regard to the rules governing property distribution) must contend with the counterargument just implied. A large proportion of equalization measures enacted by the modern state comprise in fact just such types of legislation as those enumerated above. Not all subsidies aid the economically disadvantaged but most aids

[42] See *Calculus of Consent*, p. 127 ("If minorities feel more strongly on particular issues than majorities. . . .").

[43] See Jack Lively, *Democracy* (Oxford: Basil Blackwell, 1975), pp. 18-20.

to the economically disadvantaged enjoy the political benefit of having their cost spread widely and indeterminately.[44]

It may be then that the class of "general legislation" is
small. However this may be, let us consider the arguments
pro and con. On the one hand, the putative rational individual, at a constitution-making stage, may reflect that
change is the law of modern society and that anything
which handicaps government in facilitating change or ad-
justing to it is likely to obstruct rational action and the
maximization of preference-recognition. He might note too
that many, perhaps most, people tend to have an irrational
fear of change and that therefore, for his own sake and
others', he should guard against strengthening the hands of
the timid. Both of these arguments are powerful and are
not to be discounted.

Powerful arguments on the other side are also to be
found. For example, when government enters upon a new
activity that I do not like, I have no defense. At the very
least, I must share the cost. Moreover, if, for instance, it
compels all children to attend school, I must submit (assuming I have children) whether I like it or not. But if it
refuses to establish the kind of school I like, I may be able
to band with other like-minded people to accomplish my
purpose independently. It should be noted that this argument has special weight only under the assumption that the
majority will more likely wish to add to the activities of
government and to its compulsions than to move in the
opposite direction. Such, of course, would be the situation
at the original constitution-making stage. More to the point,
the assumption appears to have considerable validity for
the modern polity.

A related but distinct point—quite apart from any trend
toward the growth of the public sector—is that rational
men have greater objection to being members of a disadvantaged minority than they have pleasure from being mem-

[44] For documentation of this assertion, see David A. Stockman, "The
Social Pork Barrel," *The Public Interest*, Spring 1975, 3-30.

bers of a majority. This is the same point, more broadly stated, as the one used in connection with the equal-protection argument discussed above. This is not so much, as one author has suggested,[45] a matter of the majority's "ganging up" on a minority—although that is a possibility—as it is that people feel injustices done to them with special poignancy, and suffer more from having something taken away from them than they gain enjoyment from getting a similar "something" they did not have before. Accordingly, rational constitution-makers would seek to minimize the likelihood of undergoing this kind of experience.[46]

But this argument is not without its counterpart. Majorities as well as minorities may be thwarted and may be unhappy as a result. Indeed they may feel that an injustice is being done them; and, however sound may be the arguments for minority blocking power, the thwarted majority is likely to feel resentment. Not all governmental action is taking something away from someone and giving it to another. Suppose, for instance, that the majority favors a general cut in federal taxes as a means of stimulating the economy. Is the minority, disbelievers in Keynesianism, having something taken away from it? It would hardly seem so.

Whatever the balance of considerations as between the last two arguments may be, what is important, indeed crucial, to bear in mind is that our rational constitution maker

[45] Harvey Leibenstein, "Notes on Welfare Economics and the Theory of Democracy," pp. 311-313.

[46] Many of the points made in the preceding pages are overlooked, or at least not considered, in the interesting and helpful article by Douglas Rae, "Decision-Rules and Individual Values in Constitutional Choice," *Amer. Polit. Sci. Rev.*, 63 (1969), 40-56. Rae introduces an elegant mathematical model to demonstrate that "majority rule can be expected to optimize the correspondence between individual values and collective choice" (under certain assumptions). Ibid., pp. 54-55. The proof depends, however, upon the assumption, which we have seen reasons for doubting, that the rational individual would be equally concerned to have positive as well as negative power over government.

will realize he has an equal chance with every other voter of being on the winning rather than the losing side, regardless of the proportion required to win. It is sometimes argued that this is not so, that it is the supporters of the status quo who have the greater chance to be on the winning side. But this argument erroneously assumes that it is the same people who support the status quo on all or most issues. Consideration of issues chosen at random should dispel this misconception. As these lines are being written, President Carter and his supporters favor maintenance of the status quo with respect to the capital gains tax and change with respect to taxation of petroleum imports. Others take the opposite position on each issue. More generally, the phrase "supporters of the status quo" is often used to refer to those who are relatively prosperous, and it is assumed that they support the status quo. But if one concentrates on specific legislative issues—which is after all the relevant concern—the assumption does not hold. In fact, these people are often clamoring for change. They would like to cut the tax on corporate net income, to eliminate the "double taxation" of dividends, and so on and so forth.

An additional argument that the rational individual would consider in selecting decision-making rules relates to the importance of information and deliberation. It stresses the costs entailed by institutions that encourage or easily permit precipitate or ill-considered or ill-informed change. The requirement of more than a simple majority for action tends to place a greater obligation upon those who are promoting change to advance facts and arguments that are persuasive than would otherwise be the case. If the requisite number of persons are persuaded, while rationality is by no means guaranteed, it is more to be presumed than if only a bare majority concurred. This of course was Rousseau's position; yet he is rightly known as a great egalitarian. In modern times, Rousseau's argument has been put in a different and arresting fashion. Technically, when a decision is made by a majority of one, we can be absolutely certain

against careless, thoughtless, or irrational majorities?—is not completely one-sided. Respectable arguments may be mustered on both sides, although it seems to me that on balance the rational man in this position would desire some checks on simple majorities even in the general case, if only to place limits on the arbitrariness, exploitation, and uneconomic expenditure cases, which it embraces. Perhaps, however, the issue can be sidestepped by considering another question. It may have occurred to the reader, during the discussion of the case of what we may call special-interest/ general-support legislation not only that it comprises a large category but also that, while its definition is clear in principle, in practice it would prove to have vague boundaries. A requirement that legislation falling in this category should pass by a special majority would probably lead to endless bickering as to when it was applicable. In this connection, then, it will be well to consider both bicameralism and the independent executive with veto power as (in some measure) functional equivalents for the requirement of qualified majorities. In fact, as will appear, they tend to act more like qualified majorities in just those cases where the latter are especially desirable than they do in other cases.[48]

Either in a direct democracy or under a representative government, the malignant results of raising issues that enable (and thus entice) voters to vote for their own (or their constituents') special interests arise out of the fact that voters find it easy to align themselves according to these special interests. And the alignments may vary from issue to issue. But, with representative government, and with a legislature consisting of two houses, *so constructed that the constituents of any given legislator in one house are scattered at random among the constituencies of the second house*, no such result would be possible. Or, take the follow-

[48] The following discussion leans heavily upon Buchanan and Tullock's analysis (*Calculus of Consent*, Chap. 16) for its principles, but greatly simplifies the demonstration.

ing extreme case; suppose one house has five districts, while the other house for simplicity's sake may be supposed as elected "at large." Special benefits of one sort and another are available for each district. No one of them, we shall assume, is worth its cost to the nation. Let us say that each costs $7, and is worth $5 (all to the district in question). Districts 1, 2, and 3 combine to appropriate funds for projects for themselves. Each gets a project worth $5 to it. The cost to each will be $4.20 $\frac{3 \times 7}{5}$. Districts 4 and 5 get nothing, at the same cost per district. To prevent this exploitation, District 4 and 5 will offer one or more of the others some form of compensation to be let in on the deal. Further trading will take place and the net result, as explained in the original discussion of this process, will be that each district gets some benefit, but that their total cost will exceed their total value. Everybody loses. On the other hand, if the country is one single district, as it is for the purpose of the upper house as described above, no project the cost of which exceeds its worth will be authorized. The second house has here blocked this uneconomic expenditure. One majority has blocked another. Multiple constituencies have produced a more rational, more just result than would have been obtained by the use of a single set of constituencies. Nor would use of a single-constituency chamber alone achieve the same result, for such a nationwide winner-take-all system would be a constant invitation to majority tyranny.

In talk of majority rule and, especially, of "blocking" majorities, the point brought out by this example is too often overlooked. When we are dealing with representative government, it is a mistake to suppose that a majority of representatives will necessarily represent the "will of the majority" even if we assume that the electorate is completely informed, interested, and rational and that their representatives do their best to vote as their constituents would have them do. The fact of division into constituencies affects their interests and thus their preferences; different ways of dividing up the electorate will produce different effects; and no single one of them is the "correct" way. This important point is more profound than Calhoun's argument based upon regional minorities, for it is a product of the representative system per se. Its importance, of course, is increased both by regional differences and, as has been indicated, by functional (interest-group) differences.

To return to the example, if, on the other hand, the legislature is confronted with an issue that is "profitable" to all (and it need not be *equally* profitable to all—simply Pareto-optimal), the result should be favorable in both houses.[49] It should be noted, too, that the "benefits" need not be appropriations. They may comprise any kind of legislation favoring some group or interest more than others, where the cost (whether in terms of taxes, higher prices, inconvenience, burdensome restrictions or requirements, or whatever) is imposed generally and the groups receiving benefits are distributed unevenly throughout the country (so that certain groups tend to dominate certain districts). If one thinks of the normal legislative agenda, it is easier to think of examples than of exceptions. Price guarantees, support for the SST, school subsidies for "impacted areas," public housing (but presumably not public health, since the demand for it is so generally distributed), and so on. (It is not being said of course that legislation of the kinds represented by these examples could not be enacted—only that it could not be enacted *unless it was worth its cost to the country as a whole*, or, more precisely, was deemed so by a majority.)

At least two important qualifications must be noted. The argument has been cast in terms of two houses with completely diverse representative bases. Of course that never

[49] This amounts to an application of Rousseau's principle that, if nothing but general questions are put to the General Will, the answer will be in the general interest. Here the fact of two houses constructed on different bases serves automatically to sort out the general from the particular interests.

happens. It would perhaps be most nearly approximated if one house were elected on a geographical basis and the other on a functional (or "interest") basis. Or, as was suggested above, one house "at-large." To a substantial extent, the United States has the latter arrangement in the case of the president, whose veto power places him in the position of a second (or, in this case, third) house. Barring the distorting effect of the Electoral College, he is elected "at-large." It is probably true, however, that various factors, notably the president's dependence upon the support of congressmen and senators for the success of his own program, place considerable constraints upon his exercise of the veto power. As between the two houses of Congress, it would be very difficult to estimate the amount of diversity in constituency bases. About all that can be said is that it is bound to operate in some degree in the manner outlined above, but the degree may be quite limited, as compared with the ideal case.

Another qualification is that bicameralism inevitably leads to "internal" decision-making costs. Again, the means of estimating the extent are not at hand. But these costs are not all for naught. Not only does further debate putatively involve further education and clarification. Also the fact of adding to the number and variety of individuals who participate in the discussion and decision brings added value. By all odds the most thorough-going case to this effect has been stated by Charles E. Lindblom in various places, but especially in his *The Intelligence of Democracy*.[50] As he says, "A multiplicity of decision makers brings new energies and skills to the task of co-ordination."[51] It also brings additional insights, information, ideas, and awareness of in-

[50] (New York: Free Press, 1965), esp. Chap. 10. Interestingly enough, Mr. Justice Douglas has argued against nonunanimous juries on the ground that "the fact that the nonunanimous juries need not debate and deliberate as fully as must unanimous juries" leads to "diminution of verdict reliability." Johnson v. Louisiana, 406 U.S. 356, 388 (1972).

[51] *Intelligence of Democracy*, p. 162.

404

individualist. Its ability to discriminate between general-interest and special-interest legislation must bulk large in the light of the present analysis. The presidential veto supplements it and, to a degree, may act as a substitute for it.

About the matter of delay, and the related and more serious possibility of deadlock, something more needs to be said. It is quite commonly held that requirements for qualified majorities and, more especially, bicameralism and the separation of powers are seriously flawed by the inability of the necessary numbers to agree on a particular decision even though the great majority favor some change. As it is frequently put, this argument is fallacious. It rests upon the false assumption that because more voters favor change than favor the status quo, more voters support some *particular* change than favor the status quo. Clearly, that conclusion does not follow. If 40 percent of the electorate believe we should be tougher on criminals and 25 percent believe we should be softer on them, clearly a majority favors change. Just as clearly, "change" harbors a critical ambiguity; for, assuming the remaining 35 percent are satisfied with the status quo, it is clear that the majority prefer the status quo to any possible change. Likewise nearly everybody may have a preference for tax reform; but this heterogeneous grouping may include those who would reform by doing away with depletion allowances but would not touch personal exemptions (perhaps because of the desirability of having a maximum number of people conscious of the costs of public spending) as well as those whose interest centers on increasing incentives by moderating the progressive features of taxation, and also those who take the opposite lines from those just mentioned. Everybody is against tax loopholes; but one man's loophole is another man's justice or socially desirable incentive. Where, in fact, a number of possible policies (or candidates) have supporters, the way to be most sure of maximizing the effect of individual preferences is to discover one preference that can defeat each of the others (including, in this case, the status quo) in single combat.[52] (In fact, something like this happens in the normal legislative process, by means of the consideration of a series of amendments.) The arguments advanced in this paragraph do not demonstrate anything about either qualified majorities or bicameralism; they merely negate the presumption that deadlock, even where most of the voters desire change, proves that the preferences of the majority are being thwarted.

To be sure, a deadlock *may* occur even where a majority (or whatever number is required for action) does favor change in a particular direction. Such a deadlock would result from a breakdown in the bargaining process. Perhaps each group within the contending majority holds out for its view, in ever-springing hope that the other side is about to give in. The more complicated the decision-making process the more likely is this to happen; just as the more nearly it approaches simple-majority rule the greater is the likelihood of precipitate, exploitative, or uneconomic decisions.

5. SUMMARY

Thus far, we have been concerned to discover what decision-making rules and related machinery the rational man would be prone to adopt for managing his political affairs. As was noted earlier, this is simply another way of asking what political decision-making rules it would be rational for men contemplating an enduring constitution to adopt. (In both cases, we are adopting the radical individualist's assumptions about the political motivation of the rational man.) Looked at the first way, it becomes a behavioral theory, but one of a special kind—a theory of the behavior of rational men. Considered the second way, it becomes a kind of normative theory—a theory of how men ought to behave under the assumptions of radical individualism; that is to say, a theory of how men ought to behave in order to

[52] See Duncan Black, *The Theory of Committees and Elections*, p. 57.

maximize the chances of securing their preferences. Unlike Buchanan and Tullock, I have used the second approach.

In the first place, it has been argued that in a fairly large and extremely important class of actions, democratic governments should not act at all. Since, for certain practical reasons, it seems undesirable to try to impose absolute restrictions on the electorate itself (in this case, on the electorate when exercising the "constituent power"), the rational solution seems to be to place these "no-noes" in a special category, alterable only by quite extraordinary majorities, or by a combination of extraordinary majorities and other institutional checks. The clearest type of action that falls in this class is any action which tends to undermine democracy itself—the process, that is to say, whereby the individual is enabled to express and secure his preferences. Under this heading come the First Amendment freedoms and protections against political persecutions. Other limitations that rational democratic constitution makers would seek to impose include protections against arbitrariness and guarantees of the rule of law, of "equal protection."

In a different category, the radical individualist finds reason to believe that some limitation on the freedom of simple majorities to do as they please is likely to promote his long-term ends. Here we find a large class of cases where differential benefits are obtained for particular localities or groups at the general expense. Bicameralism and the separation of powers were found to provide a means of checking undesirable legislation of this kind, at some cost, while not seriously interfering with that which could be justified on the basis of maximizing the satisfaction of preferences.

6. Variants of Radical Individualism

It is time now to drop our consideration of the strict theory of radical individualism and to consider certain variants that still come under the heading of individualism.

First, we shall relax the personal-benefit theory of individual motivation and desire. The initial step is simply to interpret "benefit" more broadly. Thus we may assume that people are self-seeking but that they are less concerned with material gain than with social status and with gaining the acceptance and approval of their fellows.[53] It is difficult to generalize from this type of theory. In many societies, including the United States, an important—perhaps the most widespread—means for gaining social status and approval is to be financially "successful." Insofar as this is the case, the Harsanyi theory (that men will support justice for others if it is not *very* costly for themselves) would not change our conclusions. It would appear, however, that a society of status- and approval-seekers would be less atomistic (less "radically individualistic") than a society in which economic gain was the primary motive, and would be more characterized by cohesive groups of various kinds. Social pluralism would be stimulated, as individuals sought the acceptance of like-minded individuals and the status associated with group membership. What the implications of such a social order are for decision-making rules is more difficult to say. Everything would appear to depend upon the characteristics of the groups. If overlapping membership was extensive and the groups were highly permeable, the very existence of these groups, insofar as they were politically oriented, would tend to serve the purposes of encouraging deliberation and limiting the power of bare majorities. On the other hand, if they tended to be mutually exclusive and to be relatively permanent in their membership, the situation would be very different. Trading would be more difficult and the intensity problem would consequently be exaggerated. Even more to the point, the existence of permanent or semipermanent coalitions would be encouraged, making more probable the exploitation of

[53] See John C. Harsanyi, "Rational-Choice Models vs. Functionalistic and Conformistic Models of Political Behavior," pp. 521-524.

409

minorities and so likewise increasing the need for qualified majority requirements, or their equivalent.[54]

Another variant on the personal-benefit theory is the "expressive" theory. As in the case of the status-acceptance theory, this is intended to supplement, not to replace, economic gain as the criterion of personal benefit. In particular, it is contended that a desire to express oneself, to declare one's affiliations or commitments, or simply to vent one's feelings, quite apart from any consideration of consequences, is an important part of the average voter's motivation.[55] This or some other variation from the assumptions of radical individualism becomes highly plausible when we reflect that otherwise the mere act of voting, for most voters most of the time, would be irrational. That is to say, if one takes the gain that the average voter might reasonably anticipate from obtaining his (public) policy objectives (as contrasted with those favored by the other candidate or party) and discounts it by the likelihood that his vote will be the deciding vote, the figure is almost certain to be so small that it is less than the cost of voting. It has recently been pointed out that this argument as it stands is not entirely fair. It assumes that voting is an all-or-nothing process, while in fact the closeness of the decision may influence its effect. Thus President Kennedy's power was almost certainly curtailed by the fact that he had won by the miniscule margin of about 100,000 votes, and President Carter is weakened by the fact that he generally trailed his party-mates on the same ticket.[56] Even making allowance for this argument, however, the "paradox of voting" would appear to remain less than wholly resolved. But if voting itself is a "gain" rather than a cost—whether because it is expressive, or because it leads to social approval, or because it is believed to be an obligation and thus is a gain in the sense that it

---

[54] The subject of coalitions will be discussed below, Chap. 10, Sec. 4.

[55] See Murray Edelman, *The Symbolic Uses of Politics*.

[56] See George J. Stigler, "Economic Competition and Political Competition," *Public Choice*, 13 (1972), 91-106, 103-104.

410

avoids the cost of guilt feelings—the apparently "irrational" behavior is readily explained.[57] Insofar as some such theory is valid at the voter (much more than at the legislative) level, it does not appear that it would significantly affect our reasoning. It helps explain why people take the trouble to vote, and so minimizes net decision-making costs; but it does not appear to explain *in any systematic way* why they vote the way they do. Unless it does that, it does not disturb the validity of the arguments advanced above.[58]

Finally, let us suppose that to a significant degree in matters political, the individual is not "self-interested" at all, in the usual sense of that term, but rather, because of sympathy, conscience, or plain benevolence, he behaves altruistically. This modified version of individualism takes on much of the character of the public-interest theory, to be discussed in the following chapter. As will become evident in that chapter, insofar as this theory of behavior is valid, rational decision-making rules would be less restrictive than would otherwise be the case. The rational constitution maker, in attempting to evaluate the external-costs function for any particular kind of decision, would arrive at a lower estimate of them, because he could expect that rules imposed by others would take his preferences into account.

[57] See the symposium in *Amer. Polit. Sci. Rev.*, 69 (1975), 908-928, for a recent discussion of the subject and for references to earlier literature.

[58] For a somewhat different, but not contrary, conclusion, see A. Bruce Cyr, "The Calculus of Voting Reconsidered," *Pub. Opinion Quar.*, 39 (1975), 19-38.

CHAPTER X

Decision-Making Rules and Machinery:
Other Theories

On the matter of decision-making rules and machinery for democracy, these tasks remain: first to consider the matter in the light of the three remaining motivational types of democratic theory; second, to discuss the bearing of political parties on the whole question; and finally, to consider further the relations between decision-making rules and power theories of democracy. The present chapter will take up these matters in that order.

1. Decision Making and the Theory of the Public Interest

For this topic, it will be possible in large measure to build upon ground already cleared in the preceding chapter. In brief, if we ask how much and in what direction the decision-rules called for by the other theories differ from those that seemed to be indicated by radical individualism, the answer appears to be not much, in either direction. The public-interest theorist, like the radical individualist (*vide* the case of Hobbes) need not be a democrat. He may think it is possible to establish a ruling group that will pursue the public interest more faithfully than any democratic regime. But we are concerned with democratic theorists. They may believe in democracy because they think democratic decision making is more likely to lead to the adoption of policies that are in the public interest than any other kind of decision making, or they may believe democracy has other values that justify it—the advancement of human dignity through recognition of equal rights and through participation, the development or "realization" or even transformation of the individual, and so on—even if its policies are not superior, possibly even inferior, to those of some other form of government. In either case, they will seek rules and machinery for decision making that will be most likely to promote the public interest.

The definition of the public interest is a notoriously controversial subject.[1] Fortunately, the issues need not be resolved here. Two points alone, differentiating it from radical individualism, are significant for present purposes. First, it is a theory of interest, as distinct from desire or preference. Enough has been said about this in Chapter Five to require no further discussion here. Second, it admits the possibility of interpersonal comparisons. As we recall, a person may have an interest in voting per se as well as an interest in the outcome of the voting, so the possibility of making interpersonal comparisons adds breadth to this distinction. Not only may you be able to anticipate the consequences of my actions better than I, and thus be a better judge of my interests, but you may also be able to compare the pleasure or other benefit I will derive from a certain decision with such benefits as someone else would derive from a different decision. Consequently, you may be in a position to make a valid judgment that the second decision, for example, is better than the first. (Of course the losses incurred by each of us would also have to be estimated.)

If the "public interest" is in fact, as this theory holds, not a meaningless concept but one with a real, though vaguely defined, referent, and if this concept does in fact influence people's political behavior to a significant extent, what is its bearing on decision-making rules? In the first place, according to this theory the "public interest" is objective in the sense that different individuals will *tend*, other things being equal, to evaluate it in the same way. It is objective, that is

[1] This matter is discussed above, in Chapter Five, Sec. 5. See also the symposium on interest, with articles by Benditt, Oppenheim, and Flathman in *Political Theory*, 3 (1975), 245-288, and materials cited there.

to say, in the sense of being, at least imperfectly, intersubjective. Of course great disagreements will arise from differences in information, in calculation of consequences, in the assessment of needs and other interests, and from differing values and ideals. On a matter such as the amount of money we should spend on the exploration of outer space, consensus might be almost totally lacking. On whether it would be in the public interest to explode a hydrogen bomb over New York City, one might reasonably expect virtual unanimity. Most public issues would fall somewhere between these extremes.

Supposing then that a significant number of people feel some compulsion to act in accordance with the public interest, what are the implications for voting rules and the machinery of government? What appears to follow is simply that insofar as the notion of the public interest has any systematic effect on voting which would otherwise be directed by individual preferences, to that extent it would tend to push public policy toward the interest of the whole rather than a part, whether the part be that of a minority or a majority. Minorities would then need less protection against majorities who did not take their interests into account, for the simple reason that majorities *would* take account of their interests. In short, the need for restrictive voting rules or similar devices would be lessened. On the other hand, the same factor, tending to enlarge consensus, would make it easier to obtain extraordinary majorities in support of proposals in the public interest. Hence, while the need for restrictive voting rules would be less, they would also be less likely to block the public interest.[2] In

[2] It might appear that the existence of political parties, to be discussed below, would alter this conclusion. Under a two-party system, for instance, with some significant degree of party discipline in the legislature, it would be more difficult for the majority to obtain support of enough minority-party members to meet more than a bare-majority voting requirement than would be the case where individual legislators were completely free to shift for themselves. Once more, however, we meet with a countervailing factor. Under the assumption

414

fact, *in those very cases* where it was not needed it would to that extent be ineffective. And where it *was* needed, because the majority did *not* take sufficient account of the minority's interest, it would tend to be effective. (Of course, it might also be effective in cases where the minority was seeking to abuse its power. All one can say is that, *ex hypothesi*, the minority would be less *likely* to abuse its power to the extent that the public interest theory is realistic.) In short, under the assumptions of the public-interest theory, restrictive voting rules would have less effect, either for good or ill. The net result, then, of this aspect of the theory, as with the introduction of the assumption of altruistic human conduct into radical individualism, does not change the considerations bearing on decision rules.

Turning to the public-interest theory's stress on the satisfaction of real interests as contrasted with believed interests or desires as the proper goal of public policy, the most obvious point is that additional information and opportunity for deliberation provide the most likely means for bringing the two into harmony, in other words for making people's preferences individually and socially rational. The requirement of qualified majorities (and its functional equivalents), as was argued earlier, is designed for just this purpose. Under the radical-individualist theory, the rational man, at the constitution-making stage, would recognize this need for institutions to discourage quick responses to desires that may prove transitory or ill-considered. If so, he would presumably make appropriate provision in his constitution. In any case, the public-interest theory points to the same conclusion, arriving at it by a more direct route.

The matter of intensity, once more, does not significantly alter the balance of considerations. It is true that under the

---

of a tendency for all to be influenced by a common concept of the public interest, the differences between the parties will tend to be minimized, the position they share enlarged. Thus the losses brought about by less flexibility on controversial issues will tend to be offset by reduction in the number and intensity of controversial issues.

public-interest theory, as contrasted with the theory of radical individualism, it would be desirable to weight votes (whether of the general electorate or of their elected representatives) in proportion to the intensity of the needs or interests being expressed; for it is no longer assumed that interpersonal comparisons are impossible.[3] It must be recognized, however, that representative government, as practiced in the industrialized countries of the world, undoubtedly does take account of differing intensities in a way that direct democracy could not. For instance, in deciding how to vote, a legislator is likely to give greater weight to desires he has reason to believe are intense than to others, if only because people who feel intensely are more likely than those who do not to vote against him at the next election if he votes contrary to their views.

Also the ancient, often maligned, institution of logrolling may work to give effect to intensity. Logrolling is the political equivalent of the market. While individuals (or their representatives) cannot (legally) sell their votes, they can engage in "trade." Both the concept and the practice of trading votes are commonplace. (The practice is more likely to be implicit—relying on faith that the other party will reciprocate—than explicit.) Members of Congress, for instance, who are not greatly concerned about the distribution of foreign aid as between military and nonmilitary purposes, may willingly cast their votes on this issue in such a way as to please a group who will, in return, support some project that is of primary concern to them. In this way, the same result will have been accomplished as if each group had had extra votes to cast for its more intense interests. The intensity of desires, as well as the numbers of individuals who held them, would be reflected in the result.[4]

---

[3] A practical means that is sometimes suggested for accomplishing this result would be to give each representative a given quantum of votes. He would then distribute them as he preferred, at the extreme using his total voting power on a single issue.

[4] Of course I am not contending that vote-trading always produces optimal results. In fact, in the preceding chapter I demonstrated that

416

Other implications of the public-interest theory bear at least tangentially on the matter of decision-making rules. Certain institutions, on this theory, should focus attention upon "ideal-regarding" desires, as contrasted with "want-regarding" desires;[5] they should foster altruism or public-spiritedness, as well as responding to self-interest. There may even be some division of labor in this matter. Institutions whose officials are not accountable to localities and have reasonably long tenure are especially well qualified to deal with "ideal-regarding" matters, while those that are more responsive to localities or groups are better fitted for implementing the "want-regarding" desires. One reason underlying this division is that ideals tend to be long-run affairs and to refer to the collectivity as a whole, while wants tend to be more immediate and parochial. Moreover, for many voters the impact of expenditures on taxes is generally more direct and more observable at the local than at the national level.[6]

---

with vote trading in a pork-barrel situation, just the opposite occurs, because of the effects on third parties. But in practice, vote trading may often operate as discussed in the text. The literature on this subject is extensive. See especially William H. Riker and Steven J. Rams, "The Paradox of Vote Trading," *Amer. Polit. Sci. Rev.*, 67 (1973), 1235-1247, who argue that vote trading is often not optimal and that in any case it is inherently unstable; and Eric M. Uslaner and J. Ronnie Davis, "The Paradox of Vote Trading: Effects of Decision Rules and Voting Strategies on Externalities," who contend that, while in game-theory terms Riker and Rams are correct, actual practice often does not follow the theory.

[5] These terms are borrowed, with modification, from Brian Barry, *Political Argument*, pp. 38-41. Barry refers to the "ideal-regarding" concerns of individuals as "principles" rather than as "desires."

[6] The generalization and reasoning advanced in this paragraph are certainly not without exception. The case of school prayers, for instance, provides a counterexample. (I am indebted to Robert Lyke for this suggestion.) Incidentally, the school-prayer issue, via the history of the Becker Amendment, seems to be an example of a case where simple-majority rule, without benefit of the Madisonian checks that provided opportunity for education, deliberation, and the mobilization of forces by groups originally in the minority, would have led to the

417

It is worth noting that the further we go in the direction of disregarding present wants, the more important it becomes to insure ultimate accountability. Democracy does not mean that the average man should formulate the standard for public policy; but he should ultimately approve it. He should have the final say, even if only by way of a *post hoc* review.

People's values are not given once and for all. They are changed by the institutions under which they live and by their life experiences, as collectivists especially are prone to remark. Desires and interests change and the self grows, is transformed—or may be—by public policy itself. It even makes sense (under the public-interest theory) to say that such transformation may be to a person's interest. One of the problems of democratic politics then is how to create institutions that permit and encourage this kind of development compatibly with human dignity and protection against the abuse of power. This consideration provides one more argument in favor of institutions that both call forth education, deliberation, and leadership—as some check on quick response to majority demand or opinion tends to do —and that give time to those who seek to change the value constellation of a society for their efforts to succeed and be tested—as again the greater stability of policy attendant upon the use of qualified majorities or their equivalent tends to do. The check is needed not only to give government time for the consequences of governmental acts to be judged fairly. Also it is called for when, as in the case supposed, it is a question of using the power of government not simply to conciliate conflicting interests, in the narrow sense of that term, a process which can usually be reversed if it proves unsatisfactory, but rather to develop new tastes and new values, to transform people.

---

opposite result from what eventually prevailed. See William M. Beaney and Edward N. Beiser, "Prayer and Politics: The Impact of *Engel* and *Schemp* on the Political Process," *Jour. of Pub. Law,* 13 (1964), 475-603.

To be sure, tender, incipient new values may have difficulty making headway against special-majority requirements. They might do better if they had only a simple-majority to persuade. It is at this point that bicameralism and
the independent chief executive enter the scene. The
chances of new values gaining representation, and even
ascendancy at one level or another, are multiplied by the
use of multiple constituencies, an advantage that may more
than offset the additional hurdles which must be cleared.
This argument appears to have particular weight as applied
to the independently elective presidency, which provides a
natural center for leadership that appeals to the most general ("public") interests. Also, on the institutional side,
one should mention the independent regulatory commission. Once a policy has secured a substantial degree of
approval, its implementation and elaboration may be the
more safely committed to such an agency, whose accountability is protected against easy reversal by what might prove
to be transient majorities. Even a "dependent" bureau or
agency may enjoy considerable insulation. An Environmental Protection Agency, for example, may initiate and
implement particular policies that could not have negotiated the hurdles of the legislative process on their own.
So it is with an Office of Equal Employment Opportunity.

Before leaving the subject of the public-interest theory,
a possible variant should be noted. The theory we have
been considering holds that interpersonal comparisons and
judgments of the public interest can and should be made,
and that they should and do influence our conduct. However, suppose one believes that judgments of this kind can
be made and are made and that although they ought to
provide a standard for our conduct, in fact they do not,
that we are fundamentally seekers after personal benefit,
that the public interest is something everybody pays lip
service to but nobody does anything about. (This theory,
in other words, would be designated "descriptive individualism" and "prescriptive public interest theory." It would

average legislator is more likely to be right than wrong, no matter by how narrow a margin—say 51 percent of the time—then the probability is that a majority vote will be right.[8] With a body of 100 individuals, each of whom is 51 percent likely to be right, then a 51 percent majority has a 51.99 percent chance of being right; and a 60 percent majority will be right 69 percent of the time. With a larger legislative body the chances of correct decisions go up rapidly; but the significant fact for present purposes is the striking increase of probably correct decisions produced by increasing the required majority.

Now it is true, to be sure, that the requirement of more than a bare majority puts a minority in a position to exercise a veto. The general question of whether such a veto power is equivalent to positive power was discussed in the preceding chapter. In the present context, however, it also needs to be pointed out that while a qualified-majority requirement makes it easier for a selfish or otherwise ill-willed group to use their power to maintain an unjust status quo, by the same token it also makes it more difficult for such a group to force action that would make the status quo *less* just than it is at present.[9]

2. DECISION MAKING AND THE RIGHTS AND DUTIES THEORY

We turn now from "maximizing" theories to deontological theory, that which we have denominated the rights and duties theory. What are the implications of such a theory for decision rules and related matters?[10]

[8] If this assumption is not made, the whole case for democracy is seriously damaged.

[9] I am indebted to Arthur Kuflik for this point.

[10] We assume of course that the rights and duties involved in this theory include those implicit in liberal democracy. As has often been pointed out, even the most utilitarian of democratic theories must rest in part upon an asserted right: the right of each to count equally with every other one in the basic matter of the franchise. At the very

For the most fundamental rights, including especially those essential to democracy itself and to the dignity of the human being, the answer is clear. Here, as in the case of the theories considered up to this point, the argument for giving these rights the benefit of special protections in the voting rules would be strong.

What about areas of decision making other than that of fundamental rights? Much depends on the nature of the moral obligations in question, on the intensity with which they are held, the amount of agreement or disagreement as to their substance, and the dynamics of the forces making for stability and instability. *A priori*, however, it would appear that if the prevailing ethic is individualistic, placing a high value on individual liberty and autonomy, the arguments and conclusions about decision-making rules would be similar to those derived from radical individualism. On the other hand, if the society manifested a more communal ethos, it might be more inclined toward simple-majority rule and that device might serve its purposes. At the same time, we meet again here the phenomenon we have encountered before: the factors that make qualified majorities less necessary also make the requirement less restrictive in operation, diminish its drawbacks. Thus insofar as the voters behaved in an individualist manner, the arguments considered up to this point would suggest the desirability of qualified majorities (or their equivalent); and insofar as voters sought consensual or communitarian values they would not be hampered by such a requirement: it would merely be redundant.[11]

---

least, it must assert such a right, whether or not it holds that it can be derived from utilitarian principles. Other commonly asserted democratic rights, such as the right to freedom of expression, may more readily be derived from utilitarian principles, found to be essential to the support of democracy, or held to be rights on other grounds.

[11] The analysis set forth finds support in the work of Rawls, a leading exemplar of this type of theory. In discussing the status of majority rule, he makes two points relevant to our concerns. In the first place, he classifies it as a subordinate principle—subordinate to the

Pursuing the subject from a slightly different perspective, one comes to a similar conclusion. If the society manifests serious dissensus on fundamental notions of right affecting political issues, and if the holders of a particular set of views are heavily concentrated in a given geographical area, some form of federal decentralization (a kind of limitation on overall majority rule) may provide the answer. But if they are not so distributed, it is obvious that the health of the polity is precarious and it is doubtful whether any decision-making rules can be of much assistance. A two-thirds rule, or its institutional equivalent, may maintain a reasonably satisfactory political process for a time. If, during this period, the dissensus is substantially moderated, all is well. But if it is not, if persuasion fails, the pent-up forces making for change may lead to violence or other disruptive tactics. At the extreme, civil war may result. In such a situation, simple-majority rule also has serious problems. If used with restraint, the crisis may be tided over. But again, if persuasion fails, or if a majority uses its power with a heavy hand, it may provoke a revolt,

---

background principles of political liberty, such as the First Amendment freedoms. Moreover, even with these background conditions, he points out, there is no assurance that majority rule will produce just legislation. Rawls, *A Theory of Justice*, Sec. 54.

One is tempted to speculate about the significance of the mood of modern youth for the question of majoritarianism, but it is difficult, indeed impossible, to find any clear direction in it. Or, rather, one finds clear, but mutually opposing, directions in it. Surely today a strong egalitarian spirit is abroad; and, whether or not this logically implies majoritarianism, it is widely so interpreted. On the other hand, part of the modern temper appears to be a stiff moralism—one that breeds contempt for majority decisions as well as other expressions of authority if they go counter to the reactor's sense of right. If anything, it would appear that the latter tendency is likely to prevail over the former in any contest between the two. Still another aspect of the modern temper, as it manifests itself in some quarters at least, is the desire for unity, for consensus. Clearly this is, or may be, at odds with both of the other tendencies; but, whatever it is, it is not majoritarian.

or it may resort to repressive measures that destroy private rights. In a society where people are used to acting in terms of right and wrong (as this one is, by definition) rather than by calculation of interests, it seems likely that differences, being more than matters of degree, would be held particularly strongly. Under these circumstances, decisions made by bare majorities might be especially resented by the losers.

In this matter of popular reaction to political decisions, we must note a point of some importance that has not previously been relevant to the discussion. People tend to grow attached to the decision rules under which they have grown up. Thus not only do people react to decisions in terms of their notions of right and wrong, but also they tend to think they are right if they have been reached in accordance with decision-making rules which, by habituation, they have come to value or think right. Perhaps this puts the matter too strongly. They may not consider the decisions to be objectively right simply because a majority, or two-thirds, or two houses of a legislature, or whatever is called for, voted for them; but they may feel it is now their duty to obey them. A procedural consensus of this sort naturally lessens the danger of the kind of difficulty we have been discussing, but it would appear to apply equally to either a majoritarian or a qualified-majority system.

On the matter of moral sentiments, what was said above (pages 418-419) about changes in this area could be repeated here. Even assuming, however, that simple-majority rule would help the forces which are at work in any society, and especially in a modern, dynamic society, to modify the ethical code, including even basic ideas of justice, the significance is not clear. It might help to maintain a "moving consensus." But also it might tend to hurry a process that takes time to mature, and in doing so it might even disrupt and slow the processes of change. On moral issues, it appears, most people are conservative; their attitudes change slowly and they think the presumption should be in favor of prevailing ethical beliefs and standards. Even when a bare majority is won over to a new view, the minority is likely to be recalcitrant and resentful of majority action to convert the new ideas to legal compulsions. As large numbers, predominant numbers, adopt the new view, it becomes easier for the rest to adopt them.[12]

One area that is especially likely to evoke moral attitudes is foreign policy. British sentiment, for instance, was sharply divided over the Suez affair; and a strong case can be made that this debacle might have been avoided under a system in which power was somewhat more dispersed than it is in Britain. American intervention in Korea, on the other hand, although quick, was based upon wider consultations and received firmer domestic support. It would appear that the known dispersion of authority in our form of democracy encouraged the procedure which was followed. At the same time, in the case of South Vietnam our institutions did not enable us to avoid a situation that strained our moral consensus in a way we have seldom experienced. It is not at all clear, however, that a different decision-making procedure would have altered the result. Not only the leaders of both parties in Congress but a majority vote of both houses gave successive presidents authority to take the steps that involved this country more and more deeply in warfare.

At this point it would appear that a particular institution of the American system—a complement to the system of qualified majorities—is, or may be, particularly helpful: the institution of judicial review. The record of the United States Supreme Court on race relations and the protections of the accused has always been as good as that of the majority of voters or of Congress; and, for the middle period

12 A current example of this process is provided by the rapid change in attitudes, and legislation, regarding abortion. Perhaps even more relevant, because it involves use of the qualified majorities required to amend the Constitution, is the adoption of the amendment providing for the franchise, in state elections, of eighteen-year-olds.

of this century at least, it was a good deal better.[13] To a significant degree, its success appears to be grounded on the high degree of "legitimacy" accorded in our society to courts of justice. In no small measure, it would appear, they enjoy this legitimacy precisely because they are not accountable to the majority, and because they have the independence that permits them, and the role that directs them within broad limits, to see that justice is done.

In general, the conclusions derivable from this section have been set forth in the preceding paragraphs and need not be recapitulated. In situations where the evolving sense of right is increasingly egalitarian, it may be true that simple-majority-rule institutions are sometimes more favorable to equality and less favorable to individual liberty than are those that qualify the power of simple majorities. But what was said above about the institution of judicial review must be taken into account in this connection. In this country in the past two or three decades, that nonmajoritarian institution has favored equality at least as much as liberty, although it has not always worked that way in the past. Finally, one must not forget that while responsiveness to majorities bears no necessary relation to rights, welfare, and social justice, the same logic from probability theory that was developed in the preceding section also applies here; the larger the majority required to enact legislation the more likely will the result be correct, always assuming that the average legislator has a better than even chance of being right.

3. DECISION MAKING AND COLLECTIVIST THEORY

Turning to the question of what decision-making rules would be called for by collectivist theory, it appears that little needs to be added to what has already been said in

[13] This, of course, is an evaluative judgment. It would, I believe, be strongly supported by most people who are favorably inclined toward individual rights.

connection with the other theories, particularly the theory of the public interest and the rights and duties theory. If in fact, in accordance with empirical collectivist theory, people tend to identify with the community or state and adopt its welfare as their own, consensus should be high. Requirements that go beyond simple-majority rule might be less needed than according to radical individualist theory, but, in the same measure, they would be less obstructive. To be sure, voters might disagree about means; their judgments as to what would be in the best interests of the collectivity might differ. But insofar as they did so, the best rules and machinery for resolving these differences would not seem different from what has been previously outlined. If anything, it might appear that the democratic collectivist would feel the need for rules and machinery to encourage deliberation even more than would the radical individualist. The latter is trying to aggregate preferences; but the democratic collectivist desires voters not only to seek the welfare of the whole but also to agree on the means for accomplishing that purpose. This normative goal would cause him to favor maximum deliberation even if he believed that in fact people agreed on the ends. It would also cause him to favor institutions that allowed considerable leeway for professional politicians and administrators to make policy, subject to ultimate review by the electorate.

For a theorist who is a normative collectivist but who believes that most people are not motivated as he thinks they should be (but are, on the contrary, quite self-centered), again the situation with regard to the most desirable decision-making rules remains substantially unchanged. If anything, it is less favorable to bare-majority rule, for such a person would naturally fear an aggregation of self-interested voters who might act against the interest of the collectivity. This conclusion is reinforced by the fact that the same argument from probability theory which applies to the public-interest theory and to rights and duties theory also applies to democratic collectivism.

427

The question can be looked at from a slightly different perspective. Suppose that most people behave in accordance with collectivist theory. Minorities would have less to fear from the self-interested behavior of majorities, because these majorities would be less self-interested. The danger of exploitation of the few by the many would be minimized. On the other hand, those who are less self-interested may be more self-righteous. Convinced that their values are the right values and that the dissenters are mistaken as to their own interests, a collectivist majority might well impose its will upon minorities, even overriding what the latter firmly believed were their fundamental rights, or what were in fact their real and deep interests. For those who believe that a collectivist majority is likely to be mistaken or who value highly the privilege of the minority to make its own mistakes, this will be a strong argument for protective machinery and restrictive voting rules; but of course it will not persuade those who do not share these beliefs but who have great faith in the majority will that emerges from a collectivist society, and relatively little regard for the right of individual self-determination.

In summary, it seems fair to say that in placing a high value upon community and upon consensus, the antiindividualist approaches do at least as much to weaken as to strengthen the case for bare-majority rule. In this connection, it is well to remind ourselves that Rousseau, whose theory leans heavily in the collectivist direction, insisted that decisions on important questions, at least in the absence of great urgency for prompt action, should be made only with the concurrence of a qualified majority.[14]

[14] Jean-Jacques Rousseau, *The Social Contract*, Bk. IV, Chap. 2. Rousseau, in this respect, seems to me to have been more logical and more realistic than many modern collectivists, who frequently are highly critical of any checks upon simple majorities. Whether that is because they have great faith in the correctness of the majority will, even without institutions for checking impetuous action, or whether it is because they have less concern for the rights of individuals and minorities, it would be difficult to say.

428

4. Political Parties and Rules for Decision Making

Occasional references have been made above to political parties (and also to "fixed coalitions," which, for present purposes, amount to the same thing), but at no point has their impact on the arguments about rational decision-making rules been systematically treated. Moreover, the analysis has been largely in terms of the individual voter, assuming that he, or his representative in the legislature, is free to vote any way on any question. Yet in all modern democratic societies political parties play an important role. They appear to perform important functions in facilitating the enforcement of accountability and in educating and informing the public, to mention only their most obvious and perhaps most significant contributions to a healthy polity. But for our purposes the most important fact is simply that they exist and operate. The question we must consider is whether this fact alters the considerations affecting the operation of decision-making rules.

Looking first at the legislative level, a party system may operate in one of three ways: (1) it may exist largely for election purposes only, allowing representatives in the legislature to cross party lines freely in the effort to respond to constituency interest; (2) it may maintain fairly strict party discipline, but arrange its legislative program in such a way (perhaps involving inconsistencies) as to appeal to various groups with divergent interests (higher subsidies for farmers, higher minimum wages for labor, higher social security payments for the elderly, and sugaring the pill of higher taxes by granting concessions to various groups); or (3) it may have a rigid discipline and a consistent program in accordance with some ideological pattern. Insofar as a party system approaches the first pattern, it would operate substantially the same as a completely individualistic system. It would in other words not alter the thrust of my arguments about decision-making rules and machinery. Parties of the second type might interfere somewhat, but

429

probably not very extensively, with responsiveness to individual wants. That is to say, to the extent that the intraparty program development was less efficient at duly recognizing all wants than the free organization of ad hoc legislative groups, this type of party system would increase the likelihood that majority voting might lead to inequitable results.[15]

Finally, ideological parties are almost by definition highly disciplined rather than flexible, and furthermore construct their programs in accordance with their basic principles rather than in an attempt to maximize response to preferences or wants. Under these circumstances, it would appear that simple-majority rule would very likely result in minority rule on certain issues.[16] An obvious example is Britain's Labour party. Not highly ideological as ideological parties go, it has yet committed itself in a doctrinaire fashion to considerable nationalization of industry. At the same time polls show that a majority of the country, including a sizable minority of the Labour party itself, opposes this degree of nationalization. The result of course is that when Labour is in power, the minority rules on this

[15] In a monograph written after *Calculus of Consent*, Gordon Tullock has introduced political parties into the model used by himself and James Buchanan in that book and has relaxed the assumption that only a single issue was open. Although the line of argument differs from that of the earlier work, the conclusion is similar. Majority rule leads to suboptimal results. The requirement of more than a simple majority would tend to improve the situation. This improvement would have to be discounted by the additional cost of securing more than a simple majority, but this cost, with the leaders or parties acting as entrepreneurs (in the development of platforms calculated to secure the required proportion of votes), would be far less than under a system in which voters had to carry out their own negotiations. Gordon Tullock, *Entrepreneurial Politics*, Research Monograph 5, The Thomas Jefferson Center for Studies in Political Economy, University of Virginia, February 1962, processed.

[16] For a game-theoretic proof that political parties with binding commitments increase the extent to which a majority may exploit a minority, see Robin Farquharson, *Theory of Voting* (New Haven: Yale University Press, 1969), Appendix III.

issue, a result that could be prevented only by the requirement of more than a simple majority or by some power dispersion system which achieved a like result.

The conclusions to which the last paragraph leads call for qualification. Members of the Labour party, so far as they vote rationally, must be supposed to prefer Labour rule with nationalization to Conservative rule without it. Their preference for certain parts of their program over the program of their opponents must be assumed to outweigh their dislike of, or disapproval of, nationalization. If this is so, one can charge the system with producing minority rule only if it is assumed that various policies are separable, as they tend to be with less highly disciplined parties, so that individuals, through their representatives, can pick and choose from the policies of each of the major parties. Now to an important degree this assumption would be sound as applied to the American system, as is well known. The question is, would the Labour voter be losing something if he were operating under a different system? One thing is clear: under a disciplined two-party system a requirement for qualified majorities would make government extremely difficult; it would amount almost to a unanimity requirement. On the other hand, a power-dispersion system is most unlikely to be acceptable where parties are significantly ideological. In other words, further discussion of what decision-making system would be desirable where ideological parties prevail, in a relatively evenly balanced two-party system, is fruitless. Nothing but simple-majority rule, or some fairly close approximation to it, is likely to be acceptable and workable under these circumstances, regardless of what might be desirable under different circumstances.

5. DECISION-MAKING RULES AND THE POLITICAL CULTURE

I have been dealing in the most general terms with the considerations supporting either simple-majority rule or a

431

system that qualifies simple-majority rule, whether by the requirement of more than a simple majority for decision or by some power-dispersion system that accomplishes a like result. In conclusion, it would be well to say a few words, drawing upon earlier statements and implications, about what conditions especially call for one system or another. Perhaps a more accurate way to put it, since it has been concluded that the presumption favors some limitation upon simple-majority rule under almost all conditions, and in accordance with the assumptions of any of the four motivational theories of democracy, is to say that I shall try to specify certain conditions which would appear to strengthen the case for limiting simple majorities and certain conditions that weaken the case. The latter would call for less limitation upon the action of bare majorities; but it must always be remembered that the same rule need not apply for all decisions in the same society.

The most general consideration favoring resort to some limitation on majoritarianism is that of a high degree of individualistic particularism, for which either radical individualism or rights and duties theory is an appropriate complement. Where public morale is low and individual self-seeking prevails, the case is relatively strong for qualified majorities or their equivalent—likewise where localism, as contrasted with nationalism, is a powerful force. Where many pressure groups supporting differential legislation are powerfully organized, the same conclusion obtains.[17]

On the other hand, if most legislation is by custom or constitutional requirement of a very general nature, the advantages of simple-majority rule are maximized and the disadvantages are minimized. (With respect to this point, however, one must note that the history of the modern

[17] Conversely, where the population tends to be homogeneous or fragmented into a number of groups that are themselves internally homogeneous, it appears that the case for simple-majority rule is strong. See Norman Schofield, "Ethical Decision Rules for Uncertain Voters," *Brit. Jour. of Polit. Sci.*, 2 (1972), 193-207. These are not conditions that widely prevail.

polity manifests a trend in the opposite direction.) Also, where public spirit on a nationwide basis is strongly developed, the issue is less important, the arguments on both sides being weakened.

In these concluding remarks, I have distinguished between conditions (like the existence of strongly ideological parties) that may in effect dictate the decision-making rules that will be adopted, or at least place substantial limitations upon constitution makers in this regard, and conditions (like the presence of particularism) that affect the relative desirability of one system or another. In part, this is a false distinction. A highly particularistic people— especially if their particularism takes the form of localism —is not likely to accept rule by a bare majority, while if the political culture is characterized by high consensus and public spirit, limitations upon majorities are less likely to be insisted upon. The degree of choice left open to a given society after these limiting factors are taken into account is an empirical question that would require careful study in each particular case.[18]

In this discussion, it has generally been assumed that such conditions as the prevalence of "individualistic particularism" and "public spirit" are independent variables. This assumption is probably not entirely accurate. In fact, decision-making rules and systems may influence the political culture as well as reflect its influence. It would be very helpful if we could learn more about this relation. As is so frequently the case, it is much easier to find correlations than it is to establish cause-and-effect relations that explain them. It may be that a majority system, or one that leans in that direction, encourages the development of the

[18] For a relevant theoretical study with empirical examples, see Ronald Rogowski, *Rational Legitimacy*. In particular, he argues that a society which is factionally divided and whose factions are few in number and unequal in size will not accept majority rule as rationally legitimate but will insist on legislative procedures that "weight the probabilities of the outcome in rough proportion to the membership of the various factions." Ibid., p. 95.

433

kind of public spirit which makes dependence upon power-dispersion devices unnecessary. This, in turn, may lead to a high valuation on common interests and on communal action. However, if such a system gets off to a poor start—whether because the lack of a majority (in a multiparty cabinet system) leads to deadlock or because a permanent, consolidated majority comes into being and leads to the alienation of the "outs"—the spiral might go in the opposite direction; that is to say, the operation of the voting system might undermine the supporting political culture. By the same token, a qualified majority or a power-dispersed system may encourage self-seeking minorities and particularistic individualism at the expense of the common interests that are so easily overlooked in such an environment. But it may also lead to a more variegated society as well as to the more efficient satisfaction of "want-regarding" desires.

In a somewhat different context, Mancur Olson has suggested that the "sociological" emphasis upon consensus tends to produce stability combined with economic stagnation, while the economists' emphasis upon competition and mobility—all of which go with individualism—produce growth at the price of social disruption.[19] It may be that, in this matter of decision-making rules and machinery, we are faced with a similar tension, the resolution of which would generally fall between the extremes (in this case of majority rule and rule by unanimous consent). In our case at least, however, the constitution maker would need to consider not only the best balance in the abstract, and not only his personal preference in the matter of harmonious conformism versus disharmonious variety, but also the level of government at which he was operating and the ethos already prevailing in the society in question.

---

[19] Mancur Olson, Jr., "The Relationship between Economics and the Other Social Sciences: the Province of a 'Social Report,'" pp. 137-162, esp. 146-152, in Martin Seymour Lipset, *Politics and the Social Sciences* (New York: Oxford University Press, 1969).

6. In Conclusion: Decision-Making Rules and Types of Democratic Theory

Of our two sets of democratic theories, the two chapters dealing with decision-making rules, to this point, have dealt almost solely with the motivational theories, for reasons set forth at the outset. And, in dealing with them, it has not been a question of finding what support the argument of the chapter gave to one or another of these theories; rather it has been a question of discovering what rules and machinery for decision making are supported by the various types of democratic theory. It appeared that each of the motivational theories tends to support some decision-making process which has stricter requirements— one more difficult to fulfill—than simple majority rule. This might take the form of requiring more than a simple majority for decision; but in practice some combination of power-dispersing devices, bicameralism, independently elected executive, and the like, is generally used either as a supplement to or a substitute for a special-majority voting rule. In short, acceptance of any one of the four theories in question tends to imply the acceptance, as a normative theory, of a power-dispersion theory, and more specifically of a theory of constitutionalism (which of course is not incompatible with the acceptance also of a theory of social pluralism). While the fact that any one of the motivational theories tended to support a particular system for decision making would be far from conclusive, the fact that all four theories seem to converge at this particular point, that they all support some form of constitutionalism, provides powerful support for the superiority of such a system.[20]

[20] Amartya K. Sen, in arriving at a similar conclusion, has some interesting and amusing things to say. "If a majority wants me to stand on my head for two hours each morning," he writes, "the MMD [method of majority decision] will make this a socially preferred state no matter how I view this exacting prospect." Again, with respect to the MMD, "While its grossness jars somewhat, its simplicity, symmetry,

435

It is now apparent why an extended discussion of power-dispersion theories was unnecessary for the subject of these two chapters—decision-making rules and machinery. In large measure, they are the same thing. That is, the power-dispersion theories *are* theories about the rules and machinery for making governmental decisions. In the cases of populist and constitutionalist theory this is obvious. Elitist theory is hardly an exception. True, elitist democrats are less concerned about how power is dispersed or concentrated than they are about the quality of the people in whose hands it resides. As is well known, however, they tend, like Madison, to favor constitutional devices that will check the simple will of the majority, depending rather upon devices that will "refine" this will. Finally, the social pluralist *may* also be an exception; he may believe that social pluralism itself, unaided by constitutional devices, will achieve the result Madison sought.[21] But of course nothing about social pluralism dictates this position, as the case of Madison himself clearly demonstrates. This is not the place to argue the matter at length, for that would be the subject of another discourse. It may, however, be pointed out that the case of the fall of Weimar Germany to Hitler's regime is clear evidence that even as pluralistic a society as was Germany in the 1920s is not immune from capture by an antidemocratic movement. To be sure, Germany was also not without constitutional protections, albeit less strong, it would appear, than those which have

---

and primitive logic would seem to appeal to many." And finally, he argues that "pure" systems of collective choice, such as majority rule, are the most interesting for theoretical study, but not the most useful. "While purity," he remarks, "is an uncomplicated virtue for olive oil, sea air, and heroines of folk tales, it is not so for systems of collective choice." *Collective Choice and Social Welfare* (San Francisco: Holden-Day, 1970). The quotations, respectively, are taken from pages 161-162, 163, and 200.

[21] This is the view of Robert A. Dahl, as expressed in his *A Preface to Democratic Theory* (Chicago: University of Chicago Press, 1956), esp. Chap. 5.

been developed in this country. But, as John Plamenatz put it, "if an American Hitler were to win as many seats in Congress as the German Hitler won in the *Reichstag* in the last free elections of the *Third Reich*, would he not be further from getting power?"[22]

[22] John Plamenatz, "Some American Images of Democracy," p. 257.

437

CHAPTER XI

Participation

1. THE MEANING OF POLITICAL PARTICIPATION

Among those who theorize about democracy today, the in word is "participation," or, in many cases, "participatory democracy." Not that the two are identical. The former is more inclusive and more indeterminate than the latter. At the minimum, participation in politics may mean no more than registering as a voter and, from time to time, casting a ballot. Today critics of the contemporary scene widely believe that even this kind of participation is too low in this country and that it is declining. Moreover, these critics believe that the decline reflects "alienation," a feeling on the part of the nonvoters that voting is futile because they don't like any of the realistic options or because they feel powerless to affect the result in any significant way. (A third possibility—that they are content with the way things are going and see no reason to vote when they are sure the outcome will be satisfactory anyway, is seldom considered by the critics.) Much empirical work is done in this field, but rarely do empiricist and theoretical critic join hands, or even arguments. The fact appears to be that when due allowance is made for those who are prevented from voting by circumstances beyond their control (e.g. illness, absence from home for business or other reasons with no provision for absentee voting, ineligibility because of recent removal from previous voting district), 80 percent or more of the qualified voters exercise their franchise in presidential elections. Nor does the evidence clearly indicate that this proportion is declining.[1]

[1] James D. Barber, *Citizen Politics* (Chicago: Markham, 1969), pp.

438

Critics would be quick to point out that the figures just given pertain to presidential elections and that participation falls off rapidly when it comes to off-year and local elections, not to mention party primaries. Moreover, many citizens who do cast their ballots do little else in the way of political participation. They do not campaign, attend political meetings, or engage in more regular partisan activities. Nor do they discuss politics, or perhaps even expose themselves to the political debate as it is conducted in the media. Moreover, in spite of considerable improvement in recent years, their level of political information tends to be dismally low.[2] Few are active in political organizations, few seek to communicate with or otherwise influence their

5-6. It is true that the percentage of the voting-age population who cast their ballot in the presidential election of 1972 showed a marked drop (from 60.9 to 55.4) between 1968 and 1972. For most states, 1972 was the first year in which eighteen-year-olds were eligible to vote. It is known that their participation rate was and continues to be very low. This drop showed up even more markedly in the congressional election of 1974, at the height of post-Watergate disillusionment. The presidential election of 1976, however, showed a slight gain. (*Statistical Abstract of the United States*, 1976, pp. 462, 452, and U.S. Dept. of Commerce, Bureau of the Census, Ser. P-25, No. 626, 66.) On the other hand, the Committee for the Study of the American Electorate has reported that the turnout for the November 1978 congressional elections was the lowest since World War II. *New York Times*, December 19, 1978, p. A13.

2 Philip Converse, of the University of Michigan's Survey Research Center, and one of the country's leading experts on this subject, writes as follows: "While hypothetical numbers risk being taken too literally, the difference between the two periods [the fifties and the sixties] might well be thought of in terms of a first period in which some 10 or 15 percent of the electorate is attentive and engaged enough to fit the expectations of the most naive assumptions about democratic participation, whereas in the second period the proportion of the attentive electorate has risen to 25, 30, or even 40 percent." "Public Opinion and Voting Behavior," in Fred I. Greenstein and Nelson W. Polsby, eds., *Handbook of Political Science* (Reading, Mass.: Addison-Wesley, 1975), 4: 75-168, 156. On the following page he adds his own assessment that although the improvement is substantial, even the improved condition is rather bleak.

439

representatives or other public officials.[3] And of course fewer still run for public office. Obviously participation as measured by activities of this kind is much lower than is participation measured by voting.

Those who talk about "participatory democracy," however, have in mind more than these matters, more than all of them put together. They mean the use of direct democracy in various ways and at various levels. They wish to maximize the opportunities for all citizens to take part themselves, to share in making the decisions that will affect their lives, and of course in the deliberations and group activities of all kinds that lead to these decisions. Thus, according to one writer, "meaningful participation may be defined as occurring when a person has a sense of his involvement in a total enterprise, a sense of where his efforts fit into an overall plan, when he identifies with the collective goals, has a feeling of efficacy with respect to the accomplishment of the goals, and has a stake in the results of the total enterprise."[4] (Of course it is clear that this concept, while finding an important, perhaps crucially important, application to government, is also applicable to the whole range of social organization, notably including the workplace.) The most extreme ideal calls not only for universal participation but also for equal participation. The following descriptive statement speaks for itself:

> Participatory democracy involves such techniques as running meetings without agendas or presiding officers (or, at worst, rotating presiding officers); allowing officers minimal decision-making powers away from the general meetings; running meetings by consensus or sense-of-the-meeting decision-making; refusing to limit discussion or

[3] See generally, Norman H. Nie and Sidney Verba, "Political Participation," in Greenstein and Polsby, *Handbook*, 4: 1-74.

[4] Rosabeth Moss Kanter, "Some Issues in the Community Development Corporation Proposal," in C. George Benello and Dimitrios Roussopoulos, eds., *The Case for Participatory Democracy*, pp. 65-71, 65.

440

debate; letting as many executive-administrative decisions flow from the whole body as possible, without delegation of responsibility to agents or committees; and encouraging the body to act immediately on decisions taken, that is, dropping the artificial division between meeting and non-meeting so that in the extreme the meeting is a community and the community is virtually a constant meeting."[5]

As appears from this statement, equal participation entails participation that is both strenuous and enduring.[6] It is valued for its assumed contribution to self-development as much as for its advancement of personal interests through public policy.

2. REASONS FOR ADVOCATING INCREASED PARTICIPATION

If the possible degrees and meanings of political participation are various, the reasons advanced in its favor are equally so. The most simple and obvious reason, whether or not sound, is to achieve improved governmental output —better policies more efficiently and fairly administered. The connection between greater participation and improved output can be established, or at least contended for, in a number of ways, some quite different from others, and some similar and overlapping. Greater participation may provide more effective checks on the power of sinister interests. It may also give increased assurance that no interests are excluded from the governmental process and left out of account. If those most directly affected make the decisions, it may be presumed that their desires will be

[5] Martin Oppenheimer, "The Limitations of Socialism," in Benello and Roussopoulos, *Case for Participatory Democracy*, pp. 271-282, 277-278.

[6] For a good, and much fuller, discussion of the meanings of "participation," see Lawrence A. Schaff, *Participation in the Western Political Tradition* (Tucson, Ariz.: University of Arizona Press), 1975.

reflected in public policy, at least as far as is compatible with the desires of others similarly affected. Moreover, if citizens are less than all-wise and completely informed, yet they may make up for each other's deficiencies in these respects; and their "collective wisdom," in Aristotelian fashion, may exceed even that of the wisest and most virtuous individual. This argument applies particularly to participation in the fullest sense, where citizens pool their information and their insights, deliberate together, criticize each other's ideas, and arrive at a collective and near-unanimous decision.

The arguments for improved public policy resulting from broader and more intensive participation run beyond securing a more accurate reflection of desires even as refined by the process of collective deliberation. If people become actively involved in the processes of government, so the arguments run, they will be motivated to obtain more, better, and more coherent information on public affairs. Also, feeling more responsible for their political actions and the consequences thereof, their self-interested desires will tend increasingly to be tempered by moral concern for the well-being of others, not to mention a heightened awareness of their own true interests.

A second and closely related type of reason for seeking to maximize political participation is not so much to improve the governmental product as to make it more acceptable and hence more readily enforceable. In short, participation in an activity tends to increase the sense of legitimacy of its results, with consequences that are favorable both to the system (compliance and general system support) and to the individual units (avoidance of frustration and alienation).

For many of today's participatory democrats, however, these instrumental reasons for making political participation as nearly universal as possible and also for increasing the extent and intensity of participation by each individual citizen are wholly inadequate. It is the direct effects of participation upon the participant rather than the improvement of governmental processes and output that these theorists celebrate. To be sure, this line of argument is not new. John Stuart Mill, not to speak of Rousseau or Aristotle, relied heavily upon it. To give a person a share of the responsibility for governing the society of which he is a part was, Mill argued, a most effective way of contributing to his moral and intellectual development; while, on the contrary, to deny a man power over his government was a sure way of discouraging his interest in it and his concern for it. Men without power become apathetic and privatistic, or else rebellious. Today, it is often argued, most states are so populous that one citizen's vote seems so slight as to approach complete powerlessness. The answer then must surely be to organize society and mobilize power in smaller units, so that individuals will feel it worthwhile to participate and will enjoy the fruits that Mill envisaged. This kind of participation not only has educational and moral benefits, but it also gives the active citizen a feeling of power and efficacy, and a sense of making a contribution that increases his own sense of dignity and of moral worth, and, in the current terminology, of "authenticity." To Mill's argument for educational benefits Tocqueville added the point that "town meetings are to liberty what primary schools are to science: they bring it within the people's reach and teach how to use and how to enjoy it."[7]

Much more in the spirit of today's proponents of maximum participation, however, was Karl Marx. Vague though he was on many aspects of the ultimate stage of communism, certain things were clear. Men would share equally and fully in the political process. Man, Marx believed, would become whole, no longer alienated, only by the fullest participation in determining the conditions and conduct of communal life. He would, then, be transformed, not by the deliberate pursuit of some preconceived goal,

[7] Alexis de Tocqueville, *Democracy in America*, 2: 61.

443

except in the vaguest sense, but by the revolutionizing process through which old institutions were destroyed and a new society was created.[8]

As with Marx, today's enthusiasts for participatory democracy stress its contributions to individual development and enrichment. Equally important in their view, and closely related to individual development, is the creation of real community. In the latter, the individual becomes more keenly aware of the interests he shares in common with his fellow-citizens. In working with them he becomes attached to them, he finds the sense of community a satisfying and enriching thing and therefore comes to value the community for its own sake. It satisfies his need to "belong" and to achieve personal "identity" by becoming an integral and valued part of a collective entity and enterprise. He discovers his real needs "through the intervening discovery of himself as a social human being."[9] Under these circumstances, the community itself becomes more effective in serving the shared purposes of its members and thus the whole process is cumulative and self-reinforcing. In some respects the result is like the communitarian ideal of Plato's cited earlier—the society in which each individual felt as though he had complete empathy with all his fellows, as though they all sensed with a common sensorium. But the participatory democrat is distinguished by his insistence that individuals remain not only distinct and various, but "open," spontaneous, and fluid. Whether such an ideal is even theoretically possible is debatable, but it is important to understand it in order to appreciate fully the peculiar combination of the individualistic and the social (or "collectivistic," as I have been using that term) that informs

---

[8] The substance and, in large part, the words of this paragraph are borrowed from my introduction to *Participation in Politics*, Pennock and Chapman, eds., NOMOS XVI (New York: Lieber-Atherton, 1975), p. xiv.

[9] Peter Bachrach, "Interest, Participation, and Democratic Theory," in Pennock and Chapman, eds., *Participation in Politics*, pp. 39-50, 40.

444

the goals of supporters of participatory democracy in its fullest sense.[10]

3. RELATIONS OF THE VARIOUS TYPES OF DEMOCRATIC THEORY TO PARTICIPATION

Before examining the problems and merits of participation theories, it will be well to examine the presumed reactions of various types of democratic theory toward participatory theory. As in our previous discussions of this kind, one important objective will be to discover the extent to which various theories come to the same practical conclusion and the extent to which they point in different directions. Of course, it is never a question of being for or against participation. Democracy involves popular participation by definition. It is always a question of how much participation and, in particular, whether a great increase is such a desideratum that we should make radical structural changes so as to create greater incentives and opportunities for participation of a much more active, involved kind, and perhaps at the extreme virtually to compel increased participation.

a. Motivational Theories

In connection with individualism, it is more important than with most of the previous applications of motivational theory to distinguish among its subtypes. The "rational man" of the strict form of this theory (radical individualism) would probably not favor attempts to increase political participation. He would think that we should accept the desires of others as they feel and express them. If men wished to participate more for participation's sake, presumably they would do so. Similarly, if they had de-

[10] For a fuller discussion of this topic, especially with regard to political participation as a means of developing "citizenhood," political man in the full Aristotelian sense, see Donald W. Keim, "Participation in Contemporary Democratic Theories," in Pennock and Chapman, eds., *Participation in Politics*, pp. 1-38.

sires the polity could satisfy, they would exercise their democratic rights to change the situation. That is to say, they would do so if they thought satisfying those desires would be worth the time and effort required to take the appropriate political action. The rational-man theorist is quite conscious of the costs of political action and is likely to conclude that they would exceed the probable reward. He is not likely to assume, although logically he might, that citizens will place a positive value on political activity for its own sake. Also this theorist is forced, by his assumption of the incommensurability of values, to accept the valuation that each citizen places upon the satisfaction of desires and the costs of achieving such satisfaction.

The last point is of special importance because it means that the rational-man theorist would not presume to say what others *should* desire. Doubtless he would favor equal education and equal access to the media and would oppose any conditions that tended to interfere with the operations of human rationality. But the radical individualist is not likely to assume that institutions are so perverted that revolutionary action by a self-selected minority is required to effect substantial change and to create the conditions for rational behavior.

The Tocquevillean individualist is easily disposed of. For him participation is simply a means to the end of self-protection and self-advancement. He does not seek community; on the contrary he despises it, preferring privacy. He tends to be self-sufficient and does not feel the necessity of encouraging political participation. Let each adult person fend for himself as he sees fit.

The modified individualist, that is to say the individualist who relaxes the assumption of self-interest and of no interpersonal comparisons, does not seem likely to differ substantially from the radical individualist in respect to political participation. At most he might be somewhat more responsive to appeals to vote or otherwise participate politically for the sake of the polity as a whole.

Finally, the romantic individualist is in a rather different position. He does not accept the individual as he is as a given, as the rationalist tends to do. Like John Stuart Mill or T. H. Green, he believes the individual has great potentialities for development. Mill in particular stressed the role of political activity in contributing to this development. The romantic individualist also tends to see this development as being characterized by moralization and socialization. That is to say, this type of individualist moves some distance toward the collectivist ideal. At exactly what point someone moving in this direction ceases to be a romantic individualist and starts being a collectivist is somewhat arbitrary. However this may be, the romantic individualist would clearly favor such political participation as would contribute to individual development. Moreover, he might look with favor upon all kinds of cooperative and collective activities, so long as they did not interfere with individual autonomy. In fact, it was Green's position that freedom, "the greatest of blessings," involves "the power or capacity of doing or enjoying something . . . in common with others."[11]

The public-interest theorist presents a simpler case, at least in principle. Insofar as participation gives effect to interests that might otherwise be neglected or frustrated it is a good thing. Beyond this, he has a special concern for those interests—they might be called political externalities—that tend to be overlooked by individuals acting independently. For this reason he would favor at least enough participation to get individuals involved in thinking and talking about public policies so that interests like the satisfaction which may be produced by conjoint activity and common accomplishments are given due recognition, not to mention the private interest each person has in avoiding economic externalities, such as polluted atmosphere or water supply. Once more it is clear that the line between the

[11] T. H. Green, *Works*, 3rd ed. (London: Longmans, Green, 1891), 3: 371.

public-interest theorist and the collectivist becomes extremely fuzzy.

The position of the rights and duties theorist is somewhat similar to that of the public-interest theorist but with a bit more of an individualistic bent. He would of course demand enough participation to protect private rights. Beyond this he would be concerned to develop, as well as to effectuate, the sense of justice. Justice is of course a social concept. It relates to behavior in society; it develops in society. Yet its principles may be quite individualistic, and, if the Rawlsian theory of justice be accepted, its etiology is individualistic, at least in the sense that its principles are those which would be arrived at by rational individuals, deliberating together on the best way, from the viewpoint of each individual, to organize society. Its equalitarianism is thrust upon those who accept the contract as the necessary means for obtaining what one would desire for oneself. Liberty remains the primary goal; hence political participation is likely to be valued chiefly as a means rather than for its own sake. Some may find inherent value in political participation, but Rawls's principles of justice permit rather than entail such an outcome.

Finally, the collectivist—at least the modern, egalitarian collectivist—would presumably support the most extensive political participation possible, for most of the reasons discussed above. Especially, he would support it as contributing to the development of community, as indeed an essential part of community, and as equally requisite to the spontaneity and "authenticity" that the democratic collectivist believes to be not only compatible with community but essential to it. The democratic collectivist, in his condemnation of "privatism" and insistence on equal sharing in all decisions affecting more than the person deciding, is at the opposite extreme from the Tocquevillean individualist. The most extensive and intensive political participation possible is for him a *sine qua non* of the good life.[12]

[12] At least this is true of the egalitarian collectivists. What I have

448

It is clear that, unlike the application of the motivational theories of democracy to the issues discussed in the two preceding chapters, the application of these theories to political participation is not mutually reinforcing. Rather they lead to differing results. It is not of course a matter of whether or not—but it is a matter of how much, what kinds, and under what circumstances.

b. *Power Theories*

The power theories, also tend to lead to different conclusions. Almost by definition, democratic elitism would not look with favor at efforts to maximize participation. The elitist is not only content with representative government, he believes that the process of selecting representatives provides an important, not to say crucial, opportunity for those who possess the best political talents to be selected for governing, while allowing the less active and less politically qualified sufficient power, by choosing between competing elites, to protect and advance their interests. (This is the Lippmann-Schumpeter view, often referred to as democratic revisionism.) The elitist puts little stock in the value of participation as a means of contributing to individual development. Rather, he sees it as a tool, which the average man can use when and as he sees the need for it. It is a utilitarian political instrument, no more.

The populist, being in one sense the ideological opposite of the elitist, would of course favor general and active, informed participation. However, it is still, for him, a means. His concerns are not for self-development through political activity, nor does he share the almost mystical faith of the collectivist that participation will somehow produce both a new community and a new man. But he has a deep and

---

called hierarchical collectivists, in the Hegelian tradition, lay less stress upon widespread political participation, presumably because they have less confidence in the ability of the masses to profit by it and to achieve a high level of development, not because they do not believe that high-level development could be obtained without it.

abiding belief in "the people" as a source of political wisdom. Such devices as the initiative and referendum are dear to his heart. Somewhat paradoxically, the populist tends to favor centralization, especially as between legislature and chief executive. The legislature, a deliberative body, tends to develop ideas of its own, to "refine" the popular will, perhaps beyond recognition. An elected chief executive, on the other hand, is seen more as the chosen instrument of the people. He can be held directly accountable. Responsibility is clearly defined and easily enforced.[13]

Clearly the constitutional democrat places no special premium on participation. It should play its allotted role within the constitutional scheme, and no more. "Refining" the popular will, as well as checking one center of power against another, is precisely what constitutionalism is all about. The constitutionalist might—or might not—believe in the developmental as well as the instrumental value of political participation. Thus he might—or might not— favor efforts toward political education and toward maximizing participation in political parties, voting, and so on.

Finally, the social pluralist, whose thesis is, of course, that popular participation in all sorts of organized groups constitutes a highly important kind of political activity. Even within groups that have no political objectives, that make no attempt to influence public policy and do not in fact influence it, the activities which take place are in the broad sense political. They contribute to the development of talents, to the broadening of interests, to a recognition of and concern for the interests of others, and to group loyalty and to the "sense of belonging" that is so important to most people. Beyond this, certainly, the more politically oriented groups are effective political instruments and contribute to

[13] See, for example, William H. Riker, *Government in the United States*, pp. 346-363. Whether those who maintained this position in the fifties and early sixties remained faithful to it during the "arrogance of power" of the late Johnson and Nixon administrations would be an interesting topic for investigation.

the group members both by helping them gain their objectives and by giving them that sense of political efficacy without which the feelings of dignity and equality are stunted at best.

In many ways, in short, the social pluralist may see the same values to be derived from political participation as does the democratic collectivist. He may, however, place less emphasis upon cooperation for its own sake, and tend less to idealize community. In any case, he will be much less concerned to achieve the values of political participation through the forms of government itself. In fact, he would look with grave doubt upon a government that sought for all-inclusive community. In his view, human wants, needs, and values are (and he might add "ought to be") so various that they cannot receive adequate expression through a single set of institutions. Moreover, they must have outlets through associations that are not solely, or perhaps even mainly, political. This variety of groupings is important not only to provide for people of different natures and for the differing interests and purposes of the same people, but also to check the abuse of power. For the social pluralist, informal groups and nongovernmental organizations play the constitutionalizing role of the constitutionalist's forms of government—or at least supplement it.[14]

It appears, then, that no one of the power theories of democracy would be completely in tune with the more extreme forms of political participation, specifically with what is known as participatory democracy. The populist would come closest. Yet even he does not necessarily have that quasi-mystical concern for community, for working together, that marks the adherent of participatory democracy.

[14] Social pluralists may differ among themselves on the extent to which they believe in the self-developmental aspect of associations. What is most important to their position is the belief that a large number of voluntary associations, participating in varying degrees in the political process, constitute important avenues of political influence and access to government.

Among the motivational theories, the egalitarian collectivists are strongly committed to the most extensive and intensive forms of political participation. Thus, collectivist theory (in its egalitarian forms) and populist theory, between which there is a fairly close kinship, are the two theories among the eight that most strongly support participatory democracy. And as between these two, collectivism has the greater bent in this direction.

This last conclusion is to be expected, for the power theories are primarily descriptive and instrumental, while the motivational theories, by definition, have a strong ethical component, as generally do theories of democracy that stress participation. It is indeed arguable that democratic collectivism, in its egalitarian form, should be classified as a power theory as well as a motivational theory, in which case it would add a fifth type to the former classification. Theorists of this type would, like the populists, favor the widest possible distribution of actual political power, but with emphasis upon a great deal of decentralization and with the aim of changing the participants fully as much as changing the governmental output. The alternative, followed here, is to consider this type of theory a subdivision of populist theory.

4. THE INSTITUTIONALIZATION OF PARTICIPATION

Thus far, little has been said about the mechanics of participation. Beyond education and hortatory injunctions to make use of all existing opportunities for participation, what can be done? Compulsory voting would be a possibility. Although it is practiced in a few countries with reasonable success, I know of no studies that try to evaluate the results in terms of the various arguments for increased participation. It would be difficult to do. Even among those who lay greatest stress upon the value of political participation, this particular device is seldom advocated—perhaps because resort to compulsion seems to run counter to the spirit of many of the reasons for attempting to increase and intensify participation, and certainly runs counter to one of democracy's key values. It is true that if people knew they were going to be compelled to vote they might try to find out more about the issues and personalities involved than they would otherwise bother to do. It is well known that people often tend to become interested in what they are doing even though they are not doing it by choice. But surely some of those who would otherwise not cast their ballots would simply go through the motions, adding to the number of politically ignorant voters. On balance, it is not strange that advocates of greater political participation seldom propose compulsory voting.[15]

The organization of drives against entrenched political machines on the local level often meets with considerable success not only in attaining their expressed objectives but also, as a necessary means, in securing the active and often enthusiastic support of many people who have not hitherto been active. Given an effective leader with an organization, even if an amateur one, many citizens who have hitherto either not thought about politics at all or who were dissuaded from participating because of the apparent hopelessness of their cause will become willing and often effective workers. On the national scale, the candidacies of Eugene McCarthy and George McGovern illustrate this phenomenon, while in New York City, for example, reform Democrats in the fifties and sixties operated similarly in ousting the Tammany machine in district after district. Public-interest pressure groups, such as Common Cause or The Sierra Club, provide further examples of organized popular and effective political activity.

But as the examples suggest, movements of this sort and the heightened participation they bring about are often short-lived. Hence the demand for more fundamental

[15] Alan Wertheimer has made a strong statement of the case *for* compulsory voting in "In Defense of Compulsory Voting," in Pennock and Chapman, eds., *Participation in Politics*, pp. 276-296.

453

change. What could such change be? Many suggestions have been made, although few of them have been worked out in satisfying detail. Essentially, they are of three types. One type attempts to inject a vast amount of participation into national as well as local policy making. Nearly fifty years ago, Mary Parker Follett developed a scheme of government based upon this objective.[16] The basic political units were to be neighborhood groups, which she seemed to visualize as sort of enlarged committees or small town meetings. These groups would send the results of their deliberations, via representatives, to the next higher layer of government, which would operate in similar fashion, and so on to the highest body for national government. Participation had to be fully active and deliberative, for it was the process of group interaction upon which she depended for the development of a general will, embodying sound policy.

A contemporary example is provided by Harvey Wheeler. He proposes a rather elaborate setup for the government of what he calls "an intentional society."[17] Although he speaks of citizen groups at all levels of government "conducting hearings and deliberations in conjunction with their local government officials," no attempt is made to cope with the details of how this would operate.[18] The chief organizational departure from our present pattern appears to be a distinction between governmental bodies that would agree upon and establish policy in the broadest terms ("intentional law") and those that would enact legislation. "A three-stage cycle of deliberation, enactment, and enforcement," we are told, "can involve widespread citizen participation at each turn."[19]

The second type of organizational change designed to maximize political participation concentrates on the local level and greatly adds to the powers and responsibilities of

[16] See her *The New State* (London: Longmans, Green, 1926).

[17] See his *The Politics of Revolution* (Berkeley, Cal.: Glendessary Press, 1971), esp. Chap. 6.

[18] Ibid., p. 251.

[19] Ibid., p. 250.

454

governments at lower levels. In short, the prescription is for radical decentralization. An example is provided by the movement, especially strong in New York City a few years ago, for neighborhood control of the public schools. Here, as in numerous other cases, the demand for decentralization is fueled in large measure by black and other ethnic interests, wanting self-determination for their own group. But it has also found support from those whose commitment to participatory democracy proceeds from the general theory outlined above rather than from the self-interested motivation of group politics.[20]

The most thorough-going participatory democrats are not satisfied with either or both of the types of organization change just outlined. They believe that the decisions made in the formally nonpublic sector of our society are so important, and control so much of the lives of average men, that the principles of participatory democracy must be extended to them as well. In particular, students (and presumably teachers) should govern, or at least share in the government of educational institutions; and workers should govern, or share in the government of industry. Only thus, it is argued, can the average person adequately control the conditions of his or her own life; and only thus can such men and women attain the dignity and autonomy that enables them to achieve the true human potential and to participate with others on equal terms in making the decisions that control their lives. As in the case of the other two types of theory, it is clear that this theory admits of being held and put into effect in widely varying degrees. G.D.H. Cole's plan for a (guild) socialist society would represent one extreme. At a far remove from Cole's scheme would be many devices now in effect at various places for

[20] For two excellent selections of excerpts from articles and books on the theory and practice of participatory democracy, see Terrence E. Cook and Patrick M. Morgan, eds., *Participatory Democracy* (San Francisco: Canfield Press, 1971), and Benello and Roussopoulos, eds., *The Case for Participatory Democracy*.

giving some participation in decision making to students and workers. An intermediate, but still moderate proposal for worker representation and consumer representation in industry has been proposed by Robert A. Dahl in his *After the Revolution?* He proposes that the boards of directors of corporations include representatives of both labor and consumers. Clearly participation at this level, unless it were supplemented by representative devices much farther down the line, would not amount to much from the point of view of the participatory democrat, although it might have significant effect in bringing other interests to bear upon important decisions.

5. PROBLEMS

The problems that face the advocate of drastically increased political participation are numerous and serious. In large measure they become evident to the thoughtful student of affairs who merely reflects on common knowledge. Without too much forcing, it may be suggested that the most serious problems derive from one or the other of four basic facts. First is the simple arithmetic of the situation. To appreciate the implications of this point, one need only think of the requirements for having all the important collective decisions that affect one's life determined by collective action in which he participates. Ideally, at least, this means face-to-face groups. The arithmetic is staggering. The point would soon be reached where all of one's time would be taken up with attending meetings, deliberating, and deciding. The costs are stupendous. One can readily understand why Saul Alinsky, perhaps the most successful of mass organizers, said that his greatest success involved less than 3 percent of the neighborhood's population at the height of the crisis.[21]

Further on the matter of the arithmetic of participatory

[21] Daniel Thursz, "Community Participation—Should the Past Be Prologue?" *American Behavioral Scientist*, 15 (1972), 733-748, 743.

democracy, Robert Dahl has made some interesting remarks. He points out, for instance, that if an association were to make only one decision a day and were to meet for ten hours a day and allow each member to speak for ten minutes, its maximum membership would be sixty. Of course, many people would not insist on speaking on each issue, or for that matter, on attending meetings. But insofar as some people regularly did not participate the believed advantages of direct democracy would be lost. Soon a self-selected few would in effect constitute the government, as apparently happened in Periclean Athens. Also the point would soon be reached where most of the work of governing, even of making basic decisions, would be done by professionals and all semblance of direct democracy would be lost, rendering the whole affair self-defeating.[22]

Those who have been involved, either as students or as faculty members, in attempts to achieve a radical democratization of the decision-making process for a college or university know how demanding the effort is, how much time and energy is diverted from the main purpose of the institution, how frustrating it becomes, and how, after an initial burst of enthusiasm, interest wanes on the part of all but a committed few. Yet of course the problems of governing an institution with a relatively narrow set of purposes is incomparably easier than that of governing the modern state, not to mention the economic system as well.

A corollary of the arithmetic problem is radical decentralization. The object is to bring the point of decision closer to the people affected, to allow variety among variously minded localities. In view of the steady progression toward more and more centralization of governmental (as well as other) power in this and other industrialized countries, it is no wonder that many people would like to see the trend reversed. Especially is this true because of the inefficiencies and other evils of bureaucracy. While it is no doubt true that some substantial decentralizations can be

22 See Dahl, *After the Revolution?*, pp. 67-77.

effected, the brave promises and meager results of the Eisenhower, Nixon, and Carter administrations in this vein give some idea of how difficult the task is to accomplish. The fact is that good reasons and powerful forces have brought about the centralization, and in large measure the reasons are still valid and the forces still effective. These reasons and forces relate to the notorious fact of an increasingly interrelated national economy. High minimum wages in one area will merely drive industry to other areas, unless a national standard is established. Rigid enforcement of antipollution controls in one city, when other cities do not follow suit, operates in similar fashion, creating unemployment and related evils.

Even where the case for decentralization appears to be strong, the question of the appropriate local unit often poses a near-insoluble riddle. It is easy to say that the unit should correspond to the "interest" involved; but not many problems involve a single interest only. Consider for example the dispute about control of the New York City school system already referred to—especially the demand of the predominantly black Ocean Hill-Brownsville residents to control their own schools. This demand ran headlong into the counterdemand of the United Federation of Teachers of New York City, whose geographical base was the whole of New York City and whose interests were in sharp conflict with those of the Ocean Hill-Brownsville residents. And should each subject matter have its own geographical base —schools, water districts, conservation districts, and so on— each with its own taxing power? If they have no taxing power, they cannot be independent, and if they have, confusion is rampant and overall fiscal control an impossibility. Or if, alternatively, regional governments are to replace our present divisions, or some of them, what will be the basis for regionalism? Should the aim be to create relatively homogeneous regions, as would be desirable for, say, forestry control or school systems, or should it be to create heterogeneous regions, with a nice balance of urban and rural, as might be desirable for a banking system?

And as for other governmental powers, decentralization tends to be either unjust or unworkable. "To generalize," writes Amitai Etzioni, "a truly decentralized participatory system will tend to be highly responsive to the needs of the members in each participatory locality, but will tend to neglect interlocal, interregional, and national needs, both of the allocative (e.g. social-justice) type and those that are best served collectively (e.g. a priming of the economy)."[23]

The second basic fact from which the problems facing participatory democracy derive is simply that on most of the questions facing the polity and the economy consensus, even a majority is not easily attained. It was contended earlier that "the public interest" is not so vague a concept as to be meaningless; but it is nonetheless true that even persons who are disinterested and benevolent will disagree on what would be best for the country, for their region or city, or even for themselves. Add to this the fact that men are not generally disinterested but biased in their own personal, group, or class interest, and it becomes obvious—if it was not already—that participatory democracy is a recipe for interminable discussion and rancorous conflict. As we saw in our earlier discussion of interest representation, territorial representatives normally have to represent so many different interests that they are biased toward compromise at the outset. This is not the case with members of a small, self-governing entity. In the latter case, one of several possibilities is likely to occur. First, the differences of opinion may be such that not only is discussion interminable, but also nothing gets done; deadlock ensues. Or, if discussion is limited and majority rule is adopted, minorities may be ridden over roughshod, producing small-scale majority tyranny. If the units are small enough to permit of face-to-

[23] Etzioni, "The Fallacy of Decentralization," *The Nation* (August 25, 1969) , 145-147, 145.

face discussions, the issues that can be delegated to them are likely to be so trivial that most members will lose interest. Meetings will be ill-attended and a small minority will dominate. Perhaps it will be a minority that has a special interest at stake or an ideological position to advance; perhaps it will simply be those people who happen to enjoy "politicking." In neither case is there any reason to assume that what they do will represent either the desires or the true interests of the people in the district.

A further point, the smaller and more specialized the community, the more likely its interests are to clash with those of other communities. No community wants to have a power plant, whether nuclear or fossil-fueled, in its back yard; but if all communities are successful in fending off the would-be intruder, people in the city will suffer. In fact, it may even be that people in each of the nay-saying communities will suffer. Such is the logic of the prisoner's-dilemma situation in which we so often find ourselves. It is a situation bred of mistrust and narrow self-interest, both of which are likely products of the creation of separate political entities, a point exemplified in the large by the history of sovereign states.

Finally, if factionalism and particularism (both geographical- and interest-centered) do breed *immobilisme*, whipping up hysterical enthusiasm for some single objective will likely be resorted to.[24] In this way it may happen that for a time a broad consensus emerges. But the process is not only likely to be short-lived, it is also unhealthy while it lasts. Dissenters are inevitable, and mass movements are notoriously careless of the rights of minorities. Equally important is the fact that hysteria and careful analysis of problems are incompatible.[25] Sometimes the former may be

[24] At this point the criticisms of participatory democracy coincide with those voiced in an earlier chapter with respect to democratic collectivism (Chapter Three, Sec. 6).

[25] Lewis Feuer writes in point as follows: "Participatory democracy is the contribution of the New Student Left to political theory. It was

460

essential to bring about revolutionary change in the face of deeply entrenched vested interests, but as a prescription for normal government it is an invitation to chaos or worse.[26] Clearly it is not conducive to deliberation, nor does the atmosphere of public debate promote careful thinking. Consider the case of a political convention, e.g. a presidential nominating convention or one of the annual party conferences in Great Britain, or of a general election in any country. P. H. Partridge puts it well:

> So far as governments are concerned, there are some solid reasons for being distrustful of too much publicity. Continuous public clamour and a multitude of public pressures do not necessarily provide a favorable atmosphere

born of their meetings, small and large, minute and mass, where the speaker, heckler or chairman would feel that he had articulated in words what was trying to emerge from a long, often inchoate discussion. Suddenly the mass seemed inspired; words passed to action; the spontaneity of the mass broke through the formal paraphernalia of formal democracy with its parliamentary rules." *The Conflict of Generations* (New York: Basic Books, 1969), p. 408, n.3. A study of the politics of fluoridation of water supplies in several cities is relevant here. The authors concluded that "the cities with participative governments behave no more 'rationally' than those without." Robert L. Crain and Donald B. Rosenthal, "Structure and Values in Local Political Systems: The Case of Fluoridation Decisions," *Jour. of Politics*, 28 (1966), 169-195, 191.

26 An observer of the use of participatory democracy by the Youth Movement has written as follows: "Participatory democracy is unsuited for steady activities in which careful reason predominates, clear policy statements are important, and dissonant minorities would become conspicuous. The method is best suited to an action movement, mobilizing and focussing the moral energies of young people in brief, one-event actions. In such a milieu a leader's declaration of intent is a policy, his actions a decision; all currents move toward a crescendo, overwhelming discordant notes." Bradford Lytle, "After Washington?—Three Views," in *Committee for Nonviolent Action Bulletin* (August 27, 1965), quoted by Feuer, *The Conflict of Generations*, p. 408. This and the preceding quotation from Feuer are included in Cook and Morgan, eds., *Participatory Democracy*. The editors' Introduction to this volume provides a well-balanced discussion of the subject.

461

in which solutions can be worked out and decisions taken. Incessant publicity and public debate can confuse and obstruct coherent and disinterested governmental thinking. Much policy making and administration depend upon gaining of information, upon exchange of views with other organizations, where confidentiality is a condition of the whole process. . . . It would seem plausible to assume that in what some recent American writers have been calling 'the knowledgeable society'—the society in which social decision and action are increasingly based upon complicated bodies of information and upon social and other scientific theories—the gap of incomprehension between decision makers and administrators (in all large organizations) on the one side, and the general or lay public on the other, will be increasingly hard to bridge.[27]

In some measure, to be sure, these considerations point to a general problem of democracy. They indicate a tension between the needs for publicity and consent on the one hand, and the needs, on the other hand, for confidentiality and for technical discussion. Even more, however, it suggests that modern democracy requires a balance between electoral and other highly participatory processes and political and governmental processes less directly linked to the general public. Attempts to increase popular participation in governmental processes may constitute healthy counters to apathy and oligarchy, while also contributing to the enrichment of the participants. Carried beyond a certain point, however, they may threaten the quality of government by upsetting the balance just referred to and injecting the participatory element into realms for which it is not fitted. Its most serious threats are anarchism, *immobilisme*, and rule by a self-selected and self-serving minority (elitism at its worst).

The third basic fact that places limits on effective partici-

[27] Partridge, *Consent and Consensus* (New York: Praeger, 1971), p. 145.

462

pation is simple ignorance. I have in mind not so much general ignorance as ignorance of the complicated and often highly technical matters with which government must deal. To handle the ever-increasing dimensions of this problem democratically is of course one of the most challenging issues facing democracy today. Without discussing this matter in detail—the subject for a book in itself—it may be suggested that the principle of hierarchy, of levels of competency, places serious limits on participatory democracy. Public opinion needs to be refined through successive levels of expertise. To be sure it can and should be given direct access to more than one level. Moreover there should be opportunity at numerous points not just for opinions to be voiced but for policies to be discussed, with a two-way flow of information and ideas. But final decisions in all but the most fundamental matters must be made by those who can devote full time to learning what needs to be learned about the question at issue and deliberating upon it in a way that enables decisions to be made in the light of (as nearly as possible) all relevant considerations.

The final basic fact has already been adverted to. It is disinterest. I am not thinking here primarily of the person who has no serious interests outside of his own petty concerns. I am thinking rather of the person who may have many interests, profound interests, but not in politics. The musician or artist, the chemist or astronomer, or perhaps even the church worker, who may even live a life of selfless pursuit of knowledge or of man's spiritual and moral welfare, but who, at least in normal times, is quite willing to allow others to run the ship of state: what of these people? Are we justified in trying to change their lives and make them political beings? Can we be so sure they would be happier or in any sense better people if we effectuated such a transformation? And do we have any grounds for thinking that any alteration in our institutions would effect this change? If not, would we be right in setting up participatory institutions that might make them feel they would *have* to

463

participate at great cost to the satisfaction of their other interests simply to protect themselves from what might be done in their absence?

Both of the last two points suggest that we must not lose sight of the importance of the postaudit. The opportunity to "throw the rascals out" if we don't like the results of what they did must, I suggest, remain the keystone of the democratic arch. It is the safeguard for the person whose other (laudable) interests for him take precedence over politicking. It is also part of the answer to the problem of ignorance. Those of us who do not know enough about economics to tell the Federal Reserve Board how to regulate the money supply can yield this power the more safely if we have an effective avenue of expression for our view of the overall results of public policy.

6. THE QUESTION OF EVIDENCE

The reference above to the effects of participation upon the participants, which provides the heart of the case for participatory democracy, is a reminder that little has been said about the evidence in support of the claims for this salutary effect.

What, in fact, are the effects of increased participation in government, whether of the polity or of a segment of industry, a particular enterprise or even simply a workplace? Unfortunately, the evidence is meager. Is alienation diminished? Is the self developed? Do individuals become less selfish, more community-minded? Does unselfish concern for the public interest become their major driving force? The great weakness of the case for radically increased political participation, by whatever means, is the dearth of information bearing on these questions, plus the dangers of the theoretical and practical obstacles just discussed. Dennis Thompson has analyzed the functions of participation as posited by citizenship theory and tried to find out how and in what ways they are fulfilled in contemporary democratic society. Reasoning principally from common knowledge supplemented by certain specific studies, he concludes that political participation does contribute to (1) making sure that sinister interests do not prevail, (2) seeing that no interests are excluded from the political process, (3) insuring that citizens are not politically ignorant, (4) developing political legitimacy (here he claims only that participation and satisfaction with the system seem to go together), and (5) realizing the self. Consideration of the evidence, he says, suggests at least a weak case for bringing about an increase in participation.[28]

Other evidence comes largely from experiments with worker participation in industry. One student of the subject reports that "there is hardly a study in the entire field [he examined seventeen studies] which fails to demonstrate that satisfaction in work is enhanced or that other generally acknowledged beneficial consequences accrue from a genuine increase in workers' decision-making power."[29] This finding is of interest, but it does not go far. It relates only to "satisfaction in work." Whether the results carry over to politics and other areas of life is not reported.[30] And the experiments studied were of far more modest proportions than the complete worker control of industry visualized by some advocates of participatory democracy. They related generally to schemes for permitting workers in the shop to have some say in how their work was to be performed.

In Yugoslavia, where by all odds the most ambitious at-

[28] Thompson, *The Democratic Citizen* (Cambridge: Cambridge University Press, 1970), Chap. 3.

[29] Paul Blumberg, *Industrial Democracy* (New York: Schocken Books, 1969), p. 123.

[30] There is, however, some evidence to the effect that when persons from the lower classes become more active within voluntary organizations, they become more active in politics. What the effect on *them* is is not known. See Norman H. Nie, G. Bingham Powell, Jr., and Kenneth Prewitt, "Social Structure and Political Participation: Developmental Relationships, II," *Amer. Polit. Sci. Rev.*, 63 (1969), 808-828, esp. 821-823.

tempt at giving workers substantial control of industry is being made, the record is decidedly mixed. Blumberg reports that in many, perhaps most, cases it is little more than a form. Yet he also finds that in some cases "it has actually begun to operate in line with law and ideology."[31] In view of the fact that it has been in operation for only a few years and that Yugoslavia is a relatively undeveloped country, this may be viewed as an optimistic conclusion from the point of view of the participatory democrat.

Both among blue-collar workers and, even more, among the administrative staffs, efforts are being made increasingly in American industry to enlarge the sphere of participants' control over the activities of the organization. These efforts in large measure stem from management, indicating at least their belief (hope?) that the results will be increased worker satisfaction and productivity.[32]

Finally, and most in point, another student of the subject finds that the evidence gives considerable support to the theory that worker participation *at a low level* does increase their sense of efficacy, make them happier, and lend support to democracy. The author is careful to note the modest extent to which her findings support the case for participatory democracy. In the first place, they deal with participation at a low level of problems. The only three examples she found of "industrial democracy" at a higher level (all in the United Kingdom) were not very encouraging. She also points out that the development of a sense of political efficacy, valuable though it may be, is far short of the wider educational effects of democracy that Millean theory, for instance, would lead one to anticipate.[33]

These bits of evidence support little in the way of generalization. Although not exhaustive, they are typical, and

[31] Blumberg, *Industrial Democracy*, p. 231.

[32] See Chris Argyris, *Integrating the Individual and the Organization* (New York: Wiley, 1964).

[33] Carole Pateman, *Participation and Democratic Theory* (Cambridge: Cambridge University Press, 1970), Chaps. 3-4.

466

concerning the distinctly political effects of participation on the participants, not much else appears to be available. The case for any radical increase beyond present levels finds little support in the evidence. Probably the strongest case is to be made in terms of diminishing alienation. This in itself is certainly important for the health of the body politic; but it is far short of the transformation of the quality of life that is a major objective of the proponents of participatory democracy. And even here the evidence is slight. Another argument of some, but of uncertain significance, is that if people who would not otherwise do so are persuaded to participate they will develop skills and self-confidence which will improve their chances of benefitting from participation in the future—providing not too many do so.

All of what has been said so far in this section relates to the effect of participation on the individual. To be sure, increased participation is also urged by those who look to its effect upon government, upon policy outputs. The most thorough study of this subject has been made by Sidney Verba and Norman H. Nie.[34] They find that in fact increased participation does induce leaders' greater responsiveness to the demands of the participants. But they also find, and to a far greater extent, that in the United States persons from low social and economic groups participate much less than those of higher social status. Thus if one seeks greater responsiveness in order to help those who are worse off, the strategy of trying to secure increased participation is not an encouraging one. They also find evidence supporting the belief that (again for the United States) nonelectoral politics (i.e. lobbying and similar activities by individuals and special groups) tend to skew public policy in favor of the groups in question and away from the modal preferences of the public.[35] This finding at once

[34] Verba and Nie, *Participation in America* (New York: Harper & Row, 1972).
[35] Ibid., pp. 335-342.

supports Lowi's attack on pluralism (by which he means the politics of special-interest groups) and is disheartening to those who would try to remedy the defects of the present system by encouraging the organization of more interest groups.

7. IN CONCLUSION

It was noted earlier in the chapter that participatory democracy is today urged with particular vigor by the egalitarian collectivists. For them it appears to be a *sine qua non.* Hence the weakness in the case for radically increased participation appears to be a weakness in the case for democratic collectivism. Certainly in this aspect, democratic collectivism cannot (and does not) claim to be descriptive of how democracy, in Britain and the United States at least, actually operates. Nor does the available evidence indicate that the motivational theory upon which it is based is sound. This does not entirely negate its possible validity as a prescriptive theory, but the value of an impossible ideal, a Quixotic dream, is open to question. Its prescriptive validity depends upon finding more factual support for its motivational theory than has yet been discovered.

Populism, as was noted earlier, naturally tends toward a similar, if less extreme, stance toward participatory democracy, as does collectivism. Hence what has just been said applies alike, or almost alike, to it.

Some historical perspective at this point is in order. The equalitarian ideal was present in Western culture for centuries before it gained acceptance as the underlying principle for government.[36] Only after such circumstances as the invention of the printing press and of gunpowder (enabling the man on foot to compete for power with the man on horseback) did the Judeo-Christian ideal of human equality find widespread application to government. Be-

[36] Perhaps Athens, for a brief period, and a few other city-states should be named as exceptions to this generalization.

lievers in collectivist democratic theory might contend that the participatory-communitarian ideal is similarly circumstanced. Today, the argument might run, modern technology is at least approaching the point where work for nearly everyone will be so minimized that ample time will be available to meet the demands of greatly increased political participation, including the time for necessary education. Under these circumstances, the unfeasible is becoming feasible and possibly the unattractive (to most, apparently) may become attractive.

This is certainly a possible line of development; but the last, crucial point is unsupported by any evidence I know of. It must be observed, too, that we are still far from the point where most people have the amount of leisure contemplated by these theorists. Moreover, the very groups that appear to be most alienated (at least who participate least) are the ones who have the heaviest work demands and the poorest educational resources. One is forced to conclude with Lisa Newton that in most situations, successful experiments in participatory democracy must await the creation of communities.[37]

[37] Lisa H. Newton, "The Community and the Cattle-Pen: An Analysis of Participation," in Pennock and Chapman, eds., *Participation in Politics*, pp. 233-245.

CHAPTER XII

Leadership

An important aspect of any form of political organization is the congeries of functions and qualities known as leadership. In democracy, it involves an especially complicated set of problems, because it is of the essence of the democratic ideal that individual liberty and equality should be maximized and domination avoided. At the same time, it is frequently contended that democracy, even more than other forms of government, depends upon vigorous leadership for its success. One writer declares that "in a democracy everything depends on the character and ability of leaders and officials."[1] Clearly, between this widely held belief and the democratic ideal some tension exists. No wonder it has been the stock-in-trade of conservative critics in all ages to assert that one of democracy's inherent flaws is weakness of leadership. From their outlook, today's stress on broad participation in politics and government merely underlines this point.

Leadership is not a simple phenomenon, and much of this chapter will be devoted to its analysis and to a discussion of the institutional ramifications of its various aspects. It will also be considered in relation to the various theories of democratic government that make up the two typologies which have been followed throughout this volume. But also this penultimate chapter assumes a more argumentative stance than have previous chapters. At an early stage in the discussion, I take a stand in favor of the pluralistic theory of democracy that is so widely under attack today. No attempt is made to discuss the issue thoroughly, but appli-

[1] Hamilton Fyfe, "Leadership and Democracy," *The Nineteenth Century and After*, 129 (1941), 465-484, 465.

cations of the discussion of leadership and of participation that bear on the subject are pointed out. Later in the chapter, it is also appropriate to apply leadership theory to the argument between supporters of the power-concentration theory of democracy (best exemplified by the British form of parliamentary government) and the power-dispersion theory, of which the American form of government is a prime example. This argument has been discussed already, in Chapter Seven, but here it is approached from another angle, that of leadership theory.

The concept of leadership is highly amorphous.[2] If one treats it without careful definition and subdivision as to its kinds and dimensions, the result will almost certainly be vacuous. But once one embarks upon a more discriminating approach he risks losing both his readers and himself in a mare's nest of complexity and confusion. This risk must be run. The following analysis moves from the general to the particular. More specifically, it begins with definitions and models, examining at this stage some "first approximation" relations, then explores more fully the nature and dimensions of leadership, and discusses its institutionalization and its relations to certain American institutions. Finally, the subject is discussed against the background of general democratic theories.

1. DEFINITIONS

Perhaps the simplest definition of a leader is "one who regularly influences others more than he is influenced by them." This definition is suggestive but too general to be adequate. Normally a leadership situation, unlike the relations between Robinson Crusoe and Friday, involves more than two people. The leader has numerous followers.

---

[2] Beginning here, the bulk of this chapter is borrowed (with permission), with some revisions, from my "Democracy and Leadership," in William N. Chambers and Robert H. Salisbury, eds., *Democracy in the Mid-Twentieth Century* (St. Louis, Mo.: Washington University Press, 1960), pp. 95-125.

471

Moreover, they constitute a group having a common purpose, shared with the leader. Although it may be the leader who in the first instance generates the common purpose, the relations between leader and led are thenceforth reciprocal. To be sure, the leader does influence more than he is influenced, at least in his relations with any particular individual—conceivably barring some rather covert relation with a person not in the public eye. In a sense he may be said to direct and control their behavior, although generally only within a restricted sphere, the area being determined by the nature of the shared purpose. A better way to put it perhaps is that the behavior of the leader structures or patterns the behavior of the group. He may not achieve complete integration: some members of the group may be stirred to opposition. Leadership is not the same as authority. A person whose commands are obeyed because of the law (or his position) is not, *as such*, a leader, although the possession of authority is likely to increase a person's ability to lead.

Similarly, for present purposes, I would also distinguish leadership from domination, while recognizing that in many cases domination, in varying degrees, is mixed with leadership. In the case of domination, commands are imposed, by means of force or otherwise, and the purposes to be pursued are chosen by the dominator. Moreover, persons who act in response to domination, as contrasted with followers of leaders, lack autonomy (with respect to such actions). Manipulation may be distinguished as a special type of domination. Here the patterning of behavior is achieved by more subtle psychological means than is the case with the simple dominator. Command gives way to to suggestion, insinuation, conditioning, and the like. But, as with domination, the relationship is a one-way affair, and the purposes of the manipulator are imposed upon those whose conduct he controls. The followers of a leader accept his leadership willingly, not against their will and not automatically (i.e. as automatons). Accordingly, leadership may be defined as the influencing and guiding of the conduct of others in a situation where the followers act willingly, not automatically, and with some (at least latent) consciousness that the leader is acting in pursuit of purposes they all hold in common.

This discussion, of course, refers to "pure types," such as never appear in real life. In practice, the distinction between leadership and domination is a matter of degree. Dominators perform many functions of leadership; most leaders rely in some measure on domination.

The definition of leadership here adopted departs from that advocated by Lasswell and Kaplan by including influence (power) not "formalized by the perspectives of authority."[3] For present purposes the broader definition appears preferable, because it is leadership in this sense, not simply in the sense of "legitimate power," that many critics maintain democracy lacks. Also it should be noted that in defining leadership as I have, I do not disregard the fact that in a continuing relationship of leading and following, the leader is eventually given the benefit of the doubt by his followers and often has less need to exercise the arts of persuasion than he did at the outset. Where to draw the line between willing followership and coerced or automatic response to domination or manipulation is never easy to determine. What makes the vision of B. F. Skinner's *Walden Two* so dreadful is that we might get there without knowing it.

2. LEADERSHIP AND MAJOR GOVERNMENTAL TYPES

The concept of leadership requires further elaboration, in terms of its types and of the various functions it performs and the processes by which it performs them.[4] Before

[3] Harold D. Lasswell and Abraham Kaplan, *Power and Society* (New Haven: Yale University Press, 1950), p. 152f.

[4] For this definitional discussion, the following sources have been heavily relied upon: Richard Schmidt, "Leadership," in *Encyclopedia*

embarking upon this enterprise, however, it may be useful to examine schematically the relation of leadership to major governmental types, using a simple typology. (This first approximation of a schema will be substantially modified at a later stage of the argument.) At one extreme along the spectrum of societal forms we shall place autocracy, and at the other, anarchy. The latter might also be referred to as a "voluntaristic" society, a term that would emphasize its significant features from our point of view. At the first extreme, the autocrat completely dominates. Accordingly there is no need, indeed no room, for political leadership. In the impossible ideal-type at the other extreme there would likewise be no need for political leadership, or at least for any specialization in it. Not only would all adult members of the society have equal residual (potential) political power, but through equality of opportunity and under the benign influence of democracy itself (strictly, "voluntarism" or "anarchism") as an educating and developing contrivance (as classically set forth by John Stuart Mill), each would have gained the knowledge of his real interests and of how

---

of *Social Sciences*, ed. Edwin R. A. Seligman and Alvin Jonson (New York: Macmillan, 1937), 9:282-287; Alvin W. Gouldner, ed., *Studies in Leadership* (New York: Harper & Row, 1950), esp. pp. 17-18; Paul Pigors, *Leadership or Domination* (Cambridge, Mass.: Houghton Mifflin, 1935), Part I; and *International Encyclopedia of the Social Sciences*, ed. David L. Sills (New York, Macmillan and Free Press, 1968), "Leadership" articles by Cecil A. Gibb, Arnold S. Tannenbaum, and Lester G. Seligman, Vol. 9. Glenn D. Paige quotes a number of definitions covering a wide spectrum. One from Dwight D. Eisenhower comes close to the definition adopted here. "Leadership," said Eisenhower, "is the ability to decide what is to be done, and then to get others to want to do it." Paige, *The Scientific Study of Political Leadership* (New York: Free Press, 1977), p. 65. Paige's own definition is broader than mine, including an element of coercion: "political leadership comprises decisional initiative, pacific and coercive persuasion, the exacerbation or reduction of conflict, follower-need satisfaction as related to task accomplishment, and action within an influencing but influenceable situational context." Paige, *The Scientific Study of Political Leadership*, p. 66.

to attain them that was postulated by James Mill.[5] In this situation, to repeat, leadership would not be required. All would be equally influencers and influenced. To be sure, some division of labor in political matters might be resorted to, so that even though all might share alike in making laws, certain individuals would be charged with their administration. But in our model these tasks, while they would require authority, would not entail leadership. (According to the definition above, the exercise of legal authority does not in itself constitute leadership.) Moreover, in accordance with its fundamental equalitarian premise, and to make assurance doubly certain in this matter of the balance of influence, the society might decide to resort to rotation in office and the device of the lot for all governmental positions.[6]

Before continuing the exposition, a slight digression is in order. The word *democracy* was used in the preceding paragraph in connection with "voluntarism" or "anarchism." The democratic ideal, as set forth in Chapter One and distinguished from the procedural definition of democracy, keeps pushing the democratic reality in the direction of equality not only of *access* to power but also of the *exercise* of power, participation. The logical limit of this process would seem to be a society in which no individual or group exercised power over others. It would be anarchy, after the fashion of William Godwin. To be sure, in any but the simplest society at least, this condition would be

[5] Cf. Anthony Downs's demonstration that, in his model democracy, leadership would not be needed if there were no uncertainty arising from lack of information. Downs, *An Economic Theory of Democracy* (New York: Harper & Row, 1957), p. 87. It should be noted, however, that Downs is speaking only of a limited kind of leadership and does not postulate conditions that would eliminate the necessity for all leadership as here defined.

[6] See Francis E. Lowe and Thomas C. McCormick, "A Study of the Influence of Formal and Informal Leaders in an Election Campaign," *Pub. Opinion Quar.*, 20 (1957), 651-662. This study indicates that opinion leaders tend to have least influence among the politically alert.

unattainable. (That, at least, is my conviction.) Technically, it would not be a type of government at all. It would, however, represent the fullest attainment of a major element of the democratic ideal. But democracy is a form of government. It must govern, or at least maintain order. That is its first order of business. Then it may attain to such a degree of democracy as is compatible with governing well. The demands of government—of maintaining liberty and equality themselves—push in the opposite direction from any such complete equality as is visualized above, so that normally and properly the equilibrium point will be a considerable distance from the equalitarian extreme.

Obviously tension, not to say contradiction, exists between participation in the form of "participatory democracy" and "leadership." One purpose of this chapter, however, is to show that "leadership" and "participation," properly conceived, are complementary rather than antagonistic concepts.

Returning to our main theme, we have now established the two extreme points of a continuum along which societies may be ranged, neither of which needs or indeed admits of the phenomenon of leaders. (See Fig. 1.) At one end, the relationship of ruler to ruled is entirely one of domination. At the other, political relations are essentially cooperative. Both domination and cooperation may be thought of as diminishing gradually as one moves along the line until it disappears entirely at the opposite extreme. Political leadership, on the other hand, in varying degrees and of various types, exists at every point along the continuum between the pure types at the end points.

We may think of the midpoint perhaps as indicating the situation in a large constitutional (and "liberal") democracy with all the complex problems of a modern industrialized state. Here the pattern of voluntarism is unworkable: the need for leadership, *ceteris paribus*, is at its maximum. It would also be proper to visualize an elitist democracy, one in which political leadership is infused with a

476

FIGURE 1: Cooperation, Domination, and Leadership

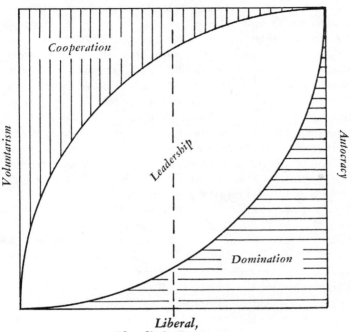

Voluntarism

Autocracy

Cooperation

Leadership

Domination

Liberal,
Pluralistic Democracy

SOURCE: Pennock, "Democracy and Leadership," in Chambers and Salisbury, eds., *Democracy in the Mid-Twentieth Century*, p. 102.

considerable amount of domination, as being located somewhat to the right of the center of the scale, while a "participatory democracy" would be to the left of the center.

Actually, this first approximation is pushing the schema too far, for numerous reasons. In the first place, the assumption that the same amounts of activities coordinated by or through the government would exist under all circumstances is unrealistic. The larger and more complex the society and the greater the sphere of governmental action, the more of such activities will be required. Conse-

477

quently any one of the three factors we have been dealing with—cooperation, leadership, and domination—may vary in amount without a compensating variance in either of the others. A high degree of domination is not incompatible with a high degree of leadership. They may even be exercised by the same person—Brezhnev, perhaps, or Sadat. Moreover, as will appear, leadership has other dimensions, such as its concentration or diffusion, that are equally as important as its net amount or extent. Accordingly, any attempt to take our schema at all literally, especially in the area between the extremes, is bound to be misleading. Subject to these caveats, however, the diagram attempts to portray graphically the schema just described. The total area encompassed by the rectangle represent the sum of activities coordinated by or through government.

At this point it is necessary to guard against misunderstanding by repeating that what has been called democracy's "ideal-type" refers to what is designated on the diagram as "voluntarism" not to "liberal democracy." It is not meant that for any likely political situation such an arrangement would be practicable. What is stressed is that a *bias* away from domination and toward cooperation is implicit in the notion of democracy; for that way lies the greatest reliance on individual autonomy.

3. LEADERSHIP AND POWER THEORIES OF DEMOCRACY

Theorists of democracy by no means always recognize or approve of this bias, as a consideration of power theories makes clear. Elitist democratic theory is much closer to the autocratic than the voluntaristic pole. To an important degree the theories of John Stuart Mill and of Walter Bagehot, of Henry Jones Ford and of Walter Lippmann, have accepted the autocratic theory of leaders and masses, or, to use the terms of Daniel Bell, of "mindless-masses" and "strong-willed leaders."[7] Perhaps the name of Joseph

[7] For Bell's references, see his "Authoritarian and Democratic Lead-

Schumpeter should be added to this list, although he was more inclined than the other writers mentioned to confine himself to descriptive theory.

The extent to which Mill relied on his faith that the masses would follow the leadership of their betters is well known. A similar assumption underlies the classical theory of parliamentary government to the effect that the legislative body does no more than say yes or no to the proposals submitted to it by the Government. Henry Jones Ford and many others have set forth this theory as the model to which American government should aspire, or at least as the standard by which it should be judged. More recently Walter Lippmann declared: "The executive is the active power in the state, the asking and the proposing power. The representative assembly is the consenting power, the petitioning, the approving and the criticizing, the accepting and the refusing power."[8] And in England John Plamenatz once remarked that "it has always been widely admitted, though not by everyone, that the role of the people in government is negative."[9]

The overtones, indeed the implications, of all these statements suggest a type of leadership that is heavily tinged with domination. As normative theory they are not pleasing to the democrat; for, from his point of view, they underrate the key value of equality. They rely too heavily upon hierarchy and make too little allowance for human dignity and for the development of individual growth through political participation.

---

ership," in Alvin W. Gouldner, ed., *Studies in Leadership*, pp. 395-408, 396. Bagehot's famous distinction between the "ceremonial" and the "efficient" functions of government has strongly elitist overtones. Mill is notoriously ambivalent on this question.

[8] Walter Lippmann, *The Public Philosophy* (Boston: Little, Brown, 1955), p. 30.

[9] Plamenatz, "Electoral Studies and Democratic Theory, I: A British View," *Political Studies*, 6 (1958), 1-9, 1. As a matter of fact, Plamenatz's own view as set forth in this article ascribes a more understanding and perhaps more active, though not more articulate, role to the voter than is fully in keeping with elitist democratic theory.

479

Here, however, the tension in democratic theory between norm and reality is perhaps at its maximum. The idea, suggested above, of citizens taking turns to perform leadership functions (as with Aristotle's definition of the ideal constitution as one under which the citizens take turns ruling and being ruled)[10] is a far cry from the reality of modern democracies. It is well known that the citizens of modern democracies run the gamut from disinterested nonparticipants in politics to full-time professional politicians.[11] It is equally notorious that the former far outnumber the latter. Here, incidentally, we have the explanation for much of the controversy among democratic theorists during the last quarter century. Theorists from Walter Lippmann and, especially, Joseph A. Schumpeter to Robert A. Dahl have insisted that this imbalance truly exists and have developed an operational theory of democracy, in which the role of the average citizen is confined to a choice at election times between (preferably only two) competing political parties.[12] Increasingly of late they have been attacked by a new generation of theorists who do not so much dispute the facts of those they term "revisionists" as allege that in building a theory upon those facts, the revisionists tacitly tend to approve of them, while, from the standpoint of normative democratic theory, they should deplore them. Much of the discussion among democratic theorists in recent years runs along these lines, which have the characteristic of parallel lines in that they never meet.

If we turn to the theory of populism, we see the reverse side of the coin. According to the theories associated with the names of Bentham, James Mill, Andrew Jackson, and Jean-Jacques Rousseau, the people should rule. A modest education for all would be enough to enable each to know

[10] *Politics*, III, xiii, §12.

[11] See Robert Dahl's classification of citizens as the powerful, the power-seekers, the political, and the apolitical. *Modern Political Analysis* (Englewood Cliffs, N.J.: Prentice-Hall, 1963), p. 56.

[12] For Schumpeter's theory, see his *Capitalism, Socialism, and Democracy*, pp. 243-249 and Chap. 22.

480

his own interest and to see how to exercise his franchise in such a way as to maximize that interest. In more recent times, proponents of this theory have sought to give it operational effect by adopting such devices as the initiative, referendum, and recall. Today proponents of participatory democracy carry the argument to even greater extreme, as we have seen. Once more the tension between normative and empirical theory assumes major proportions. Curiously enough, some populists, or theorists who appear to accept some of the populistic assumptions, seek to bridge the gap between the normative ideal of popular participation and popular wisdom on the one hand and the patent need for leadership on the other hand by calling for a single strong (dominant?) leader, for a "hero-president."[13] As these lines are being written, however, that call is seldom heard.

What then of constitutionalism and social pluralism? (The two will be treated together, since for present purposes what is true for one is also true for the other.) Here, I believe, is where a satisfactory power theory of democracy may be found, and this not least because it is accommodative of the essential role of leadership. (By "satisfactory" is meant being both operationally realistic and normatively acceptable.) Neither the model of a single, great leader nor that of no leaders at all is satisfactory. The first fails to satisfy the normative claims of democratic theory, while the latter is operationally unrealistic. Between these extremes one finds pluralistic theory.

But here it is important to make a distinction. Much pluralistic theory is cast in terms of competition and strife among self-seeking groups, each treated as an individual. Just as Rousseau assumed that the errors of individual wills would cancel one another out and so allow the General Will to prevail, and as Bentham too easily accepted the Smithian doctrine of the Unseen Hand in his faith that the summation of special interests would be identical with the

---

[13] For an example, see William H. Riker, *Government in the United States*, pp. 201-202, 346-365.

general interest, so much of modern group theory accepts the same principle with nothing more than the substitution of groups for individuals.

The theory of group-equilibrium is less easy to identify with a particular writer than are those previously discussed. Writers like David Easton, who discuss its value for analytical purposes, do not use it as a model of how democracy ought to operate. But, in the works of many political scientists from Bentley to Truman, one finds strong overtones of the suggestion that pressure-group politics, properly channeled by institutional devices, works in much the same beneficent fashion as radical individualists ascribe to the politics of individual self-interest. Robert A. Dahl, for instance, appeared to accept the group-equilibrium theory as a reasonably accurate description of American democracy (or "polyarchy," in his terminology) when he concluded that the American political system "appears to be a relatively efficient system for re-enforcing agreement, encouraging moderation, and maintaining social peace in a restless and immoderate people operating a gigantic, powerful, diversified, and incredibly complex society."[14]

This kind of pluralism has tended merely to substitute the group for the individual in classical individualist theory. In doing so, it is true, pluralism supplied an essential "organizing idea" that was missing from the individualistic theorists. But more than this, more than the political parties, pressure groups, labor unions, and churches, for which pluralism found a place—more than all of these was overlooked by the earlier theories, and by the kind of pluralism discussed above, as well. The latter was so concerned with the role of groups in the state that it gave insufficient attention to what goes on *within* the group. The organizations and informal groups that proliferate in a modern democracy are characterized, in varying degrees, by flows

[14] Dahl, *A Preface to Democratic Theory*, p. 151. Some of Dahl's subsequent works suggest considerable alteration in this point of view. See especially *After the Revolution?*

of information, ideas, sentiments, loyalties, and influence that move up as well as down. They provide a natural home for leadership as contrasted with domination. Moreover, they facilitate, indeed require, participation rather than stifle it.

The brand of pluralistic theory just described stresses discussion more than consent and voting. It is keenly aware of the need for continuous intercommunication of both ideas and feelings. It realizes that this process tends to go on at all levels, from top to bottom, making use of all sorts of media and organizations, nonpolitical as well as political. It not only insists that the communication must be a two-way process but it also holds that it must be mutual to the utmost. In any full statement of the theory, words like "feedback" and "integration" come in for tiresome reiteration. But such processes are neither started nor continued without leadership—leadership in practically every cell and every significant substructure of the whole complex organization. Such a theory is neither individualistic nor collectivistic, in the full sense of either term. Both are qualified in the recognition given to a quasi-organic group process.[15] It is within the group and its quasi-organic process, this theory holds, that the responsible individual can attain his fullest development. Thus voluntary associations (as with "the corporation" in Hegel's theory) are expected to accomplish much of what the participatory democrat seeks in the formal political process.[16]

[15] See, for instance, A. D. Lindsay's *The Essentials of Democracy* and Mary Parker Follett's *Creative Experience* (New York: Longmans, 1924).

[16] Hegel's discussion of the corporation is to be found in *The Philosophy of Right*, trans., Knox (Oxford: Clarendon Press, 1949), Pars. 250-256 and 308. See especially Hegel's Addition to Paragraph 255, where he writes as follows: "Under modern political conditions, the citizens have only a restricted share in the public business of the state, yet it is essential to provide men—ethical entities—with work of a public character over and above their private business. This work of a public character, which the modern state does not always provide, is

As has been indicated, the group process that is so central to what we may call "organic-pluralistic" theory is normally dependent upon and infused with leadership. Indeed, it may be suggested, it is increasingly by way of the reciprocal influences of leader and led in all sorts of groups and organizations that coherence (in the sense of consistency of policy) is to be obtained in a democracy. As electorates become more informed and less willing to follow the lead of their "betters," the older devices for achieving coherent policies become less effective. Elitist democracy works less well or becomes less elitist. Popular demands that may be mutually inconsistent tend to break through the dikes of party discipline and effectively assert themselves at the policy-making level. Alternatively, the parties, anticipating such developments, preserve discipline by yielding to pressures that entail departures from the standard of coherence. Leadership, operating through the group process, provides no panacea for this problem. But it does provide an important means for combining individual self-expression and self-development with rational adjustment of conflicting interests willingly accepted. In other words, with the development of organic pluralism, it becomes increasingly necessary and also increasingly possible to achieve a greater measure of rationality and coherence at lower levels in the political hierarchy than is assumed by elitist theory or is possible with a less participant public.

4. The Nature of Leadership Further Considered

The discussion to this point has been rather general and abstract. If now we examine the nature of leadership in greater detail, the argument can be made more concrete.

---

found in the Corporation." By "the Corporation" Hegel refers to the guilds, the modern counterpart of which would be the trade unions; but his argument applies with even greater force to voluntary associations of all kinds, especially those with a broader than vocational base.

In doing so we shall go beyond the "first approximation" of a model essayed in the diagram.

First, then, what functions does a leader perform? And how, at least in a general way, does he or she perform them? Leadership comprises four main functions. First, is the role of aiding the thought of others. In part this is simply a matter of identifying and pointing out problems for which political action is appropriate. The problems may already exist in the sense that the public welfare is in some respect suffering, or its improvement is being hampered; or the leader may be anticipating problems. Having noted a large influx of young married couples in a particular community, the leader points out that the school facilities, adequate now, will be woefully wanting in a few years. At this level, and in the case of other, more subtle, examples of anticipation, the need for a leader to identify problems is greater than when the matter has already become obvious. Next, but still under the heading of aiding the thought of others, comes the stage of analyzing the problems, of seeking causes, identifying the most likely points and means of attack, of calculating the probable effects of various possible courses of action, of showing what values are involved in each case, and by insightful and dramatic presentation, of helping individuals to weigh these values and to reach judgments that are sound from the standpoint of their own interests.

Leadership's second function, after people's opinions are formulated, is that of enabling these opinions to be effective. The leader provides goals, sets of ideals, which like-minded people can rally to support, and is the standard-bearer of a flag around which followers can gather, unite, and organize for effective action. The leader also articulates their views. He is indeed their representative. And if it is true that no one can completely represent another, it is equally true that for particular purposes—and these may be very broad—a skillful leader may present the interests

485

and views of someone else far more effectively than that person could do it for himself. Finally, he proposes a plan of action. The leader's success is determined in no small measure by his ability to anticipate how his would-be followers will react to his plan. He must represent them, although in doing so he may propose lines of action they did not know they wanted or favored until he put them forth.[17]

Thus far we may have many leaders, each with his own band of followers, marching off in as many different directions. The next task is to obtain the agreement of an effective combination on a single policy in each problem area and on an order of priorities among different problems. Assuming a lack of such agreement in the first place, it is clear that minds and wills are going to have to be changed. Here the leader must both initiate and facilitate changes in group purposes. He may modify the purpose of his own group. He may persuade other leaders to alter their purposes and those of their followers. Or he may appeal directly to the followers of other leaders to gain their support for the objectives of his group or at least to make them more ready to accept some modification of their original goal. Better yet—and this is as applicable to in-group as to out-group leadership—he may discover and suggest means for integrating apparently contradictory purposes. All the arts of persuasion combine with intellectual analysis to aid the leader in this role. A great capacity for empathy is an incomparable asset to this kind of leadership. Beyond this, a combination of qualities that characterize the most spectacular leaders defies analysis; hence we call it charisma.

Finally, even after a large area of agreement is attained it remains to be translated into action. For this, more than assent, and more than will itself, is required; the will must be strong, energetically determined. The task of energizing his followers is by no means the least important of the leader's functions. To be sure, the extent to which even the

[17] See Karl Deutsch, *The Nerves of Government* (Glencoe, Ill.: Free Press, 1963), pp. 157-160.

486

most talented leader is likely to succeed in accomplishing either this or the preceding function will depend on other factors than those that are personal to him. Specifically, it will be a function of the extent to which human impulses are being thwarted. But, granted the evidence of such thwarting, leaders will differ greatly in their ability both to canalize and to energize the latent potential.[18] Here their dramatic ability, their capacity to appeal to basic emotions, their understanding of the values held by their would-be followers, and their own infectious enthusiasm and self-confidence (the latter to convince followers that inspiring goals are attainable) will be important among the factors determining their success.

A particular leader may concentrate his efforts on some one or two of these functions. Moreover, the first function, especially, might almost be said to be ancillary rather than central to leadership per se. It is most easily delegated or its results borrowed from persons we would not normally think of as leaders. The identification or even solution of problems may be carried out by obscure scholars, for example, whose efforts would bear no fruit unless picked up by others. In other words, it is essential to leadership that this function be performed, but it need not be performed by the leader himself, and unless it is combined with other functions of leadership it could hardly be called a part of leadership.

With respect to all that has been said above about the nature of leadership, it must be remembered that the true leader will be the object of influence as well as its subject. Doubtless, leaders vary tremendously in this respect. Some seem to do little more than select and magnify the feelings of the crowd. Obviously, however, a leader who performs all of the functions enumerated above will do much more than this. On the other hand, if he is to avoid domination, he must be a receiver as well as a giver. Not only will he be influenced by people as he finds them, but also he will

[18] See Paul Pigors, *Leadership OR Domination*, pp. 3-6.

inspire and enable them to become greater sources of in-fluence—on him and on others.

In discussing leadership, it is clear we are dealing with a very complicated phenomenon. It has many dimensions. For instance, one may try to measure the *extent* of leader-ship—in a given society, or, more practically, in a given situation. How much is one person influencing others? It is obvious, however, that the way in which leadership shades off into manipulation or domination means that any measurement will be extremely difficult and at best a crude approximation.

Fully as significant is the *distribution* of leadership. At any given time, at the extreme, all political leadership may be concentrated in one man ("big" leadership). More char-acteristically it may be widely distributed, both vertically and horizontally, functionally (*i.e.* by specific type of in-terest) or on a geographical or other basis. A widely dis-persed leadership pattern ("little" leadership) may or may not be pyramidal in form. The pattern of leadership and the persons in whom it chiefly resides may remain constant over fairly long periods of time, or it may be subject to fre-quent changes. Leadership may also be variously distribut-ed as between those with official governmental capacity and those without it (unofficial leadership). Likewise, leader-ship may be highly institutionalized or it may be purely personal. And this distinction does not necessarily follow that of official versus unofficial.

Simplifying slightly this account of the nature of leader-ship, it can be said that acts of leadership may be classified as to whether they are initiating, coordinating, or energiz-ing. Another dimension of the subject relates to the levels at which the leadership in question is operating. Or, if we are considering a society as a whole or in all its political aspects, the dimension has to do with the distribution of leadership among these levels.

Leadership types may be classified in various ways. An obvious possibility is to categorize them by the relative emphasis they place on each of the three types of leadership acts just enumerated. Thus we have the initiating leader, the innovator. Franklin Roosevelt quickly comes to mind. Or possibly de Gaulle. Such a person may innovate by finding new means to satisfy old wants and needs, or he may generate new desires or inspire his followers to accept new ideals. He may bring together people who had been at odds with one another, politically, in pursuit of a common ideal, such as the greater glory of France.

Other leaders play their major role in coordinating the desires and efforts of others so that they are mutually consistent. This result may be accomplished in any of various ways. At the lowest level, it may be by the simple process of trading, the art of political brokerage. Or, in more subtle and refined fashion, a leader—Clement Attlee, for instance —may build an administrative organization that aids in channeling disparate demands so as to produce harmony.

In addition to the initiator and the coordinator there is the energizer. Both Franklin Roosevelt and Winston Churchill qualify for this classification; but, like all *great* political leaders, they were outstanding in more than one of the categories. The energizer may have no claim to originality or initiation. Accepting other people's ideas, he puts them across by arousing, exciting, and inspiring many people.

Such a leader may act democratically; he may be a demagogue; or he may impose his will upon large numbers of people. By the sheer force of his personality he may virtually compel them to follow a course of action that is, let us say, both against their real interests and against their own better judgment. Insofar as such a "crowd-compeller" succeeds in this fashion he is more dominator than leader, as those terms are used in this chapter. Finally, it may be noted that problem solving may be used by all three types (whether performed by themselves or by someone else for them) but especially by the first two.

Many other bases for classifying leadership types have

489

been suggested. A good deal of what has been said up to this point suggests that leadership plays an innovative or at least a dynamic role; but this is not necessarily so. It may also be conservative. Nor does this category embrace only the leader who actively organizes opposition to an innovative leader. More distinctively, conservative leadership may be primarily symbolic. A conservative leader may achieve his conserving purposes by seeming to embody and symbolize the values for which the status quo, or something closely approximating it, stands in the minds of a great many people. While such a person may do very little under the first of the four headings discussed under the nature of leadership, he may lead very effectively in the other three aspects considered there. Among recent American presidents, "silent Cal" Coolidge—who emitted more words for the record, per year, than any previous president—is perhaps the clearest example.[19]

Finally, it may contribute further to understanding the complexity of leadership phenomena to suggest one other basis of classification. Some leaders, such as Ronald Reagan, or George McGovern during his presidential campaign, are "extremists." They adopt a position far from the mode of existing attitudes and unyieldingly seek to gain support for it and will settle for nothing less. Others have definite policy views that they seek to have carried out, but they are willing to compromise, if necessary, as the price of some

[19] See Elmer Cornwall, "Coolidge and Presidential Leadership," *Pub. Opinion Quart.*, 21 (1957), 265-278. To be sure it may seem somewhat paradoxical to extend the concept of leadership this far. Nothing in the argument of this chapter depends on doing so. Bertrand de Jouvenal uses the term *authority* for something close to what I have called leadership, and then applies the term *dux* ("leader") to one who exercises authority intermittently and actively, while the *rex*, or rectifier, is more passive though more constant in his exercise of authority by such means as laying down rules of conduct, enforcing contracts, and arbitrating disputes. Bertrand de Jouvenal, *Sovereignty*, trans. J. F. Huntington (Cambridge: Cambridge University Press, 1957), Chap. 2, esp. p. 34.

degree of success. Perhaps Harold Wilson and Gerald Ford belong in this category. These may be denominated "agitational" leaders. Finally, there are the "facilitative" leaders, who are neutral as to policy and whose concern it is simply to get agreement on something, to remove the source of conflict.[20]

5. The Institutionalization of Leadership

In view of the vast variety of functions leaders must perform, even granted that they need not necessarily be combined in the same persons, it is virtually inevitable that in today's immense and complicated societies leadership should be institutionalized. This means not only that there are certain settled expectations about the modes of behavior and the jobs to be performed by people in certain situations, but also that large staffs are built up to aid the leader in playing his role. Obviously certain types of leadership activity, or at least preparation for them, are more easily delegated than others. But even the intensely personal ones can be greatly facilitated by staff work that builds up a certain image of the leader's personality. The most obvious example of institutionalized political leadership is the American presidency. The ways in which the Executive Office of the President, some forty-five hundred strong, provides the raw materials and creates the environment for leadership need not be detailed here. Of course a great deal still depends upon the capacities and inclinations of the president himself, but to an ever-increasing extent the presidency has been built up to a point—partly by the very device of institutionalization and partly because of the expectations created by the actions of past presidents, especially their use of the newer mass media—from which retreat is virtually impossible. As Elmer Cornwall puts it,

[20] Harry M. Scoble, "Yankeetown: Leadership in Three Decision-Making Processes," mimeographed paper presented at meetings of the American Political Science Association, Sept. 6-8, 1956.

491

"While in the nineteenth century the man made the office over in his image, in the twentieth, more and more, the giant public image of the office will mold the man to its demands."[21]

In the office of the president we simply see writ large what on a smaller scale is happening everywhere. In one sense, to be sure, Franklin Roosevelt was his own secretary of state. Moreover, under Eisenhower, John Foster Dulles made minimal use of the staff facilities of the State Department. But the self-sufficient Nixon had Kissinger, and Kissinger himself, while still within the White House, had a staff of approximately 120. In Congress, too, the same process is in full swing, with staffs for majority and minority leaders, for committee chairman (and ranking minority members), and for individual congressmen.

Nor is it only official leadership that seeks this kind of implementation. The same device is used by all kinds of private organizations, whether it be the Council on Foreign Relations, the National Planning Association, the Committee for Economic Development, the National Council of Churches, the AFL-CIO, the American Farm Bureau Federation, the United States Chamber of Commerce, or Common Cause. Of ever-increasing importance in this category are the private foundations. Indeed they play a rather distinctive role in that they seek to lead especially by discovering, stimulating, and encouraging leaders outside of their own organization. Here the search for leadership, innovative leadership in particular, has itself been institutionalized.

Doubtless the institutionalization of official leadership, inevitable though it is, has its dangers. The leader's staff may become more of an obstacle than an aid. Parkinson's Law contains more than a modicum of truth, and it is not confined to the "line" side of bureaucratic structures. Whenever it becomes necessary—or is thought necessary—to "clear" each move through innumerable staff members, dry rot has begun to set in. Resultant delays, at best, are likely

[21] Cornwall, "Coolidge and Presidential Leadership," p. 278.

to spoil the timing of leadership moves. Spontaneity is lost, character and personality are smudged.

It would be wrong to assume that such costs represent the necessary price of leadership on the grand scale in modern society. On the contrary, this is an important area for research. We need studies of the institutionalization of leadership in various contexts and at various levels, executive, legislative, and in party organizations. What can such institutionalization at best accomplish? How well is it actually doing the job? What are the effects on the leader, on his relations with his followers and with other leaders and their followers? Does it have an effect on the type of person who tends to be selected for leadership offices?

6. DEMOCRATIC LEADERSHIP IN MODERN STATES

Leadership in modern, industrialized states is especially difficult and complicated. This is particularly so if the states are large, as is the United States. But it is the multiplication of tasks assumed by modern governments as much as the size of some of them that complicates the task of leadership. The more layers, whether of bureaucracy or of political organization, the greater the degree of specialization, the greater is the psychological distance between the ordinary citizen and the top leadership. Between the needs of healthy individuals and the demands of formal organization, tension always exists. This tension becomes greater as the tasks and size of the organization expand. Conflicts inevitably arise and these conflicts become more serious as the individuals at the bottom of the pyramid (and at intermediate levels as well) become more aware of their interests and rights. We have here a major explanation both for the difficulties of widespread and intense participation and, at the same time, for the need to find ways to involve more people in the process. People at the bottom will see the actions of those at the top that impinge unfavorably upon them as "ripoffs," and will react accordingly, unless

493

they can be made not only to feel a share in the purposes of the organization but also to see the relation between the actions taken and those purposes.[22] Thus the very conditions of modern society, especially its need for educated, self-aware people, both complicate the task of leadership and make its democratization essential.

The last statement leads directly to considering those aspects of the leadership problems of modern states that relate especially to democracy. Not all that has been said in the preceding pages about the nature and dimensions of leadership and concerning its institutionalization in large modern states provides bases for distinctions between leadership in a democracy and leadership in any other kind of polity. But much of it does. For instance, among the functions of leadership enumerated above, democratic leadership especially must develop the first: aiding the thought of the people by identifying and analyzing problems and showing the consequences of various possible courses of action in terms of popular values—and almost equally the second—enabling people to make their opinions effective. In the case of the third function—getting widespread agreement on policy—the nature of democracy demands that to the greatest extent possible this end be obtained by interaction. The emphasis, that is to say, is on the kind of leadership which involves the maximum of discussion, or give-and-take, between leader and led. Just as leadership is to be preferred to domination, so, within the broad ambit of leadership, that which is farthest from charismatic leadership most nearly approaches the democratic ideal. This means more emphasis on the intellectual approach and less on the emotional. It also means that the leader will be more open to influence from those he is leading; and not just influenced out of considera-

[22] Although it does not deal specifically with *political* leadership, useful material on this aspect of the subject may be found in Chris Argyris, "Organizational Leadership," in Luigi Petrulla and Bernard M. Bass, eds., *Leadership and Interpersonal Behavior* (New York: Holt, 1961), pp. 326-354, esp. 331-332.

tions of immediate self-interest, but also and especially by gaining new insights in the process of interaction. From all of this it follows that democratic leadership tends to be widely distributed in all the ways suggested above. Finally, with respect to institutionalization of leadership, democracy may impose what superficially look like opposing demands. The point just made indicates that it is vital for leaders and led in a democracy to have a great deal of direct personal contact. On the other hand, the leader's staff members may get between him and his public, or even between him and his line subordinates, as was the studied policy of President Nixon. But this need not be so. If staffs operate as they should, they will aid rather than interfere with the objective of maximizing direct personal contact between leader and followers.

7. APPLICATION TO PARTICULAR DEMOCRATIC SYSTEMS

The foregoing discussion provides the foundation for an extensive examination of any particular set of democratic institutions. Clearly, no more than a few hints at what such an inquiry might disclose can be attempted here. In the pages that follow I shall give a cursory glance at the leading British and American political institutions from this point of view.

In a general way the practical implications of the theory of leadership's role in a modern, Western democracy have already been adumbrated. It calls for a loosely integrated and highly pluralistic society with the maximum opportunity for, and the actual performance of, leadership functions of one kind or another, at virtually every pore. What about formal political institutions? Does our analysis throw any light on the relative preferability of a parliamentary (majoritarian) or a presidential (check-and-balance) system? The former facilitates the formation of majorities and places the fewest obstacles in the way of their will, while the latter relies more heavily upon what is sometimes called "the

495

politics of adjustment" and upon what Lindblom describes as reconciliation of conflicts "without high-level overview." Here we encounter once more, but in a new context, the common assumption that a majoritarian system is more democratic than any other. The equalitarian premise of democracy calls, so runs the argument, for the simplest and surest method for letting the majority have its way. By the same token, according to the usual manner of thinking, the presidential, or American, system must be defended, if it is to be defended at all, on the ground that democracy needs to be curbed. Our analysis of democratic leadership, however, appears to point to the opposite conclusions.[23] If we accept the goal of self-development or self-actualization as an important part of the democratic ideal and if we agree also with the organic-pluralist model of power distribution defended earlier in this chapter, we should seek to maximize dispersed, "little" leadership. This directive calls for close contact and small group operations. Moreover, the lieutenant leaders in such a system, since to be democratic leaders they must be open to influence as well as influencing, must have the maximum of independence, not subject to the discipline of the top command. It is of course no accident that totalitarian "leaders" everywhere oppose those independent groups that are like "worms within the entrails of the state." Nor is it because such groups may become conspiratorial revolutionary societies. Rather, they recognize them as the heart of the democratic system to which they are opposed. Once more, then—this time from a consideration of the democratic ideal in the light of leadership theory—we find ourselves drawn toward the kind of loose and relatively undisciplined party system that tends to go with the dispersion of power characteristic of checks and balances and a federal system of government.

[23] This issue was discussed in connection with our treatment of decision-making rules and machinery in Chaps. 9 and 10, as well as in the chapter on responsiveness (Chap. 7). Here a different set of considerations is brought to bear upon the same issues.

For still another reason, democracy calls for dispersed leadership. If we accept the Millean principle that a major argument for adopting democratic institutions follows from the developmental effect on the citizens of political participation, then the institutions should be such as to encourage more than a mere choice of leaders and the rather unrealistic debates that grow out of a situation where the alternatives are always sharply structured. But a balance must be maintained. Too great fragmentation of the decision-making process may be self-defeating. As long as important policies are to be made centrally (and it would be hard to imagine the contrary) not all leadership can or should be dispersed. Moreover, competition for central leadership positions—in the form of electoral campaigns—will play a most valuable educational and developmental role.

These arguments do not find universal support among democratic theorists. Samuel H. Beer, for instance, takes a somewhat different point of view. He likes the greater power of British party leaders.[24] Apparently he sees here no threat of antidemocratic "domination," or of elitist control. Or if he sees such a tendency he does not consider it a threat. He welcomes the coherence he believes it gives to British policy, and deplores the "incoherence" of American policy. I shall limit myself to two observations in this connection. In the first place, with respect to trends, as Beer himself notes, there are signs of pluralistic developments threatening the party duopoly in Britain. He concedes that the increase of state intervention in the economic system has led to greater participation by interest groups in the policy-making process and has forced greater dependence upon their consent. He also admits the possibility that the use of public campaigns by pressure groups may be on the increase. My own observation supports his belief in both instances, that these trends are likely to continue, and that they must inevitably tend to weaken the power of the political parties, especially of the party leaders. As this happens, a decline in the co-

[24] See his "New Structures of Democracy," pp. 45-79.

herence of party programs would be a natural, almost inevitable result. It is my impression that this decline is occurring.

My second point raises a question about the facts of the case. Few would deny that coherence of policy (in some sense at least) is desirable. Beer believes that "centralized power means that there is a chance for deliberate and coherent solutions," while the vice of the American system of fragmented and dispersed power is incoherence. If true, these propositions are certainly significant, although not necessarily determinative. How can they be tested? It is sometimes thought to be self-evident that central direction must be more rational in its results than a system making great use of dispersed, partly independent decisions, but this need not be so. Are centrally fixed prices necessarily more rational (in terms of the allocation of resources they produce) than those resulting from the higgling of a competitive market? May not political decision making, within certain limits, operate in a fashion analogous to the decision making of the market? And may this not tend especially to be true if abundant opportunity is provided for the operation of relatively independent leadership within groups at all levels?

Comparing the coherence of policies and programs is no easy matter. Is it clear that the United States is so inferior to Britain in this respect? The evidence seems to be lacking. It may be noted in passing that examples of what appears to be incoherence sometimes disappear on closer examination. The American system of tariffs supplemented by financial aid to foreign governments is not necessarily an example of incoherence. The two by no means completely defeat each other. Nor is it self-evident that the net effect of the two is in any sense irrational. Incidentally, too, the erstwhile British combination of agricultural subsidies with Dominion preference might be attacked on similar grounds.

More fundamentally, perhaps, it must be pointed out that coherence is a test which should be applied vertically over time as well as horizontally. Whatever British policies gain during a given Government's tenure of office they may lose at the next general election. Switches from private to public ownership and back to private in the cases of steel and road transport may be cited as examples. If the programs of American major parties tend to be somewhat more alike than are their British counterparts, as is widely believed to be so, this should make for greater coherence of legislative and administrative action in the United States in the long run. Furthermore, it is more than possible that this greater degree of agreement or consensus in the United States reflects the results of dispersed "little" leadership, operating at all levels and in all sorts of groups, as contrasted with the more centralized British system.

One final caveat under this heading. All that has been said rests on the assumption that maximum attainment of democratic ideals is a major objective. Also, it presupposes the existence of conditions that will enable the pluralistic system to achieve a reasonably satisfactory solution for the country's problems. If this system does not result in sufficient agreement for action to be taken, or if it does not call forth ideas equal to the tasks that are faced, the whole situation is changed. Under such circumstances of crisis it is to be hoped that "big" leadership, even charismatic leadership, will take over where the other variety has failed. That it has generally done so in the past may be more than an accident and yet less than a guarantee that it will always do so in the future. This is not a counsel of either irresponsibility or despair. The more closely a democracy approaches its ideal type, the less is the need for big leadership and the less the willingness to accept it. Conversely, when the need is there, when human impulses are being seriously frustrated on a wide front, the temper changes. It is not that such circumstances magically bring forth leadership equal to the occasion; but it does appear to be true, and in accord with well-known phenomena of social psychology, that people in deep trouble select and listen to leaders who have conviction, determination, the ability to sense the needs of the situation, and the other leadership qualities required. Indeed it may be suspected that charisma is as much a product of the situation and of the followers as it is an independent personal quality.[25]

8. LEADERSHIP AND CERTAIN AMERICAN POLITICAL INSTITUTIONS

In the following necessarily sketchy discussion of certain particular institutions of American democracy in the light of what has been said up to this point, the presidency demands first attention. Here it is not a question of explaining the importance of dispersed leadership. Rather, we are here dealing with the primary American institution for centralized power, overview, and focus for popular attention on national policy. Division of power requires a counterpoise; and dispersed leadership, grading upward from molecular to molar in pyramidal fashion, needs a focal point and indeed a climax. The eminence and uniqueness of the president's position assure him an almost unequaled leverage for

[25] An experiment that was once conducted with military personnel seems to support the argument of the last two sections. Twenty-four squadrons were trained in accordance with the traditional concept of military leadership, that is to give unquestioning obedience to officers. An equal number of squadrons were trained, we are told, "in the idea that leadership is a set of group functions channeled through a salient member and requiring the initiative and cooperation of all group (squad) members." It was further explained to them that "one of the reasons for high levels of combat deaths is the inability of unassisted formal authority figures adequately to process combat-relevant information." The two groups were then put through a set of simulated combat exercises, both of the groups having had their formal leaders (sergeants and corporals) removed at the last minute. Not a single traditionally trained squad scored as well as any squad trained in the idea of leadership as a set of functions. In the latter, despite the surprise element of the situation, various individuals took over the leadership functions and the results were almost as good as when the leaders were present. Paige, *The Scientific Study of Political Leadership*, p. 76.

leadership. His constitutional and political powers are great. It is arguable of course that they are not great enough. But it cannot be denied that they are very great indeed if, as Max Lerner puts it, "he has grasp, contagion, political artistry, and a mastery of his purposes and methods."[26] It is true too, as Lerner also declares, that even the strongest president "is helpless except insofar as he can win the people's confidence."[27] (The presidential career of Lyndon Johnson came close to illustrating both of these propositions.) Significantly, Lerner attributes this fact not to the separation of powers or other constitutional limitation but to certain characteristics of the American people, especially a general skepticism of political power and an emphasis on individual self-reliance which, whatever its origin, is today nurtured and reinforced in the American pattern of family life and by our school system.

It is sometimes felt that the job is too big for any person, or at least for any but the rarest of presidents. But could more people—i.e. a cabinet system—do it better? Could they, for instance, keep a closer eye on all significant aspects of national policy and keep it unified, coherent? Even in Britain, the facts of modern political forces are tending to defeat the theory of collective leadership. L. S. Amery, member of several British cabinets, criticized that institution, even as it operates with a secretariat, for failure to co-ordinate departmental policies. "There is very little cabinet policy, as such, on any subject," he declared. "No one has time to think it out, to discuss it, to co-ordinate its various elements, or to see to its prompt and consistent enforcement. There are only departmental policies."[28] The major

[26] Lerner, *America as a Civilization* (New York: Simon & Schuster, 1957), p. 374. President Eisenhower effectively demonstrated the power that resides in the presidential office even when Congress is controlled by the opposition party and when the incumbent is ineligible for reelection.

[27] Ibid., p. 376. One is reminded, too, of Harry Truman's lament that the only power he had was that of persuasion.

[28] Amery, *Thoughts on the Constitution* (New York: Oxford Uni-

job of coordination is done in England by the prime minister and two or three others. Much the same—substituting the president for the prime minister—is true for the United States. Even President Eisenhower's strenuous efforts to achieve "team" policies achieved only limited and temporary success.

One other aspect of the presidency calls for brief discussion: selection. Ever since Lord Bryce wrote his famous chapter on "Why Great Men are not Chosen Presidents," numerous students of politics have lamented this same alleged fact. To cite Max Lerner once more, "the conditions for reaching the Presidency are so haphazard and opportunist that the way is too often open for a genial mediocre man who means well, commands a popular following, and will not be too intractable."[29] It can hardly be denied that mediocre men have not infrequently been elected to the presidency. But if the implication is that the British system does it better, a glance at the record will raise some doubts. Since the turn of the century we can count McKinley, Theodore Roosevelt, Taft, Wilson, Harding, Coolidge, Hoover, Franklin Roosevelt, Truman, Eisenhower, Kennedy, Johnson, Nixon, and Carter. (Ford, not having been elected, hardly belongs on this list.) For the same period the roll of English prime ministers runs as follows: Balfour, Campbell-Bannerman, Asquith, Lloyd George, Bonar Law, Baldwin, MacDonald, Chamberlain, Churchill, Attlee, Eden, MacMillan, Wilson, Heath, and Callaghan. Can it be said with any assurance that the latter list includes more "great leaders" or a greater sum total of leadership ability than the former?

Of Congress, perhaps the most general remark possible is that the substantial differences between the Senate and the House provide the beginning of one of the avenues

---

versity Press, 1947), p. 87. The statement is probably even more valid today than it was when Amery made it.

[29] Lerner, *America as a Civilization*, p. 372.

down the line from big to little leadership. The Senate, with its small size and consequent great opportunities for each member to make an effective bid for influence, produces many leaders of national stature. Its peculiar rules and customs may sometimes thwart the popular will; but the fact that "Senatorial courtesy" makes of each senator a little king in a certain area has the great advantage, as Arthur Krock once remarked, that "it makes it worth a man's while to be a United States Senator." And as Lyndon Johnson demonstrated, and Taft before him, it retains ample scope for effective democratic leadership.

In the House, the opportunities for leadership in matters of national policy are notoriously limited, although an effective committee chairman may have a powerful impact both within the chamber and in the country at large, especially in his dealings with the representatives of groups regularly appearing before his committee. In some measure the effectiveness of his leadership in his own constituency will be a function of the stature he attains in Congress. One of the most frequently mentioned obstacles to effective leadership in the House, the seniority rule, has now been substantially reformed. Further, a four-year term of office would doubtless do something to free congressmen from parochial interests.

Of the federal system little need be said. Whatever else may be its merits and demerits, it clearly multiplies the opportunities for leadership and the extent of practical participation in politics. Thus both participation and the kind of dispersed leadership that has been supported in this chapter gain by it. Federalism also contributes to the kind of democratic system that has here been argued for in yet another way. This has to do with political parties. We have found reason at earlier points (especially in Chapter Seven) to find a system of loose, weak political parties conducive to the most satisfactory operation of democratic institutions. The study of leadership buttresses that conclusion. Disciplined, programmatic national parties, even if they are at-

503

tainable, would bind the American political process in a straitjacket entirely incompatible with the kind of leadership (flexible, permeating the whole social structure, and with the balance between leader and led never too one-sided) herein espoused. Among the many factors contributing to the kind of weak-party system that characterizes American politics, federalism must rank high; for it is in the organizations formed to conduct state elections and nourished by the benefits controlled by state and local governments that our national party system has its foundations. The latter are indeed little more than loose federations of these state organizations. The presidency and the importance of national issues are of course powerful nationalizing forces in American politics, but the centralizing tendency in politics is also stoutly checked by the federal structure.

9. In Conclusion

A good deal has been said in this chapter about the power theories of democracy and practically nothing about the motivational theories. The fact is that their whole approach is based upon the nature of the individual citizen, whether considered individually or collectively. The subject of leadership, by definition, deals primarily with a select (although it may be quite populous) group. Yet the motivational theories are by no means wholly without bearing upon the subject of leadership in a democracy. In particular, public-interest theorists, generally recognizing that men tend to be concerned chiefly with matters closer to home than the national scene, normally rely upon strong leaders to raise the sights of the common man, to appeal to his "better" nature, to understand his real interest, and, especially, to discern the public interest. It might be thought that collectivists would take the same line, and indeed they may. Hierarchical collectivists, in particular, tend to lay great stress upon "big" leadership, as with

Hegel's "world-historical individuals." On the other hand, egalitarian collectivists have such confidence in the inherent "goodness" and community-minded nature of man, once he is freed from oppressive and privatizing institutions, that they believe a community can manage itself with a minimum of "big" leadership, although all but the most radically egalitarian of them would feel the need to rely—perhaps more than others—upon "little," dispersed leadership. Rousseau, once his Legislator had succeeded in getting a good constitution installed, took the radical line. And while Rousseau was dealing with a small city-state, Karl Marx imposed no such restrictions and yet had faith in a communist commonwealth with minimal leadership, as many of his followers do today. Contemporary egalitarian collectivists, even though only vaguely Marxist, tend to stress collective deliberation and action, eschewing anything in the way of *formalized* leadership, at least. The individualist would appear to be committed, by his confidence in each individual, to little, dispersed leadership; while the rights and duties theorist seems to be in a neutral position.

CHAPTER XIII

Conclusion

In this concluding chapter I shall deal primarily with certain themes that have frequently recurred throughout the book. No attempt will be made at a complete summary, but I shall try to provide a framework for a more systematic view of these subjects than would otherwise be apparent. First, I shall say something about the general theory of human nature on which I have frequently relied, explicitly for the most part but without much argumentation. Indeed to give much argumentation would be the subject of another book, but what can be done here is to pull together various parts of this theory and give some indication of the kinds of evidence I believe support it.[1]

Certainly one of the features distinguishing man from the lower animals is that his nature is more flexible than theirs. Some writers, especially among collectivists, would urge that human nature is not only flexible but that it is completely plastic, infinitely alterable. Without resorting to such artificial measures as drugs as yet undiscovered or the insertion of electrodes into the brain, this seems to me extremely unlikely. I speak of man as we know him and as he appears to have been throughout the ages. None of this is to say that human behavior is not vastly affected by its environment, by its training and conditioning, and so on. The point rather is that a constant human nature often helps *explain* changing patterns of behavior.

[1] For further exposition and analysis of this vast subject, see Pennock and Chapman, eds., *Human Nature in Politics*. Among other things, this volume contains a substantial bibliography and an encyclopedic discussion, "Toward a General Theory of Human Nature and Dynamics," by John W. Chapman.

This point can be made in another way. An economist, seeking a theory of property rights, has examined the development of the institution of private property in certain Indian tribes.[2] The Montagnes of Labrador have private property in land. The Indians of the American Southwest did not. Does it follow that nothing in human nature dictated this development? Demsetz's study gives no support to that conclusion. The Labrador Indians, before the development of commercial fur trade, also had no private property in land. But it appears that as the demand for furs increased, fur became more valuable, hunting increased, fur-bearing animals became more scarce—and private property developed as the best way to prevent overhunting. In the Southwest, the conditions were quite different. There was little commercial trading and the topography and the types of animals inhabiting the region made it difficult to confine them to a given territory. Hence no private property in land was called for. "Human nature" led each group of Indians to develop institutions that were in their rational self-interest, at least as far as concern the matter of private property in land.

Another point that may lead the unwary astray in this matter of the constancy of human nature: our natures develop, as a child becomes an adult and as a society achieves favorable conditions.[3] Thus what the unmindful observer sees as random variability are rather stages in a developmental series.

[2] The reference is to H. Demsetz, "Toward a Theory of Property Rights," *Amer. Econ. Rev.*, 57 (1967), 347-359, reprinted in Eirik G. Furubotn and Svetozar Pejovich, *The Economics of Property Rights* (Cambridge, Mass.: Ballinger, 1975), Chap. 3.

[3] Three references will provide a small sample of the literature and guides to more. They are: Lawrence Kohlberg and Carol Gilligan, "The Adolescent as a Philosopher: The Discovery of the Self in a Post-Conventional World," *Daedalus*, Fall 1971, 1051-1086; Daniel Yankelovich, "The Idea of Human Nature," *Social Research*, 40 (1973), 407-428; and James C. Davies, in Pennock and Chapman, eds., *Human Nature in Politics*, Chap. 6.

In this catalogue of circumstances that may lead to misunderstanding, a final fact relates to the ambivalence of human nature. It is the (sometimes unfortunate) nature of man to want different and incompatible things at the same time: privacy and sociability; safety and excitement and adventure; liberty and security. Thus if one person eats and another hoards it does not necessarily mean that their natures are sharply opposed to each other. They are opposed to themselves. As Charles Frankel remarked on a recent telecast, "Man is the social animal that seeks privacy."

In dire circumstances, men look out for themselves and their loved ones before giving aid to strangers no worse off than they are. A minimum of physical needs must be satisfied, in all but the rarest cases, before love becomes an effective force in society.[4] But, granted that minimum, sociability and some concern for the welfare of others develops. So does self-esteem and the desire for approval of others (approbativeness), on which self-esteem feeds. In certain respects the demand for some freedom seems to be almost as primordial as the physical needs. (A baby cries when its arms or legs are held still.) But once the basic minima of social life are achieved this desire to be free, to experiment —and also to compete and to excel—expands. And here too we soon encounter the phenomenon of ambivalence. Men's desire to be free often leads them to take chances, thus conflicting with their basic need for safety, for self-preservation. Also the desire to excel may run counter to the pleasure they obtain from cooperative activity. Expand as it may, the concept of the self seldom if ever reaches the point where self-love and love of others never conflict. At least in part, it is these conflicts that lead to the development of a sense of justice and of the bent toward equality which informs that sense. Yet, as Locke noted, even while they accept these rules, men tend to be partial to themselves in their interpretation and application. Also, as Aristotle made clear in

[4] Moreover, in the absence of basic need satisfaction, selfishness completely displaces altruism.

classic terms, the meaning of equality to a person—absolute or relative—will depend upon his or her circumstances.

These brief remarks must suffice to summarize the general theory of human nature that has been relied upon, mostly expressly, at many steps throughout the argument of this book. Certain basics are constant, and those are sufficiently at odds with each other that human beings frequently manifest ambivalence. All of this is very simple; yet it is either denied or overlooked by some of the theorists who have been discussed in the preceding pages.

The following pages are devoted primarily to the discussion of the two themes that have been developed recurrently throughout this volume. Although the main thrust of the book does not relate to the controversy between pluralists and their critics, it is impossible to discuss democratic theory for long and not become involved in it, for today attacks upon "pluralistic" or "liberal democratic" theory, the two terms generally being used interchangeably, are rife.[5] While I have said a good deal about this controversy,

[5] In spite of the interchangeable usage of these terms, it makes sense to distinguish them. In point of fact, the critics of pluralism are attacking the "old" liberalism, as distinguished from the "new" liberalism, as the latter is described in the following passage:

A *new liberalism* has now grown up. Nurtured by a climate of affluence in which such values have been significantly realized, it places less emphasis upon economic well-being and security, is less materialistic. It rather more emphasizes civil liberties and civil rights. It looks to a more participant, less hierarchical society. It stresses the importance of self-development of the individual, even at the cost of some further economic expansion if that is necessary. It is less attentive to the demand for economic growth, stressing environmental costs of such growth. Not rejecting governmental nationalism, it is nonetheless much less sympathetic to it than is the old liberalism, and reveals a suspicion of the state and of the workings of bureaucracy not found in the latter. The new liberalism shares the equalitarian commitments and flavor of the old (surely the only excuse for attaching "liberal" to both positions); but its equalitarianism is more sensitized to the needs of deprived (often ethnic) minorities. The new liberalism is attracted to the socially and culturally avant-garde, to experimentation and change in life styles, personal values,

509

and, I believe, made my own position clear, I have nowhere dealt with it in overall fashion. Although the critics of pluralism do not always seem to recognize the fact, democratic theory, even "liberal democratic" theory, is not a unity, as has been amply demonstrated in this volume. Even here, then, we must refer to the various types of democratic theory.

I shall examine the attitude of the critics, by inference where it is not expressed, toward each of the forms of democratic theory treated in this book, starting with motivational theories and, within this classification, the individualistic theories. In general, the critics of whom I speak are critical of all of the theories I have called individualistic, with the exception of romantic individualism. The latter, as we have seen, takes as its "individual" a self so expanded, so inclusive of others, that it borders on "collectivism." But radical individualism, Tocquevillean individualism, and modified individualism all are included in the camp of the enemy. So also, for many of the critics at least, with methodological individualism. All, among other things, are too "privatistic" for the antiindividualists.

Rights and duties theories, as has been noted, may lean either in the individualist or in the collectivist direction. Insofar as they stress "rights," it is difficult for them to escape the strictures (as least implied) that are leveled against individualists.

Public-interest theory is in a somewhat different category vis-à-vis the critics of liberalism. Here again adherents to

---

and ethical or normative codes. Everett Carll Ladd, Jr. with Charles D. Hadley, *Transformations of the American Party System* (New York: Norton, 1975), p. 340.

It will be noted that the "old" liberalism the authors describe is New Deal liberalism, rather than that of J. S. Mill, which in some respects (e.g. its suspicion of bureaucracy) is more like the "new" liberalism. Partly because of the ambiguity of the term *liberalism*, my remarks will be addressed to the discussion relating to the slightly less ambiguous term *pluralism*.

this theory (like the other theories, capable of variations) may lean to one side or the other. If the public interest is viewed as a sort of summation of private interests, as Bentham would have it, the critics of whom we speak are by no means satisfied. For them the "public" interest must differ in kind from that of "private" individuals. It must lay major stress upon goods that are collective, sharable, and incapable of enjoyment in isolation.

The critics of liberalism and pluralism then are themselves to be classified either as extreme public interest theorists, or perhaps in most cases more accurately, as being on the other side of the thin line that separates these theorists from democratic collectivists. Certainly it is safe to say without qualification that with the collectivists they have no quarrel, and they are themselves likely to belong in that category.[6]

[6] No attempt will be made here to list the contemporary writers who fall in this classification. Many have been discussed earlier in this volume. One might note, as an example, the work of Robert J. Pranger. See his *The Eclipse of Citizenship* (New York: Holt, 1968). For collections of antipluralist writings see William E. Connolly, ed., *The Bias of Pluralism* (New York: Atherton, 1960); John Playford and Charles A. McCoy, *Apolitical Politics* (New York: Crowell, 1967), and Part III ("Challenges to Democratic Revisionism") of Henry S. Kariel, ed., *Frontiers of Democratic Theory.* See also Kariel, *The Decline of American Pluralism* (Stanford, Cal.: Stanford University Press, 1961); Kariel, *Open Systems* (Itasca, Ill.: Peacock Publishers, 1969); and Kariel, *The Promise of Politics* (Englewood Cliffs, N.J.: Prentice-Hall, 1966). C. B. Macpherson represents quite a different point of view in some respects, but also belongs in this category. See his *Democratic Theory* and his *The Life and Times of Liberal Democracy.* Finally, from a still different point of view, the work of Ellen Meiksins Wood should be mentioned. See her *Mind and Politics: An Approach to the Meaning of Liberal and Social Individualism* (Berkeley and Los Angeles: University of California Press, 1972). As her subtitle hints, Wood would classify herself as a social individualist rather than as a collectivist. Indeed she is protesting the appropriation of the term *individualism* by adherents of the Lockean-empiricist tradition (which she equates with liberal individualism). But the distinction is semantic only; she is opposed to individualism as I have been using that term.

511

The attitude of the critics of pluralism toward the power theories requires little discussion, the only case about which any question could possibly arise being that of constitutionalism. One of their major criticisms of much individualistic theory is that it is elitist. And, since their attack is phrased in terms of opposition to "pluralism" (sometimes "liberal democracy" or simply "liberalism"), "social pluralism" is also ruled out. Finally, constitutionalism is so closely identified with liberalism that it is hard to see how a critic of the latter could consider himself, or be considered, a member of the "constitutionalist" school. He might of course favor certain constitutional devices—it is hard to see how he could avoid it. But most of what is associated with constitutionalism is far too much concerned with the protection of individual rights and with the protection of minorities against majorities to suit the tastes of the writers under discussion.

That leaves populism. If they had to choose among these four, here clearly the critics of liberal democracy (or pluralism) would find their most congenial home. "Power to the people" is a slogan that certainly fits the populists and likewise many or most of the critics under discussion. Is it power to "the people," envisaged as a collection, a mass of individuals? Or is "the people" thought of, as might be the case with the more extreme democratic collectivists, as an entity that has transcended the individuals whom it comprises? In the case of the latter, they might not be happy with the designation "populist." But since such theorists, to the best of my knowledge, have not worked out a theory of how power would be exercised in their ideal state (except to say that it would be for "the common good"), they must for the time being remain outside the classification of power theories.[7]

[7] The work of Harvey Wheeler, discussed above (Chap. 11, Sec. 4), should perhaps be mentioned as an exception to this generalization. Wheeler, whether or not properly classified as a collectivist, at least shares many features with them, including not only an attack on

From what has been said thus far, it follows that much of what was written about democratic collectivist theory (especially in Chapter Five) and about populist theory and participatory democratic theory in Chapters Eleven and Twelve is applicable to the critics of liberal democracy (and pluralism). But, since that material is scattered in several places throughout this book, I shall attempt here to sketch a more systematic approach, including some remarks not previously made.

The attack on liberal democratic theory is a mixture of empirical claims and moral arguments. Liberal democracy, in its modern form of pluralism, is held to depend upon the "group theory of politics." This theory, in turn, is alleged to view groups as narrowly self-interested and to view democratic politics as a process of combined bargaining and struggling among these groups and to hold that the result of this process will be the advancement of the public interest.[8]

This view of the operation of democracy is attacked on numerous grounds. It is argued that many, probably most, citizens participate so little in groups having any political influence that they are effectively debarred from the benefits of the group process. Consequently these citizens feel, and are, politically powerless. They tend to become alienated from politics, and they are deprived of the advantages of political participation that Mill and others have attributed to the democratic process and counted as one of its great virtues. Community spirit lags. Self-interest and selfishness of

---

American democracy as it now is, but also strong support of the "intentionalist" philosophy so characteristic of collectivists. He also favors maximum popular participation in the political process at many levels. But, as was indicated previously, he has sought to develop a sketch of constitutional machinery that might be used to implement his ideas. He is then in some sense a constitutionalist, while also sharing much of the outlook of populism.

[8] This point of view has been given forceful expression by Theodore J. Lowi in his *The Decline of Liberalism* (New York: Norton, 1969).

individuals ("privatism") and also of the groups is encouraged by the theory that defends the process. Moreover, it is pointed out, even if everyone was involved in the group process, the sum of group desires, as of individual desires, "may be that which is desired by nobody."[9] (This is the "prisoner's dilemma" that was discussed in Chapter Seven.)

Against the claim of the pluralists to be dealing only in the realm of descriptive theory, the critics reply that the pluralists are in fact covertly prescriptive. They hold that the pluralists are at least complacent about the apathy and political ignorance of the masses and that this tends to become a defense of existing elitism and more than a suggestion that this is what is to be desired. Even if the theory is not intended to be prescriptive, some argue, the inevitable effect of its "description" of "democracy," a word that is "inescapably commendatory," amounts to praise of the elitism it embodies.[10]

Not only is liberal democracy associated with pluralism, it is also associated with capitalism. This of course is historically true; and many, although not all, defenders of this faith would claim as well that the relation between political and economic individualism is not simply coincidental but actually necessary. In the eyes of many of its critics this becomes an additional count against liberal democratic theory. They desire a political system that encourages cooperation rather than competition, and community spirit and public selves rather than privatism.

This then is a highly compressed sketch of the nature of the critics' attack. In describing it, most of the arguments in favor of some alternative form of democracy (generally not specified in any detail) have been at least implied. The alternative polity would be more inclusive, more egalitarian. It would engage its citizens much more fully in the

[9] Barry Holden, *The Nature of Democracy*, p. 165.

[10] See Quentin Skinner, "The Empirical Theorists of Democracy and Their Critics: A Plague on Both Their Houses," *Political Theory*, 1 (1973), 287-306, 298-301.

processes of government. It would do everything possible to develop a rich community, or series of communities, which would be a "training ground for altruists."[11]

In short, the critics of liberal democracy and of pluralism seem to prescribe for the ills of democracy and for the ills of pluralism more pluralism. This may take the form of urging deliberate efforts to organize the unorganized and also encourage those who do belong to organizations to participate in their governance. Alternatively, and more characteristically, a la Rousseau, they may deplore specialized organizations, and urge instead radical decentralization of the state and of industry, in such a way that the basic units could govern themselves by direct democracy.

Lastly, collectivists generally, and so most of the critics of pluralism, uphold an ideal of the individual as a completely socialized being, in the fashion of Marx. They see socialism as a necessary means to making the economic power centers of present society responsive, and to increasing the number and power of political power-centers. In this connection it may be remarked that they seldom deal with the economic problems this might entail. They tend to assume, contrary to Adam Smith's great insight, that the economy is a zero-sum game, that profits are always at the expense of others and that they can be redistributed without diminishing the total output of industry, and that state ownership of the means of production would be more efficient than the capitalist system. These highly controversial assumptions are left without more support than mere assertion by the writers in question.[12]

[11] Jack Lively, *Democracy*, p. 121.

[12] See, for instance, Michael J. Parenti, *Democracy for the Few* (New York: St. Martin's, 1974), especially pp. 184-185. Protesting against individualism and privatism, he declares: "The commitment is, or should be, to communal, collective and responsible decision making and toward the elimination of poverty and pollution, the end of imperialism, the equalization of life chances, the bettering of the lives of millions of needy working people. Once the creative energies of people are liberated from the irrational social purposes of a capitalist system, the

515

It is interesting, at least as a semantic footnote, that the critics of contemporary (descriptive) pluralists, when pressed for positive suggestions, sound strangely reminiscent of the (prescriptive) pluralists of yesteryear, men like Harold J. Laski, G.D.H. Cole, and Hugo Krabbe, who advocated decentralization to achieve decisions made by those directly affected, and believed in the real personality of groups, especially (in the cases of Laski and Cole) if freed from the bonds of capitalism.[13]

The general form of the con side of this debate has been largely implied already. Pluralists classify their critics as Utopians, point to the lack of evidence in support of their positive proposals and to a very considerable amount of evidence, largely garnered from Russia, China, Cuba, and Yugoslavia, that attempts to implement these proposals do not support the claims of their proponents. Moreover, pluralists contend that the groups by which they set such great store include "cause" groups and other public-interest organizations as well as those whose function is related to the material welfare of their members. They also make the point, following Hegel and various neoidealists in the Hegelian tradition, that membership in groups of all sorts contributes to the education and the socialization of men

---

potentialities for human advancement and individual initiative [sic] will be greatly increased, as has happened in a number of Third World countries that have liberated themselves from imperialism." Ibid., p. 296. C. B. Macpherson uses similar arguments, also relying upon the purported experience of Third World countries, ignoring the fact that, far from manifesting the features attributed to them, those countries appear to be sinking farther and farther into a morass of poverty, corruption, and undemocratic regimes. See his *The Real World of Democracy*. It is notable that in his more recent works, *Democratic Theory* and *The Life and Times of Liberal Democracy*, while adhering to the same ideal, and finding other grounds for some optimism, his reliance on the experience of Third World countries is muted.

[13] See Francis W. Coker, "Pluralistic Theories and the Attack upon State Sovereignty," in Charles E. Merriam and H. E. Barnes, eds., *A History of Political Theories* (New York: Macmillan, 1924), 80-119.

and to the development of loyalties that take people beyond the realm of the private. Even organizations formed for the promotion of specific economic interests find themselves compelled to take into account differences among the interests of their own members. The arguments in favor of pluralism in the chapters on responsiveness and responsibility (Seven) and representation (Eight) and the discussion in the chapter on participation (Eleven) of the problems inherent in participatory democracy need not be repeated here.

Finally, along this line, one must note the relevance of theories of human nature. The collectivist relies upon his faith that human nature is capable of a complete transformation, if only institutions are altered—a transformation that eliminates the sources of competitiveness, selfishness, and strife. The pluralist or liberal democrat, on the other hand, finds no evidence to support this faith and advances a great deal of history and more immediate experience to the effect that human nature is irrefragably ambivalent.

More central to the purpose of the chapters on the various problems of operational democratic theory than an appraisal of pluralism has been their use as bases for appraising the power and motivational theories of democracy. In each of these chapters, I have posed the question, with respect to each of these theories: How well does it fit the facts? How well does it serve as description and explanation? The prescriptive aspect of the theories is of course to be judged in terms of the democratic values discussed in the earlier chapters of the book. However, in some cases the discussion of one of the problems casts doubt upon the workability of particular prescriptions; suggests, in short, that the values sought to be obtained by a particular theory cannot in fact be obtained in the way the theory proposes. Thus the prescriptive and the descriptive aspects of the theory are often closely linked.

I shall begin with the power theories, since they are more closely related to the so-called pluralistic theory that has just been canvassed. For each of these theories the first question then is, Was the theory, as a descriptive and explanatory model, supported, contravened, or unaffected by the various problems of democratic government to which consideration has been given in the foregoing chapters? (The chapters dealing with decision-making rules and machinery fall in a special category, and will be discussed separately.)

The theory of democratic elitism received some support from a consideration of the conditions of democracy. The evidence from developing countries supports the conclusion that, without a group, an elite, of relatively well-informed, educated, and democratically committed political activists, a democratic regime has little chance of surviving. On the other hand, consideration of the subjects of responsiveness, and of responsibility in its various senses, suggested that democratic elitism, whether taken descriptively or prescriptively, was in itself inadequate, at most only of some subsidiary applicability. It was likewise found wanting in conjunction with representation, in that it was unrealistic except as a partial explanation. Consideration of participation and of leadership also led to unfavorable conclusions for this theory. Descriptively, some degree of elitism is unavoidable, but too much is unworkable. Prescriptively, because of the minimal weight it gives to the ideal of equality, it must be limited by constitutional restraints, social pluralism, and (what tends to go with both of these) dispersed "little" leadership, as an important complement to "big" leadership.

Populism comes out with a similar score. Except for the fact that the discussion of conditions of democracy yielded no implications for this theory whatever, its boxscore is precisely the same. It is simplistic and unrealistic, and because of its threat to liberty, prescriptively undesirable.

Turning to the other two power theories, constitutionalism and social pluralism, the findings are precisely the opposite. Here in fact the analysis of each of the problems studied has given support to the two theories in question. That is to say, the institutions described by each of the theories appear to play a role in the successful functioning of democracy from the point of view of both ideal and procedural definitions. This outcome is hardly surprising, in view of the more general remarks about liberal democracy and pluralism made in the first part of this chapter as well as at appropriate points throughout the book. Nonetheless, it does add weight to these conclusions.

The power theories, practically by definition, are closely akin to the institutions of government, with which in large measure the "problems of democratic government" chapters of this book have dealt. Accordingly, from another point of view than that just rehearsed, the close harmony of findings indicated above was to be expected. The motivational theories, on the other hand, being theories of how men behave or ought to behave politically rather than about the institutionalization and organization of their political behavior, proceed at one stage removed. Therefore, as we view their various implications for the problems or aspects of the democratic process discussed in the preceding chapters, we might anticipate a looser fit among the conclusions than appeared in the case of the power theories. However that may be, let us have a look. We are faced at the outset with the fact that our four theories are not so much single theories as sets of theories. In some instances each member of a given set seems to point in the same direction, for our purposes, but in others not so.

Let us begin with individualism, and first with a few remarks about its varieties. Individualism as a starting point for analysis (an aspect of methodological individualism), which was discussed at some length in Chapter Two because of the collectivists' attack upon it, has not been mentioned in the "problem" chapters, with which we are now primarily concerned. The reason is simple: methodological individualism, as such, leads to no particular conclusions about these subjects. It is relevant only insofar as it gives support to radical individualism or to one of the other subbranches of substantive individualism as starting points for analysis, contrary to the arguments of collectivists. Consideration of it was a prerequisite to proceeding with any individualistic theories. Radical, Tocquevillian, and modified individualism can, for present purposes, be treated together. Insofar as they differ from the other motivational theories, they have the same tendencies; modified individualism naturally has them in lesser degree. Romantic individualism, on the other hand, tends to differ from other brands of individualism in relevant ways, being in many respects closely akin to collectivism. In spite of this fact, in the case of only one problem area is it necessary to distinguish it from the other individualisms, or the level of generalization appropriate here.

No one of the problems discussed has led us to conclusions that are sharply incompatible with individualism. On the other hand, in some cases, and especially in the discussion of the conditions of democracy and of responsiveness and responsibility, it has seemed clear that individualistic theory by and in itself is inadequate to explain what happens. Also, at least in its more extreme versions, it weighs the scales too heavily in favor of liberty and against equality. It calls for supplementation by one of the other theories. Obviously this would be less true of modified individualism, for by definition that form of the theory has moved some distance toward public-interest theory. In the case of political participation, it is necessary to note some differences. Here Tocquevillian individualism would occupy the extreme position, being unfavorably disposed to more than minimal participation. Consequently the normative arguments of Mill and others would be least favorable to that version of individualism. On the other hand, the criticism levelled in Chapter Eleven against the feasibility of maximal political participation (i.e. participatory democracy) would be entirely compatible with either radical or modified individualism. Romantic individualists, on the other hand, would be less happy with it. The writers I have placed in this category, certain British idealists, notably T. H. Green, have much in common with the collectivists. While of course they do not discuss participatory democracy, a phrase that had not been coined in their day and an idea that was scarcely entertained, their emphasis upon self-realization through developing an all-inclusive self would naturally lead them in the direction of supporting this concept—certainly much further than other types of individualists would be willing to go.

The theory of the public interest appears to emerge with flying colors if, as a descriptive theory, it is considered as an overlay on individualism, a highly modified individualism. Nothing that came out of the discussion of the problems was in any way incompatible with the theory thus interpreted. Consideration of the conditions of democracy, and of responsiveness and responsibility, decidedly reinforces the public-interest theory on both the descriptive and the prescriptive side, and what was said under the heading of participation favors it, especially insofar as the emphasis on increased participation means giving effect to interest that had been hitherto neglected.

The rights and duties theory also receives considerable support, and no opposition, from the problems chapters. Especially in the case of the discussion of responsiveness and responsibility, this theory appears to provide valuable supplementation to other theories, although it could not stand alone as *the* descriptive theory of democracy. The study of the conditions of democracy was the other main area that gave positive support to this theory.

Finally, as to collectivism, it clearly emerges as the least favored of the four motivational theories. Study of the conditions of democracy does give it some support, but it also indicates the need for qualification. The responsiveness-responsibility complex gives it some vindication as long as, and only so long as, it plays a subsidiary role. It is in the discussion of leadership, and especially participation, that

521

opposition to collectivism as a theory of democracy is most pronounced. As an ideal, a normative theory, to lead democratic practice *somewhat* more in the direction that now prevails in the leading democracies in the world, it can play a valuable role. But, as either a theory of how democracy does operate (which it does not claim to be) or as a normative theory in a stronger sense than was suggested above, it is not to be commended.

To the last statement, the collectivist would reply by arguing that the nature of man can be transformed in such a way that what is now unworkable would become workable, that competitive man would be completely subordinated to cooperative man, and that self-interest would yield to altruism. I have previously given reasons for disbelieving this proposition, and they need not be repeated here. However, a few further remarks seem to be in order. How far people do modify their self-interest, narrowly construed, in favor of altruism or justice is an empirical question, and undoubtedly the extent to which it could be answered in completely general terms is severely limited.[14] It must be remembered, however, that our concern is with political behavior only. Three arguments, two empirical and the other theoretical, may be advanced against giving more than a modestly qualifying weight to nonself-regarding motives in politics. On the empirical side, it is notorious that politicians, in their party platforms, their public pronouncements, their appeals, whether to voters or to fellow legislators, cater heavily to self-interest. Certainly "justice" and "the public interest" also figure importantly in their oratory, nor is it to be assumed that this is mere window-dressing; yet it is notorious that all possible efforts are

---

[14] Doubtless it would not only vary from society to society but quite likely also from one level of government to another. Charles E. Gilbert has suggested that the self-interested individualist type of reasoning might be more applicable at local than at national levels. See his "Two Academic Models," in Lynton K. Caldwell, ed., *Politics and Public Affairs* (Bloomington, Ind.: Institute of Training for Public Service, 1962), pp. 65-70.

made to make it appear that the general interest coincides with the particular interest of whatever group is being addressed. My second point is more directly pertinent to the collectivists' position. It is simply that the full-scale efforts which have been made in various countries since the first World War to create a "new man" are, to say the least, not encouraging.

The theoretical argument runs to the effect that in large aggregations of people, the presence of only a few self-seekers will drive the others, even though more altruistically inclined, to resort to selfish behavior in self-defense. Among early writers in the modern era, Thomas Hobbes made this point. After denying that he assumed all men were wicked, he argued as follows: "Though the wicked were fewer than the righteous, yet because we cannot distinguish them, there is a necessity of suspecting, heeding, anticipating, subjugating, self-defending, ever incident to the most honest and fairest conditioned."[15] This classic theme is put in modern dress by Buchanan and Tullock in their example of the roads. They argue persuasively that the existence in a community of even a few individuals who are out to maximize their own individual benefit ("maximizers"), the rest being committed to the principle of having the government treat others as well as it treats them ("Kantians"), creates an unstable situation. The Kantians will ultimately be so exploited by the maximizers that they will be forced to adopt the maximizing policy in self-defense. It is a case of Gresham's law in politics.[16] The argument has special force where benefits are particularized and costs generalized; but as we have seen that is a very large category.

Finally, it is important to recall the one problem area, the subject of Chapters Nine and Ten, that has not been

[15] Thomas Hobbes, *De Cive, or the Citizen*, edited with an introduction by Sterling P. Lamprecht (New York: Appleton-Century-Crofts, 1949), p. 12.

[16] Buchanan and Tullock, *Calculus of Consent*, pp. 135-140.

mentioned in this summary review. What seemed to be important in the discussion of rules and machinery for decision making in a democracy was not what motivational theory that discussion vindicated or contravened, but rather what kinds of rules and machinery gained support from each of the theories. Something of the same sort is true of the consideration of representation (Chapter Eight). In these three chapters, and only in them, the question for study relates to forms of government, constitutional matters; and it is on such matters that theories should be able to make recommendations.

To begin with representation, all the motivational theories, with the exception of the egalitarian form of collectivism, support my general conclusions regarding representation. This refers both to the general theory of representation advanced in that chapter and to the condemnation of interest representation. In the case of proportional representation, perhaps a qualification is called for.

In the case of rules and machinery for decision making, a similar convergence of recommendations from the various theories emerges—with possibly the same exception. That is to say, except for egalitarian collectivism, the weakness of which I have sufficiently discussed, all of the theories concur in providing support for institutions that call for qualification of simple majority rule. The qualification may take the form of the requirement of more than a simple majority for voting purposes, or it may take the form of machinery that makes use of multiple constituencies and multiple points of access to government, with any of a great variety of provisions for checking power against power. Whether the case of egalitarian collectivism does in fact amount to an exception is not at all clear. If my analysis in Chapter Ten is correct, its premises would not seem to make it an exception but rather the contrary. On the other hand, egalitarian collectivists tend to believe so strongly in the transformation of human nature that they believe can be achieved, and in the consensus that can then be arrived at, that they may not believe individuals and minorities would any longer need special protections, or for that matter that voting would even need to be resorted to.

What the significance of the findings recapitulated in the preceding pages is for any particular motivational theory depends upon the manner, the tone, in which it is offered, the claim that is made for it. And these vary from theorist to theorist. Any one of the theories (except for radical individualism) may be offered as the sole and sufficient theory to explain both how democracy does operate and how it should operate. At the other extreme it may be offered only as descriptive or only as prescriptive theory, and in either case not as completely accurate but as an approximation that may be of value as a guide either to understanding or to recommending or evaluating. When the spectrum of democratic theories, and now especially the motivational theories, is viewed in this perspective, it becomes apparent that one should not expect to be forced to choose one and forsake all others. It need not be a question of marriage, although there are those whose passions, even in this field, cannot otherwise be assuaged. And even if marriage is indicated, for most a modest bigamy, or even polygamy, perhaps obeying the Muslim injunction of giving precedence to one will provide the happiest solution. Especially so since the Muslims make a change of mind (or heart) a simple and unilateral affair.

To be a bit more specific, with respect to the motivational theories, the first three types all receive some support on the descriptive side. On the prescriptive side, the first and fourth types, taken by themselves, seem respectively undesirable and unattainable, while the second and third types are both desirable and mutually compatible. That one should conclude with the conviction that no one theory does justice both to the facts and to a justifiable ethical position, or to put it another way, that a sound theory must be pluralistic in its assumptions about human nature,

525

seems to me not a weakness but a proper recognition of the complexity of man.

More than once throughout these pages I have referred to the problem, broadly stated, of the prisoner's dilemma—a problem faced by all democracies, at least from time to time and in varying degrees. It used to be thought that it was man's irrationality which posed the greatest threat to democracy. A threat it undoubtedly is, but my contention is that man's rationality, in the sense of pursuit of individual self-interest, presents an equally serious problem. It is to be hoped, then, that this ineradicable self-seeking may be sufficiently moderated by concern for the public interest and by the Kantian (or a similar) ethic of respect for the individual and acceptance of duties toward other individuals compatible with such respect, to make the democratic ideal increasingly practicable and increasingly widespread.

Bibliography

Adelman, Irma, and Cynthia Taft Morris. "A Factor Analysis of the Interrelationship between Social and Political Variables and Per Capita Gross National Product." *Quarterly Journal of Economics*, 79 (1965), 555-578.

Allardt, E., and Y. Littunen, eds. *Cleavages, Ideologies and Party Systems*. Helsinki, Transactions of the Westermarck Society, 1964.

Almond, Gabriel A., and James S. Coleman, eds. *The Politics of the Developing Areas*. Princeton, Princeton University Press, 1960.

Almond, Gabriel A., and Sidney Verba. *The Civic Culture: Political Attitudes and Democracy in Five Nations*. Princeton, Princeton University Press, 1963.

Alt, James A., Bo Särlvik, and Ivor Crewe. "Partisanship and Policy Choice: Issue Preferences in the British Electorate, February 1974." *British Journal of Political Science*, 6 (1976), 273-290.

American Political Science Association. "Toward a More Responsible Two-Party System," A Report of the Committee on Political Parties. Supplement to the *American Political Science Review*, 44 (1950).

Amery, L. S. *Thoughts on the Constitution*. New York, Oxford University Press, 1947.

Ames, Barry, "Bases of Support for Mexico's Dominant Party." *American Political Science Review*, 64 (1970), 153-167.

Apter, David E. *The Politics of Modernization*. Chicago, University of Chicago Press, 1965.

Apter, David E., and Charles F. Andrain, eds. *Contemporary Analytical Theory*. Englewood Cliffs, N.J., Prentice-Hall, 1972.

527

Argyris, Chris. *Integrating the Individual and the Organization.* New York, Wiley, 1964.

———. "Organizational Leadership." In Petrulla and Bass, eds. *Leadership and Interpersonal Behavior.* New York, Holt, 1961, pp. 326-354.

Aristotle. *The Politics of Aristotle.* Trans. with an introduction by Ernest Barker. Oxford, Clarendon Press, 1946.

Arrow, Kenneth J. *Social Choice and Individual Values.* 2nd ed. New York, Wiley, 1963.

Avineri, Shlomo. *The Social and Political Thought of Karl Marx.* Cambridge, Cambridge University Press, 1967.

Bachrach, Peter. "Interest, Participation, and Democratic Theory." In Pennock and Chapman, eds. *Participation in Politics,* pp. 39-50.

Bailey, Stephen Kemp. *Congress Makes a Law: The Story Behind the Employment Act of 1946.* New York, Columbia University Press, 1950.

Baker, Kendall L., and Oliver Walter. "Voter Rationality: A Comparison of Presidential and Congressional Voting in Wyoming." *Western Political Quarterly,* 28 (1975), 316-329.

Banks, Arthur S. "Modernization and Political Change: The Latin American and American-European Nations." *Comparative Political Studies,* 2 (1970), 405-418.

Barber, Benjamin R. *Superman and Common Men: Freedom, Anarchy, and the Revolution.* New York, Praeger, 1971.

Barber, James D. *Citizen Politics: An Introduction to Political Behavior.* Chicago, Markham, 1969.

Barker, Ernest. "The Breakdown of Democracy." *The Contemporary Review,* 145 (1934), 18-31.

Barry, Brian. *Political Argument.* London, Routledge & Kegan Paul, 1965.

Barry, Brian M. "The Use and Abuse of 'The Public Interest.' " In Carl J. Friedrich, ed. *The Public Interest*, pp. 191-204.

Bay, Christian. *The Structure of Freedom*. Stanford, Cal., Stanford University Press, 1958.

Beaney, William M., and Edward N. Beiser. "Prayer and Politics: The Impact of *Engel* and *Schemp* on the Political Process." *Journal of Public Law*, 13 (1964), 475-603.

Beckner, Morton. *The Biological Way of Thought*. New York, Columbia University Press, 1959.

Beer, Samuel H. "New Structures of Democracy: Britain and America." In Chambers and Salisbury, eds. *Democracy in Mid-Twentieth Century*, Chap. 2.

Bell, Daniel. "Authoritarian and Democratic Leadership." In Alvin W. Gouldner, ed. *Studies in Leadership: Leadership and Democratic Action*, pp. 395-408.

Benello, C. George. "Group Organization and Socio-Political Structure." In Benello and Roussopoulos, eds. *The Case for Participatory Democracy*, pp. 37-54.

Benello, C. George, and Dimitrios Roussopoulos, eds. *The Case for Participatory Democracy*. New York, Grossman, 1971.

Benn, Stanley I. "Egalitarianism and Equal Consideration of Interests." In Pennock and Chapman, eds. *Equality*, pp. 61-78.

———. "Freedom and Persuasion." *The Australian Journal of Philosophy*, 45 (1967), 259-275.

———. " 'Interests' in Politics." *Proceedings of the Aristotelian Society*, n.s. 1959/60, London, Harrison & Sons, 1960, 60: 123-140.

Bennett, Stephen Earl. "Consistency among the Public's Social Welfare Attitudes in the 1960's." *American Journal of Political Science*, 73 (1973), 544-570.

Bennis, Warren G., and Philip E. Slater. *The Temporary Society*. New York, Harper & Row, 1968.

Bentham, Jeremy. *A Fragment on Government and an In-*

troduction to the Principles of Morals and Legislation.
Ed. Wilfred Harrison. Oxford, Clarendon Press, 1970.
———. *An Introduction to the Principles of Morals and
Legislation.* Ed. Wheelwright. Garden City, Double-
day, 1935.
Berelson, Bernard, and Gary A. Steiner. *Human Behavior:
An Inventory of Scientific Findings.* New York, Har-
court, Brace and World, 1964.
Berelson, Bernard R., Paul F. Lazarsfeld, and William
N. McPhee. *Voting.* Chicago, University of Chicago
Press, 1954.
Berlin, Isaiah. *Four Essays on Liberty.* New York, Oxford
University Press, 1969.
———. "Two Concepts of Liberty." In *Four Essays on
Liberty.* London, Oxford University Press, 1969.
Bernholz, Peter. "Logrolling, Arrow Paradox and Decision
Rules: A Generalization." *Kyklos,* 27 (1974), 49-61.
Birch, A. H. *Representative and Responsible Government.*
Toronto, University of Toronto Press, 1964.
Black, C. E. *The Dynamics of Modernization: A Study of
Comparative History.* New York, Harper & Row, 1966.
Black, Duncan. *The Theory of Committees and Elections.*
Cambridge, Cambridge University Press, 1958.
Blumberg, Paul. *Industrial Democracy: The Sociology of
Participation.* New York, Schocken Books, 1969.
Bosanquet, Bernard. *The Philosophical Theory of the
State.* London, Macmillan, 1930.
———. *The Principle of Individuality and Value.* London,
Macmillan, 1927.
Boyd, Richard W. "Popular Control of Public Policy: A
Normal Vote Analysis of the 1968 Election." *Ameri-
can Political Science Review,* 66 (1972), 422-449.
Bradley, F. H. *Ethical Studies.* 2nd ed. Oxford, Clarendon
Press, 1927.
Braybrooke, David. *Three Tests for Democracy: Personal
Rights, Human Welfare, Collective Preferences.* New
York, Random House, 1968.

Braybrooke, David, and Charles E. Lindblom. *A Strategy of Decision*. Glencoe, Ill., Free Press, 1963.

Brody, Richard A., and Benjamin I. Page. "Comment: The Assessment of Policy Voting." *American Political Science Review*, 66 (1972), 450-465.

Brown, Keith C., ed. *Hobbes Studies*. Oxford, Blackwell, 1965.

Buchanan, James M. "An Individualistic Theory of Political Process." In Easton, ed. *Varieties of Political Theory*, pp. 27-38.

Buchanan, James M. "The Relevance of Pareto Optimality." *Journal of Conflict Resolution*, 6 (1962), 341-354.

Buchanan, James M., and Gordon Tullock. *The Calculus of Consent: Logical Foundations of Constitutional Democracy*. Ann Arbor, University of Michigan Press, 1962.

Buchanan, William. "An Inquiry into Purposive Voting." *Journal of Politics*, 18 (1956), 281-296.

Budge, Ian. *Agreement and the Stability of Democracy*. Chicago, Markham Publishing Co., 1970.

Burke, Edmund. *The Works of the Right Honorable Edmund Burke*. 6 vols. The World's Classics, Vol. LXXXI. London, Oxford University Press, 1906.

Burnham, Walter Dean. *Critical Elections and the Mainsprings of American Politics*. New York, Norton, 1970.

Butler, David, and Donald Stokes. *Political Change in Britain: Forces Shaping Electoral Choice*. London, Macmillan, 1969.

Caldwell, Lynton K., ed. *Politics and Public Affairs*. Bloomington, Ind., Institute of Training for Public Service, 1962.

Carlyle, R. W. and A. J. *A History of Medieval Political Theory in the West*. Edinburgh and London, William Blackwood & Sons, 1915, III.

Chambers, William N., and Robert H. Salisbury, eds. *Democracy in the Mid-Twentieth Century: Problems and*

531

Prospects. St. Louis, Mo., Washington University Press, 1960.

Chapman, John W. "Toward a General Theory of Human Nature and Dynamics." In Pennock and Chapman, eds. *Human Nature in Politics,* pp. 292-319.

Cicero, *Republic.*

Cnudde, Charles F., and Donald J. McCrone. "The Linkage between Constituency Attitudes and Congressional Voting Behavior." *American Political Science Review,* 60 (1966), 66-72.

Cochran, Clarke E. "Political Science and 'The Public Interest.'" *Journal of Politics,* 36 (1974), 327-355.

Cohen, Carl. *Democracy.* Athens, Ga., University of Georgia Press, 1971.

Coker, Francis W. "Pluralistic Theories and the Attack upon State Sovereignty." In Merriam and Barnes, eds. *A History of Political Theories,* pp. 80-119.

Cole, G.D.H. *Guild Socialism Re-Stated.* London, Parsons, 1920.

————. *Social Theory,* London, Methuen, 1920.

Coleman, Andrew M., and Ian Pountney. "Voting Paradoxes: A Socratic Dialogue." *Political Quarterly,* 46 (1975), 304-309.

Coleman, James. "Collective Decisions and Collective Actions." In Laslett, Runciman, and Skinner, eds. *Philosophy, Politics, and Society,* pp. 208-219.

Connolly, William E., ed. *The Bias of Pluralism.* New York, Atherton, 1960.

Connor, Walker. "Nation-Building or Nation-Destroying?" *World Politics,* 24 (1972), 319-355.

Converse, Philip. "Public Opinion and Voting Behavior." In Greenstein and Polsby, eds. *Handbook of Political Science,* 4: 75-168.

Cook, Terrence E., and Patrick M. Morgan, eds. *Participatory Democracy.* San Francisco, Canfield Press, 1971.

Cornwall, Elmer. "Coolidge and Presidential Leadership." *Public Opinion Quarterly,* 21 (1957), 265-278.

Coulter, Philip. *Social Mobilization and Liberal Democracy. A Microquantitative Analysis of Global and Regional Models.* Lexington, Mass., Heath, 1975.

Crain, Robert L., and Donald B. Rosenthal. "Structure and Values in Local Political Systems: The Case of Fluoridation Decisions." *Journal of Politics,* 28 (1966), 169-195.

Cumming, Robert Denoon. *Human Nature and History: A Study of the Development of Liberal Political Thought.* Chicago, University of Chicago Press, 1969.

Current Opinion. Roper Public Opinion Research Center, Williams College, Williamstown, Mass. 1, Issue 8 (August 1973).

Cutright, Phillips. "National Political Development: Measurement and Analysis." *American Sociological Review,* 28 (1963), 253-264.

Cyr, A. Bruce. "The Calculus of Voting Reconsidered." *Public Opinion Quarterly,* 39 (1975), 19-38.

Dahl, Robert A. *After the Revolution? Authority in a Good Society.* New Haven, Yale University Press, 1970.

———. "Governments and Political Oppositions." In Greenstein and Polsby, eds. *Handbook of Political Science,* 3: 115-174.

———. *Modern Political Analysis.* Englewood Cliffs, N.J., Prentice-Hall, 1963.

———. *Polyarchy: Participation and Opposition.* New Haven, Yale University Press, 1971.

———. *A Preface to Democratic Theory.* Chicago, University of Chicago Press, 1956.

Daniels, Norman, ed. *Reading Rawls: Critical Studies of "A Theory of Justice."* New York, Basic Books, 1975.

Davies, James C. *Human Nature in Politics: The Dynamics of Political Behavior.* New York, Wiley, 1963.

———. "The Priority of Human Needs and Stages of Political Development." In Pennock and Chapman, eds. *Human Nature in Politics,* pp. 157-196.

Davis, J. Ronnie, and Charles W. Meyer. "Budget Size in

Democracy." *Southern Economic Journal*, 36 (1969), 10-19.

Demsetz, H. "Toward a Theory of Property Rights." *American Economic Review*, 57 (1967), 347-359.

Deutsch, Karl. *The Nerves of Government*. Glencoe, Ill., Free Press, 1963.

DeVries, Walter, and Lance Tarrance, Jr. *The Ticket-Splitter: A New Force in American Politics*. Grand Rapids, Mich., Eerdmans Publishing Co., 1972.

Dewey, John. *Reconstruction in Philosophy*. Enlarged edition. Boston, Mass., Beacon Press, 1966.

A Dictionary of the Social Sciences. Ed. Julius Gould and William L. Kolb. London, Tavistock Publications, 1964.

Dodge, Guy H. *Jean-Jacques Rousseau: Authoritarian Libertarian?* Lexington, Mass., Heath, 1971.

Dorsey, Gray, ed. *Equality and Freedom: International and Comparative Jurisprudence*. Dobbs Ferry, N.Y., Oceana Publications, 1977.

Douglas, Roger. "Economy and Polity in Australia: A Quantification of Common Sense." *British Journal of Political Science*, 5 (1975), 341-361.

Downie, R. S., and Elizabeth Telfer. *Respect for Persons*. London, Allen & Unwin, 1969.

Downs, Anthony. *An Economic Theory of Democracy*. New York, Harper & Row, 1957.

———. "In Defense of Majority Voting." *Quarterly Journal of Economics*, 69 (1961), 192-199.

Dray, W. H. "Holism and Individualism." In *Encyclopedia of Philosophy*, 4: 53-58.

Durkheim, Emile. *The Division of Labor in Society*. Trans. George Simpson. Glencoe, Ill., Free Press, 1947.

———. *Selected Writings*. Ed. and trans. Anthony Giddens. Cambridge, Cambridge University Press, 1972.

Dye, Thomas R. "Malapportionment and Public Policy in the United States." *Journal of Politics*, 27 (1965), 586-601.

Easton, David. *A Systems Analysis of Political Life.* New York, Wiley, 1965.

———, ed. *Varieties of Political Theory.* Englewood Cliffs, N.J., Prentice-Hall, 1966.

Eckstein, Harry. *Division and Cohesion in Democracy: A Study of Norway.* Princeton, Princeton University Press, 1966.

Edel, Abraham. "Humanist Ethics and the Meaning of Human Dignity." In Kurtz, ed. *Moral Problems in Contemporary Society.* Englewood Cliffs, N.J., Prentice-Hall, 1969.

Edelman, Murray. "The State as Provider of Symbolic Outputs." International Political Science Association, IXth World Congress, 19-25 Aug. 1973, nr. 1, 3, 11, p. 1 (mimeographed).

———. *The Symbolic Uses of Politics.* Urbana, University of Illinois Press, 1964.

Elliott, Ward. "The Los Angeles Affliction: Suggestions for a Cure." *The Public Interest* (Summer 1975), 119-128.

Emerson, Rupert. "Nationalism and Political Development." *Journal of Politics,* 22 (1960), 3-28. Reprinted in Millikan and Blackmer, eds. *The Emerging Nations,* pp. 572ff.

Encyclopedia of Philosophy, Paul Edwards, ed. New York, Macmillan and Free Press, 1967.

Encyclopedia of the Social Sciences. Edwin R. A. Seligman and Alvin Johnson, eds. New York, Macmillan, 1937.

Epstein, Leon. "Electoral Decision and Policy Mandate: An Empirical Example." *Public Opinion Quarterly,* 28 (1964), 564-572.

Etzioni, Amitai. "Basic Human Needs, Alienation and Inauthenticity." *American Sociological Review,* 33 (1968), 870-884.

———. "The Fallacy of Decentralization." *The Nation* (August 25, 1969), 145-147.

Eulau, Heinz, and Kenneth Prewitt. *Labyrinths of Democ-*

racy: Adaptations, Linkages, Representation, and Policies in Urban Politics. New York, Bobbs-Merrill, 1973.

————. "Political Matrix and Political Representation: Prolegomenon to a New Departure from an Old Problem." *American Political Science Review*, 63 (1969), 427-441.

Ewing, A. C. *The Individual, the State and World Government.* New York, Macmillan, 1947.

Farquharson, Robin. *Theory of Voting.* New Haven, Yale University Press, 1969.

Feigl, Herbert, and May Brodbeck, eds. *Readings in the Philosophy of Science.* New York, Appleton-Century-Crofts, 1953.

Feinberg, Joel. *Social Philosophy.* Englewood Cliffs, N.J., Prentice-Hall, 1973.

Festinger, Leon. *A Theory of Cognitive Dissonance.* Evanston, Ill., Row, Peterson, 1957.

Feuer, Lewis. *The Conflict of Generations.* New York, Basic Books, 1969.

Field, G. Lowell, and John Higley. "Elites and Non-Elites: The Possibilities and Their Side Effects." Module 13, Warner Modular Publications, Andover, Mass., 1973, pp. 1-38.

Finer, S. E. *Anonymous Empire: A Study of the Lobby in Great Britain.* Rev. ed. London, Pall Mall Press, 1966.

Fiorina, Morris P., and Charles R. Plott. "Committee Decisions Under Majority Rule: An Experimental Study." *American Political Science Review*, 72 (1978), 575-598.

Fishburn, Peter C. "Single-Peaked Preferences and Probabilities of Cyclical Majorities." *Behavioral Science*, 19 (1974), 21-27.

Fitzgibbon, Russell H. "Measuring Democratic Change in Latin America." *Journal of Politics*, 29 (1967), 129-166.

Flathman, Richard E. *The Public Interest: An Essay Concerning the Normative Discourse of Politics.* New York, Wiley, 1966.

Follett, Mary Parker. *Creative Experience.* New York, Longmans, 1924.

————. *The New State: Group Organization and Popular Government.* London, Longmans, Green, 1926.

Friedland, Edward I. "Introduction to the Concept of Rationality in Political Science." University Programs Modular Series. Morristown, N.J., General Learning Press, 1974.

Friedrich, Carl J., ed. *The Public Interest*, NOMOS V. New York, Atherton Press, 1962.

Friedrich, Carl Joachim. *Man and His Government.* New York, McGraw-Hill, 1963.

Furubotn, Eirik G., and Svetozar Pejovich. *The Economics of Property Rights.* Cambridge, Mass., Ballinger, 1975.

Fyfe, Hamilton. "Leadership and Democracy." *The Nineteenth Century and After*, 129 (1941), 465-484.

The Gallup Opinion Index. American Institute of Public Opinion, Princeton, N.J., March 1973 and June 1975.

The Gallup Poll—Public Opinion, 1935-1971. New York, Random House, 1972.

Gardiner, Patrick, ed. *Theories of History.* Glencoe, Ill., Free Press, 1959.

Garvin, Lucius. *A Modern Introduction to Ethics.* Boston, Houghton Mifflin, 1953.

Gauthier, David. "Justice and Natural Endowment: Toward a Critique of Rawls' Ideological Framework." *Social Theory and Practice*, 3 (1974), 3-26.

Gellner, Ernest. "Holism versus Individualism in History and Sociology." In Gardiner, ed. *Theories of History*, pp. 489-503.

Gerth, H. H., and C. W. Mills, eds. *From Max Weber: Essays in Sociology*, New York, Oxford University Press, 1946.

Gibb, Cecil A. "Leadership." In *International Encyclopedia of the Social Sciences*, 9: 91-100.

Gilbert, Charles E. "Two Academic Models." In Caldwell, ed. *Politics and Public Affairs*, pp. 55-89.

537

Glass, S. T. *The Responsible Society—The Ideas of Guild Socialism*. London, Longmans, 1966.

Goldschmidt, Maure L. "Rousseau on Intermediate Associations." In Pennock and Chapman, eds. *Voluntary Associations*, pp. 119-137.

Goodin, Robert E. "Cross-Cutting Cleavages and Social Conflict." *British Journal of Political Science*, 5 (1975), 516-519.

Gough, J. W. *John Locke's Political Philosophy*. Oxford, Clarendon Press, 1950.

Gouldner, Alvin W., ed. *Studies in Leadership: Leadership and Democratic Action*. New York, Harper & Row, 1950.

Graham, A. C. "Liberty and Equality." *Mind*, 74 (1965), 59-65.

Green, Thomas Hill. *Works*. 3rd ed. Vol. 3. London, Longmans, Green, 1891.

Greenstein, Fred I., and Nelson W. Polsby, eds. *Handbook of Political Science*. Vols. 3, 4. Reading, Mass., Addison-Wesley, 1975.

Griffiths, A. Phillips. "How Can One Person Represent Another?" *Aristotelian Society*, Supplementary Vol. 34 (1960), 182-208.

Halévy, Elie. *The Growth of Philosophical Radicalism*. New York, Macmillan, 1928.

Hanson, Royce. *The Political Thicket: Reapportionment and Constitutional Democracy*. Englewood Cliffs, N.J., Prentice-Hall, 1966.

Harsanyi, John C. "Cardinal Welfare, Individualistic Ethics, and Interpersonal Comparisons of Utility." *Journal of Political Economy*, 63 (1965), 309-321.

———. "Rational-Choice Models vs. Functionalistic and Conformistic Models of Political Behavior." *World Politics*, 21 (1969), 513-538.

Havelock, Eric A. *The Liberal Temper of Greek Politics*. New Haven, Yale University Press, 1957.

538

Hayek, F. A. *The Constitution of Liberty.* Chicago, University of Chicago Press, 1960.

———. *Law, Legislation, and Liberty: A New Statement of the Liberal Principles of Justice and Political Economy.* Vol. 2, *The Mirage of Social Justice.* Chicago, University of Chicago Press, 1976.

Hedlund, Ronald D., and H. Paul Friesema. "Representatives' Perceptions of Constituency Opinion." *Journal of Politics,* 34 (1972), 730-752.

Hegel, G.W.F. *The Phenomenology of Mind.* Trans. J. B. Bailie. New York and Evanston, Ill., Harper & Row, Harper Torchbooks, 1967.

Hegel, Georg Wilhelm Friedrich. *The Philosophy of History.* Trans. J. Sebree. Rev. ed. New York, Wiley, 1900.

———. *The Philosophy of Right.* Trans. Knox. Oxford, Clarendon Press, 1949.

Held, Virginia, *The Public Interest and Individual Interests.* New York, Basic Books, 1970.

Herodotus. *History of the Persian Wars.* Trans. Rawlinson. Modern Library edition, New York, Random House, 1942.

Hobbes, Thomas. *De Cive, or the Citizen.* Ed. Sterling P. Lamprecht. New York, Appleton-Century-Crofts, 1949.

———. *Leviathan.* Ed. Oakeshott. Oxford, Basil Blackwell, 1946.

Hocking, William Ernest. *Man and the State,* New Haven, Yale University Press, 1926.

Holden, Barry. *The Nature of Democracy.* New York, Barnes & Noble, 1974.

Homans, George C. *The Nature of Social Science.* New York, Harcourt, Brace and World, 1970.

———. *Social Behavior.* London, Routledge and Kegan Paul, 1961.

Hook, Sidney. "The Philosophical Presuppositions of Democracy." *Ethics,* 52 (1942), 275-296.

Hoselitz, Bert F., and Myron Weiner. "Economic Development and Political Stability in India." *Dissent*, 8 (1961), 172-179.

Hsu, Francis L. K., ed. *Psychology and Anthropology*. Homewood, Ill., Dorsey Press, 1961.

Humboldt, Wilhelm von. *The Limits of State Action*. Ed. J. W. Burrow. Cambridge, Cambridge University Press, 1969.

Hume, David. *An Enquiry Concerning the Principles of Morals*. LaSalle, Ill., Open Court, 1947.

———. *Treatise of Human Nature*. Ed. L. A. Selby-Bigge. Oxford, Clarendon Press, 1896.

Huntington, Samuel P. *Political Order in Changing Societies*. New Haven, Yale University Press, 1968.

Inkeles, Alex. "Making Modern Men: On the Causes and Consequences of Industrial Change in Six Developing Countries." *American Journal of Sociology*, 75 (1969), 208-225.

———. "National Character and Modern Political Systems." In Hsu, ed. *Psychology and Anthropology*, Chap. 6.

International Encyclopedia of the Social Sciences. Ed. David L. Sills, New York, Macmillan and Free Press, 1968.

Ionescu, Ghita, and Ernest Gellner, eds. *Populism*. London, Weidenfeld and Nicolson, 1969.

Jackman, Roger W. *Politics and Social Equality*. New York, Wiley, 1974.

Jackson, John E. "Issues, Party Choices and Presidential Votes." *American Journal of Political Science*, 19 (1975), 161-185.

Janowitz, Morris, and Dwaine Marvick. "Competitive Pressure and Democratic Consent, an Interpretation of the 1952 Election." *Public Opinion Quarterly*, 19 (1955/56), 381-401.

Johnson, Nevil. "The Place of Institutions in the Study of Politics." *Political Studies*, 23 (1975), 271-283.

Jones, Bryan D. "Competitiveness, Role Orientations, and Legislative Responsiveness." *Journal of Politics*, 35 (1974), 924-947.

Jouvenal, Bertrand de. *Sovereignty: An Inquiry into the Political Good.* Trans. J. F. Huntington. Cambridge, Cambridge University Press, 1957.

Just, Marion R. "Causal Models of Voter Rationality: Great Britain, 1959 and 1962." *Political Studies*, 21 (1973), 45-56.

Kant, Immanuel. *Critique of Pure Reason.* Trans. Kemp Smith. London, Macmillan, 1953.

———. *The Metaphysics of Ethics.* Trans. Semple. Edinburgh, Clark, 1886.

Kanter, Rosabeth Moss. "Some Issues in the Community Development Corporation Proposal." In Benello and Roussopoulos, eds. *The Case for Participatory Democracy*, pp. 65-71.

Kariel, Henry S. *The Decline of American Pluralism.* Stanford, Cal., Stanford University Press, 1961.

———, ed. *Frontiers of Democratic Theory.* New York, Random House, 1970.

———. *Open Systems: Arenas for Political Action.* Itasca, Ill., Peacock Publishers, 1969.

———. *The Promise of Politics.* Englewood Cliffs, N.J., Prentice-Hall, 1966.

Keim, Donald W. "Participation in Contemporary Democratic Theories." In Pennock and Chapman, eds. *Participation in Politics*, pp. 1-38.

Kendall, Willmoore. *John Locke and the Doctrine of Majority-Rule.* Urbana, University of Illinois Press, 1941.

Kendall, Wilmoore, and George W. Carey. "The 'Intensity' Problem and Democratic Theory." *American Political Science Review*, 62 (1968), 5-24.

Key, V. O., Jr. *Public Opinion and American Democracy.* New York, Knopf, 1961.

———. *The Responsible Electorate: Rationality in Presi-*

dential Voting, 1936-60. Cambridge, Mass., Harvard University Press, 1966.

Kohlberg, Lawrence, and Carol Gilligan. "The Adolescent as a Philosopher: The Discovery of the Self in a Post-Conventional World." *Daedalus,* 100 (Fall 1971), 1051-1086.

Kovenock, David M., Philip L. Beardsley, and James W. Prothro. "Status, Ideology, Issues, and Candidate Choice: A Preliminary Theory-Relevant Analysis of the 1968 American Presidential Election." Specialist Meeting B:XI, Eighth World Congress of the International Political Science Association, Munich, 31 August-5 September 1970.

Kramer, Gerald E. "Some Procedural Aspects of Majority Rule." In Pennock and Chapman, eds. *Due Process,* pp. 264-295.

————. "Short-Term Fluctuations in U. S. Voting Behavior, 1896-1964." *American Political Science Review,* 65 (1971), 131-143.

Kuflik, Arthur. "Majority Rule Procedure." In Pennock and Chapman, eds. *Due Process,* pp. 296-332.

Kurtz, Paul, ed. *Moral Problems in Contemporary Society.* Englewood Cliffs, N.J., Prentice-Hall, 1969.

Ladd, Everett Carll, Jr., with Charles D. Hadley. *Transformations of the American Party System.* New York, Norton, 1975.

Laslett, Peter, and W. G. Runciman, eds. *Philosophy, Politics, and Society.* 3rd series. Oxford, Basil Blackwell, 1967.

Laslett, Peter, W. G. Runciman, and Quentin Skinner, eds. *Philosophy, Politics, and Society.* 4th series. New York, Barnes & Noble, 1972.

Lasswell, Harold D., and Abraham Kaplan. *Power and Society: A Framework for Political Inquiry.* New Haven, Yale University Press, 1950.

Leibenstein, Harvey. "Notes on Welfare Economics and the

Theory of Democracy." *Economic Journal,* 72 (1962), 299-319.

Lemos, Ramon. "A Moral Argument for Democracy." *Social Theory and Practice,* 4 (1976), 57-79.

Lerner, Daniel. *The Passing of Traditional Society.* Glencoe, Ill., Free Press, 1958.

Lerner, Max. *America as a Civilization.* New York, Simon & Schuster, 1957.

Lewis, Ewart. *Medieval Political Ideas.* New York, Knopf, 1954.

Leys, Wayne A. R., and Charner Perry. *Philosophy and the Public Interest.* Chicago, Committee to Advance Original Work in Philosophy, 1959.

Lindblom, Charles E. *The Intelligence of Democracy: Decision Making through Mutual Adjustment.* New York, Free Press, 1965.

―――. *Politics and Markets: The World's Political-Economic Systems.* New York, Basic Books, 1977.

Lindsay, A. D. *The Essentials of Democracy.* Philadelphia, University of Pennsylvania Press, 1929.

Lipman, Matthew. "Some Aspects of Simmel's Conception of the Individual." In Simmel. *Essays on Sociology, Philosophy, and Aesthetics,* pp. 119-183.

Lippmann, Walter. *The Essential Lippmann: A Political Philosophy for Liberal Democracy.* Ed. Clinton Rossiter and James Lare. New York, Random House, 1963.

―――. *The Phantom Public.* New York, Harcourt, Brace, 1925.

―――. *The Public Philosophy.* Boston, Little, Brown, 1955.

Lipset, Seymour Martin. *The First New Nation.* New York, Basic Books, 1963.

―――. *Politics and the Social Sciences.* New York, Oxford University Press, 1969.

Little, I.M.D. *A Critique of Welfare Economics.* 2nd ed. Oxford, Clarendon Press, 1957.

Lively, Jack. *Democracy.* Oxford, Basil Blackwell, 1975.

Locke, John. *Two Treatises of Government*. Ed. Laslett. Cambridge, Cambridge University Press, 1960.

Lowe, Francis E., and Thomas C. McCormick. "A Study of the Influence of Formal and Informal Leaders in an Election Campaign." *Public Opinion Quarterly*, 20 (1957), 651-662.

Lowi, Theodore J. *The End of Liberalism*, New York, Norton, 1969.

———. *The Politics of Disorder*, New York, Basic Books, 1971.

Lucas, J. R. "Against Equality." *Philosophy*, 40 (1965), 296-307.

———. "Against Equality Again." *Philosophy*, 52 (1977), 255-280.

———. *The Principles of Politics*. Oxford, Clarendon Press, 1966.

Lukes, Stephen. "Alienation and Anomie." In Laslett and Runciman, eds. *Philosophy, Politics, and Society*. 3rd series, pp. 134-156.

———. *Individualism*. New York, Harper & Row, Harper Torchbooks, 1973.

Lyons, David. "The Weakness of Formal Equality." *Ethics*, 76 (1966), 146-148.

Lytle, Bradford. "After Washington?—Three Views." In Committee for Nonviolent Action *Bulletin*, 27 August 1965, 408.

Macaluso, Theodore F. "Parameters of 'Rational' Voting: Vote Switching in the 1968 Election." *Journal of Politics*, 37 (1975), 202-234.

Macleod, A. M. "Equality of Opportunity: Some Ambiguities in the Ideal." In Dorsey, ed. *Equality and Freedom: International and Comparative Jurisprudence*, 3: 1077-1084.

Macpherson, C. B. *Democratic Theory: Essays in Retrieval*. Oxford, Clarendon Press, 1973.

———. *The Life and Times of Liberal Democracy*. Oxford, Oxford University Press, 1977.

544

————. *The Real World of Democracy*. Oxford, Clarendon Press, 1966.

Mandelbaum, Maurice. *History, Man, and Reason*. Baltimore, Johns Hopkins University Press, 1971.

————. "Societal Facts." In Gardiner, ed. *Theories of History*, pp. 476-488.

Marcuse, Herbert. "Repressive Tolerance." In Wolff, Moore, and Marcuse. *A Critique of Pure Tolerance*, pp. 81-117.

Marshall, Geoffrey. "Enforcing Equality: Two Statutory Attempts." In Dorsey, ed. *Freedom and Equality*, 3: 933-939.

Marx, Karl. *Capital*. Trans. from 3rd German edition by Samuel Moore and Edwin Aveling. Ed. Friedrich Engels, revised and simplified according to 4th German edition by Ernest Untermann. New York, Modern Library, 1906.

Maslow, A. H. *Motivation and Personality*. New York, Harper & Row, 1954.

Mayo, H. B. *An Introduction to Democratic Theory*. New York, Oxford University Press, 1960.

McCallum, R. B., and Alison Readman. *The British General Election of 1945*. London, Oxford University Press, 1947.

McCrone, Donald J., and Charles F. Cnudde. "Toward a Communications Theory of Democratic Political Development: A Causal Model." *American Political Science Review*, 61 (1967), 72-80.

McKeon, Richard, ed. *Democracy in a World of Tensions*. Chicago, University of Chicago Press, 1951.

Mead, George H. *Mind, Self, and Society*. Ed., with introduction by Charles W. Morris. Chicago, University of Chicago Press, 1934.

Megill, Kenneth A. "The Community in Marx's Philosophy." *Philosophy and Phenomenological Research*, 30 (1970), 382-395.

Melanson, Philip H., and Lauriston R. King. "Theory in

Comparative Politics: A Critical Appraisal." *Comparative Political Studies*, 4 (1971), 205-231.

Merriam, Charles E., and H. E. Barnes, eds. *A History of Political Theories—Recent Times*. New York, Macmillan, 1924.

Mill, John Stuart. *A System of Logic*. 7th ed. London, Longmans, 1868.

———. *Utilitarianism, Liberty, and Representative Government*. New York, Dutton, 1926.

Miller, David L. *Individualism: Personal Achievement and the Open Society*. Austin, University of Texas Press, 1967.

Miller, Warren. "Majority Rule and the Representative System of Government." In Allardt and Littunen, eds. *Cleavages, Ideologies and Party Systems*, pp. 345-376.

Miller, Warren E. "Party Government and the Saliency of Democracy." *Public Opinion Quarterly*, 26 (1962), 531-546.

Miller, Warren E. and Donald E. Stokes. "Constituency Influence in Congress." *American Political Science Review*, 57 (1963), 45-56.

Millikan, Max F., and Donald L. M. Blackmer, eds. *The Emerging Nations: Their Growth and United States Policy*. Boston, Mass., Little, Brown, 1961.

Milne, A.J.M. *Freedom and Rights: A Philosophical Synthesis*. New York, Humanities Press, 1968.

Mises, Ludwig von. *Human Action—A Treatise on Economics*. London, Hodge, 1949.

Mogi, Sobei. *Otto von Gierke*. London, King, 1932.

Murakami, Y. *Logic and Social Choice*. New York, Dover Publications, 1968.

Nagel, Thomas. *The Possibility of Altruism*. Oxford, Clarendon Press, 1970.

Natchez, P. B., and J. C. Bupp. "Candidates, Issues and Voters." *Public Policy*, 17 (1968), 409-437.

Nathan, N.M.L. "On the Justification of Democracy." *The Monist*, 55 (1971), 88-120.

Neubauer, Deane E. "Some Conditions of Democracy." *American Political Science Review*, 61 (1967), 1002-1009.

Newton, Lisa H. "The Community and the Cattle-Pen: An Analysis of Participation." In Pennock and Chapman, eds. *Participation in Politics*, pp. 233-245.

Nie, Norman H., and Kristi Anderson. "Mass Belief Systems Revisited: Political Change and Attitude Structure." *Journal of Politics*, 36 (1974), 540-591.

Nie, Norman H., G. Bingham Powell, Jr., and Kenneth Prewitt. "Social Structure and Political Participation: Developmental Relationships, II." *American Political Science Review*, 63 (1969), 808-828.

Nie, Norman H., and Sidney Verba. "Political Participation." In Greenstein and Polsby, eds. *Handbook of Political Science*, 4: 1-74.

Nisbet, Robert A. *The Sociological Tradition*. New York, Basic Books, 1966.

Nozick, Robert. *Anarchy, State, and Utopia*. New York, Basic Books, 1974.

Oakeshott, Michael. *On Human Conduct*. Oxford, Clarendon Press, 1975.

Olafson, Frederick A. *Principles and Persons: An Ethical Interpretation of Existentialism*. Baltimore, Johns Hopkins University Press, 1967.

Ollman, Bertell. *Alienation: Marx's Conception of Man in Capitalist Society*. Cambridge, Cambridge University Press, 1971.

Olson, Mancur, Jr. *The Logic of Collective Action: Public Goods and the Theory of Groups*. Cambridge, Mass., Harvard University Press, 1965.

―――. "The Relationship between Economics and the Other Social Sciences: The Province of a 'Social Report.'" In Lipset, ed. *Politics and the Social Sciences*, pp. 137-162.

O'Neill, John, ed. *Modes of Individualism and Collectivism*. London, Heinemann, 1973.

Oppenheim, Felix E. "Democracy—Characteristics Included and Excluded." *The Monist,* 55 (1971), 29-50.

———. *Dimensions of Freedom.* New York, St. Martin's Press, 1961.

Oppenheimer, Martin. "The Limitations of Socialism." In Benello and Roussopoulos, eds. *The Case for Participatory Democracy,* pp. 271-282.

Orbell, John M., and L. A. Wilson, II. "Institutional Solutions to the N-Prisoners' Dilemma." *American Political Science Review,* 72 (1978), 411-421.

Ordeshook, Peter C. "Extensions to a Model of the Electoral Process and Implications for the Theory of Responsible Parties." *Midwest Journal of Political Science,* 14 (1970), 43-70.

Paige, Glenn D. *The Scientific Study of Leadership.* New York, Free Press, 1977.

Parent, William A. "Some Recent Work on the Concept of Liberty." *American Philosophical Quarterly,* 11 (1974) 149-167.

Parenti, Michael J. *Democracy for the Few.* New York, St. Martin's, 1974.

Pareto, Vilfredo. *The Mind and Society.* Vol. 4. Ed. Arthur Livingston. New York, Harcourt, Brace, 1935.

Partridge, P. H. *Consent and Consensus.* New York, Praeger, 1971.

Pateman, Carole. *Participation and Democratic Theory.* Cambridge, Cambridge University Press, 1970.

Pennock, J. Roland. "Democracy and Leadership." in William N. Chambers and Robert H. Salisbury, eds. *Democracy in the Mid-Twentieth Century,* pp. 122-158.

———. "Hobbes's Confusing 'Clarity'—The Case of 'Liberty.'" In Brown, ed. *Hobbes Studies,* Chap. 5.

———. *Liberal Democracy: Its Merits and Prospects.* New York, Rinehart, 1950; reprinted by Greenwood Press, Westport, Conn., 1978.

———. "The 'Pork Barrel' and Majority Rule: A Note." *Journal of Politics,* 32 (1970), 709-716.

―――. " 'Responsible Government,' Separated Powers and Special Interests: Agricultural Subsidies in Britain and America." *American Political Science Review*, 56 (1962), 621-633.

Pennock, J. Roland, and John W. Chapman eds. *Due Process*, NOMOS XVIII. New York, New York University Press, 1977.

―――. *Equality*, NOMOS IX. New York, Atherton, 1967.

―――. *Human Nature in Politics*, NOMOS XVII. New York, New York University Press, 1977.

―――. *Participation in Politics*, NOMOS XVI. New York, Lieber-Atherton, 1975.

―――. *Privacy*, NOMOS XIV. New York, Aldine, 1971.

―――. *Representation*, NOMOS X. New York, Atherton, 1968, Chap. 1.

―――. *Voluntary Associations*, NOMOS XI. New York, Lieber-Atherton, 1969.

Penrose, L. S. "The Elementary Statistics of Majority Voting." *Journal of the Royal Statistical Society*, 109 (1946), 53-57.

Perry, Ralph Barton. *Puritanism and Democracy*. New York, Vanguard Press, 1944.

Petrullo, Luigi, and Bernard M. Bass, eds. *Leadership and Interpersonal Behavior*. New York, Holt, 1961.

Pigors, Paul. *Leadership or Domination*. Cambridge, Mass., Houghton Mifflin, 1935.

Pitkin, Hanna Fenichel. *The Concept of Representation*. Berkeley and Los Angeles, University of California Press, 1967.

Plamenatz, John. "Democracy." In Richard McKeon, ed. *Democracy in a World of Tensions*, pp. 302-327.

―――. *Democracy and Illusion*. London, Longmans, 1973.

―――. "Electoral Studies and Democratic Theory, I: A British View." *Political Studies*, 6 (1958), 1-9.

―――. *Man and Society*. New York, McGraw-Hill, 1963.

―――. "Some American Images of Democracy." In *The Great Ideas Today, 1968*, eds. R. M. Hutchins and

M. J. Adler. Chicago, Encyclopedia Britannica, 1968, pp. 251-300.

Plato. *The Republic of Plato.* Trans. Cornford. New York, Oxford University Press, 1945.

Playford, John, and Charles A. McCoy. *Apolitical Politics: A Critique of Behavioralism.* New York, Crowell, 1967.

Pomper, Gerald M. *Elections in America: Control and Influence in Democratic Politics.* New York, Dodd, Mead, 1968.

―――. "From Confusion to Clarity: Issues and American Voters, 1956-1968." *American Political Science Review,* 66 (1972), 415-428.

―――. *Voters' Choice: Varieties of American Electoral Behavior.* New York, Dodd, Mead, 1968.

Pranger, Robert J. *The Eclipse of Citizenship: Power and Participation in Contemporary Politics.* New York, Holt, 1968.

Pride, Richard A. *Origins of Democracy: A Cross-National Study of Mobilization, Party Systems, and Democratic Stability.* Beverly Hills, Cal., Sage Publications, 1970.

Prothro, James, and Charles M. Grigg. "Fundamental Principles of Democracy: Bases of Agreement and Disagreement." *Journal of Politics,* 22 (1960), 276-294.

Putnam, Robert E. *Politicians and Politics: Themes in British and Italian Elite Political Culture.* New Haven, Yale University Press, 1970.

Pye, Lucian. *Personality and Nation Building: Burma's Search for Identity.* New Haven, Yale University Press, 1962.

Rabushka, Alvin, and Kenneth A. Shepsle. *Plural Politics in Plural Societies.* Columbus, O., Merrill, 1972.

Rae, Douglas. "Decision-Rules and Individual Values in Constitutional Choice." *American Political Science Review,* 63 (1969), 40-56.

―――. "Political Democracy as a Property of Political Institutions." *American Political Science Review,* 65 (1971), 111-119.

Rae, Douglas W., and Michael Taylor. *The Analysis of Political Cleavages*. New Haven, Yale University Press, 1970.

Raphael, D. D. *Moral Judgement*. London, Allen & Unwin, 1955.

Rawls, John. *A Theory of Justice*. Cambridge, Mass., Harvard University Press, 1971.

RePass, David E. "Issue Salience and Party Choice." *American Political Science Review*, 65 (1971), 389-400.

Resnick, David. "Due Process and Procedural Justice." In Pennock and Chapman, eds. *Due Process*, Chap. 7.

Richards, David A. J. *A Theory of Reasons for Action*. Oxford, Clarendon Press, 1971.

Riker, William H. *Government in the United States*. New York, Macmillan, 1953.

———. "Voting and the Summation of Preferences: An Interpretative Bibliographical Review of Selected Developments During the Last Decade." *American Political Science Review*, 55 (1961), 900-911.

Riker, William H., and Peter C. Ordeshook. *An Introduction to Positive Political Theory*. Englewood Cliffs, N.J., Prentice-Hall, 1973.

———. "A Theory of the Calculus of Voting." *American Political Science Review*, 62 (1968), 25-42.

Riker, William H., and Steven J. Rams. "The Paradox of Vote Trading." *American Political Science Review*, 67 (1973), 1235-1247.

Ripley, Randall B. *Party Leaders in the House of Representatives*. Washington, D.C., Brookings, 1967.

Rogowski, Ronald. *Rational Legitimacy: A Theory of Political Support*. Princeton, Princeton University Press, 1974.

Rose, Richard. *Politics in England*. 2nd ed. Boston, Little, Brown, 1974.

Rothenberg, Jerome. *The Measurement of Social Welfare*. Englewood Cliffs, N.J., Prentice-Hall, 1961.

Rousseau, Jean-Jacques. *Émile*. Trans. Barbara Foxley. London, Dent, n.d.

———. *The Political Writings of Jean-Jacques Rousseau*. Ed. C. E. Vaughan. Oxford, Blackwell, 1962.

———. *The Social Contract and Discourses*. Trans. G.D.H. Cole. Everyman's Library. London, Dent, 1923.

Russett, Bruce M. "Inequality and Instability: The Relation of Land Tenure to Politics." *World Politics*, 16 (1964), 442-454.

———. *Trends in World Politics*. New York, Macmillan, 1965.

Russett, Bruce M., and others. *World Handbook of Political and Social Indicators*. New Haven, Yale University Press, 1964.

Rustow, Dankwart A. *A World of Nations: Problems of Political Modernization*. Washington, D.C., Brookings, 1967.

Sabine, George H. "The Two Democratic Traditions." *Philosophical Review*, 61 (1952), 451-474.

Sait, E. M. *Democracy*. New York, Appleton-Century-Crofts, 1929.

"Sartre at Seventy: An Interview." *New York Review of Books*, 7 Aug. 1975, 10-17.

Saseen, Robert F. "Freedom as an End of Politics." *Interpretation: A Journal of Political Philosophy*, 2 (1971), 105-125.

Schaff, Lawrence A. *Participation in the Western Political Tradition: A Study of Theory and Practice*. Tucson, Ariz., University of Arizona Press, 1975.

Schmidt, Richard. "Leadership." In *Encyclopedia of the Social Sciences*, 9: 282-287.

Schofield, Norman. "Ethical Decision Rules for Uncertain Voters." *British Journal of Political Science*, 2 (1972), 193-207.

Schumpeter, Joseph A. *Capitalism, Socialism, and Democracy*. New York, Harper & Row, 1942.

Schwartz, Sayre P., and S. I. Edokpayi. "Economic Attitudes

of Nigerian Businessmen." *Nigerian Journal of Economic and Social Studies*, 4 (1962), 257-268.

Schwartz, Thomas. "Collective Choice, Separation of Issues and Vote Trading." *American Political Science Review*, 58 (1964), 876-887.

Scoble, Harry M. "Yankeetown: Leadership in Three Decision-making Processes." Mimeographed, paper presented at the annual meetings of the American Political Science Association, 6-8 Sep. 1956.

Scott, Robert E. *Mexican Government in Transition*. Urbana, University of Illinois Press, 1959.

Self, Peter, and Herbert J. Storing. *The State and the Farmer*. London, Allen & Unwin, 1962.

Seliger, M. *The Liberal Politics of John Locke*. London, Allen & Unwin, 1968.

Seligman, Lester G. "Leadership." In *International Encyclopedia of the Social Sciences*, 9: 107-113.

Sen, Amartya K. *Collective Choice and Social Welfare*. San Francisco, Holden-Day, 1970.

————. "Rawls versus Bentham: An Axiomatic Examination of the Pure Distribution Problem." In Daniels, ed. *Reading Rawls*, pp. 283-292.

Shaffer, William R., and Ronald E. Weber. "Political Responsiveness in the American States." Paper delivered at the annual meetings of the American Political Science Association, Washington, D.C., 5-9 Sep. 1972.

Shapiro, Michael J. "Rational Political Man: A Synthesis of Economic and Social-Psychological Perspectives." *American Political Science Review*, 63 (1969), 1106-1119.

Shepsle, Kenneth A. "Theories of Collective Choice." In *Political Science Annual*, 5 (1974), ed. Cornelius P. Cotter. Indianapolis and New York, Bobbs-Merrill, 1974, pp. 22-44.

Shils, Edward. *Political Development in the New States*. The Hague, Mouton, 1962.

Shklar, Judith N. *Freedom and Independence: A Study of*

the Political Ideas of Hegel's "Phenomenology of Mind." Cambridge, Cambridge University Press, 1976.

Simmel, George. *Essays on Sociology, Philosophy, and Aesthetics.* Ed. Kurt H. Wolff. New York, Harper & Row, 1965.

Simon, Herbert. *Models of Man: Social and Rational; Mathematical Essays on Human Behavior in a Social Setting.* New York, Wiley, 1957.

Simon, Yves. *Freedom and Community.* New York, Fordham University Press, 1968.

Skinner, B. F. *Beyond Freedom and Dignity.* New York, Knopf, 1971.

Skinner, Quentin. "The Empirical Theorists of Democracy and Their Critics: A Plague on Both Their Houses." *Political Theory,* 1 (1973), 287-306.

Spengler, J. J. "Economic Development: Political Preconditions and Political Consequences." *Journal of Politics,* 22 (1960), 387-416.

Stigler, George J. "Economic Competition and Political Competition." *Public Choice,* 13 (1972), 91-106.

Stockman, David A. "The Social Pork Barrel." *The Public Interest,* Spring 1975, 3-30.

Stokes, Donald E. "Area and Party in Representation: Britain and the United States." Mimeographed, paper presented at the annual meetings of the American Political Science Association, Chicago, 5-9 Sep. 1967.

Stokes, Donald E., and Warren E. Miller. "Party Government and the Saliency of Congress." *Public Opinion Quarterly,* 26 (1962), 531-546.

Stone, Julius. "Justice in the Slough of Equality." Mimeographed, paper presented to the World Congress on Philosophy of Law and Social Philosophy, Sydney and Canberra, 14-21 Aug. 1977.

Strawson, P. F. *Individuals.* London, Methuen, 1965.

———. "Social Morality and Individual Ideals." *Philosophy,* 36 (1961), 1-17.

Sullivan, John L., and Robert E. O'Connor. "Electoral

Choice and Popular Control." *Comparative Political Studies*, 2 (1969), 7-67.

Sundquist, James L. *Politics and Policy: The Eisenhower, Kennedy, and Johnson Years.* Washington, D.C., Brookings, 1968.

Tannenbaum, Arnold S. "Leadership." In *International Encyclopedia of the Social Sciences*, 9: 101-105.

Tawney, R. H. *Equality.* New York, Harcourt, Brace, 1931.

Thompson, Dennis F. *The Democratic Citizen.* Cambridge, Cambridge University Press, 1970.

Thucydides, *History of the Peloponnesian War.* Trans. Richard Crawley. New York, Dutton, 1910.

Thursz, Daniel, "Community Participation—Should the Past Be Prologue?" *American Behavioral Scientist*, 15 (1972), 733-748.

Times Guide to the House of Commons, 1966. London, Times Office, n.d.

Tocqueville, Alexis de. *Democracy in America.* 2 vols. Ed. Phillips Bradley. New York, Knopf, 1945.

Tribe, Laurence H. *American Constitutional Law.* Mineola, N.Y., Foundation Press, 1968.

Tufte, Edward R. "Determinants of the Outcomes of Midterm Congressional Elections." *American Political Science Review*, 69 (1975), 812-826.

Tullock, Gordon. *Entrepreneurial Politics.* Research Monograph 5, processed. The Thomas Jefferson Center for Studies in Political Economy, University of Virginia, February 1962.

Turner, Julius. *Party and Constituency: Pressures on Congress.* Baltimore, Johns Hopkins University Press, 1951.

Ulich, Robert. *Education of Nations.* Cambridge, Mass., Harvard University Press, 1961.

Ulmer, S. Sidney, ed. *Political Decision-Making.* New York, Van Nostrand-Reinhold, 1970.

Unger, Roberto Mangabeira. *Knowledge and Politics.* New York, Free Press, 1975.

Uslaner, Eric M., and J. Ronnie Davis. "The Paradox of

Vote Trading: Effects of Decision Rules and Voting Strategies on Externalities." *American Political Science Review*, 69 (1975), 929-942.

Verba, Sidney, and Norman H. Nie. *Participation in America—Political Democracy and Social Equality*. New York, Harper & Row, 1972.

Wahlke, John C. "Policy Determinants and Legislative Decisions." In Ulmer, ed. *Political Decision-Making*, pp. 76-120.

Wahlke, John C., Heinz Eulau, William Buchanan, and LeRoy C. Ferguson. *The Legislative System*. New York, Wiley, 1962.

Ward, James F. "Toward a Sixth Party System? Partisanship and Political Development." *Western Political Quarterly*, 26 (1973), 385-413.

Warrender, Howard. *The Political Philosophy of Hobbes: His Theory of Obligation*. Oxford, Clarendon Press, 1960.

Watkins, J.W.N. "Historical Explanation in the Social Sciences." In Gardiner, ed. *Theories of History*, pp. 503-514.

———. "Ideal Types and Historical Explanation." In Feigl and Brodbeck, eds. *Readings in Philosophy of Science*, pp. 723-743.

Wertheimer, Alan. "In Defense of Compulsory Voting." In Pennock and Chapman, eds. *Participation in Politics*, pp. 276-296.

Wheeler, Harvey. *The Politics of Revolution*. Berkeley, Cal., Glendessary Press, 1971.

Wild, John. "Authentic Experience." *Ethics*, 75 (1965), 227-239.

Wilson, James Q., and Edward G. Banfield. *City Politics*. New York, Vintage Books, 1963.

———. "Public-Regardingness as a Value Premise in Voting Behavior." *American Political Science Review*, 58 (1964), 876-887.

Winham, Gilbert P. "Political Development and Lerner's

Theory: Further Test of a Causal Model." *American Political Science Review*, 64 (1970), 810-818.

Winter, Gibson. *Elements for a Social Ethic*. New York, Macmillan, 1966.

Wolff, Robert Paul. *In Defense of Anarchism*. New York, Harper & Row, Harper Torchbooks, 1970.

———. *The Poverty of Liberalism*. Boston, Beacon Press, 1968.

Wolff, Robert Paul, Barrington Moore, Jr., and Herbert Marcuse. *A Critique of Pure Tolerance*. Boston, Beacon Press, 1969.

Wood, Ellen Meiksins. *Mind and Politics: An Approach to the Meaning of Liberal and Social Individualism*. Berkeley and Los Angeles, University of California Press, 1972.

Woodhouse, A.S.P., ed. *Puritanism and Liberty*. Chicago, University of Chicago Press, 1951.

Wootton, Barbara. *Freedom under Planning*. Chapel Hill, University of North Carolina Press, 1945.

Worsley, Peter. "The Concept of Populism." In Ionescu and Gellner, eds. *Populism*, Chap. 10.

Wright, Georg Henrik, von. *Explanation and Understanding*. Ithaca, N.Y., Cornell University Press, 1971.

Yankelovich, Daniel. "The Idea of Human Nature." *Social Research*, 40 (1973), 407-428.

Index

LIBRARY OF CONGRESS CATALOGING IN PUBLICATION DATA

Pennock, James Roland.
  Democratic political theory.

  Bibliography: p.
  Includes index.
  1. Democracy.   I.   Title.
JC423.P348   321.8   78-63596
ISBN 0-691-07604-9
ISBN 0-691-02184-8 pbk.